LECTURES IN
CHRISTIAN DOGMATICS

LECTURES IN CHRISTIAN DOGMATICS

JOHN D. ZIZIOULAS

EDITED BY
DOUGLAS KNIGHT

t&t clark

Published by T&T Clark
A Continuum imprint
The Tower Building   80 Maiden Lane
11 York Road   Suite 704, New York
London SE1 7NX   NY 10038

www.continuumbooks.com

British Library Cataloguing-in-Publication Data
A catalogue record for this book is available from the British Library

ISBN-13: HB: 978-0-567-03314-7
          PB: 978-0-567-03315-4
ISBN-10: HB: 0-567-03314-7
          PB: 0-567-03315-5

Typeset by Newgen Imaging Systems Pvt Ltd, Chennai, India
Printed and bound in Great Britain by CPI Antony Rowe, Chippenham,
Wiltshire

To my students
in the Universities
of Edinburgh,
Glasgow,
King's College London
and Thessalonica.

CONTENTS

Preface	ix
Introduction	xi

Chapter 1
DOCTRINE AS THE TEACHING OF THE CHURCH

I.	The Church and the Formation of Doctrine	1
	1. Theology and hermeneutics	3
	2. The purpose of doctrine	5
	3. Scripture and doctrine	7
II.	Knowledge of God	9
	1. Knowledge in general	16
	2. Knowledge through the Son	22
	3. Knowledge through Personhood	25
	4. Knowledge through Faith	33

Chapter 2
THE DOCTRINE OF GOD

I.	Beginnings	40
II.	The Being of God	47
	1. One and Many	50
	2. *That, what and how* God is	54
	3. Augustine	65
III.	Theology and Economy	69
IV.	*Filioque*	75

Chapter 3
CREATION AND SALVATION

I.	The Doctrine of Creation	83
II.	Creation *ex nihilo*	88

III.	The Significance of the Doctrine of Creation	91
IV.	The Fall	98
V.	Christology	101
VI.	Salvation	105
VII.	Communion	115

Chapter 4
THE CHURCH

I.	Identity of the Church	120
II.	Gathered Church	126
III.	The Church of God	132
IV.	The Church as Image of the Future	135
V.	The Church and the Churches	139
VI.	The Church around the Bishop	145
VII.	Son and Spirit	148
VIII.	Eschatology and History	153
IX.	Reception	161

| Index | 165 |

PREFACE

The present volume contains material from my lectures on Christian Dogmatics which were given to students of theology in the Universities of Edinburgh (1970–1973), Glasgow (1973–1987), London (King's College 1984, 1989–1998) and, finally, Thessalonica (1984–1998). These lectures were tape-recorded by my students in Thessalonica and widely circulated. From this text a group of young scholars in Greece took the initiative to produce an English translation, which Douglas Knight has edited to produce the present volume. I am grateful to Katerina Nikolopoulou, Anna Nevrozidou, Thomas Dritsas and their colleagues at the Outlet for Dogmatic Enquires (OODE) who produced the first text, and also to Liviu Barbu in London. As to Douglas Knight, I find no words to express my appreciation for the hard labour and, above all, the enthusiasm with which he has edited these lectures. The Introduction he has provided for the book will certainly be of help to the reader.

This book does not claim to be a systematic theology, and unlike my previous books, does not contain references to other authors, except to Biblical and Patristic sources. It is written primarily for undergraduate students, although I hope that other theologians may find it useful too.

Orthodox theology in our time must operate in an ecumenical context and so in dialogue with other Christian traditions. And it cannot take place in a cultural vacuum that ignores current philosophical trends, and it cannot simply repeat the traditions of the past. It is unfortunate that much of today's Orthodox theology is in fact nothing but history – a theologically uncommitted scholar could have done this kind of 'theology' just as well or even better. Although this kind of 'theology' claims to be faithful to the Fathers and tradition, it is in fact contrary to the method followed by the Fathers themselves. For the Fathers worked in constant dialogue with the intellectual trends of their time to interpret the Christian faith to the world around them. This is precisely the task of Orthodox theology in our time too.

In the lectures contained in this volume Christian doctrine is
approached as a tradition that comes to us from the past but which is
interpreted in a way that answers the needs of human beings in our own
time, particularly in the context of Western culture. It is an attempt at
dogmatic hermeneutics that aims to answer this question: what would the
Fathers say to us today in response to our own concerns, as these are
shaped by our Western culture? In this attempt faithfulness to history
is presupposed and care is taken not to deviate from it. But this does
not exhaust our purpose which is to offer an interpretation rather than
simply a repetition of Christian doctrine. In the inspired words of the
late Father Georges Florovsky, the message of the Fathers must be
phrased today 'in such a way as to secure an ecumenical, a truly universal appeal. This obviously cannot be achieved by any servile repetition of
the Patristic letter . . . servility is alien both to the Bible and to the
Fathers. . . . The East must face and meet the challenges of the West, and
the West perhaps has to pay more attention to the legacy of the East . . .
Theological tradition must be reintegrated, not simply summed up and
accumulated'. *This *neopatristic synthesis*, as Florovsky termed it, is the
task to which Orthodox theology is called today.

These lectures are dedicated to my students in the Universities in
which they were given. For they are the result of constant and creative
dialogue with them over the many years of teaching, for which I whole-
heartedly give thanks and glory to the merciful God, Father, Son and
Holy Spirit.

+Metropolitan John (Zizioulas) of Pergamon

---

* George Florovsky, 'The legacy and the task of Orthodox theology', *Anglican
Theological Review*, 31 (1949) 65–71.

INTRODUCTION

In these lectures on Christian dogmatics the celebrated Orthodox theologian John Zizioulas gives us a comprehensive introduction to the Christian faith. He shows that the Christian doctrine of God is intimately linked to the Church, the living community that is the embodiment of the love and communion of God. By articulating its faith as doctrine, the Church gives an account of this love for the world. Within this communion human beings may participate in the friendship shared by the triune persons of Father, Son and Holy Spirit.

The lectures come in four chapters, discussing doctrine, God, the economy of God for man, and the Church. Zizioulas not only tells us what the Church teaches, but also why, and what difference it makes to us. He lays out profound and complex ideas with great simplicity, to show us how Christian doctrine integrates issues of communion, freedom and personhood. These lectures explore the relationship of the individual Christian to other Christians, and so introduce us to life and discipleship in the communion of the Church. Since few other thinkers are able to show that communion and freedom are as fundamental as this, a more lucid and profound exposition of Christian teaching would be hard to find.

I. DOCTRINE

Christian doctrine, which is the teaching of the Church, sets out what the Christian community says in its worship of God. The Church teaches us that Christ is always with the Holy Spirit, and that he may be known only within the community that the Spirit sanctifies for the purpose. Christ cannot be isolated or separated from his people, so we have to receive Christ from them. The Christian people experience the reality of the new communion opened by Jesus Christ and affirm the truth of the teaching about that communion. The Church distinguishes its own teaching from all rival accounts in order to protect this communion and re-state its truth clearly for each new generation.

Life within the communion initiated by God is the source of knowledge of God. Communion is fundamental to all knowing, for we have no real knowledge of a person as a *person* until we are in relationship with them. We may come to know them as they open themselves to us, and we open ourselves to them: since we do not know what any relationship will lead to, this is to take a risk. Relationship with God also brings us into relationship with all his creatures: knowledge of God cannot be merely spiritual or intellectual, for it is made present to us through all the many persons who make up the communion of the Church.

II. GOD

The doctrine of God sets out what is revealed to the Christian community in the incarnation of Christ, recorded in Scripture and celebrated in its worship. Worship is simply the acknowledgement that God is God and that we are not, and this acknowledgement is the basis of all further knowledge. God has brought the Church into being for this purpose, and he sustains it as the community that is able to acknowledge him, together with all his creatures, and to do so in freedom.

When we talk about God, and even more when we pray, we refer ourselves to the Father of Jesus Christ. God is the particular person whom we may know by the name of 'Father'. The Father begets the Son and sends the Spirit and they affirm him as Father, so he is never Father without them. The divine persons give to one another and receive from one another, so this Trinity of persons is the way God is who he is.

The concept of the person enables us to explicate the doctrine of God, and in particular to point to the fundamental importance of love and of freedom. The doctrine of God teaches that God secures all unity and plurality, and that God extends both unity and plurality to creation through mankind.

When the stress is put on unity *before* plurality, such as when God has been understood on the basis of analogies with an individual mind, the doctrine of God lurches between two misrepresentations. It is possible to misrepresent the unity of God in such a way that God becomes an impersonal and incommunicative monad, or it is also possible to misrepresent the persons as three independent consciousnesses ('gods') in order to promote 'communion' (which is itself an abstraction) over them. This is sometimes known as a 'social' doctrine of the Trinity.

Such accounts of the doctrine ignore the way the persons freely order themselves to the Father. There is an order in God, in which the Father is first and last, because all the persons so order themselves to one another. The Father is the single source from whom the persons of God come, and consequently he is the single source of all that is. Freely the Father loves and begets the Son, and is loved and worshipped by him, and loves the Spirit who proceeds from him and glorifies him through the Son. The Father is never without the Son and Holy Spirit: their mutual deference confirms the order and eternal unity that is the free act of the persons of God.

It is easier to see how the persons of God order themselves to one another when we examine how God acts for us. The Son and the Spirit do the Father's work, and they present their work to the Father for his approval. The Son regards us as his own body and presents us to the Father as though we, and all creation, were integral to himself. Christ raises us continually to God, and he will present us to God finally and, because the Father receives us from him, our existence is affirmed. Only God, who is free and does not seek our recognition for himself, can truly give us recognition and so establish who we are. The Holy Spirit binds us to Christ, so that the Son's acknowledgement of God becomes our act of acknowledgement too; his worship becomes our worship, and issues in our truthful appreciation and knowledge of all God's creation. It is finally due to its reception and acknowledgement by the Father that anything has the identity and existence that it has.

Zizioulas shows us how the Church learned how to avoid explanations that restricted the freedom of God. The Church insisted that it is God who makes himself known to us: the true God, the Father, has made himself known in the Son. He initiated the whole plan of our creation and redemption, so we are the outcome of his act of love, and in love he will recognise us. Because God affirms our knowledge of him, gained through Christ and the teaching of the Church, we do indeed know the otherwise unknowable God; the result is that our knowledge of creation is reliable and the possibility of all our science is secure.

If God had not revealed himself, our identity would be in crisis. We would have to create an identity of our own, but we would be unable to do so. When we are able to acknowledge that God reveals himself in Christ we have no need to assert or exalt ourselves over one another or in any other way to attempt to fill God's place. One inference is that, though we may have real knowledge of other people, we cannot know them or master them utterly, because they belong primarily not to us, but to God. The doctrine of God gives us the truth of man, but it cannot be abstracted from the truth about God and turned into a theory about man alone. God is knowable only to the extent he makes himself known, and this is true also of man, the creature of God. The secret of being human, is hidden with God, and only in communion with him, can we be human, together with other humans. The assessment of God is that we, along with rest of the world, are worth waiting for, and the existence of the Church is the demonstration that this remains God's good judgment. God is not threatened by the existence of anything, since it is by his will that anything comes into existence. He is free to love and confirm all his creatures without limit, and in love he extends his freedom to us, so that in Christ we are able to give each creature our recognition, and to say that all the works of God, even those that seem darkest to us, are good. This is the significance of the Christian doctrine of God for us.

However, when the contribution of the Church is left on one side, the Western philosophical tradition takes us in a different direction. We assume that other people are a threat to us, and that we have to assert ourselves against them. Fear takes the place of love in our account of the social and natural worlds. If we define our freedom without reference to love, we may believe that we have to make ourselves free by separating ourselves from others on the one hand, and from our embodiment in nature on the other. The Church insists that love, along with all forms of fellowship and society, is essential to any account of human being. Freedom and communion are both fundamental. Without a concept of person, either communion is given undue weight over freedom, or freedom over communion.

When it is disciplined by all Christian doctrine, the concept of person determines that communion and freedom are equally important. The result is that we are not tempted to believe that *being* is prior to persons, or that the question w*hat?* is more fundamental than the question *who?* Persons are not an afterthought in the great order of being, and only a person has the freedom to respond to love with love.

Zizioulas shows us that it is not enough just to say what the Christian doctrine of God is, but we also have to demonstrate its underlying logic, so we can clearly differentiate it from all that it is not saying. One implication of the doctrine of God is that, in God, 'one' is not prior to 'many', and unity is not prior to plurality. This single insight has huge ramifications. Human freedom and the individual person are just as fundamental as existence itself. When unity is placed before plurality, individuals are set before society: then society must control the individual to prevent him destroying society, and the individual has to assert himself against society to establish his freedom.

A second result of this assumption that unity is more primal than plurality is the possibility that plurality will eventually collapse back into unity. Then the profusion of creatures and persons that make up this world would disappear and it would be as though creation had never been. However, the logic of the Christian doctrine of God suggests that diversity is not temporary, and that the universal and collective will not overwhelm the particularity of any single entity. A world full of particular things and unique people will endure against all threats to its existence. 'Person' is the concept that holds together these three fundamental concepts of *being, communion* and *freedom,* and which establishes that plurality is not subordinate to unity.

In the teaching of the Church, all human persons exist within one person – Christ. This particular person gives room to a multitude without limit, and allows them to discover each other and to flourish. Since Christ receives his identity entirely from the Father he does not need the recognition of created persons for himself: he is able to be the 'other', who can freely acknowledge what is not himself, and give each created person the confirmation that establishes their identity. He is able to be the 'person' of humanity because the Father's acknowledgement of him makes him 'more than' humanity: he is the person in whom all created persons may truly be persons.

God loves us for ourselves. He can receive us because it was he who initiated the project of creation and called us into being in the first place. He has the authority to acknowledge us, and that will satisfy us that we are rightly identified and our existence is finally secured. When we come to him, we will know that we exist because he invites us to, and that this is all the justification that is needed.

The Son of God, who is eternally this divine person, has assumed human nature. In Christ, human life is raised to participate in the life of God, and to become free and God-like, 'the likeness of God'. Only when we are together with God may we be together with all other human beings and so be properly human. Christ does not desire to be known apart from his body, that is, apart from us. Because the Father receives him together with this body, made up of all whom the Spirit has united to Christ, the whole human race is one, in relationship with God. The Christian doctrine of God brings with it the most sophisticated and fundamentally positive teaching about man.

The Economy

Zizioulas brings the doctrines of creation and incarnation together under the heading of the work, or 'economy', of God for man. His discussion of God's coming to man brings dramatic new clarity to the doctrines of salvation and creation, and to the relationship of man to the natural world.

Since it is not the source of its own life, creation has no means of sustaining itself. It came from nothing and remains liable to dissolve back into it. All created things, left to themselves, tend to break apart and drift towards isolation, dissolution and eventual death. Aware of his vulnerability, man is fearful, and fear makes him a misery to himself and a terror to his fellow creatures. He needs to be liberated both from the confines of nature and from the fear which drives him to devour his fellow men.

If the world is to live, death must be overcome. But only a relationship of love, freely willed on both sides, can overcome the constraints on our life, including the ultimate limit that is death. Created beings are safe from death as long as they are in communion with the life that, being uncreated, has no limit. Man is made for relationship with God, who always intended to be with man, and intended that man should know this and be glad of it. From the first, God meant to be incarnate for man: had he not fallen, man would have been transformed incrementally into Christ, that is, *man-with-God*.

Man was given the freedom of God to decide freely, and on behalf of all creation, for participation in the communion and life of God. Because all creation makes up his body, materiality participates in man's decision. Man unites created materiality to the communion of God that overcomes all limits and so secures creation's continued life. Christ is the one who is able to establish and sustain relationship with all men, and brings each into relationship with all others, and unites within himself all creation to God. He is the truth of man and creation, sustained through all limits by the invincible communion of God.

Although Christ is the whole reality of human being, he does not force himself upon us, but appears amongst us as one person amongst others, and so as someone we can reject or accept as we like. We can withhold our acknowledgement of him or, in faith, we can recognise him for who he is. When we concede Christ his otherness, and acknowledge that he shares the freedom of God, this opens the possibility that we understand that all persons are different from us, not *our* creatures but creatures *of God*. As we concede the otherness and freedom of every human being we gain our own true freedom.

THE CHURCH

In the fourth part of these lectures Zizioulas turns to the Church. The Church is the communion and love of God truly present to us, and from it all human fellowship and society flow. By bringing us into his fellowship, God enables us to pass beyond the limits given by our creatureliness and enter fellowship with one another. Since this communion can never be exhausted, the Church cannot be divided, comprehended or threatened by any created thing. In spelling out this communion Zizioulas deals with discipleship, sanctification, the gathered community, the Eucharist, eschatology, order and hierarchy, scripture and worship and relations between churches. He shows us again that plurality is as fundamental as unity: the complementarity of distinction and unity is developed through every part of his account, which he sets out together with his account of Christ and the Holy Spirit.

Through centuries of debate, the Church developed a theology of the gathered community and of the growth of the individual Christian. Through discipleship, each of us purified of our aggression and turned outwards towards others, so the Christian is transformed from one degree of Christ-likeness to another, from partial to whole and perfect, and so made a catholic person.

Left to ourselves, however, we separate ourselves from one another and attempt to establish our own rival kingdoms and so divide the world between us, so that each part holds out against all others. None of us is able to let other people be truly different from himself; our inadequate love means a failure of otherness. Our partial kingdoms are premised on the exclusion of some, and thus our kingdoms are not the kingdom of *God*. Without the Church, the world attempts to close down of the otherness of others; in particular it attempts to suborn the Church and to reduce the difference between Church and world. But because it is the act of God, the Church will never be assimilated, the distinction between Church and world will remain, and the Church will continue to baffle the unreconciled world.

The Church, which is a single assembly made up of all Christ's people, is the embodiment of the renewal and redemption of creation. It includes those who, for us, are in the past or in the future. Each local gathering of Christ's people is that complete assembly, diffidently making present to us what will only be finally complete at the fulfilment of all ages. But it will be our future only because we desire that it be so and are ready to receive and love all whom Christ has in store for us.

With infinite power, Christ sustains his body so that it resists all contrary voices, and remains unified, and with infinite patience he calls all humanity into reconciliation in this body so that no part is any longer at war with any other. The unity and order of this assembly can be seen in the way that its members order themselves to one another in love. The fellowship of God creates in the Eucharist that mutual deference that brings down the walls between creatures and initiates reconciliation and good order within human history. As all kingdoms and all times are reconciled in the body of Christ, we will cease to assert ourselves against all others, and the world will no long be a place of warring camps: the communion of God which is 'in heaven' will become the truth 'on earth'.

THE SON AND THE SPIRIT

The Holy Spirit glorifies Christ and is always with him. The Spirit glorifies him both by distinguishing Christ from all others, and by uniting all others to him as members of his body. Christ cannot be isolated or separated from the whole people of God, whom he regards as his own glory, so we cannot know Jesus Christ (the one) without simultaneously acknowledging his community (the many). He cannot be known as Christ outside that body which the Holy Spirit sanctifies, or apart from its saints and teachers whom the Holy Spirit has pressed into our service. We can know Christ only through the life of the Church, its worship, sacraments, tradition, gifts and offices.

The Spirit situates us 'in Christ'. The same Spirit who makes Christ indivisible and unassailable also makes each of us indivisible in him. Christ is the person, which is to say, the fundamental unit, in whom we may become persons who can never be broken into any smaller constituents. Christ and the Spirit together are responsible not only for our unity, but also for all the distinctions that makes us different from one another. He differentiates us from one another, establishing us as unique and irreplaceable particulars, so each human being will become catholic, anointed with the whole plurality of Christ. Christ makes his people one indivisible whole, and the Church is this future whole, making itself present to us in time. God sends us instalments of this whole which make it publicly present within the world, in the form of the gathered communion of this people. God does not let the world come to rest until it comes together into the kingdom of God. The kingdom of God interrupts the world's claim to be self-sufficient or complete, and the Eucharist is the form that this interruption takes. The Eucharist prevents the parts, of which the present world is made up, from prematurely determining themselves against the much larger whole that is promised and therefore still to come.

Jesus Christ comes to us accompanied by the entire company of his people: we cannot have him without receiving them too. Christ has an unbreakable person-to-person relationship with each member of this company, so that, through him, each of us is related to all of this vast assembly. The Christian people arrange themselves around the apostles and all their successors, who as witnesses of the resurrection, are themselves gathered around Christ. The way the Church stations itself around these witnesses makes the Church an image that will not change until Christ, who is its original, returns. The kingdom of God is the good-ordering of all things around Christ, and the Church is its public image.

God intends that we be free and his invitation to freedom is what the future is. If the future were fixed or necessary, it would not be *future*, but simply more of the present. No future can be foisted on us. We can only be said to be beings with a future if we become, and remain, free: we must be willing contributors to it, for our identity will not be decided without our collaboration. The future is the invitation Christ issues to us to share life with him and with all his people. If God were a universally manifest and inescapable fact it would make freedom impossible. So God withholds his glory, so that that it is *mystery*, revealed and known only in faith. In this faith we look for the resurrection that will make his body, and his glory, complete.

But it is not enough that Christ *gives* us our identity, but we must also *take* it up. Our identity becomes truly ours as we love him and love his people as our own. Christ does not regard himself as complete without us, so he waits for us; the saints and whole communion wait for us with him, and so we must also wait for each other. Our lives are therefore part of a process and a history, enabled by the Holy Spirit which, because we must all participate in it, unfolds through time. Waiting for other people is what time is.

In the prayers of the Eucharist we ask God to give us all whom we are waiting for, along with all the grace to receive them, and so make this body complete. We mourn for those who are not yet present, for their absence means that we are not yet present as we want to be. The whole Christ, and our own very being, is waiting for them. Christ calls us and listens for us, and regardless of how long it takes, waits for each particular person to hear and answer in freedom. However deep we have been buried, he hears us, and can uncover and restore us. He is able to wrest us out of one another's grasp, tell us apart from all other persons and confirm who we are. As creatures, we are divisible by time and so located by it, so we presently see the body of Christ strung out across time, like stragglers in a race, its unity hidden from us. But time cannot ultimately divide this body: though events chafe away, they will never prevail against it, but only serve to purify this body until it is finally revealed as eternal and indivisible. Because it is the communion of God, the Church will stand forever: now the mutual love of its members demonstrates its undefeated good order at every Eucharist.

The resurrection will bring us face to face with all men. The resurrection that raises us to God will also raise to them, and them to us, so that we will receive Christ together with all whom he brings with him. He now sends us all these people ahead of him to us, so we may receive him by learning to receive them.

Our resurrection, imperceptibly underway since our baptism, consists in meeting these saints who already make up the glorified body of Jesus Christ. The Eucharist, which is the union of God with man taking place before us, is gathering us together and making us fully present and available to one another at last.

EUCHARIST

In each place that it meets, the Church is the evidence that Christ is drawing all men to himself, bringing each into connection with all. This future and final assembly makes itself present to the present world in this hidden form of the Church. In the Eucharist each church intercedes for its own locality, speaking on its behalf to God. Each Christian prays for those members of his own family and society, past and present, and through these prayers they become present in this assembly: in Christ we are the presence of persons other than ourselves.

The Church participates in the manyness of Christ, and passes his plurality on to the world. The whole Church receives the diversity of the people of Christ from each of the many local churches. The whole Church passes on the holiness of Christ to each local church, so that Christ's indivisible unity is present in each part of the world, to reconcile and draw it into his body. The Church supplies the world simultaneously with both unity and plurality, identity and difference. Without the

Church, present in every part of the world and making every part of the world present in its prayers, both the unity and diversity of the world, and so its very existence, would be in doubt.

Christ's people embody creation. Each of the bodies which make us visible and present to one another, constituted of all the vegetable and animal bodies we consume, is itself a gathering of the material elements of creation. Each of us embodies a particular part of the earth, so creation exists within the body, or as the body, of each member of Christ's assembly. Creation lives in and through us, just as much as we live in it. In Christ we are the 'person' of creation, the indivisible unity that preserves creation immune from time and death. In the Eucharist, material creation is able to sing the praises of God and so participate through us in the freedom of God.

Since Christ clothes himself with his people, in him all persons and all material creation are forever present with God. In his liturgy to God and service to man, Christ unites all creation with God. This work of bringing these many into one, is what is going on in the great eucharistic prayer of offering, the *anaphora*. For the benefit of the world, the saints who are assembled behind Christ participate publicly in his office of raising and embodying the world to God. As Christ and his body speak for it and present it to God, creation's divisions disappear, there is reconciliation between the social and the natural worlds, and so we are able to live with, rather than against, the order of creation. As the Eucharist is the reconciliation of mind and body, intellect and materiality, so the Church is the union of nature in humanity and nature, and freedom come to creation.

CATHOLICITY

Communion involves persons who are different from one another. The preservation of the distinctiveness and otherness of each of these persons requires order and authority. The distinctions incorporated and affirmed within the body of Christ are protected by offices within the Church. Christ sanctifies specific office-holders in the body in order to serve us and do us good: they ensure that we do not form into narrower, less tolerant groups; their discipline enables us to accept the ordering of the whole catholic body within which all differences are established and enabled to flourish. Just as the whole Church is under the discipline given by Christ, each congregation is under the discipline of the whole Church, worldwide and of all generations. Thus there is no gap between the local and universal churches, or between the people and the institutions of the Church: all must demonstrate the simple truth that we are ordered to one another, and made finally distinct from one another, in Christ.

Just as no disciple is under his own authority, no church can ordain its own leaders, but must receive them from the whole Church. Communion consists in receiving apostles, together with their teaching and their discipline, from other parts of the Church, and in sending them to other parts of the church. By giving and taking in this way, each church exists in relationships with other churches and is part of the whole catholic body. Each of these apostles represents the oversight of the whole Church for this particular church; each overseer brings to each church the deposit of faith found good by the long historical experience of the Church as a whole. Each community must receive this overseer and his discipline willingly, as a gift from the whole body. Through mutual subordination in love we receive the shaping of the whole Christ as it comes to us from the whole Church.

Each church participates in the one catholic Church by sending and receiving apostles. Any community that does not receive these apostles and their gifts from the rest of the Church will be held together by a spirit of nation, class or age-group, or by a merely intellectual, aesthetic or sentimental spirit. It will fortify itself against other parts, and so represent only the division of the body and the falsification of the gospel.

We cannot turn away from other churches without shutting ourselves off from Christ and from our own future in his body. Thus every event of ecumenism, like every Eucharist, is an event of judgment and repentance, and of forgiveness and reconciliation, in which we are joined to those we have shunned. Every church must humbly offer its faith to every other, submit itself to the questioning of every other church, and attempt to learn from them all. The one Church exists as each church gives and receives the instruction and oversight of every other.

The Church is constituted by the whole Christian people, gathered around their bishops, and their agreement demonstrates that the one and the many are one Church. The Church is the catholic body: all other communities are partial, and so not yet the whole truth. Our way into this truly universal communion is through the cross of Christ which removed all false universals from us. We may now know Christ only together with every single one of those whom he brings with him. When Christ is all in all, *all* will be all in all.

John Zizioulas, Metropolitan bishop of Pergamon, has led many of the exchanges between Eastern and Western churches. He believes all ecumenical efforts are mutually enriching, and he expresses his gratitude to the Western churches for them. Some Eastern churches are wary of Western 'influence' and critical of those involved in such ecumenism. But Bishop John tells us, every act of ecumenism must be based in the truth and thus hear the judgment of God with repentance and in the hope of reconciliation. The whole Church eagerly looks forward to its redemption and the fulfilment of all things in Christ, so it must be the prayer of the churches 'that they may be One'. These lectures represent an unrivalled opportunity to learn the faith of the whole undivided Church, which is the embodiment of the love of God for us.

Chapter 1

Doctrine as the Teaching of the Church

I. THE CHURCH AND THE FORMATION OF DOCTRINE

Theology starts in the worship of God and in the Church's experience of communion with God. Our experience of this communion involves a whole range of relationships, so theology is not simply about a religious, moral or psychological experience, but about our whole experience of life in this communion. Theology touches on life, death and our very being, and shows how our personal identity is constituted through relationships, and so through love and freedom. What makes man different from any other creature? Can humans be truly free? Do they want to be free? Can humans be free to love?

Theology is concerned with life and survival, and therefore with salvation. The Church articulates its theology, not simply to add to our knowledge of God or the world, but so that we may gain the life which can never be brought to an end. Christian doctrine tells us that there is redemption for us and for the world, and each particular doctrine articulates some aspect of this redemption. We have to enquire how each doctrine contributes to knowledge of our salvation. Rather than isolating each doctrine, we have to set each doctrine out in the context of all other doctrines. Theology seeks a living comprehension of the Christian faith, of our place in the world and relationship with one another. It does not just want to preserve the statements of the Church as they were originally made, but also to provide the best contemporary expression of the teaching of the Church.

Christian theology sets out the teaching of the Church. The worship of God, the Eucharist and baptism were the immediate origins of Christian teaching, which took a variety of forms even in the Scriptures. The New Testament shows us how the faith was confessed by the first

Christian communities. The Christology which gave shape to the teaching of the Apostle Paul can be seen in the Christ hymn of the letter to the Philippians (2.5-11). Many consider the Gospel of John to be a eucharistic and liturgical text, because its prologue at least is comprised of liturgical material used in worship. The letters of Peter probably also have a liturgical context: the first letter resembles a baptismal liturgy. The same is true of the eucharistic references of the first centuries, which represent forms of liturgical theology of the bishops who led the Eucharist, and who were initially free to improvise as they led the worship of their congregations, as can be seen from the *Didache* and Justin Martyr.

Baptism, and the catechising that prepares candidates for it, was another context for theology. All the earliest creeds originated in baptism, and the first Council of Nicaea used the baptismal creeds of the local churches as the basis of its creed. Another context was given by the need to respond to the rival alternative accounts of the faith that were offered by other teachers outside the Church. This form promoted the development from baptismal confessions to a broader range of creeds, in order to confront Gnosticism, Arianism and other deviations from the faith of the Church. This was the background of theological writers such as Irenaeus, Athanasius, Cyril of Alexandria and Maximus the Confessor who wrote because they were asked to respond to opposing views of the gospel, rather than because they set out to compose comprehensive statements of the faith.

Origen in the third century was the first to offer a comprehensive presentation of the Christian faith, setting out a systematic arrangement of the doctrine of the Church in his 'On Principles'. Saint John of Damascus did the same, five centuries later, in 'The Exposition of the Orthodox Faith', while the 'Summa Theologica' of Thomas Aquinas represents the high point of the subject's development in the mediaeval period. Nonetheless, there is no particular reason why Christian theology should be presented as a system.

Theology also originated in the councils of the Church. Councils were called in order to respond to deviations from the faith of the Church, and as one council followed another, faith was expressed by increasingly detailed statements given in creeds and canons. Theology also had its origin in the reflection of Christians on their own lives, and particularly reflection on the lives of the monks. These are expressed in the sayings of the Desert Fathers recorded, for example, in the works of Saint John Climacus (sixth century), Maximus the Confessor (seventh century), Simeon the New Theologian (tenth century) Gregory Palamas (fourteenth century) and those spiritual Fathers we know as the Hesychasts.

These various elements of liturgy, baptism, the need to respond to distortions of the faith, councils and finally the ascetic experience of the Christian life, mean that Christian theology is the expression of the experience of the living Church, rather than of intellectual perception or the logical arrangement of propositions. Theology affirms truths which come, not from the intellect alone, but from the whole relationship of man with God.

1. *Theology and Hermeneutics*

The task of re-stating Scripture and Christian doctrine is termed 'hermeneutics'. All theology is a matter of hermeneutics, that is, of deciding how to receive and re-state the teaching of Scripture for the Church and the world. Scripture is silent until it is read and interpreted to the world, so we could say that all Christian teaching is simply interpretation of Scripture. Christian doctrine would be no more than an archaeological artefact until the Church goes on to interpret and re-state it for the world.

There are two aspects to the interpretation of Scripture and doctrine. One is the attempt faithfully to understand the context in which Scripture and the teaching of the Church was first expressed. Good historical scholarship will present the historical reality without anachronism. It asks a certain range of questions: what challenges did the Church face in each period? How did it do so? What written and oral traditions, Scripture or doctrinal, were available to it? Each council used the traditions it had inherited. What vocabulary and conceptuality were available within the intellectual and cultural environment of each period? To take one example, by tracing the decisions that led the fourth century Church to adopt the term 'homoousion' – unknown to the New Testament – we learn something about the logic of the revelation that the Church intended its teaching to manifest.

All biblical interpretation requires good historical scholarship. Any account of a doctrine is open to challenge until we offer some description of the original historical setting within which it emerged. What was the relationship to Christian worship and discipleship of each doctrine? How did martyrdom relate to Christian life and worship within the New Testament, for instance? What role did icons and apophaticism play in worship for the Seventh Ecumenical Council. In the same way, we need to identify the issues that brought about the drafting of a doctrine. We have to decide which textual and philosophical sources the

Fathers used, and what experience of worship and the Christian life any particular doctrine represented.

We have to examine the terminology and conceptuality of that period of history. The Fathers of the Church did not remain fixed to the letter of the New Testament. Although it does not change in essentials, the worship and life of the Church varies in form and emphasis so, for example, in some periods the Church experiences public martyrdoms, while in others worship and spirituality take a more interior form. We can see the influence of monasticism on the worship of the Church through observance of the canonical hours, and then gradual disengagement from this in the twentieth century. These shifts in the experience of worship and the ascetic life have consequences for the Church's interpretation of doctrine.

But interpretation of Scripture and doctrine also requires that we interpret our own situation. This means that we must analyse contemporary intellectual movements, and the challenges thrown up by economic, technological, ecological and other changes. But theological interpretation of doctrine demands that its relationship to other currents of thought, and thus to philosophy, must be established too. A theologian must be familiar with the intellectual climate of his or her own time. But he or she must also be a philosopher in the sense of being a truly enquiring mind, and in the wider sense of being sensitive to the deepest needs of human beings. The theologian must also be familiar with the liturgical experience and the life of the Church, including the institutional forms established by the canons of the Church. Perhaps no individual can be expert at all of these, but whoever aspires to be a theologian must be aware of each of these disciplines. Theology requires expertise at a range of disciplines, accompanied by a moral sensitivity and intellectual curiosity.

We have said that theology is first worship of God and that the fundamental logic of theology is given in the event of baptism and eucharistic worship. The Creed sets out the confessional structure which corresponds to the relationship with Christ that God has provided for our salvation. Problems start to occur when the arrangement of the individual doctrines of God, Christology, salvation and so on, does not relate to the logic of public confession represented by the Creed. The structure of any work of theology has to be flexible enough to allow all the relationships between each doctrine to emerge. For example, the chapter on the triune doctrine of God must establish connections to the Church, the sacraments and the eschaton. We cannot examine each doctrine in isolation from the whole to which it belongs, or we would be reproducing the individualising approach to dogmatics of the Scholastics and rationalists.

Then we must set out the significance of a doctrine for the period in which it emerged. What problems were met by those who first gave expression to the new doctrine and what conceptual means were available to them to meet these new challenges? Christian theology must always set out a plausible account of the development of each doctrine, so we need a set of principles by which we can interpret doctrine as a whole. We have to ask how Christ was worshipped and encountered within the Church. Then we have to relate the teaching of the Church to the problems faced by each historical period, and by making explicit the relationships between each Christian doctrine and the human search for love, freedom, and the hope of overcoming death, we have to relate our doctrine to the deepest problems of our own contemporaries. Though this is the job of theological ethics, theologians must at least offer the principles by which ethicists can tackle this task. Finally we must establish the relationship of doctrine to the wider contemporary issue of knowledge, particularly as it is posed by philosophy and the natural sciences.

2. *The Purpose of Doctrine*

Christian doctrine is the teaching of the Church. 'Doctrine' simply means 'what is taught', from the Latin *doceo*, to teach. *Dogma*, the word used by the Greek Fathers, comes from *dokein*, 'seeming' or 'believing', derived originally from that which was good or right. So dogma is related to belief, consensus, faith, principles and a wide range of similar meanings. So Plato refers to 'making use of the many *dogmas* and words' (*Sophist* 256C). From this original sense of 'personal opinion' the term was used of various views of the philosophical schools, so when Plutarch talked of 'the *dogmas* about the soul' (*Ethica* 14B) he meant the wide range of teachings offered by ancient philosophy on this subject.

This term was also employed to signify the decisions or decrees that bore the authority of the state, and so it meant something authoritative. In Plato's *Laws* for example we read of 'the city *dogma*' (*Laws* 644D), and in the Gospel of Luke 'a decree (*dogma*) was issued by Caesar Augustus to conduct a census of the population' (Luke 2.1). In the Old Testament and Judaism, it had a legal or mandatory sense. The Apostle Paul says that Christ has 'cancelled the written *dogmas* that were against you' (Colossians 2.14) and that Christ has abolished the enmity in his Body, by 'abolishing the *dogma* of the law of the commandments' (Ephesians 2.15). For Luke, dogma has a positive sense: 'As they passed through the cities, they delivered to them the decrees (*dogmas*) approved by the apostles and the elders' (Acts 16.4). So 'dogma' came to refer to authoritative decisions about the faith, received by the Church and linked to the presence and the inspiration of the Holy Spirit. For example, in a conciliar letter quoted in Acts, the Apostles wrote, 'It seemed good to the Holy Spirit and to us' (Acts 15.28).

The dogma or teaching of the Church relates to worship rather than to preaching. We see this in Saint Basil's statement that 'Dogma and proclamation (*kerygma*) are two distinct things: doctrine we confess without argument, but our preaching we make known to all the world' (*On the Holy Spirit* 27.65). Basil means that doctrines are what the worshipping community of the Church has to learn, and 'honour in silence', whereas 'kerygma' exists in order that it can proclaim the truth to those outside the Church, which does of course involve arguing with them about what is true. The community of the Church and its worship is the context that gives doctrine its authority.

The Fathers take it for granted that dogma is only for those within the Church. Gregory of Nyssa said, 'Let us reason within our own borders' (*Against Eunomius* 10.4), by which he means 'within the Holy Land, rather than in Egypt', that is, within the Church rather than on the foreign territory of philosophy. The authority of a doctrine does not come from a simple obedience to reason, though it certainly does not come from any refusal of reason. The reason it points towards is that renewed reason that corresponds to the relationships embodied within the community of the Church.

Dogma is the doctrine that, through its councils, the Church confesses as the truth that brings salvation for every human being. This truth brings us into particular relationships with one another, and it brings the Church into a particular relationship with God and with the world. The Church expects that through their own experience its members will recognise the truth of this teaching, and therefore its authority too. The preaching of the Church is addressed to the wider world. When people become Christians and members of the Church, they will have experienced the truth for themselves and so they will confess that what the Church has taught is true.

The preaching, and teaching, of Christians becomes doctrine when it is confirmed by the Church. Since the Church is a living body, it may set out new statements of its teaching for each generation. The Holy Spirit acted not only in its earliest period, but he acts through every period of the Church, now as much as in what we refer to as the Patristic period. For this reason there is no upper limit to the number of dogmas the Church can affirm in its history. It can make whatever statements are required to preserve the faithfulness of the Church in each age. The Holy Spirit enables Church councils to make, and the whole Church to acknowledge, these re-statements of the Church's teaching. The teaching of a particular spiritual teacher or academic theologian can only become binding when it has been confirmed by the whole Church, led by its councils.

3. *Scripture and Doctrine*

It is the task of the Church to judge how to understand the teaching it has received in Scripture and doctrine and set it out in each new situation. From the Reformation on, Western theologians asked whether divine revelation has one source or two. Protestants rejected the authority of the tradition of the Church and introduced the principle of '*sola scriptura*', Scripture on its own, without the experience of all previous generations of the Church in expounding that Scripture. In Orthodox theology, the problem arrived with the so-called 'Orthodox Confessions' of the seventeenth century, which were shaped by the encounter with Roman Catholicism in the case of the confession of Peter Mogilas (1597–1647) and with Calvinism in the case of the confession of Cyril Lucaris (1572–1637). The West tends to regard Scripture and doctrine as two distinct sources and tries to arbitrate between what it understands as their rival claims. If we understand that the continuity of the apostolic tradition is the work of the Holy Spirit, there is no problematic relationship between tradition and Scripture, for each serves the other.

There are two reasons why Western churches saw the relationship of Scripture and doctrine as a problem. The West tended to regard revelation as primarily rational or intellectual, and the Scriptures and the Church simply as a repository of truths, available as individual units of inert information. In the Orthodox tradition, however, Scripture and the Church are regarded as the testimonies of those prophets and apostles who have experienced the truth of Christ. But truth is not a matter of objective, logical proposals, but of personal relationships between God, man and the world. We do not come to know truth simply through intellectual assent to the proposition that God is triune. It is only when we are drawn into the life of God, which is triune, and through it receive our entire existence and identity, that we have real knowledge. Then we may realise that the Church's trinitarian doctrine of God faithfully articulates the truth of our experience in this communion that is the Church. Through such living experience, every member of the Church experiences the communion of God and is able to affirm that the doctrine of the Trinity is the truth of that reality. The revelation of God is an event in which man comes to experience, and share in, the life of God and of his fellow-man and the world, and this revelation brings new light and sense to all life. The Scripture that brings this revelation is complete, and this revelation makes sense of every part of the canon of Scripture.

The revelation of the one true God is the person of Christ given to us. Revelation is of course always personal, for God revealed himself to Abraham, Moses, the Apostles, the Fathers and so on. Consequently, we have no *new* revelation and no *addition* to the revelation of Jesus Christ given in Scripture. Though it is personal, this revelation takes a variety of forms. The epiphanies of the Old Testament, such as the event of Mount Sinai in the Book of Exodus, reveal Christ. In the New Testament, revelation of God has taken an unrepeatable form. With Jesus Christ, we are allowed not only to see and hear God, but to actually touch and feel him and relate to him physically. It is not merely communion of the mind or the heart, but a communion of vision, hearing and touch, with him 'whom our hands have touched' (1 John 1.1). Nothing is superior to the revelation of Christ, for 'whoever has seen me, has seen the Father' (John 14.9). The Fathers insisted that this communion was final and complete. The New Testament is the record of the experience of those who had this physical communion with God. It sets their experience above Old Testament appearances of God, and above whatever revelations have been given to the Church since the time of the Apostles.

The incarnation has given us a fuller revelation than that represented by the Old Testament. The Church attributed this superiority to the physical and tangible relationship Christ shared with the disciples, and understands the Eucharist and sacraments as the continuation of this fully physical form of communion. Ignatius, Cyril of Jerusalem and Cyril of Alexandria insisted that those who worthily participate in the divine Eucharist see God better than Moses did. Saint Maximus summed up Saint Irenaeus' teaching about their relationships with the phrase 'the Old Testament is the shadow, the New Testament is the image, the things to come are the truth' (*Scholia on Dionysius' Ecclesiastical Hierarchy* 3.3.2).

The entire life of the Church lives from the revelation of God in the historical event of Christ recorded for us by the Scriptures. The New Testament is the fundamental doctrine, or dogma, of which all other forms of revelation, the Old Testament and all subsequent teaching of the Church, are renditions. A further revelation could only be an entirely different revelation, and different religion, altogether. So to sum up what we have said so far, the New Testament and all subsequent Christian doctrine simply point to the person and event of Jesus Christ. The teaching of the Church, taken together with the whole canon of Scripture, enables us to experience this new relationship between God, mankind and the world.

The divine Eucharist is the complete revelation of him 'whom our hands have touched' and direct communion with God in personal and tangible form. Every revelation of God, in whatever form it comes, manifests Christ. All revelations are appearances of Christ, and thus of the uncreated light which shines from the historical body of Jesus Christ. As John of Damascus and Theodore the Studite insisted, it is the incarnation of Christ that makes the icons revelations of Christ.

To return to the relationship of Scripture and doctrine, we can see that all doctrine essentially recalls the event of Christ. It reveals that we have been brought into a living relationship with God and so with all truth. Jesus Christ is the whole knowledge of God, Father, Son and Holy Spirit and this is the reason why, in the course of setting out the truth of Christ, the Council of Nicaea set out an entire theology of the Trinity. All subsequent ecumenical councils were concerned to elucidate Christ as the truth of God, and thus the truth of our salvation, even when it may seem that they were concerned with issues not directly connected to Christology. The experience of the Apostles, recorded in the New Testament, is the doctrine which all subsequent teaching has to set out. Doctrine only ever restates the experience of the Apostles and restores the clarity of their witness to Christ. The continuity of doctrine is sustained by the dogmas set out by the ecumenical councils of the Church; these dogmas are themselves icons of Christ, painted by each new generation, each with all the means that it has at its disposal. This continuity is both external, because it represents a fidelity to all preceding tradition all the way back to the period in which Scripture was written, and it is internal, because it preserves our living relationship of God with humankind and the world, fulfilled and revealed in Christ.

II. Knowledge of God

Jesus Christ is the revelation of God, so Christology is theology. The doctrine that articulates this revelation of Christ presents us with two fundamental issues. The first is the need to account for the period of time between Christ in history, and the Apostolic era and subsequent historical periods in which christological doctrine was formulated. What accounts for the continuity of the revelation of Christ through time?

The second problem is that within the historical revelation of Christ there is a tension between the present and the future, the 'already' and the 'not yet'. In the historical Christ and the experience of the first Apostles, God's revelation is a poor reflection 'as in a mirror' rather than the whole reality that the eschaton will reveal 'face to face' (1 Corinthians 13.12). Christ now presents an image and foretaste of that complete and direct personal knowledge of God for us, though, according to 1 John 3.2, until that kingdom arrives, no prophet or saint has full or final knowledge of God. How can we attain a foretaste of heaven, the complete knowledge of God, and be confident that Christian teaching is the faithful and accurate expression of this foretaste? Truly to portray Christ as the revelation of God, Christian teaching has to be faithful in two respects: It has to portray truthfully the historical Christ of the past, and the future, eschatological Christ and his kingdom.

Christian doctrine must hold together the past, historical revelation of Christ and the future advent of Christ in glory, and this union and transformation of past and future is the particular task of the Holy Spirit.

'It seemed proper to the Holy Spirit and to us', concluded the council of the Apostles in Acts 15. It is the conviction of the Church that, just as Scripture is 'God-breathed' (2 Timothy 3:16), the teaching of the Church is equally the work of the Holy Spirit. There are a number of ways in which we could understand this. The presence and action of the Holy Spirit could be understood as some kind of mechanical or magical intervention of God. For the ancient Greeks, 'divine inspiration' was involuntary, manifesting itself through divination and oracles, often without the consent of the individual who was caught up in prophetic rapture. But such an understanding as this would make the authors of the bible and the Fathers of the councils the involuntary tools of the Spirit. Another possibility would be to understand the presence and the effect of the Spirit in terms of the development of the human spirit through time, and the consequence of humanity's efforts towards its own amelioration. A third possibility is that the work of the Holy Spirit is an event of communion that centres on a community, and which has a horizontal as well as a vertical dimension.

The first of these possibilities can be excluded straightaway. The Holy Spirit is the Spirit of freedom, so he does not force himself upon us. Christ's revelation fully respects the freedom of the person. The second possibility at least fits the spiritual experience of the disciple and ascetic, for without being purified from sin, it is not possible for anyone to see

God, for 'whoever hates his brother cannot see God' (1 John 2.11). The Eunomians claimed that sin does not present any obstacle to immediate knowledge of God. Saint Gregory Nazianzus argued that they had thereby created a theology of the disembodied intellect which allowed anyone to 'do theology', as though theology were just another topic of conversation that would pass the time between the races and the theatre. Gregory insisted that theology is not open to anyone, but only to those 'who have been tested, having spent their life in contemplation (*theoria*) of God, cleansed in soul and body, or at least undergoing such a purification' (*First Theological Oration, Against Eunomius,* III). But equally to isolate spirituality from all other considerations and make it the sole requirement of the theologian would be individualism and moralism. We would be mistaken to think that God reveals himself to those individuals who isolate themselves in order to advance to a higher degree of spirituality.

The third option we could call the ecclesial action of the Holy Spirit. Wherever he works, the Holy Spirit brings the communion of Christ. We need to rid ourselves of the belief that the Holy Spirit acts upon us as isolated persons and leaves us as isolated afterwards as before. This perception that the Spirit takes persons away from community is so widespread that we must reject it emphatically. Those who defend this view overlook the fundamental distinction between the action of the Holy Spirit in the Old Testament and in the New Testament. In the Old Testament, the Spirit is given to particular persons, prophets and kings, but not to the whole nation of Israel. But in the New Testament the Messiah gives the Holy Spirit to the entire people of God. In his account of Pentecost Luke quotes the prophet Joel, 'In the last days I shall pour my Spirit forth on all flesh, says the Lord Almighty' (Acts 2.17–18).

The New Testament teaches that all baptised Christians have the Holy Spirit, and with him, his charisms and gifts. The Apostle Paul explains in 1 Corinthians 12 that being a member of the Church means the possession of some particular gift and office of the Spirit for that Church. Paul clearly rejects the view of the Corinthians that some people may be more spiritual or more charismatic than others; he insists that everyone has some spiritual gift, even if it takes the form of an unostentatious service like administration. Paul rejects every manifestation of a spiritual elitism, saying that even if someone has faith enough to 'move mountains', he will be nothing if he has no love.

What does the Apostle mean by 'love'? If we take a look at chapters eleven to fourteen of the first letter to the Corinthians, we see that love is the communion created by the community of the Church. Love here does not refer to an emotion or to good will but refers to the mutual relationship between the members of the Church, for it is this mutual relationship that makes this communion one. No one says that they 'do not need any other parts of the body' (1 Corinthians 12.21), for love means that all offices and ministries are exercised interdependently and in union.

The Apostle relates this fellowship to the Holy Spirit. The phrase that ends his second Letter to the Corinthians, 'the fellowship of the Holy Spirit' (2 Corinthians 13.13) appears to have been part of the liturgy of the first Churches, prior to Paul, and it has remained part of the divine Eucharist ever since. Wherever the Spirit blows, he brings an end to individualism and elitism, and creates a community. We could point to a multitude of quotes from the Fathers of the first centuries. Gregory of Nazianzus refers to the Holy Spirit's focus on personal contemplation (*theoria*). He says that though we may desire solitude and purification of mind in order to achieve contemplation of God, this is not the direction the Spirit leads us in. The Spirit brings into being a congregation and makes each member of that congregation fruitful, so that each, 'being helped by helping others makes public the Spirit's enlightenment' (*Twelfth Oration,* 4). This is why the experience of the gathered Church is, Saint Gregory believes, greater than the experience of contemplation 'just as the skies are greater than a single star, or as a garden is greater than a single flower, or an entire body is greater than any particular part of it' (*Twelfth Oration,* 4). The Fathers tell us that it is the Spirit's chief work to lead us towards the gathered Church, and not towards an isolating individual experience.

It is not simply the rarer or more cerebral charismas, but all the charismas of the Church that belong to the revelation of God. Each gift should be understood within the symphony made up of all gifts. Not everyone is intellectual, or has the ability to treat the sick and heal them, not everyone can speak more than one language, or excel as a leader and we cannot all be prophets. But no one can approach God by his own effort, without the many charismatic gifts that the service of our fellow Christians makes available to us. The Spirit calls together this community, and all the Spirit's acts and gifts serve the unity of the community of the Church. Our conclusion is that revelation of the truth always brings about communion, the particular communion of Christ. Christian doctrine points to this communion and teaches us that this communion is the truth itself.

Now we have come to the part that the Church plays in the formation of doctrine. Christ is the reality of a new relationship between God, mankind and the world, and the Church is the community within which this new relationship is manifested for the world. In the Church, the entire world, with Christ the new Adam at its head, acknowledges God as Father. The new relationship expressed by this acknowledgement, is the world's salvation from dissolution and death. Knowledge of the revelation of God is an empirical reality within the body of the Church, which enjoys the relation of the Son to the Father, in which the entire world is embodied, making it the body of Christ. The relationships that constitute this community and make it this body are the actualisation by the Spirit of the revelation of God in the world.

All members of the Church constitute this communion that is the living knowledge of God. It is only *together* that all baptised members of the Church constitute the body that reveals Christ. The people (*laos*) created by baptism, laity and clergy together, are the revelation of the Son who is the truth of the new relationship of the world with God. Christ, together with his Apostles, stands at the head of this people. Christ makes himself present to the Church in the person of his ministers. They must ensure that the community preserves the original form of the body of Christ, as experienced by the whole people of God from the earliest moments to which Scripture bears witness. This is the particular ministry of the head of the eucharistic community, the bishop who, accompanied by his presbyters, represents the image of Christ surrounded by his Apostles. In the Eucharist, the community of the Church lives and displays the Christ-centred relationship of God and the world. The knowledge of God is given by the new, salvific relationship of God to the world, manifested in Christ and experienced as Eucharist. In the person of the bishop, the community gathered at the Eucharist expresses its faith 'with one accord', as the liturgy puts it.

Doctrine acquires its authority from its faithfulness to the truth of the relationship between God and the world. This is revealed as the communion of God, the world and mankind in Christ, which is the communion experienced by the Apostles and their communities, as the New Testament records. When all the Churches confess the same faith, the catholicity of the Church is made evident 'throughout the world'. 'The bishops in every corner of the world are of one and the same mind as Jesus Christ', in the words of Saint Ignatius of Antioch (*Letter to the Ephesians* III). The councils of bishops are the form in which the Churches express the unanimity that makes them the one Church and body of Christ. They are ecumenical because they include all primatial bishops, representing the whole world (*ecumene*). The doctrine of the Church set out in the decisions of these councils expresses the faith of the whole Church and fully reveal the knowledge of God within his relationship to the world through Christ in the Spirit.

Because Christian doctrine witnesses to the living truth it must be continuously received and transmitted by all the members of Christ's body. There are no specific procedures for this reception of doctrine by members of the Church, but this reception occurs in the 'Amen' given by the whole people of God in worship. Without this public and eucharistic affirmation there cannot be any liturgy, or preaching or teaching. Such affirmation can be withheld when there is disagreement between bishops and the laity, as it was at the Council of Florence in the fifteenth century. But above all, this giving and receiving in the entire community, by which doctrine is disseminated around the whole body, is effected through the experience of the truth of this doctrine, and maintained by the exercise of all the charisms of the Holy Spirit in the service that constitutes the Church as a unity.

Bishops have the particular office of convening councils, through which the faith can be learned and confessed as the common and unanimous acknowledgement of God by all the churches. For this reason they have to formulate the doctrine of the Church which expresses the reality of the communion created by this acknowledgement. Thus the whole people led by their bishops participate as one Church in the shaping of the dogmas as living truths that reveal God as the Father of Jesus Christ, and through him, of the entire world, with the God-man, Jesus Christ, at its head.

In order that Christian doctrine receives its proper authority, it is vital that the eucharistic community functions properly. This community must include people in all stations of life, exercising all the charisms. When the eucharistic community is properly and catholically constituted, doctrine is not unilaterally imposed from above by an institution acting with a merely judicial authority, a *magisterium*, but rather demonstrated and affirmed by the 'Amen' of the whole people. When doctrine is received in this way and becomes secure in the mind of the Church, it is irrevocable and cannot be changed, and can then only be experienced and interpreted by Christian teaching, worship, discipleship and the life of the saints. Whatever is decided by a fully ecumenical council, and is recognised and acknowledged as doctrine by the whole Church, has full authority and is then a *dogma*, which no subsequent council or theological development has the power to rescind. The task of bishops and theological teachers is only to interpret this doctrine, by formulating teaching, which may itself eventually become the doctrine of the Church, expressed in the decisions of subsequent councils of the Church.

Here we must say something about the infallibility of the doctrine of the Church. Infallibility is not the possession of any institution, either councils or bishops. It is not the possession of any individual, no matter how great his or her office or spirituality or intellectual achievement. As individuals, the saints and Fathers are not infallible. Infallibility is the consequence of the 'fellowship of the Holy Spirit', who brings about the wholeness of the Church. Without any reference to the other charisms and functions of the Church, no individual is infallible. But any individual can express the truth of the Church as it has been infallibly formulated by the councils of the bishops, as long he is faithful to this truth. A hymn writer, any martyr or outstanding disciple, and every ordinary Christian who lives faithfully and humbly as a member of the eucharistic body of the Church is a witness to the infallible truth.

Christian doctrine can claim infallibility only if it is faithful to the dogmas decreed by the councils. Many theologians have confused the teaching of the Fathers with the dogmas of the Church. You hear it said that because some particular Father taught a doctrine, that it cannot be mistaken, but this is not so. For the teaching of a Father to acquire real authority, it must be confirmed by the experience of the saints, in the furnace of the 'fellowship of the Holy Spirit' and made explicit in the ruling of an ecumenical council. Athanasius correctly articulated the faith of the Church before the Council of Nicaea, but it was only when the teaching of that council was affirmed by the Church, that Athanasius' theological teaching became dogma, compelling the affirmation of the whole Church.

What happens in those periods when there are no ecumenical councils, and no truly ecumenical dogma can be given? At such times the Church continues to live and confess the truth of God's revelation, through the whole range of lived experience and Christian confession, through the teachers given to it. The Church has its Fathers in every generation, of course: the Fathers did not come to an end in the ninth century, as is often assumed. They interpret the teaching of the Church. They do not produce dogmas, and they do not demand that the Church accept without question their account of its teaching. What we attempt, as students and teachers, is simply faithful interpretation of the teaching that has been passed down to us. We do not make any stronger claims: it would be a foolish teacher who expects his own interpretation to be *dogma*, that fully and validly expresses the teaching of the catholic Church. Each one of us is, as an individual, capable of erring, so we must learn humility and listen to one another's views, for without humility we risk setting ourselves up as judges of the Church.

The truth is revealed and secured, and in this sense becomes infallible, only as we submit to the communion of the Holy Spirit and are incorporated into the body of the Church. God is not known outside the communion of the Spirit and the love created by him, as we will see as we turn to examine the issues of knowledge and faith.

1. *Knowledge in General*

How can we know God? Is knowledge of God innate, as theories of natural revelation maintain? Are we born with some knowledge of God which we can then build upon? Or does our knowledge of God come through direct revelation? Is it possible to gain any knowledge of God from nature, or from human nature? Contrasting views of the possibility of knowledge of God developed on the Western side of the Church, in the rival accounts of Roman Catholic and Protestant theology. But theology does not need to understand the origin of our knowledge of God in either of these two ways. Before we examine patristic views of the knowledge of God, we must consider the question of knowledge more generally.

What is knowledge? Since we are not just theologians, or scientists and academics, we can start by taking a more everyday and common sense approach to knowledge, by looking at how we know anything. When we say that we know something, such as the table in the room in which we find ourselves, it means that we orient ourselves to it in a particular way: we relate it to ourselves. Aristotle introduced this idea, which became familiar to the tradition as Aristotle's 'this thing' (*tode ti*). When we identify something by pointing to it, saying *this*, rather than *that*, we are saying that we know and recognise it. Knowledge is identification: when its identity is lost to us, we have no knowledge of that object. How do we identify objects? Again this is not an issue of theology but just of epistemology generally. How do we know that this is a table? What makes us identify it in this way? First, we recognise it by a process of negation or exclusion, by ruling out all the things that it is not. We say that it is A, and not B. To define A, we exclude all other entities, so when we say 'this one', we mean none of the other objects or possibilities.

A second factor in the act of knowing is that we are obliged to 'define' this object in order to exclude other objects. The etymology of the word 'define' relates to boundaries which we place around this object to separate it from all others. The third action, consequent on the second, is that we 'describe' it by referring to its properties. In the case of our table, we might describe it by its shape, given by space and time. If it loses this shape it would no longer be a table, but something else, like a pile of wood. If there were no space, we would be unable to isolate and describe this table on the basis of its form. This table here would be one with that table over there, absorbed into it, and we would be unable to tell one table apart from another, in which case the identity of this table would be lost in a confusion of all other objects. Without space and time we would have no knowledge of this table.

As Aristotle pointed out, description gives objects those attributes we judge they have. When we say that this table is square we have begun to acquire knowledge of it. But where did the concept of 'square' come from? Plato believed that our concepts are drawn from an unchanging world of ideas and that we apply their names to our objects. Aristotle said that squareness is an attribute possessed by the object itself, so it resides within the table in some sense. But this table is not the only square thing: if it were, we could not call it square, for an attribute must be held in common by a number of other objects. The concept of 'square' is not applicable only to this table, but to a vast variety of other things too.

We describe the object by referring to its various attributes: it has a particular colour. The more attributes we add, the more we know of the object, and the more we are able to relate to it and make use of it. Its usefulness to us allows us to define it: it is a table because we can write on it, lean on it, leave things on it, walk round it. There is always a latent utilitarian or pragmatic aspect to our knowledge, because its attributes make it available to us, either to exploit in some specific way, or simply because it has some aesthetic attraction for us.

So far we have said that to have knowledge of something we must exclude it from other objects and describe it on the basis of attributes given in the context of time and space. We relate not only to what we see, of course, but also to what we cannot see. I know my father, even though I cannot see him because he is no longer alive. Time, that individuated me from him in the first place, has now separated me from him altogether. Without time there would have been no distinction between my father and myself, and without such distinction of things, I would never have been able to know my father as someone other than myself. I was able to identify him only because of the distance that time and space created between us. Time and space allows us to distinguish one thing from another and so enables us to identify things. We know them by descriptions that identify their attributes and the way we employ and value them. We make comparisons: this table is bigger and better than that one and these aspects are also part of scientific knowledge. It is our entire social and cultural context that makes this rather than that attribute of an object useful, and thus makes the object significant for us so we notice it in the first place.

Whilst for the ancient Greeks, the attributes of form and beauty were fundamental to knowledge, in our utilitarian Western culture we tend to place the emphasis on the utility of knowledge, so aesthetics and theoretical sciences are considered to be of less significance. If when you discover something new you are not able to demonstrate its usefulness, your research is regarded as of less value, even as less scientific. Why should we talk about the beauty or fittingness, of art, or of God? What can they contribute to a national economy? Humanities departments are under threat because funds go to departments that demonstrate measurable economic benefit. But how is such benefit to be measured? We can measure it only through the practices of knowledge by which we are able to define and describe it. Knowledge is given by the practices of judgment and evaluation promoted by the humanities, so without these practices we will have little idea of what is useful or worth discovering. Without considerations of value there is ultimately no knowledge at all. Finally, since relativity, and more recently, quantum theory, we have had a change in the perception that the researcher, the knower, must distance himself from the object of his knowledge. Contemporary natural sciences understand that the researcher is involved in the processes by which he comes to know his object, so the experimenter may affect his own results. Knowledge is largely or perhaps even entirely an interaction with a complex environment. So we have very briefly sketched the issues that relate to science and indeed to knowledge of any kind.

We have described what is involved in knowledge of an object. But if we apply this to the knowledge of God we will entirely fail to gain any knowledge. Why is this? First, when we apply the method of exclusion (A is not B), in order to know A we must presuppose that there is something else around, which we have to exclude. So we are obliged to accept that something exists along with God, even if that something is just 'nothing'. But when we say that God creates something out of nothing, what is that 'nothing', besides himself? For some, like Thomas Aquinas and Karl Barth, 'nothingness' seems to have some shadow existence that God rejected and removed by bringing the world into being in its place. On this basis, something is excluded in order to make a first step towards knowledge of God. We would have to suppose that there is something that is not God, which exists in parallel with God, in order to say anything about God. But is it possible to relate God to something other than God without forfeiting the very concept of

God? For God to be God, we may not assume his co-existence with anything else, so we cannot take a first step towards knowledge of him by distinguishing God from whatever he is not.

Description, the second element we mentioned, relates to our location in space and time. Any description of God would place him in time and space. But time and space presuppose a beginning and it is only creatures who have a beginning. They are given their boundaries and separated by the distance given by space. Time and space cannot be applied to God and so we are unable to produce a description of him. The Fathers called God indescribable, which means that it is not possible to ascribe boundaries or limits for him. So it appears that it is simply not possible to say anything about God.

This brings us to a perennial discussion about the attributes of God. Medieval theology taught that we may know God by his attributes, because we can say that God is good, almighty, omniscient and so on. But we know an object by its attributes because we take those attributes from our experience of other objects. We do not find the attributes simply and solely within the object we investigate. If we were to invent some word not found in any language, and then describe this table by that word, and say that the attribute named by this invented word exists only in this table, we would not be offering any description of it that would allow others to identify it. Imagine we show some new invention to someone who had never seen anything like it before, and when he has watched it working, ask him to relate it to something. Its action will remind him of something else that he is familiar with, to which he can make some comparison, however far removed. If he has truly never seen anything to which it can be compared he will be unable to offer any description of it, and so will have no knowledge of it. We comprehend what is new by analogy with things that are familiar to us, for all knowing is a matter of making connections with our existing experience. We identify what we don't know on the basis of what we do: knowledge is analogical.

The attributes that we allocate to an object are never unique to that single object: we can never know what is truly unique. We are able to know objects because they have characteristics in common, so there are degrees of resemblance or kinship between them. If someone's body was truly unique, we would be unable to relate his anatomy to our experience of any other anatomy, and so we would be unable to perceive him at all.

This being so, what can we say about God? From where can we draw his attributes? How can we say he is good, for example? Where would this attribute come from, if not from our own experience? I know various people who are good or powerful, and I know about God's goodness or power because I draw this knowledge from my experience of other persons generally. But if I attempt to reach God by extrapolating from my experience I am making God a creature; indeed, I am making him my own creature. Since attributes of goodness or power are not exclusive to God, the human race is endlessly able to substitute various phenomena or abstractions for God. If God is like these other phenomena or like other persons we know, why not replace him with them? Why should I revere God and not revere a thunderstorm, if both of them are 'powerful'?

We can see this in the case of our notion of God as Father, which is where the problem of anthropomorphism most frequently appears. We teach children to refer to God as 'Our Father'. In what sense do they, or we, understand this? It must be on the basis of those children's experience of fathers. They identify their father with certain attributes: he can do things that they cannot, perhaps, such as protecting or providing for them, and through these attributes the child receives an idea of God. When adolescence, and with it the desire for freedom, arrives children have to free themselves from subordination to their parents. The young person can only turn into an adult by shaking off some of these received ideas and undergoing a revolution against authority and dependence, and in this revolution, the childhood idea of God has to disappear.

This event of disbelief in God is the same whether viewed on a personal level, or on the level of a society or civilisation. In those moments of cultural transition where authority is contrasted with freedom, the idea of God is discarded. It has to be put aside because we came to 'know' God on the basis of experiences and attributes that we acquired from our own family and wider relationships.

We cannot give God the attributes found in other objects. Danger follows inevitably from knowledge attained by extrapolation from familiar objects and from notions abstracted from them. The knowledge of God is bound up with the results that this knowledge offers, and such knowledge will ultimately be rejected. How many people lose their faith in God because he does not answer their prayers! Just as I choose to reject and ignore this table if it is of no use to me, I will eventually reject God and ignore him as of no use to me. And the word 'ignore' does not simply mean that I know that he does not exist, but that, since he makes no difference to me one way or the other, he does not exist *for me*. I do not know him because I decide I do not need to know him.

I do not condescend to know him, that is to concede him any acknowledgement, so my ignorance of him is deliberate. You can see what kind of danger the knowledge of God – epistemology – contains, when it is based on the attributes of God. It leads to atheism, because by definition, God cannot be fitted into any of the moulds that we have available to us or in any way be made useful to us. If this were not the case, then at any given moment, just as I push a button to start up a machine, I could likewise push the prayer button and wait for the answer to come. This would demote God to the status of an object and, and worse still, demote me to the status of someone bound to such an object.

We cannot speak of God's attributes and then attain knowledge based simply on these attributes. We cannot resort to any categorisation that includes place and time, because time and space came into being at creation and do not apply to God. So how can we come to know God? Is there anything that we can find in our own experience that can point us on the way? Is it possible to know something, without going through this process of objectification and then exclusion of attributes? Either we cannot know God, or we give up trying to describe God on the basis of our experience and say simply that, though we know God, we cannot describe him.

These two options have been discovered many times over the centuries, and they are very much on offer today. The response we call negative theology insists that we cannot say anything about God. Our silence about him must be absolute, for whatever knowledge we have, we are unable to put into words. The other response is a form of mysticism that allows a certain expression of God, that involves experience and emotion which, in its most extreme form, obliterates the distinction between the one who knows and the one who is known. Through the centuries, Christians have experimented with both negative theology and mysticism. In 'The Mystical Theology of the Eastern Church' Vladimir Lossky (1903–58) tries to offer a combination of the two. If negative theology, which insists that we do not know God by nature, is the way forward, what can we say about God? It is easy to say what God is not, or to say that we cannot say anything about God. What can we say affirmatively about God?

Negative theology appears as the problem of opposition between God and the world. In order to know God, you must go beyond the world and leave it behind you. Neo-platonism represents this principle of 'beyond the essence'. In the hands of the sixth-century theologian Dionysius the Areopagite, its method was to attach the prefix 'hyper' (over or beyond) to every concept. Whatever we say about the world, we must use 'hyper' when we refer to God. So, for example, to say that God is 'good', which is of course based in our experience of the goodness of other people, we would have to say that God is *more-than*-good, or *beyond-*goodness. By this we do not mean that God is good to the maximum degree but that he surpasses goodness entirely. In the same way we say that God is not 'being' but 'beyond being' (*hyper-ousios*). Dionysius wants us to understand that all our categories represent the projection of our worldly experience onto God and so we must be taken beyond them. But despite all this rhetorical effort, we cannot definitively pass beyond ourselves to God.

2. *Knowledge Through the Son*

Now we must see what knowledge of God is offered in the teaching of the Church. To find out how the Fathers approached the knowledge of God we must examine a little patristic history.

In the middle of the second century, Justin began to use the concept of the Logos to set out the view that the human mind is the instrument of understanding. Origen (*c.*185-254) and then Evagrius Ponticus (345-399) expanded this into an epistemology in which the mind purified itself of all that was available to our powers of perception, which fitted well with Evagrius' view that the calling of the monk is to rid himself of all worldliness. According to this view, there is a direct relationship between God and the human mind, so the mind is the link between God and man, and the means of our knowledge of God.

One danger of this doctrine is that it excludes from our knowledge of God everything perceived by the human senses. Though this may seem obvious, it does not easily agree with the confession that Christ has become perceptible to human senses, and that the senses too are therefore the means of knowledge of God. The human mind appears to be able to perceive God directly, without any interaction with the material world, and so becomes the point of contact between man and God. Some of Origen's followers developed this doctrine into an entire theology. It was corrected however by another monk, Makarius the Egyptian (*c.*300–390) and eventually condemned by the Council of Constantinople (553). Makarius introduced another faculty, the heart, into the discussion. Rather than the mind, the heart was the source of our knowledge of God. Because the classical view of man understood the heart as the source of the emotions, Makarius was not always understood, but in fact he was not making a distinction between mind and emotion.

In the theology of Israel the heart was the faculty of cognition because it was the instrument of obedience. The heart represents man's obedience and so it knows God as God, since the pure in heart 'shall see God' (Matthew 5.9). The heart is the place of freedom, where we say 'yes' or 'no' to one another and to God. The obedient heart does God's will. So knowledge of God is not an issue simply of intellect or of emotion but of obedience. For those formed by the Greek worldview and coming to terms with the teaching of Scripture this was not obvious. For Greeks, knowledge had to point towards the identity and existence of something. An object must be much more than a moral summons, to which I respond with a 'yes' or 'no'. Through obedience we acknowledge that someone truly exists, so for Makarius there was an ontological aspect to this knowledge.

The breakthrough came with Saint Maximus the Confessor (580–662). Maximus was one of the great, perhaps the greatest, theologians of that time, because of the boldness with which he reconceived all the major theological issues. He used Makarian ideas to correct Evagrius, so that the theological tradition of Origen was purged of its more detrimental aspects. This did not require any aggressive confrontation: doctrinal breakthroughs seem to come without any great fury in the Patristic period. Although Origen had huge authority, Athanasius, the Cappadocians and above all Maximus amended him radically, but none of them found any need to mount great campaigns against his theology.

The first change that Maximus made was to redefine the term 'Logos'. To Maximus, Christ is the Logos of God. It is through the Logos that we come to know God, and all beings have their *logoi* and reason within the one Logos and Word of God. The breakthrough came when Maximus perceived this Logos of God as this *person*, the Son with whom God the Father has a relationship of love.

Only Christ, the Logos of God, can know God. Only the Logos is in an eternal loving relationship with God which actually reveals, discloses and makes known the identity of God as this person, the Father. As the Gospel of Matthew puts it, 'no-one knows the Son except the Father, and no one knows the Father except the Son, and anyone to whom the Son chooses to reveal him' (11.27). Maximus insists that the Son knows the Father because of the relationship of love that exists eternally between them. In this relationship the Father is recognised and revealed by the Son, who says, 'You exist as my Father.' Within this relationship of Son and Father, God reveals himself, and is acknowledged, as truth. Athanasius made the same observation in argument with the Arians: he said that the Son was forever with the Father, and that it was impossible for the Father to exist without his Son because the Son is the image and truth of the Father, and image and truth are united in him (*Against the Arians* I, 20–21).

This was a significant epistemological move. The Father knows himself as he recognises the Son as his own image. You cannot recognise yourself in isolation from another person. You need a relationship to reflect back to you who you are. The Son is the mirror of the Father, which is what Athanasius meant by calling the Son the image and truth of God. This is the conception that powered the theology of Maximus the Confessor. A relationship of persons, and therefore of love, reveals the truth, and makes known what could not be known in any other way. God is known through the Logos because the Logos is his Son. The Fathers had given up all the earlier teaching of Origen and Evagrius that the mind is the sole conduit or vehicle of knowledge. The Logos is a person, who loves and is loved, and through this loving relationship, he recognises and relates directly to the person who is his other. There is eternal knowledge of God because God is eternally recognised and known by the Son. It is not the creation of the world that makes God known. He is known in his Son in the love that exists between the Son and the Father.

Let us go back to the theological implications of this epistemological revolution. This topic was discussed again in the fourteenth century by Saint Gregory Palamas (1296–1359), though with an epistemology quite different from Origen's. Since Origenism had long receded, the Fathers were free to involve the mind in epistemology again. The mind cannot acquire knowledge on its own, without the whole person, so the heart and mind were understood as a unity. The heart knows, and the mind loves, and because it loves it is also able to know. This meeting of heart and mind was referred to as the 'descent of the mind into the heart'.

Having established that the Logos by which God is eternally recognised, is the Son, Maximus took another step. We too may gain knowledge of God through the Son, and only through him. Maximus agreed with Makarius that the heart was the source of human knowledge. No true knowledge of God comes through the mind or the heart, by either intellectual or spiritual exercises. The Son, who is his true other, and who is loved by the Father, knows and loves the Father and accepts his identity and his being from him. The only true revelation and knowledge of God is located in the loving relationship of the Father and the Son, and God reveals himself through this relationship of love. We may come to know God in Christ.

So how does love relate to knowledge? We have looked at the way in which we know objects and we have said that none of those approaches could be applied to knowledge of God because all the conditions by which God could be known as an object would directly abrogate the meaning of 'God'. We found that there is another way that is linked directly to our experience, and of course it has to be linked to our experience if it is to become knowledge for us. This way relates to the communion of the Son who, loved and known by the Father, knows and loves God.

We have said that we cannot simply repeat the theology of the Fathers word for word. We may use their terminology, but we must also do the conceptual work that is required in order to interpret them and be faithful to their meaning. If we are to learn from them, so that their theology is allowed to challenge the way we understand ourselves, we have to take the vocabulary and conceptuality of our own age and use them to interpret the Fathers' theology faithfully. Then the theology of the Fathers will change our conceptuality and influence the way we think about ourselves. This requires that we relate our own experience to Patristic theology, bringing one into the light of the other. All knowledge that is truly ours must relate in some way to our experience. What experience can we apply to God without encountering all the problems that we observed with knowledge of objects? It is the experience we know as *personal relationship*.

3. *Knowledge Through Personhood*

In order to make clear the connection between knowledge and relationship we have to examine the Fathers' discovery of the concept of *person*. A person is identifiable only within a relationship with another person. There is no person outside relationship with other persons, so one person is no person at all. No person can be substituted by another or be absorbed into another. We may know things through their attributes, but this is not how we know persons. We cannot submerge persons into attributes and classes.

We could even say that we know persons in spite of their attributes. The person you know may be in all sorts of moral trouble, but because you love him and regard him as unique you do not allow his deficiencies to define your relationship. If it is only because of their goodness that you relate to a person, you are not relating to them as a *person*. If we likewise identify God by his goodness, we are identifying him not as a person but as the sort of object which, when it proves to be not quite as we expected, we lose faith in, with the result that the relationship comes to an end.

Each person affects our own life and very existence irreplaceably. We exist in relationship to him and this relationship affects our very existence. If this person were to disappear, in some measure we cease to be ourselves. Since one person acquires his identity through his or her relationship with another person, the disappearance or death of that person affects him or her ontologically.

In terms of theology, this means that if the Son ceased to exist, the Father would not exist either. If the Father did not exist, neither would the Son. Their relationship is mutually constitutive, each of the parties in this relationship depending on the other. Now we must look at the particular significance this has for theological knowledge. This personal relationship of Christ and the Father is given in Christ to us, so we are enabled to recognise God because we are made sons, who can address God as *Father*. In teaching them to pray 'Our Father' Christ gave this privilege to his disciples, and we are brought within this relationship so we can also address God as Father. There is no one but the Son who can eternally address God as Father, therefore only the Son can bring us into relationship with himself, so we become sons of the Father and thereby able to know God as he is, as God the Father. The Christian approach to God as Father originates exclusively from this relationship of the Son to the Father, and the right that the Son bestows on us to address God as Father with him.

The concept of the paternity of God was common in the ancient world. To the Greeks, Zeus was 'the father of gods and men'. But in the bible only the Son has the right to address God as Father. Christ alone is able to reveal that the Father is the identity of God. Knowledge of God means the acknowledgement that God is the Father. This relationship that God has eternally with his Son is the relationship that is passed on to us. We do not therefore come to know God by compiling a dossier of his characteristics, in the way that some dogmatics systems do. That God is Father is the whole truth of God, so a true understanding of God is only possible within the identity of the Son of God. If we are familiar with Christian doctrine, we may even give this our intellectual assent. But really to know this is to recognise and acknowledge God as Father, which is the prerogative of the Son. A son knows *his* own father in quite a different way than he knows anyone else's father. Personal knowledge exists only within relationships that are unique and irreplaceable.

What is it that distinguishes knowledge of a person from knowledge of a thing? Freedom is one of the basic elements that distinguishes persons from things. A thing cannot be known freely. When a thing is known to me it has no freedom; indeed, neither the object nor the subject who knows it can be free. We are not free to ignore what is directly in front of us, because the object imposes itself on us, making our knowledge the function of necessity. Christian apologetics attempts to prove the existence of God, so we have no choice but to accept it. If we intend to convince someone that God exists by a logic that they cannot evade, they can only be compelled to concede their acknowledgement, and this knowledge would eradicate their freedom.

On this basis, God would become an involuntary object, to himself and to us. When God is regarded as 'supreme being' or 'higher power', this is the acknowledgement that animals, demons or idolaters are able to make of him. They understand him in this way because they are obliged to do so by consciousness of their own weakness before the all-powerful being that they cannot control. But what does it mean to know something, or rather someone, *freely*?

Saint Maximus (*Ambiguum* 9) asked in what way does God know things? What form of acknowledgement does he give the world? Does he know it as a scientist knows the laws of nature? Maximus replies that God does not know the world according to its nature, for this would mean that what he knows he *has* to know, and cannot avoid knowing it. Such a conception of knowledge does not fit God, for it is not by nature that God knows things. He knows things because they are the creatures of his own will. By willing them, he created them. The nature of things is not the condition of God's knowledge of them, for everything that is, is the product of his will. As a result, we may also know a person not because we have to acknowledge his presence and existence but because we freely identify him as the one we freely love. The 'object' of love can only be a person. It is not due to their nature that you know this person, and perhaps not due even to their presence with you, but because, like you, they are free either to refuse you and withhold themselves from you, or to return your love and enter relationship with you.

Here we have to make an effort of the imagination to see how different a person is from a thing. Imagine you are in love with someone, and you have not seen them for what seems like a very long time. Say you have arranged to meet them at a café, but when you arrive at the café can cannot see them. You scan the crowd and it is full of friends, but the one person you want to see is not there. You are oblivious of all the others who call you to join them because at that moment the absence of the person you love fills the entire café. By their physical *absence*, they determine the way you experience all the others who are present in the café. Strangely enough, the absent person you love fills the café with his or her presence, while those present become absent for you. One's person is not dependent on one's physical presence. You can be present within a personal relationship without being so physically. Absence can help us to come to know one another because this means that our knowledge of one another is not overpowered by our physical presence. There is an element of involuntariness about physical proximity. Physical presence does not entirely determine our knowledge of persons. We have to grasp this in order to realise that knowledge of God does not rely on physical presence.

We can recognise a person as a *person* only in freedom, so all the knowledge we have of persons depends on whether and how they reveal themselves. We cannot know anyone *as a person* by force, so if someone does not wish to divulge their identity, we cannot know them as persons. We may regard one another as objects of knowledge, with all the properties that we observe from one another's physical presence, but no one can finally and definitively know someone until that person is willing to make themselves known. God intends to give himself, so we may acknowledge him and gain knowledge of him without threatening his freedom. Personal knowledge is therefore always free, which means that it comes to us as a gift or a revelation. Because he desires to, God identifies himself to us through our knowledge and so reveals himself freely.

We can go a step further and say that God does not want to be known or be acknowledged by us, unless this takes place in freedom for us too. Knowledge that is imposed on us, in defiance of our liberty, is not person-to-person knowledge, and so is not the knowledge that God wishes for us. If God's existence were to be proved so that we became compelled by logic to believe in him, it would not be God who was thus believed in and known. God does not intend to be known, and therefore cannot be known, by compulsion. Man has the choice not to know God. We can tell him that we do not wish to know him. We are free to say that God may exist, but as far as we are concerned, he does not. We reject this possibility for ourselves. God wants us to know that he exists *for us*, for *me*: he looks only for that acknowledgment that can take place person to person.

When God reveals himself, he does so as *our* Father. Such knowledge encountered in freedom gives us the possibility of saying freely, 'Yes, you are there', or 'No, I don't want to know you'. Freedom both for God and for man is therefore intrinsic to knowledge of God. A relationship between persons is not determined by nature. God is known to nature only in the form of necessity: animals know of God, as do the principalities and powers, 'demons believe and are terrified' (James 2.19), but who wants that sort of knowledge?

By saying 'no' to God, and withholding acknowledgement of him, man demonstrates his freedom. If you tell me that you have no time to meet me, either now or at any time in the future, you are withholding relationship from me. 'I do not know you' (Matthew 25.12) is what Christ warned he will say to those who finally withhold themselves from him. If Christ says, 'I don't know who you are', the possibility of any personal relationship is gone. So in theology we are not dealing simply with knowledge, but with the knowledge that originates in the freedom of persons, and which is therefore personal knowledge, for only this knowledge exists in freedom.

Another fundamental constitutive element of knowledge is love. By love we do not mean an emotion or a relationship given by nature, for there is an element of compulsion to all such relationships. For the ancient Greeks for whom *eros* was a fundamental reality, love held all things in a harmony which made the cosmos as a whole beautiful. In the *Symposium* Plato speaks of love: in his view each good thing has a power of attraction, so love necessarily draws us towards it. Goodness and beauty are forms of necessity. This was so in the moral realm too, because the Greeks believed that we have to love someone who is good. Wherever there is nature and biology, the power of attraction – which is what love is – is at work. How can we demonstrate that we are free, and not utterly determined by the force of necessity that nature represents? We can show this only by breaking and reversing the force of necessity. This is the great revolution introduced by the gospel.

In his discussion of the *Symposium*, Ioannis Sykoutris, a modern Greek authority on Plato, says that if Satan asked God why he loves his human creatures in spite of their sinfulness, God would be hard put to come up with an answer. What sort of reason could there be for such a love? Where would you find a reason to justify God's love towards the man who will not give up his sin, and where everything indicates that he should be given up rather than loved? It is exactly this that demonstrates that we love of our own free will. We do not love because we have to; we love because we will to do so and so we love freely. Knowledge that is determined by love is not compelled but motivated by freedom.

We have to consider the love that is not driven by any necessity whatsoever, not even the most moral or spiritual. God loves in perfect freedom, so Christ reveals to us a love that, because it is free, is quite unconstrained by man's love of sin. If you remove the love towards a sinner from the gospel, the entire freedom in which God loves disappears. It is not difficult to love someone who is good or attractive; in fact, it is natural to do so. But to love a sinner even to the point of dying as a result of love for that sinner as Christ did, may be utterly opposed to nature or sense, but it is surely an expression of freedom.

I have said that personal knowledge is the form that complete knowledge takes, and that personal knowledge is a function of love. The third element that is contained in this love is that that we come to know God through a particular relationship. If there is no love, and no relationships of love, there would be no knowledge of God to be had at all. Several New Testament verses make the fundamental point that, we cannot know unless we love. In the First Letter to the Corinthians, where he deals with the issue of knowledge, Paul points out that many people boast how much they know, but he says, 'knowledge puffs up, while love builds up'. He continues, 'if one believes he knows something, he has never known anything whatsoever, in the way that it should be known; if one loves God, he shall be known by him' (1 Corinthians 8.1-3).

Here the apostle lays out an entire epistemology in which love is the presupposition of knowledge: 'Though he believes he knows something, he does not know anything whatsoever'. One truly knows only within a relationship of love. In the case of the knowledge of God, it is God's love that precedes our knowledge of him. 'He who loves God shall be known by Him', or even simply, 'he who loves shall be known by God.' This is repeated more clearly in the Letter to the Galatians, where Paul says, 'having known God' and then corrects this to 'or rather, being known by God' (Galatians 4.9). You cannot encounter God unless God has acknowledged you, because we cannot love him unless he first loves us, as the First Letter of St John (4.10) states.

God first knows us, and reveals himself to us. But this occurs only within a relationship of love. If man cannot love, he cannot come to know God, for as John again tells us, 'He that does not love, does not know God, for God is love' (1 John 4.8). In John the words 'he does not love' refer to the love that is given in the specific communion of the Church. Love for us means inhabiting this specific set of relationships which we call the Church. As we shall see, ecclesiology is essential to epistemology.

John goes on to explain what he means by 'God is love'. 'God's love was made apparent' because 'he sent his only-begotten Son.' God's love is not an emotion, and it does not flow from God, as though it were wine poured from a jug. The Fathers were very careful to avoid all those expressions of this sort that were commonplace in the ancient world. God's love consists of his being the Father of the Son. The Father's love is his Son, this person and this relationship, whom the Father gave to us so we can know him. Our knowledge is entirely a function of this relationship, which God is in himself, and into which he has brought us.

This relationship exists before we do, so we are not compelled to initiate it for ourselves.

Knowledge of God involves our admission into the relationship of love of the Father and the Son, a relationship that we desire in freedom for ourselves. This relationship is free because God is not obliged to love us, but does so of his own volition. Equally we are not obliged to love him, but we may either enter this relationship willingly, or we may decline it. Entry to this relationship means identifying God in the person of Jesus Christ. If we do not accede to the relationship of love that exists between the Father and the Son, we remain outside all knowledge of God. The many forms of philosophical, mystical and pagan knowledge that remain open to us are unable to identify God as he is, which is the Father of the Son.

Now we can say that love is that particular relationship that we may refer to as being 'in Christ', within which we may acknowledge God as Father. We belong to the community and the body constituted by this relationship. There is no approach to God outside the body brought into being by the Son's acknowledgement of God and consequent knowledge of him. God is known as who he is within the Church and there only. Anywhere else he could not be acknowledged as Father, but only as something else. The Father is who God is, and how God intends to receive us and does in fact receive us. God may be many other things, but we cannot know what they are because we can only know him as, in his freedom, he receives us and reveals himself, as the Father of Jesus Christ.

The knowledge of God as Father involves the re-constitution of every relationship by which we are constituted. We exist through all the relationships we know, and the many more we are unaware of. My identity is linked to all the relationships that I have with persons and things. All these relationships and our direction and desires undergo a re-ordering and purification as they are brought into this relationship with God. This represents a radical purification, which is what the life of the Christian is. The re-ordering of our relationships brings us finally into being, setting us definitively with the relationship to the persons of God that will secure our life without limit.

We heard Saint Gregory Nazianzus say that talk about God is not a general possibility, but only for those who have 'undergone testing, lived in contemplation, and have cleansed body and soul.' In another oration Saint Gregory tell us that such purification is essentially a matter of love. 'God is the ultimate light . . . which is contemplated as we purify ourselves, is loved as we contemplate it, and which is known as we love it' (*Oration* 40.5).

We may come to know God only as we love him, and we are known by him only as we are loved by him. Ascetic purification will not reveal God to us, automatically as it were, simply by re-ordering our desires. It is through love realised in communion within the body of Christ, as we come to participate in the relationships that make up this body, that God becomes known to us.

What difference is there between Christian spirituality and other forms of spirituality? Is the difference merely one of form, so that, apart from the fact that we use the name of Christ, Christian spirituality is otherwise not very different from that of other religions? If we do not refer to the community of Christ's body, these specific relationships within which we are placed, we will be quite unable to say how Christian spirituality differs from every other spirituality. A Buddhist also claims to know God by cleansing himself of his passions. But for a Christian, knowledge of God does not come until we enter this specific community of persons who, bound together by love, make up the body of Christ and in Christ know God.

We have said that Christian teaching is given and interpreted within the Church, and it is most particularly given in the event of the Eucharist, which is the fullest possible acknowledgement of God on earth. All other forms of discipleship or teaching are provisional, and although we should not minimise them, they all direct us to the relationships of love into which God freely brings us in Christ. I must have the love that God has for my brother, or I do not know God. 'If anyone says I love God yet hates his brother, he is a liar; for if he does not love his brother, whom he has seen, cannot love God whom he has not seen' (1 John 4.20). Knowledge of God is not simply a vertical line between me and God, but it connects me to all other persons, and through these persons it connects and binds together the whole world. This is why 'he who loves not, does not know God, for God is love' (1 John 4.8).

So we have said that knowledge is identification. Then we have said that there are two kinds of knowledge, of *things* and of *persons*. *Things* appear before us as givens, which we identify because their nature and ours compels us to. We distinguish them from other objects, and on the basis our experience gives us, we describe them by those characteristics that they have in common with other objects. We identify them by their location within networks so that they have value, function and represent opportunities that are there for us to take.

Then there is knowledge of *persons*, which involves identifying another being in a relationship of freedom and love. Freedom means that we are not compelled to acknowledge the identity of this being.

We will recognise particular characteristics and attributes of course, but it is the person himself who willingly reveals his presence to us and allows us to acknowledge him in freedom.

We identify each person within a set of relationships of constitutive interdependence. We come to know him as part of a relationship of love that is integral and necessary to our own existence. We know him, not as a 'thing', and thus not because this someone imposes themselves on us through their attributes and power, but because they open themselves up to us and we to them in a free relationship of love.

We have said that knowledge of God is offered to us within a loving relationship of the Father and the Son in which God is identified and known eternally, quite apart from us. We identify God in Christ as we become part of this existing relationship. This knowledge is the function of this relationship of love, so God is known within the community constituted by these relationships. The Holy Spirit sustains the relationships of love that make up the community of Christ.

4. *Knowledge Through Faith*

We must now turn to the subject of faith. We must start with the main elements of dogmatics as they are found in the Creed. Were we to adopt some other approach we would be attempting to force Christian teaching into the categories given by logic. The Creed is based on the living relationship created by baptism, and sustained by the holy Eucharist, by which man and creation are held in union with God.

The Creed begins, 'I believe..'. The relationship of faith and knowledge represents a problem to many people because they regard faith and knowledge as opposites, so we may either believe something or we may know it. If we believe, we have given up on real knowledge. An equally common perception is that we know something and then we believe it, or the other way around. Just as we asked whether love comes before knowledge, or knowledge before love, so we must ask which, of faith and knowledge, comes first.

The baptismal rite of the ancient Church was recorded for us by Justin in the second century and in more detail by Cyril of Jerusalem in the fourth century. In this rite, when someone is baptised, an act of exorcism frees them from whatever powers have had dominance over them. Then they are called to turn to face the east, so at the moment they first say 'I believe' their whole direction changes. When man is born, he has a particular orientation and perspective to life, to all other created beings and to God, that is governed by nature and destined to die. Baptism reverses this orientation and re-orients that person towards true life. We cannot say 'I believe' if our direction remains as it has been given us by birth.

The words 'I believe' are a response to a question, which means that they are not the action of an individual on their own. The baptismal candidate replies to the question put to them by the Church. No one can say 'I believe' unless as a reply to this community, so no one can come to faith whilst locked up alone in his room. Faith is possible only within the community that puts this question to us.

There is a second element to this turn to the east. The east is the direction from which the Church awaits Christ's coming, towards which the prayers of the early Christians were offered, and to which all the Church's liturgical rites are essentially oriented. We turn to the east because that is the direction from which the completion of history and true life will come with the coming of the kingdom of God. Faith is therefore an about-turn by which we turn to face the direction from which our true life comes.

A fundamental definition of faith is given in the Letter to the Hebrews. 'Now faith is the substance (*hypostasis*) of things hoped for, the evidence of things not seen' (Hebrews 11.1). Faith is the *hypostasis*, which is an ontological term, of things not yet seen. When we say that faith is this *hypostatis*, we mean that we believe *in truth*, and that through faith we are enabled to perceive reality *in truth*.

But the second element is that this identification is eschatological. It is the 'substance of things *hoped for*', which we do not possess at this moment. It is in expectation that we turn towards the culmination of all time in the future, and acknowledge the reality of things that are not yet physically present to us. The second part of the expression, 'the evidence of things not seen', clarifies the first. The things that we can see convince us of their existence. Things 'not seen' are not available to the scrutiny of all our senses, so although only vision is mentioned, all the senses can be understood here.

We cannot claim faith in those things that we already grasp by our senses, or by the processes of logic by which we perceive a coherent world through those senses. There is no faith involved when a being is an object perceptible to our senses, so that we have no choice but to be convinced about it. Where we are obliged to recognise its existence there is no mediating role for faith, so the concept of faith is about freedom once again.

My presence before you is perceived by your senses, which we conceptualise primarily in terms of sight. You cannot say that you do not recognise me, or cannot identify me, when I am standing directly before you. By being here before you I am imposing on you, so you have no choice about acknowledging my presence. Faith however is what is not imposed on us by the presence of things, or by nature, or by experience or history. Faith relates to whatever is on its way to us from the future, which is to say, from what is not yet visible or perceptible to us.

Faith allows us to move beyond such imposed and involuntary knowledge. Knowledge that forces itself on us may offer us social and psychological security, of course, just as when faith is understood as trust between two persons. A child trusts its mother, but this trust is not the same as faith because it springs from a very tangible cause. The child is certain of its mother's love because, from conception her womb has mediated that love, and after birth the child continues to experience its mother as love. A child knows who loves it: it knows 'things unseen' though nonetheless very well intuited, so we can conclude that trust is not same as faith.

Faith is more far-reaching than trust. Faith is a somersault: we land facing a new direction. Our being no longer consists in what nature makes secure and verifiable to us. This faith is not supported by experience of things already known to us, but comes from that about-turn and a new start in a direction for which we have no experience. Faith receives no support from anything that can be grasped by senses, logic or either historical or psychological experience, all of which represent some kind of compulsion.

This understanding of faith can be seen in Christian baptism, in which the believer places their security in what they can have no confirmation of. At baptism the first Christians were asked to give up their identity and receive a new one, not based on any set of known relationships. Faith implied a 'crisis' because it involved this about-turn which placed all existing relationships under judgment. The first of these are the relationships of biology and so of family which provide us with our most basic security and identity. The child is born into relationships with parents and family, and if these relationships are removed it would mean disaster for that child. A second set of relationships that determine our identity are our social and political relationships. Our security derives from the community we belong to, which vouches for us and acts as the guarantor of our identity. Without the recognition that this community gives us we would have no public identity or public existence at all. For the early Christians, as for us today, identity has a public and civil element. Let us imagine that in some violent event you are stripped of your identity: imagine your passport, driving licence, credit card and all other identity papers were taken from you, and imagine that when you try to rectify this situation you find that your bank account has been closed and national insurance number withdrawn. You have no means of entering employment or any other relationship with the rest of society, or of being acknowledged by any public institution. Your civil identity has vanished: you have no public existence.

Here we arrive at the distinctive thing about Christian faith. The first Christians were asked to do two things at their baptism. Firstly, they said goodbye to all the identity and security they received from their families. To be baptised was to obey the words of Christ, 'if you do not forsake your kindred, you cannot follow me' (Matthew 10.37) or in the even stronger words of Luke, 'if you do not hate your own family, you cannot follow me' (Luke 14.26). In other words, in baptism we are torn away from every biological root.

The second thing which was true for the first Christians, though not for us, is that when they were baptised as Christians they ceased to have any civic identity. Christians were non-persons in the eyes of the law, until Constantine granted legal recognition to them for the first time. The author of the Letter to the Hebrews says (13.14) that 'here we have no permanent city, though we seek one to come.' By 'city' we mean a state and the legal framework that enables the rule of law. 'We have no city' means that we Christians are persons without civic identity, for our citizenship is 'in heaven'.

Baptism means the loss of one identity and the gain of another that is not acknowledged by the state. We 'look for the city that is to come,' orientated to the eschaton, the kingdom and society that is yet to come, so we are the naturalised citizens of a state that has not yet established its presence in history. We do not enjoy the security of a state on earth, yet. This is indeed a giant leap into an identity that is known and secured by someone whom we are unable to see. Our identity is based on his promises about our future.

This faith takes us into a situation in which nothing is in our control. Everything is as yet unconfirmed biologically, historically, socially or by our own experience, or by logic. Indeed such security does not even come when, through faith, God reveals himself to us and we become conscious of this new relationship, and even able to say what kind of relationship it is. Faith cannot be based in such empirical experience. For often, despite the absence of any such evidence, when God is silent and we have no experience of his presence even in prayer, we are called to have faith in him.

We could then say that faith is that giant leap towards someone whom we believe loves us, no matter what. Regardless of all evidence to the contrary, we believe that he loves us and will never abandon us, and we live simply on the basis of this promise. Nothing forces us to acknowledge him, but when of our own will we confess that this loving relationship is the source of our existence, we live from the promise of God and no other security. For the first Christians who made this leap, this faith meant participation in the community of the future, the eschatological communion of God.

The Lord's Prayer tells us that our Father is 'in heaven'. In sayings such as 'call no-one on earth your Father; you have one Father and he is in heaven' (Matthew 23.9) and 'if you do not abandon your father and your mother' (Luke 14.26), the contrast with 'earth', tells us that 'heaven' means that God is beyond the grasp of our senses. Out of our reach, he cannot be compelled or manipulated. In baptism the Christians abandon their earthly parents and masters and the security they represent, and put their hope on things that they cannot control or verify. Such faith means that we are growing into a relationship that connects us to God our Father. Because our relationship is with the Father who is in heaven our life can also no longer be grasped or imposed by biology, family, society and so on.

What about the historical nature of Christian revelation? Do we have no historical evidence, 'proofs', that compel us to acknowledge God? The pagans point to the phenomena of nature, but these only point back to their own pagan conceptions of God. If nature gives no proof of God, what about the evidence of history? God has 'not left himself without witnesses' (Acts 14.17). The witness statements we have are historical records. The Old Testament points to God's dealings with his people through history, showing that God miraculously saves his people from disaster, and repeatedly asks Israel whether they are going to remain faithful to the God who so often intervened to vindicate them. Surely this is the evidence that supports our faith? Isn't the supreme proof of God that Christians have the person of Christ himself, whose life and death are historical events, giving our faith an objective basis?

All this is true, and yet no such evidence alone can be the basis of our faith. That which has already been given to us by God as evidence of his existence, cannot be ignored by faith, which is why the Creed sets out the acts of God in history. But the evidence of his existence that God gives through history, even including the resurrection of Christ, contains an element of indeterminacy or paradox. Although the events themselves are real and certain, God does not allow them to become convincing in an absolute sense. If the ascension had not taken place, but things had continued just as they were after Christ's resurrection, how could anyone *not* believe in God? If we saw the Lord among us as Thomas saw and examined him, how could we *not* believe? Then the presence of Christ would compel us to believe.

But Thomas, who is not prepared to believe until he has the evidence of his own hands and eyes, receives the rebuke 'Blessed are they who have not seen, and yet have believed' (John 20.29). Christ looks for those who believe without any such assurance or reinforcement. They are blessed because they believe and know in freedom. The moment such tangible evidence convinces him, Thomas' faith has lost its freedom.

Our freedom is made possible by the ascension of the Lord, which is followed by the gift of the Holy Spirit who is himself freedom. The ascension opens a new era in which we may know Christ but *by faith*, without compulsion. Knowledge of Christ cannot be compelled.

God now addresses our free will, and this free will is a characteristic of the Spirit and of life in the Spirit, lived by faith. God gives us signs of his presence, but of a sort that we are quite capable of not receiving if we have no wish to. The Apostle Paul could have refused to receive the light that halted him on the way to Damascus: the possibility of shrugging off what happened on that road and referring to it simply as imagination, was open to him. Our faith is supported by the witnessed presence of God, but in a way which makes it possible for us to refuse it, not in a way that closes down our freedom. God never reveals himself in a way that does not allow us to say 'no'.

Often a number of things are confused here, particularly when it comes to the sacraments of the Church. The sacraments are indeed knowledge of God and the signs in which our faith is rooted, but they do not replace the freedom represented by faith. When Christ offers himself in the form of bread and wine, he does so in such a way that we are not obliged to recognise him through them, for the sacraments are 'the substance of things hoped for, and the conviction of things unseen.'

The same is true for the greatest disciples and saints of the Church. Sometimes we are given the impression that there is a constant, almost objective holiness in the presence of a holy man or woman. But even the miracles of saints leave a margin for those who wish to doubt them. We cannot rely on miracles which would make our faith in God's presence unfree. So God offers signs of his presence amongst created things and events, without destroying our freedom, and he does this through his saints, who often know moments when God is not present for the verification of tangible experience. The lives of saints include whole periods of God's absence, through which the saint remains faithful.

Faith will pass away, for faith itself is not the goal of the Christian experience. There will come a time when the 'substance of things unseen' will be unseen no longer, but there for all to see. We will not need the 'assurance of things hoped for', for by then those things will have become reality. Love alone will remain constant through our history and into the kingdom (1 Corinthians 13.8-13).

Chapter 2

The Doctrine of God

I. BEGINNINGS

We have discussed the role of knowledge and faith in Christian doctrine. In this chapter, we shall begin our examination of the Christian doctrine of God. We must outline the historical framework within which the doctrine of God appeared, beginning from the bible, and going on to see how the doctrine took shape through the Patristic period, and finally looking at the significance of the doctrine of God for us.

Christians are not the only ones to talk about God – every religion does so. Even atheism talks about God in order to reject particular conceptions of God. Atheism may wish to reject every notion of God, but it is only possible to reject a conception you can identify. It is not really possible for anyone to avoid the question of God for even if you reject all conceptions of God, you have to describe what it is that you wish to reject.

We are going to examine the concept of God as it has been received by the Church and set out in its teaching, so we will start by examining the history of this doctrine. The Christian faith introduces no new concept of God, but follows the faith of Israel. Christ believed in the God of Israel, so he shared the same faith in the God of Abraham, of Isaac, of Jacob and all the Fathers of the Old Testament. But although Jesus Christ addresses the God of the people of Israel, in his person and teaching he also represents a modification of Israel's understanding of God. We must discover what changes this conception of God underwent as it became faith in the person of Christ.

Israel's conception of God consists in the absolute transcendence of God. God exists prior to the world, and we can never relate him to anything of what we see in the world. This is entirely different from the thought of the ancient Greeks, for whom the cosmos gives us knowledge of God. Whether their God was a rational, connective force, that holds the world together in harmony ('cosmos' means order and beauty), or a 'reason' that allowed them to explain the cosmos, for the Greeks the cosmos shows us something of the nature of God.

For Israel, this is not so. You cannot reach God by studying the cosmos, or tie God to the existence of the cosmos, or refer simultaneously to God and the cosmos as though there were some necessary relation between them. God exists prior to the cosmos, and this is represented by the doctrine of the creation of the cosmos *ex nihilo*. Although God exists always and forever, the cosmos has not always been in existence. This would be a most strange idea to the Greeks, for whom the cosmos is eternal, even though it is always in process of coming into being. Plato gives us an account of the creation of the cosmos by the Creator-God, who creates from existing ideas and elements in an existing space. The cosmos is made from something that always had existence, and is given its form by a God who is in some way bound up with its existence. For the gods of ancient Greece there is no transcendence in the strong sense found in the faith of Israel.

A second and related factor for Israel is that God is transcendent and utterly free. He is bound by no physical or other needs. Ancient Greek thinkers on the other hand took a different view. Tragic poets such as Euripides, and pre-Socratic thinkers such as Heraclitus, asked whether the gods were free to do what they wanted and their categorical reply was that they were not. The gods were bound to do what was right, for there was a natural and moral law which the gods were not free to contravene. Heraclitus taught that a single logos sustained the cosmos: if this logos failed, the entire cosmos would vanish; but because this logos is given and the gods observe it, the cosmos does not vanish. Justice was part of this cosmic order. Zeus married Themis ('Justice') to demonstrate that even the chief of the gods is not free to act arbitrarily, a theme reiterated by every Greek tragedy.

In the *Timaeus* Plato describes a God who brings this world into existence by forming it in conformity with the ideas which represent the perfection of the cosmos, and which regulate even the action of God. This God had to give the world a spherical shape because, as Plato explains, a sphere is closest to the form of beauty; if he had created an ugly world he would have transgressed against the ideas and the imperatives of justice and beauty.

Israel had quite a different conception of God. There was no thought that God could be constrained by goodness or right, for God acts entirely freely. The Old Testament is full of events that do not appear right, but which are nevertheless commanded by God. God is constrained by no cosmic principle of justice or order.

For Israel God is personal. We could say that God was personal in ancient Greek thought, of course, in that the gods are forces given personal characters. However, when we say that God is personal in the Old Testament we mean that he is acknowledged within relationships between persons. He is the God of Abraham, Isaac and Jacob. God can only be understood in relationship with these particular persons whose encounters with God make up the history of Israel and are recounted in Israel's Scripture. He is never a faceless, supreme power, and he cannot be understood in terms of a mind, or a physical force or a rational origin of existence. This does not tell us anything about the nature of God, but it does tell us that God is always related to specific persons. Israel's God is in a constant relationship of persons and he summons man to enter a relationship that is person to person.

After transcendence, freedom, and the personal character of God, a fourth aspect of the doctrine of God is the historical character of God's revelation. God reveals himself and is recognised through his involvement in history, rather than by observation of nature or the cosmos. Greeks did not give up observation of the cosmos on becoming Christians, but the Church insisted that the cosmos only leads towards God in the sense expressed in the psalms: 'the heavens declare the glory of God, and the skies proclaim the works of His hands' (Psalm 19.1). The cosmos can tell us only that it was made by someone other than itself. God exists outside the cosmos, his transcendence is decisive, so the relationship of the cosmos to God confessed by the psalms, is an historical rather than a cosmological observation. The works of God's hands are made evident by the heavens: the world is a creation, which is to say a project initiated by an agent. It is not a matter of nature, governed by laws, such as the principles of harmony, goodness or justice honoured by the Greeks. The world is not approached as nature or cosmos, but as event and history.

Another characteristic of the biblical view of God, which we could call the historical aspect of the revelation of God, is that God reveals himself through his commandments. For Israel, truth in general, and faith in God more specifically, are not a matter of theory for they do not come from observation (*theoria*) of the cosmos. Truth comes through history, and from God's interaction with the people of Israel and thus through their experience and history. They are given the law that they are to follow and they respond by following it. These are the factors that make up the biblical understanding of God, and which means that the Christian God is the God of Israel.

Nonetheless, there are certain claims that Christ makes about himself which revise Israel's understanding of God and which account for the conflict between Jesus and his contemporaries. The Apostles and their communities accepted Christ's claims, wrote the New Testament and then expounded and interpreted it, bringing into being the growing corpus of the Church's doctrine of God. Therefore, the issue for us is not whether the Church was right to accept the claims of Christ, but whether these claims still represent Israel's understanding of God, and thus whether Christ is as he presented himself, the fulfilment of Israel's understanding of God.

The first claim is that Christ addresses God as Father and that he is able to do so because he alone is Son. The claim is not that anyone can call God 'Father', but that Christ does so exclusively. With this claim of unparalleled personal relationship, Christ brings himself into a relationship with God different from that experienced by every other member of Israel, and this represents a change to Israel's conception of God.

The second claim is that Christ is the final act of God in history. To Israel, God revealed himself in historical events rather than as physical or natural facts. As these acts of God were unfolded by the Church Fathers, they were related to the cosmos and developed as the doctrine of creation. Though the distinction between history and nature is not always easy to define, we can make such a distinction and use the concept of history or nature as seems most appropriate. For Israel the acts of God were historical events rather than facts of nature. Talk about the givens of nature in Israel would raise the charge of idolatry.

To his contemporaries Christ presented the claim that he is the 'Son of Man', which in the Apocalyptic literature of the period meant that he is the one who will finally judge history. Only God himself can bring historical time to an end, for Israel, for only God can pronounce judgment on all kingdoms and all history. In the books of Daniel and Enoch the judgment of God is exercised by the 'Son of Man', and the Gospel tells us that 'when the Son of Man comes, seated on his throne of glory' (Matthew 25.31), he will give his judgment on all kings and kingdoms of this world. Since for Israel this final judgment can only be passed by

God, the 'Son of Man' is the presence of God to history. No man can pass judgment on any other man, let alone on human history as a whole: only God can give such judgment. Israel never expects to see God, for he transcends the perception of his creatures. But as the 'Son of Man', God comes to bring his judgment to all human history. Christ identified himself from the first with the Son of Man and so with faith in the future judgment of all. This created a unique relationship between the person of Christ and God, for Christ maintains that he is the one who will judge the whole history of mankind. The preaching of Christ's resurrection signifies that, in the mind of the first believers, Jesus Christ is identified with the eschatological Son of Man, who is God come to rule over all human authorities. The Church is created by this new expectation that the eschatological Son of Man, the resurrected Christ will return to bring the rule and judgment of God to all human history.

None of this represents a crisis in the doctrine of God. However, this waiting for Christ's judgment meant that the first Christians had to explain who they were waiting for and why he was making them wait. It was the need to explain the wait that resulted in the writing of the New Testament. Where is Christ between his resurrection and his return as judge of all kingdoms, and what is now his relationship with God? The answer is found in the teaching of the ascension. Christ sits at the right hand of God: 'The Lord said to my Lord, "Sit at my right hand"' (Psalm 110.1). The Christ who sits at the right of the Father enjoys the dignity that, in the theology of Israel, belongs exclusively to God. First, there is worship: 'every knee shall bow in heaven and on earth' (Philippians 2.10). No member of Israel can kneel before a creature, and yet this person sits at the right hand of the only God and receives the same praise. How is this the same God when Christ receives the sort of devotion that the leaders of pagan empires demand, but which even under torture and at the cost of their lives, Christians withhold from all other lords? Only God can make such demands as this.

The wait for Christ's coming adds a third element. We have to ask where Christ is now, and what our relationship with God is in the time before his return. How should we see our relationship with God, now that Christ is seated at the right hand of God in heaven? The answer to this urgent practical question comes with the other 'Helper' (*paraclete*) introduced in the Gospel of John. 'I will not remain here', Christ had said, and yet 'I shall not leave you as orphans' (John 14.16-18). As Christ is at the right hand of God, the Father has sent another helper, the Spirit of truth.

A new experience of the relationship with God began after Christ's ascension, with the arrival of this third person, the Holy Spirit. This person verifies the presence of God himself and, and with gifts and demonstrations of power, does what only God can do. The first disciples were compelled to find a place for their experience of the fellowship of the Holy Spirit within their understanding of God. Christ now appeared as this fellowship which breaks through the limits given by nature and creates the Church. The Spirit enables each human being to transcend his limits and go out to meet the 'other', regardless of their natural differences. Before the arrival of the Spirit of Christ the world knew of no such community that transcended all the divisions of creation.

This raises the question of whether we can still refer to God as Israel does, without referring to the Son and the Spirit. We have the person of Christ who termed himself 'the Son of God', and the person of the Holy Spirit, who makes Christ present to us in history as this fellowship of the Church. Through its experience of this communion the Church was led to confess its faith in the Father, the Son, and the Holy Spirit and this trinitarian form eventually became the proper name of God for Christians. It was its own experience which compelled the Church to give an account of this event, in which the constrictions of nature are transcended by the freedom of fellowship in Christ. You may reject the claim Christ is making, and remain with Israel's form of confession, or you can accept this trinitarian name that conveys this new communion of all creation brought into being by Christ.

This trinitarian name appears in the New Testament, in three forms, two of which are liturgical. The first context is baptism, which involves public confession of God as this Trinity of persons. St Matthew's Gospel has Christ's instruction to 'baptise in the name of the Father, the Son and the Holy Spirit' (Matthew 28.19). Some argue from the witness accounts in the Acts of the Apostles that baptism was first performed in the name of Christ rather than of the Trinity and that Justin gives us the first account we have of baptism in the name of the Trinity. However, baptism in the name of the Trinity is present in all books of the New Testament, most clearly the letters of Saint Paul, and so from being a term used in the confession made at baptism the Trinity became the name of God.

The other context in which the trinitarian formula appears is that of the Eucharist. This use is also very early, for we find it at the end of the Second Letter to the Corinthians in the familiar form 'May the grace of our Lord Jesus Christ, and the love of God the Father, and the communion of the Holy Spirit, be with you all' (2 Corinthians 13.13).

Scholars have shown that this phrase, with which Paul ends his letters, was the opening of the Eucharistic liturgy of the first churches, so from the very beginning the trinitarian formula has been part of the Eucharist.

Finally, there was also a broader theological context, for we find reference simultaneously to the Father, the Son and the Holy Spirit in the letters of the Apostle Paul and the Gospel of John. Thus, a theology of these three persons developed, and it did so without controversy until the Church's faith began to meet the questions posed by the Greek worldview in the second century.

The question was put in this way. If we are baptised in the name of the Father, the Son and the Holy Spirit, as all Christians were by then, what had become of faith in the one God of the bible? What was the status of these persons? How are they related to God? If the three persons are related to God *ontologically*, doesn't this make three gods? If we say that the persons are not ontologically related to the one God, why do Christians worship them and attribute to them acts that belong solely to God, like the judgment of history or the creation of this nature-transcending fellowship?

It would not do to say that this is simply an unfathomable mystery. If we simply declared everything to be unknowable, we would have no theology at all. There are mysteries, of course, but they are mysteries that invite us to wonder. They do not prevent thought, but invite it. The Fathers of the Church went to great lengths to show that there is no contradiction between monotheism and the trinitarian God, indeed it is only the doctrine of the Trinity that is able to safeguard the unity of God. We must discover why this is so.

It took many generations to settle the Church's account of these questions. We can divide the earliest answers that were offered into two sorts. One set of answers refer to the Logos and the Spirit as acts of God in creation and providence. God is one, but in order to create the cosmos he acts as Logos and Spirit. The difficulty with this response was that the trinitarian life of God presupposes the existence of the cosmos, which would mean that the transcendence of God would be lost.

For the second-century Apologists there was little clarity about whether Logos and Spirit are divine or part of creation. They always seemed to appear in relation to creation, but this raised the question of the transcendence of God. The Church was compelled to search for greater clarity, at least with regard to the Logos. Finally, it declared that the Logos belongs to God, not to creation, and so ruled out some of the interpretations of Logos that had been in circulation. God is not triune because he is Creator. The Council of Nicaea (325) made it clear that God is triune quite independently of creation.

The other category of responses we could call 'modalist'. Here the Son, the Holy Spirit and even the Father were regarded as the modes by which God acted in history, rather than as 'concrete' beings. This theory, chiefly represented by Sabellius, became a huge challenge until it was finally rejected. The Church insisted that these three persons are in personal relationships, each of which is different from the others. The Father speaks to the Son, and the Son prays to the Father, and thus they are two 'beings'. The Church insisted that the difference between them was more than merely functional, and it was not confined to the 'economy' of God for man. The question of how three 'beings' are not three gods remained, but the Church preferred to face this question rather than accept Sabellius's theory that there were three personal modes behind which lay God's single 'being'.

It was this challenge that was met by the theology of the Cappadocian Fathers, whom we turn to next. Though we can admit that the triune doctrine of God has its own complexities, we must not give in to the obscurantism that discourages any intellectual labour in the name of a simple faith. Theology is not the enemy of Christian faith. If we examine these issues with our minds we will find that the life and worship of God become more wonderful to us than if we attempted no intellectual engagement with them.

II. The Being of God

The Church inherited the baptismal and confessional statement 'Faith in the Father and the Son and the Holy Spirit' from the Church of the Apostles. Every Christian made this confession at baptism and, though there were differences of interpretation, the statement itself was universally accepted. The Fathers who inherited this trinitarian confession had to ensure two things. First, they had to exclude interpretations that would lead to idolatry, which meant any interpretation that would distance this confession from the truth of the God of Israel revealed by the Old Testament. Second, they had to show their contemporaries that this formula was meaningful and true. The Fathers were always concerned to demonstrate the meaningfulness of the Christian confession to the world they lived in, for the truth of Christ can never become the possession of any group that is not concerned to give an account of Christ to the world beyond them. The Fathers expounded the teaching of the Church in those categories of thought that brought them

into dialogue with contemporary intellectuals, but they also related
Christian doctrine to the Christian life with its universal appeal, so
that ordinary people could make this faith their own. We must examine
this first historically, and then as it relates to our own situation.

The Apologists of the second century made the first attempts to set
out the Christian doctrine of God in terms of the Logos. They decided
that God projected the Logos, the second person of the Trinity, in order
to create the cosmos. There was much disagreement about whether
the Logos was uncreated or part of creation. If we say that God *became*
triune or that he acquired the Logos in order to externalise himself
and create a cosmos, we link the existence of the Logos to that of the
cosmos. One Apologist who pointed in a more promising direction was
Theophilus of Antioch (*c.*180). Theophilus distinguished between the
Logos and its outward expression, going beyond Justin to say that, while
the Logos may be a projection of God outside himself for the creation
of the cosmos, nevertheless it pre-existed within him. Just as we have
intentions to which we are able to give verbal expression, so God always
has his Logos. Having decided to bring a cosmos into being, he gave
external expression to this Logos, and in this way the distinction between
God and the world is safeguarded. However, this left the question of
whether the inner logos could exist without verbal expression or was
compelled to give itself an outward expression.

Another attempt to set out the Christian doctrine of God in terms
of the Logos took the form of modalism, for which the persons of the
Trinity are roles that God takes on for the sake of creation. God played
the role of Father in the Old Testament, the Son in the New Testament,
and in our own time the Holy Spirit, adopting these three identities to
perform particular functions for us within history. This was the account
developed by Sabellius who taught in Rome at the beginning of the
third century, and whose teachings became widespread in the West.

The Church reacted intensely against Sabellianism, particularly in
the East, which regarded the West as particularly vulnerable to the
temptation of modalism. Second-century Apologists declared that the
persons of the Trinity are 'three in number'. However, they insisted
that this does not mean that God starts as a unit and then subsequently
divides or expands to become three. The one does not take on a form
external to itself, for the threeness of God is intrinsic to him. In order to
demonstrate this, the Fathers took the crucial step of distinguishing
between 'alone' and 'one'.

In philosophical Hellenism, God was understood as a monad, a self-
sufficient unit. In the religion of the ancient Greeks, represented in

demythologised form by Plato, God was simply one. However, in the Christian account, the oneness of God cannot mean that God is a monad. In first-century Alexandria, Philo, a Jewish thinker thoroughly at home with Greek thought, offered the interpretation that God is the one who is truly alone. His commentary on the verse that speaks of the creation of woman shows what he meant: 'It is not good for man to be alone; let us make for him a helper in his likeness' (Genesis 2.18). Philo says that man cannot be allowed to be alone, because God is the only one who is truly 'alone' (*monos*) (*Allegorical Interpretation of Genesis* II.1.1). That God is one means that he is utterly solitary.

However, in opposition to this view the Church believed that although God is one, he is not a monad. In the Christian doctrine of God the number three represents particular beings in relation with one another, so God is not a solitary being. The insistence, however, on such a distinction between being 'one' and being 'solitary' would keep Christian doctrine in permanent tension with other philosophical accounts of God. Were Christians talking a peculiar language of their own, or were they able to give a public account that would demonstrate the rationality of their claims? The Fathers were not content to leave any ambiguity.

First of all, the problems were tackled on the level of the vocabulary employed. How were they to choose the terms by which to say that God is three persons who are one, rather than three different aspects of a single unit? Tertullian, writing at the end of the second century, used an expression which proved decisive. God is '*una substantia, tres personae*'. With 'substance' he indicated the unity of God, and with 'persons' he indicated plurality. Tertullian's choice of terms was picked up by Hippolytus who translated them for the Greek-speaking Christians of the East. The translation of Tertullian's terms represented an immense challenge. The Latin '*substantia*' may be literally translated into Greek as '*hypostasis*'. Both words refer to what is underlying and fundamental and so denote the unchanging being found within or beneath each individual thing. Everything is based on some such unchanging being, which was termed its 'hypostasis'. Though this Greek term went through many shifts through the centuries, this basic sense was constant. When we say that a rainbow does not have a hypostasis, we mean that it is an ephemeral phenomenon, while a table has a hypostasis, because there is something substantial and enduring about it.

In general, hypostasis was used to denote that single unchanging being that God is. So what about the persons? The Greek word for person, 'prosopon', meant aspect or facade. It originally referred to the human face and then to the mask worn by actors in the very ritualistic theatre of ancient Greece, which indicated the character an actor was playing. The risk was that this term would continue to suggest a facade, which would mean that persons would be fronts for the essence of God behind or beneath them. So how did this term, taken from Tertullian, come to be accepted in the East? From Origen onwards the East began to replace the term 'person' with 'hypostasis', and so taught that God had three hypostases, that is to say, three unchanging, underlying realities. Translation of hypostasis into Latin immediately created 'tres substantiae'. However, Latin speakers who already used the expression 'una substantia', could hardly now say 'tres substantiae'. At stake in this translation issue was the unity and therefore the being of God. How could the Church use the expression 'one substance', without creating the impression that the three persons of the Trinity are 'modes' or 'faces' of the one God without real 'being', as Sabellius taught?

1. *One and Many*

The solution to the problem of the persons and unity of God came in the fourth century with the Cappadocian Fathers, and it came through a radical innovation that involved a redefinition of terms. Up until that time 'hypostasis' had meant being or substance. The Cappadocians made a new departure, by deciding to make a distinction between these two meanings so that essence and hypostasis could no longer be regarded as synonyms.

The Cappadocians now said that the meaning of 'substance' and 'nature' was the same, so both could be used to signify the oneness of God. God is one nature or one substance. From then on the Latin term 'substantia' was rendered in Greek not by hypostasis, but by 'ousia'. We can translate 'ousia' either with 'substance' or 'nature', two English words which can be used as synonyms here. However, they decided that 'hypostasis' should be understood to mean the same as 'person', so the term 'person' now referred to a distinct being, to someone who possessed true and particular being and was not simply the 'mode' or 'manifestation' of another being

This was a revolutionary move, though for some reason it has received almost no mention in the history of philosophy. It was possible only because 'hypostasis' bore several nuances which allowed this development, so this conceptual revolution was not entirely arbitrary. The term 'hypostasis', which had referred to what was most fundamental and unchanging, was now a synonym for person, which consequently was understood as an 'ontological' category. Person no longer denoted just a relationship that an entity could take on or the role that an actor would play. For this reason Saint Basil insisted we can only say that God is three 'prosopa' when we make it clear that the 'prosopon' indicates a distinct and particular entity, and not a 'face' or role in Sabellius' sense.

Now we must turn to the significance of saying that God is one being or one substance. The term substance refers to what is general, or to what is held in common, and so it implies the existence of more than one being. The term 'human nature', for instance, indicates that we are all of one sort or one nature, human nature, even though we are each individually a complete human being. Human nature has as many instances as there are human beings. There is a unity to humanity and yet there are simultaneously two, three, a thousand, a million human beings, each of whom exemplifies human nature and represents humanity. However, if there are many humans sharing one human nature, are there many gods sharing a divine nature?

The answer the Cappadocians offered was that, because we humans have been created, our nature is divisible. Human beings are not only distinct, but they are separate, owing to the intervention of time and space between them. Time and space allow us to be perceived as self-existent persons. This means that human nature is subject to mortality: when a human is born, human nature brings forth a human entity which is divided from all other human entities by time and space. Each human person is therefore a separate entity, and thus we have many people. The oneness of the human race seems to be at odds with, and even to be threatened by, the plurality of all these individual persons.

For all created beings, there is a conflict between oneness and many-ness, owing to their emergence in time and space. Without space and time everything is in danger of losing its identity. However, the many-ness of God is not in conflict with the unity of God: since God is not subject to time or space, there is absolutely no connotation of separateness, or of externality and internality for the persons of God. The Cappadocian Fathers said that the analogy of one human nature exemplified by a multitude of distinct human persons could indeed be applied to God, provided that we do not include time and space, and therefore separatedness and mortality, in the analogy. With this condition the question of three different gods disappears.

The next issue we must examine is the relationship of God to being. Does the 'being' or the 'essence' of God come before these three persons? Does God start as 'one' and subsequently become 'many'? We can ask the same question about humanity. Could it be that humanity comes first, and particular humans came along later? The ancient Greek philosophers believed that human nature, this general thing in which many participate, comes first and is followed by the more particular thing. We all come into existence from a single essence, and from this unity we diverge into separate beings with a myriad forms: on this basis nature comes first, and the individuals who exemplify that nature arrive later. Plato and Aristotle believed that no matter what each one of us is as an individual human being, we are exemplas of a common nature. For Plato, we are exemplas of the ideal human being in which we all participate, whilst for Aristotle we are exemplas of an underlying human nature in the form of the human species from which we all spring. The species precedes the individual, and so, according to Aristotle, particular individuals disappear but the species survives. If the philosophers of ancient Greece are right, 'nature' precedes the particular 'person'.

However, with its doctrine of the Trinity, the Church took an entirely different approach that opened up a new path for philosophy. One single statement made by the Cappadocian Fathers laid the basis for an entire new philosophical project: *there is no bare essence*, no nature-as-such. Nature exists only in specific instances, so we can only talk about being or essence or nature when there are particular beings. Nature is not more fundamental than any specific instance of that nature: 'Being' as such does not come before particular *beings*. It makes no sense to say that specific human beings spring out of human nature. Each particular human being is fundamental for human nature and for humanity as a whole. The Cappadocians tell us that it is not possible to use the term human nature without including this and that particular person already. We cannot refer to human nature without implying the specific persons.

The philosophical breakthrough represented by the doctrine of the Trinity has profound significance for humanity. If there is no essence as such, and we cannot assume the origin of the human species is a human essence, whether Plato's ideal human, or Aristotle's species, what is the origin of each human being? In a letter to Amphilochius, Basil agrees that since a 'bare' human essence cannot be the origin of humankind, the chief ontological predicate of a human being cannot be his essence (*Letter* 235). It must definitely be one particular being, one human. The ancient Greeks said that we derive our existence, and trace our genealogy as particular beings, from a common human nature. However, Christians respond that we each draw our existence from a single person, whom we call 'Adam'. This specific being, and not 'nature', is the cause of our being.

In God, too, it is not divine nature that is the origin of the divine persons. It is the person of the Father that 'causes' God to exist as Trinity. However, 'Father' has no meaning outside a relationship with the Son and the Spirit, for he is the Father *of* someone. This plurality and interdependence of the persons is the basis of a new ontology. The one essence is not the origin or cause of the being of God. It is the person of the Father that is the ultimate agent, but since 'Father' implies communion he cannot be understood as a being in isolation. Personal communion lies at the very heart of divine being.

Now we are in a better position to understand the expression 'God is love'. Christianity did not invent the notion that God is love. Plato believed that God is love, in the sense that love is a flow of the divine nature, a flow as involuntary as the overflowing of a cup or a crater. The Church rejected this conception of love as involuntary emotion or passion, and insisted instead that the phrase 'God is love' means that God is constituted by these personal relationships. God is communion: love is fundamental to his being, not an addition to it. Because it is directly related to the doctrine of the Trinity, this point has to be given a great deal of clarification.

It is perhaps our usual assumption that we exist first, and then that we love. However, let us imagine that our existence depends on our relationship with those we love. Our being derives from our relationship with those who love us, and if they cease to love us, we disappear. Love is this communion of relationships which give us our existence. Only love can continue to sustain us when all the material threads of life are broken and we are without any other support. If these threads are not reconnected we cease to exist; death is the snapping of the last thread. Love, or communion with other persons, is stronger than death and is the source of our existence. That 'God is love' means that God is the communion of this Holy Trinity. God the Father would lose his identity and being if he did not have the Son, and the same applies to the Son and to the Spirit. If we took away the communion of the Trinity to make God a unit, God would not be communion and therefore would not be love.

It is easy to assume that God is love because he loves the world, but the world did not always exist. God did not *become* love because he loves the world, for this would imply that he became love when the world came into existence. But God is absolutely transcendent, his existence is utterly independent of the world. God is love in his very being. It is not however himself that he loves, so this is not self-love. The Father loves the Son and the Spirit, the Son loves the Father and the

Spirit, the Spirit loves the Father and the Son: it is another person that each loves. It is the person, not the nature or essence, who loves, and the one he loves is also a person. Because divine love is a matter of personal communion this love is free: each person loved is free to respond to this love with love.

Our question was whether it is the substance or the person that is most fundamental, in God. We have seen that, in God, essence and person are co-fundamental, neither is prior to the other. Next we must see what significance this has for the doctrine of God, first by seeing what the Cappadocians made of it, then by looking at the very different answer given by Augustine to the question of the divine Trinity and the issues that it has left us with.

2. *That, What and How God is*
We have seen that, by making a distinction between substance and person, the Cappadocians made a vital development in the doctrine of God. These two terms, substance and person, allow us to distinguish between the various ways in which we use the word 'being'. We can distinguish between saying *that* God exists, *what* God is, and *how* God is who he is.

The Cappadocian Fathers dealt first with the bare fact of God's existence. To say *that* God is God is simply to affirm his existence and rule out his non-existence. By asking *what* God is we are asking about 'being' in general. When referring to any existent object, it is one thing to say that it exists, ruling out the possibility that it does not exist, and it is another thing to say *what* this particular object is. For the Greeks, the question of *what* relates to the substance, or *ousia*, of the object, and in the case of God, it refers to the essence of God. The third way of referring to things according to the Cappadocian Fathers is with the question *how*, or in *what way* it is what it is. The Cappadocian distinction between *what* and *how* was quickly adopted by the Church because it helped to set out the rationality of its teaching about God. Saint Maximus the Confessor argued that 'what' corresponds to the 'reason', or logos, for which a thing exists, while 'how' refers to the way in which it is what it is. These distinctions will help us lay out Christian doctrine with regard to the being of God.

First, *that* God Is. To say *that* God exists, is merely to indicate his existence rather than non-existence. The question of God's existence was scarcely ever asked in the ancient world, so the issue that is so pressing for us was not one that patristic writers had to engage with. The

Epicureans expressed doubt about God's existence, but they did not exercise any significant influence.

Patristic theology and subsequent Christian doctrine uses the verb 'to be' when referring to God. The neo-platonism which dominated at the time of the Fathers spoke of 'One' as being 'beyond substance, so the term 'ousia' could not be used of the 'One', but only of what derives from it. Such negative theology was widespread, and not limited to neo-platonism. Dionysius the Areopagite used the expression '*hyper-ousios*' (above essence) in order to say that God in himself is above every onto-logical category. All our categories come from our experience of created reality, but created reality cannot give us any knowledge of God. When dealing with the Greek Fathers, we refer to this as *apophatic* theology.

The doctrine of God does indeed take us beyond the common nature of things, but this does not mean that we cannot use the concept of being when dealing with God. 'Apophaticism' does not mean that we have surpassed the concept of being or gone beyond ontology. In an important passage in 'On the Holy Spirit' Saint Basil says, with reference to the phrase of St John's Gospel 'in the beginning *was* the Word', that no matter how we stretch our intellect, we cannot go beyond the word 'was'. The verb 'to be' is not only permissible in discus-sion of God, but it applies most directly and uniquely to God, for God is 'the one who truly is'. 'Being' applies primarily to God, so theology is the true ontology. God is not beyond or above the concept of 'being', but he is the genuine, the true, '*being*'.

God is 'the one who is' and he is that 'being' whom we can address in worship and the Eucharist. The beginning of the Eucharistic *anaphora* that bears St John Chrysostom's name, makes the formal declaration of the Church that God is the real, the true 'being.'

> It is only meet and right to sing praises unto thee, to bless thee, to magnify thee, to give thanks unto thee, to worship thee in all places of thy dominion. For thou art God ineffable, unknowable, invisible, incomprehensible, the same THOU ART from everlasting.

The expression 'the same' was familiar even in Plato's time, defining 'being' as what is stable and permanent. To the ancient Greeks, decay and dissolution was the fundamental problem, as indeed it is for all of us, so 'being' is what is constant and immutable. Ontology simply repre-sents our search for stability and permanence.

Division and dissolution turn 'being' into 'non-being'. Whatever has existence now will eventually disappear, so all appearances will ultimately let us down. Even though we call this river the 'Thames', and it cannot be anything else but the 'Thames', yet, as Heraclitus pointed out, we cannot cross this same river twice. But what enduring being does this river have if it is constantly changing? Like this river we are all constantly undergoing change, affected by processes that, though slower, make us equally subject to flux. What being, or what stability, does any one of us have if we are all heading towards decay and eventual death? Saint Maximus uses the concept of 'the logos of nature' to refer to whatever is stable about every being, which gives it its existence and reality. If this stability is removed its existence is threatened. Decay mocks and falsifies everything that exists, turning it into something delusory and finally non-existent. Every entity is penetrated by non-being, which is always wearing away at it until, when it has finally disappeared, it no longer has any reality at all. Non-being ultimately renders everything unreal. But we are hoping to find permanence, and we do find it, only, in God. In the Liturgy of Saint Basil we confess this stable and constant being in the prayer, 'It is very meet, right and befitting the majesty of thy holiness that we should praise thee and sing unto thee . . . who are from everlasting, invisible, searchless, uncircumscribed, immutable'.

It is therefore not true to say that there is no ontology in the theology and life of the Church. We do indeed refer to the being of God, and to his being true 'being', the 'being' who actually is. This is the significance of the confession *that* God is: we may really know this. It does not represent an absence of knowledge, and we do not require any negative theology to communicate this. As Saint Gregory Nazianzus pointed out, God is that which may not be doubted.

While our knowledge '*that* God is' is certain, things are different when it comes to '*what* God is'. The 'what' question relates to the essence of a thing. Saint Gregory Nazianzus makes this distinction between 'what' and 'that' in his Second Theological Oration. He says that we cannot give an answer to this 'what' question, for we cannot say what God's essential being is. We cannot know 'what' God is, because to know God in this sense would be to have mastery of God – which would mean that he would not be God. Gregory goes on to show us how difficult it is to know what anything is in its 'essence'. He argues that if it is difficult enough to discover the mysteries of nature and of man, but the 'essence' of God is simply beyond our conception. But what about the angels who are also spiritual beings, or what about the saints who have been made holy? Gregory tells us they can no more grasp the essence of God than we can.

All knowledge comes with an unavoidable margin of wonder and mystery. Essence denotes that stable and unchanging factor in any being whatsoever. But nobody can know the essence of anything, and so nobody knows the essence of God, apart from God himself.

Our third category represents a third way to refer to the being of God. This is the question of '*how*' something is, and this is perhaps the most significant for theology, because we are able to learn in what *way* God is who he is. The Cappadocian Fathers distinguish three ways that God is God that correspond to the persons of God. God is God as Father, Son and Holy Spirit – these persons indicate *how* God is.

Arians and Eunomians asked whether the Son is the essence of God or an energy of God. If the Church had replied that the Son is the essence, it would not have been possible to distinguish between the Son and the Father. If they had said that he was an energy, they would have reduced the Son to a creature. Saint Gregory Nazianzus insisted that the Son is neither essence nor energy, but an identity that can be described only in terms of its relationships (*Third Theological Oration* 16). He says that 'essence' is that which is self-subsistent to each single thing. It is that thing in its uniqueness, as it is distinct from every other thing. An 'energy' is shared by a number of entities just as relationship is. The essence is self-subsistent, so when we refer to the divine essence, we can do so without referring to any other essence. Though an essence may be held common by any number of beings, we can talk about it without making reference to anything beyond it.

But the person is not an essence. It does not exist without being related to other beings, and it cannot be understood in isolation from all else. When we talk about a person, we can do so only by referring to other beings, even though each person is distinct so that what is particular to this person is found in no other. Every person is unique, unprecedented and irreplaceable, even though he exists only through relation with others. The person is the identity born of a relationship, and exists only in communion with other persons. There cannot be a person without relationship to other persons, so if all the relationships which constitute a person disappear, so does that person. We cannot refer to a person without relating them to something else. Therefore, 'Father', 'Son' and 'Spirit' denote unique persons. Yet, if the Father was without relationship to the Son, there would be no Father, and if the Son was without relationship to the Father, there would be no Son.

In this communion each person has his own personal features, which cannot be transferred. The Father cannot impart his paternity to the Son.

None of these personal or hypostatic characteristics, of 'unoriginate', 'begotten' and 'proceeding from' respectively of the Father, the Son and the Holy Spirit, can be imparted or communicated. Each of the persons is a unique and singular identity. If it is replaced by something else, it ceases to be that identity. The Cappadocians used the term 'particular' (*idion*) to express this.

At first glance, the concept of the 'particular' appears to conflict with that of relationship. If we define a person by a relationship, how can we say that the person is entirely unique and particular? And yet, its particularity springs from a relationship for the relationship creates a 'particularity' which is non-communicable, and without being in communion, this 'singularity' cannot exist. Thus each person of the Holy Trinity is unique and irreplaceable precisely because each is in an unbroken relationship with the other persons. If this communion is severed, that person is lost. Communion, therefore, is a condition for the person, indeed communion creates singularity.

What principles did the Fathers introduce in employing these terms into the Christian doctrine of God? We have seen that the first principle introduced by the Fathers is we cannot know the 'what', that is the 'essence' of God. The mind cannot grasp this essence, and though this was conceded by neo-platonism to an extent, it was also a basic principle of Greek thought that we *can* come to know the essence of beings and that the mind can achieve this, by conceiving the idea and then being led to the essence itself.

To know the being of this table, according to Plato, we look for the idea of 'table' within this particular table. No matter how much the truth of the table surpasses this actual table before me, our minds reach beyond this actuality to that truth. The more my mind is purified of all materiality, the more it is able to reach the reality, which is what the form is. If we take Aristotle's view, we look for the essence of the table in this material hypostasis, within which there are certain natural laws that make it a table.

The Eastern Fathers are clear that the essence, the *what* of God, cannot be conceived or comprehended by the mind. Saint John Damascus said, 'the Divine is infinite and unintelligible, and only one thing about it is intelligible: its infinity and its unintelligibility' (*On the Orthodox Faith* 1). We cannot comprehend an essence in any way.

A second principle, offered by Saint Basil, is that the 'essence' (or 'what') does not exist without the 'how'. There is no essence or generality without hypostasis or particularity. The 'how' question is as ontologically fundamental as the 'what' question: they both refer to what we call 'being'.

Hellenic philosophy always attributed primacy to 'being' in the sense of what is universal. For this reason the Cappadocian Fathers found Aristotle of more use than Plato, because Aristotle distinguished between 'first' and 'second' substance: 'first substance' referred to the specific instance, while 'second' refers to the species, and thus to what was general and universal. For example, 'first substance' denotes George, John and Basil – these particular persons – while 'second substance' denotes humanity as a whole or the human nature which these three have in common.

However, divine essence does not come before the particular hypostases, the persons, because there cannot simply be 'being' without hypostases, just as we cannot talk about humankind without implying specific individual people. The same is true of God; one cannot talk about the *being* of God without referring to the persons who tell us 'how' God is God. The divine essence does not precede the persons logically, because the essence never exists without the persons. The being of God cannot be understood without the persons, nor can the persons be understood except as the being of God.

Nevertheless, there is an order and hierarchy to these persons, for their being and existence is a matter of *cause*. The concept of agency or causality in the existence of God is one of the most important and least recognised areas of Christian doctrine, again introduced by the Cappadocian Fathers, and for very good reason.

First, the issue of causality was introduced as a response to the Platonists, who believed that the procession from one to another, particularly in Plotinus' system of emanations, was a natural evolution outwards from the One, in a process of degeneration or disintegration. They believed that the One becomes multiple inadvertently, as it breaks up and loses its identity, and this is both an inevitability and a terrible misfortune.

On the other hand, the Cappadocian Fathers had to confront the claim that the Son is a creature, asserted most publicly by Eunomius of Cyzicus (d.393), who believed that the Father and the essence of God are one and the same thing. Given that the Father is the only one who is unbegotten, Eunomius concluded that whatever is not the Father, such as the Son, originates outside the essence of God. It was for this reason that the Cappadocians made a crucial distinction between the Father and the essence or being of God.

The question was asked whether the Son is born of the Father, or of the 'essence' of the Father. Following Saint Athanasius, the Council of Nicaea (325) decided that the Son is born of the 'substance' of the Father. If this is so, it is this 'substance' which is the source of life, and the Son is begotten by this 'substance'. 'Substance' is productive, and it begets the Son in the same way that any other productive thing gives birth to things other than itself.

When the Cappadocian Fathers introduced the concept of causality, they did so in order to dismiss the idea that the cause of this begetting could be anything other than a person, the Father. The Father is the cause. In this way they distinguished between the Father and 'substance'. Had they not been able to make this distinction, they would have remained in same position as Eunomius. The Father cannot simply be identified as 'substance'. The divine 'substance' does not produce the trinitarian persons by some inevitable process. The divine life originates in the Father, which is to say in a person, thus the Father is the principal person, while the persons of the Son and Spirit come from the Father.

Athanasius was responsible for the idea that it was the Father's 'substance' that was generative and begets the Son. The Arians challenged him. If the Son is of God's 'substance' rather than of God's will, surely the Son must be Son out of necessity? Athanasius responded that even though he is not a function of a will, he is not the Son by necessity either. His sonship is willed by the Father and will always be desired by the Father. But it is not just that the Son is willed by the Father. As Athanasius says, the Father wills his own person. He means two things by this. One is that God's 'substance' exists because of the Father. The other is that the being of the Father exists because it is willed by the Father. The Father wills his own existence as person, so his own existence is not thrust on him. Athanasius sets out the issue:

> For, just as the Father willed his own person, so the person of the Son – who is of the same being as the Father – is not unwilled by the Son. The Son is wanted and loved by the Father, so we should understand that God's being is voluntary and willed. The Son is freely desired by the Father, and the Son loves, wants and honours the Father in the same way, and the will of the Father in the Son is one and the same, so we can consider the Son to be in the Father, and the Father to be in the Son. (*Third Oration against the Arians* 66.)

That the Son of God is 'of the "substance"' of the Father does not mean that he is the Son by necessity. The Cappadocians went on to develop Athanasius' idea by saying that the Father is the cause of the Son. Since the Father willed to exist as this person, he must have willed that the Son exist as a person too.

Here we have arrived at the limits of ontology. We have asked whether God exists because he *intends* to, or because he *has to*, and we have found that he exists because he intends to, and not because he cannot do otherwise. On this principle the Cappadocians named the Father the agent, or 'cause', who is responsible for the existence of God. The Father is the agent of his own existence as Father and the existence of these other persons. Existence is the function of persons acting in freedom, and so is in no way a function of necessity.

The Cappadocians tell us that the freedom of God is the freedom of the Father. Saint Gregory Nazianzus attacked the old Platonist conception that God is like a drinking vessel (*krater*) which overflows, pouring out goodness and life, the sort of analogy conceptualises the natural overflow of a fertile nature, which cannot but give birth to new life (*Third Theological Homily: Oration* 29.2). Gregory insisted that this analogy makes the Father's begetting of the Son involuntary, which would suggest that the entire Trinity exists as a natural and necessary consequence of the essence that God is.

The Creed of Nicaea had said 'begotten of the Father, that is, of the substance of the Father.' At the Council of Constantinople (381) the words 'of the "substance"' of the Father were removed, so that our Creed simply says that 'the Son is begotten of the Father'. The debate that took place between the years 325 and 381 made it evident that the concept of 'substance' could make the begetting of the Son a matter of necessity. The accusations made by the Arians and Eunomians indicated that the begetting of the Son was involuntary and unfree, so the Church made this alteration to the Creed in order to rule out all sense of compulsion. The Council of Constantinople ruled that, in order to interpret Nicaea correctly, the concept of freedom had to be secured within the doctrine of God.

The Cappadocian Fathers made some fundamental contributions to the doctrine of God. The first of these was to provide a more appropriate conceptuality, brought about through a change in terminology. They shifted the sense of 'hypostasis' from its original sense of 'essence', and transferred it to the person, making 'person' a fundamental category. The word 'hypostasis' implies that something or someone actually exists, for whatever has no actual hypostasis has no real existence. We Greeks still use hypostasis in this sense, for instance in an expression such as 'these rumours are without hypostasis', when we want to say that there is no truth in them.

By calling hypostases 'persons', the Cappadocians attributed full ontological reality to each of the persons of God. They rejected the view that they are simply different roles enacted by the one and the same being. Then the Cappadocians attributed the cause of God's existence to the Father, so the existence of God became a matter of personal freedom.

These new terminological and conceptual tools allowed the Fathers to employ analogies in which the persons were clearly complete beings, and so to stay faithful to the tradition they had received. Sabellius viewed God as a being that extended into three separate offshoots each with its separate role, but the assumption was that this plurality would finally contract back into the one again. The belief that God's being has three extensions is termed 'modalism'. The concern aroused by the threat of modalism produced very mixed reactions to Nicaea's ruling for the term 'homoousion'. Following Athanasius, Nicaea stressed that the Son is born of the essence of the Father: the Son is not an extension of the Father's essence, but a complete and independent entity.

The Cappadocians insisted that these three persons are indeed three complete entities. They made an important characteristic alteration to one familiar analogy. In the phrase 'light from light' the Creed uses the analogy of light to represent the unity of the Father and the Son; just as light emanates rays that cannot be separated from their source, the Son is inseparably one with the Father. The Cappadocian Fathers found that this analogy needs clarification, because just as rays of light could be construed as the extension of the light source, so the Son could thus be construed as the necessary outworking of God. So rather than repeating 'light of light', the Cappadocians spoke of three suns or three torches.

We have three complete persons. What is common to these three lights? They have a common energy and substance, for they emit the same heat and light. The particularity and integrity of each person is as fundamental as what is common to them and which gives them their unity.

To refer to this relationship of persons, the Cappadocian Fathers employed another concept to refer to the unity and distinction of each person. This is the concept of 'perichoresis'. The three persons inhere in one another, so each is found entirely within the other. Each person has his own ontological integrity, and yet they are one. In a letter attributed to Saint Basil we read:

> Whatever the Father is, is also found in the Son and whatever the Son is, is also found in the Father. The Son is found in his entirety within the Father and he has the Father in his entirety within him. Thus, the hypostasis of the Son is the image

and the likeness by which the Father can be known and the hypostasis of the
Father is known in the image of the Son. (*Letter* 38)

The intention here is to set out the teaching of the Fourth Gospel
that 'Whomsoever has seen me, has seen the Father, for I am in the
Father and the Father is in me' (John 14.11). In seeing the Son we
see the Father, for the Father is fully present in the Son. The divine
substance cannot be broken up; each person possesses the whole
being of God. 'God is not partitioned,' as Saint Gregory Nazianzus puts
it. The divine being is found in full in persons who are distinct from one
another, so each person exists within the other persons. We could call
this a mystery and refuse to go any further, but, as with the whole
mystery of God, we must attempt to shed light on this too.

How is it possible for one person to be the bearer of the entire being
of God? How is it possible for a person to exist within another person,
without losing their identity? If we place human persons within
other persons, their individuality would be lost. Created nature has
a beginning, it moves within the limits of space and time, and space and
time divide as much as they unite. Human nature is composite, and it is
re-divided as each new person comes into existence, so the human
essence is being constantly re-divided. No single person can be the
bearer of the entire human essence, for if he were, at his death, all
humanity would die with him.

We are all born with this dividing and divisible nature and hence the
existence of death, and yet we can understand how a single person can
be regarded as the bearer of all humanity. When an army announces its
casualties, for example, it says that there were ten fatalities. For those of
us with no personal relationship to them, these are ten individual deaths
which scarcely touch us and have no effect on human nature as a whole.
We survive them and life goes on. But for the wife and mother of one of
these soldiers, the man who has gone now is not one of ten, but one of
one, the one and only. He represents life as a whole, so all life has gone
with him. The unity of two people is so close, that each regards the other
as representative of human being as a whole. When the relationship is
person to person, and one person vanishes, our world vanishes with him
so it seems that this death threatens the whole world. The murder of a
single person is often called a 'crime against humanity'. The more we
regard someone a person, the more we regard them as representative of
humanity as a whole. So we can see from our own existence how we
could regard all humanity through the life of a single person, as though
all the many persons of the human race were also just a single being.

With God, each person of God is the entire being, not a portion of the being of God. But God has no beginning and no mortality, and his being is not divisible. In God, the existence of the one person within the others actually creates a particularity, an 'individuality' and an otherness. Because we are made in the image of God we can see intimations of this in our own relationships. Because man is made in the image of God, we can find analogies between God and man, that are based in the relationships of the persons of God. The doctrine of the Trinity gives us the truth of our own existence.

With 'person', we refer to the way or mode in which each person of God receives his existence from the others, so that Fatherhood, Sonship and procession indicate the ways in which these three persons exist. The names of the Holy Trinity denote ontological particularity and distinctiveness, not single attributes or psychological experiences. The Father does not come into being: he simply exists as the Father, and he freely brings the Son and the Spirit into existence and does not exist without them. The Son is not the Father, and he is begotten. The Holy Spirit is neither Father nor Son, and he proceeds from the Father. If the Spirit were also begotten of the Father, we would have two Sons. Although we may not be able to say what the difference between 'begotten' and 'proceeds' is, it clearly indicates that the Holy Spirit is distinct from the Son.

Saint Cyril of Alexandria (378-444) developed the teaching of Athanasius and the Cappadocians, by showing that there is a difference between the terms 'unbegotten' and 'Father'. The Eunomians regarded 'unbegotten' and 'Father' as synonyms. But Saint Cyril pointed out that 'Father' indicates that God has a Son: God cannot be Father without the Son. 'Unbegotten' merely signifies that the Father was not born of anyone. Cyril insisted that the positive meaning of Father is that he has a Son. The Father could not be Father if he was without the Son. He is the Father eternally, for he did not *become* a Father in time, and the consequence is that the Son is also eternally the Son. In the same way, the term 'Son' does not just tell us that he is begotten, but that he is the eternal Son of the Father.

The Fathers did not attempt to express the persons on the basis of attributes, but subordinated attributes to the relationships of the persons of God. With the Cappadocian Fathers the doctrine of God was complete and there were no significant further developments. If we want to give a faithful account of the Christian understanding of God we have to learn it from these Fathers of the Church.

3. *Augustine*

We shall now take a look at theological developments in the West. The theologian who put his mark on Western thought and the Western theology of the Trinity in particular was Augustine. Augustine himself was not well known until the rise of the Franks, but thereafter he became the standard-bearer of the Western Church, and eventually the single source from which the West drew its theology.

Saint Augustine's longest treatment of the doctrine of God appears in his *De Trinitate*. Augustine wanted to help people to come to terms with this very counterintuitive Christian doctrine of the Trinity, so he was more concerned to make it accessible than to be comprehensive. But when searching for analogies from human existence, Augustine made a decision which was to impact on all subsequent theology. He found his analogy for the persons of God within the single human individual. Augustine found all that he needed to explicate the Trinity within the individual, prior to any consideration of the society of others. Augustine's intellectual inheritance encouraged him to believe that the most essential thing in a person is the mind. Your mind makes you who you are, so your ability to think and to become aware of yourself thinking is the key to understanding your existence. You may study yourself in complete isolation from whatever is around you, for once you have observed yourself thinking, you may be confident of your own existence at least. With this decision, Augustine opened the way for preoccupation with one's inner self.

The Cappadocian Fathers believed that a single individual could not possibly serve as an analogy for God. Since God can only be identified through the persons of Father, Son and Holy Spirit, our analogies must always involve a set of particular persons whom we can name, such as Peter, John and Andrew.

If the mind is what is most fundamental about us, Augustine, influenced by Platonic thought, decided that the memory is the most important aspect of the mind. Our entire existence springs from the memory, and everything we know and think about, is stored inside us, in an eternally existing storeroom of truth. Knowledge is simply the recollection of this truth; the etymology of truth (*aletheia*) is 'unforgetting'. We discover the truth at the moment that knowledge re-emerges from within us. This makes memory the source of our existence. Augustine was content with the traditional expression the 'source' of divinity and the ancient image of a spring from which divinity flows. The Cappadocian Fathers found the traditional image of source insufficient because it suggested that divinity is something that flows out involuntarily.

For Augustine, God is, above all else, *mind (On the Trinity,* books 8 and 9). The mind is the source of knowledge, and the Logos, the second person of the Trinity, is the knowledge that the mind produces. The Logos was the form which God's knowing takes. Knowledge comes from memory, and an active mind always expresses what it knows. God is an active mind: he has a Logos, from which his knowledge comes. The knowledge that is the Logos comes from the source that is the Father. But what could this be knowledge of, given that nothing exists other than God? God's knowledge must be knowledge of himself, and his awareness must be self-awareness. The object of the knowledge of the Logos is the Father, so we have a self-knowledge of God. Another basic platonic tenet is that God is goodness, so the mind must be identical with the Good. Plato maintained that the good draws love and beauty towards itself and that beauty and the good awaken love, *Eros.* But, if God is all goodness and if there is no goodness other than him, whose love does he arouse? The Logos recognises the Father, and recognises him as the 'Good', and thus love of the 'Good' is born.

In Augustine's view, the Spirit is this love of the Son and the Father. The Spirit is a third form of existence, by which the Father loves the Son and the Son loves the Father. Augustine's term for the Spirit is '*nexus amoris*', the bond of love: love is the particular attribute of the Spirit. The Son is knowledge and has knowledge, while the Spirit is love and has love. Augustine had found a way to identify a specific attribute for each of the three persons. By equating the Father with memory, the Son with knowledge and the Spirit with love, he had described an attribute and specific function for each person.

The Greek Fathers did not believe that we can describe the persons by assigning an attribute to each of them in this way. They do not say anything about the attributes of the Son or to the Spirit, just as they do not attempt to explain the difference between 'being born of' and 'proceeding from'. The Son differs from the Father simply in that he is not the Father, and the Spirit is not the Son and so on.

The Cappadocians believed it is crucial to begin with the person of the Father, and thus with the persons of the Trinity. Augustine however makes the 'substance' of God prior, and regards the persons as relations within the substance of God. He affirms first *that* God exists, and only then turns to the question of *how,* and therefore of *who,* God is. As Karl Rahner shows, under his influence, mediaeval dogmatics in the West dedicated one chapter to the one substance of God, a second to the attributes of his substance, and another to the Trinity. Works of theology ever since have listed the attributes of the one God. Augustine's decision to promote divine substance over the persons of God demotes the question of which God we are referring to. But the question of which God we are talking about is just as important as the question of the existence of God at all. It is the question of how God is that determines which God we are talking about. The Trinity is therefore primary and utterly fundamental to our discussion of God.

We have seen how, in his search for images that would express the doctrine of the triune God, Augustine resorted to the notion of the perfect metaphysical being described by Plato and his successors. We have seen that this perfect being possesses three characteristics, so allowing Augustine to establish analogies for the three persons of the Holy Trinity. The Father he equated with memory, the Son with knowledge and the Spirit with love and will. The Greek Fathers did not identify the persons of the Trinity with particular characteristics, but believed memory, knowledge and love belonged to the persons of the Trinity together. God has one knowledge, one will and love, not three. So we do not have one person representing knowledge, or one person representing love, but love and knowledge are common to the three of them. The Cappadocians insisted that, just as we cannot envisage God through introverted observation of one's self, so we cannot achieve any image of man simply by interior inspection of one man. Man is not man because of his internal characteristics, whether we identify these as mind, memory, rationality or love. In order to obtain an image of a person, we need to have a communion of more than one person.

In his *Confessions* and *On the Trinity*, Augustine portrayed the person as a thinking object. Boethius (480–524) identifies the person with the 'rational individual'. To Western thought, the person must possess the faculties of rationality, awareness and self-awareness. Descartes (1596–1650) and Western philosophy in general took self-consciousness to be the attribute that makes us persons. For the Western philosophical tradition 'person' means someone with a developed sense of self-consciousness.

This psychological approach to the person gave rise to our contemporary psychology and philosophy of mind with their interest in determining the point at which we first become persons. Is it at conception, or at some point in the development of the foetus? Is it only when one is grown up and has acquired consciousness of one's self that one becomes a person? So what of those who have no such awareness, or who, by illness or age, lose it? In what sense are they persons? Are those who have no developed self-consciousness to be considered deficient as persons? This whole discussion is generated by this linking of personhood to consciousness in the doctrine of the Trinity.

For Augustine, the psychological categories which give us knowledge of God also make each of us a person, and would do so even if we were the only one in existence. So we have seen that the concept of person is used in quite different ways in Western and Eastern thought. One's account of God has far-reaching consequences for our understanding of man. But before examining these, we must look more closely at the doctrine of God.

The priority he gave to 'being' meant that Augustine identified God with mind and substance (*On the Trinity*, book 10, 4,18). The Greek Fathers, we have seen, insisted that the Father is the true identity of God. They are faithful to the way Scripture refers to God, as 'the God, and the Father of our Lord Jesus Christ' (2 Corinthians 2.3). When the Father is acknowledged as God we are able to understand why the concept of one God is embodied by the Trinity. If the one God is the Father, a relationship is presupposed. The Father has no existence without the Son, and, albeit differently, the Spirit, so these persons are from the very first included in the concept of the 'one God'. When God is the Father, this Trinity of persons is necessarily included.

At this point we should relate our theology to the life and worship of the Church by asking one fundamental question. When you worship God, who or what are you ultimately addressing? Who or what are you praying to? Are you praying to God in general, to some deity or Divinity or Godhead? Or are you praying to specific persons, to the Father, Son and the Spirit?

Orthodox worship addresses prayers to the Father as God himself. The Holy Trinity cannot be divided of course, so where the Father is, there the Son and the Spirit are too. Yet we pray to a specific person. Many prayers are addressed to Christ and some to the Holy Spirit, or to all three persons at once. But the prayers of the divine Eucharist were originally addressed to the Father. It is clear from the liturgies of the earliest centuries that the anaphora, the offertory prayer, was always addressed to the Father. This is still clear in the Liturgy of Saint Basil where, without precluding the Son and the Spirit, the anaphora is addressed to the Father explicitly. We are addressing a particular person, as we do in the Lord's prayer, and just as, in his prayers in the flesh, the Son addressed the Father. To the Greek Patristic tradition

God is unequivocally the Father. In worship, which is fundamentally what determines theology, we pray ultimately to the Father, from whom the persons of the Trinity come and to whom they direct their own existence.

The Greek Fathers insisted that memory, knowledge, will and love are not individuated between the persons of God but common to them all. They understood that to confer individual psychological attributes to the persons of God may lead to the projection of creaturely characteristics onto God. In their anxiety to avoid such projection many Orthodox theologians have taken refuge in so-called apophatic or 'negative' theology which refers to God only by saying what he is not. They want to state that, when referring to the Holy Trinity, the concept of person in no way relates to the human person. But by doing so they have conceded that the Augustinian conception of the person, as the consciousness of the individual, is the only possible view of the person.

In view of the danger of projection that accompanies this 'personalistic' conception, many are understandably cautious in speaking about persons, and some believe that such personalism makes it best to avoid using the concept of the person altogether in referring to God. But rather than transferring human experience to God, a faithful theology will take the meaning of person from the trinitarian doctrine of God and transfer it to the human person. This is what we have to do if we are to speak of man as the 'image and the likeness' of God.

The doctrine of God is of fundamental importance if we are to understand who we are. Human beings are called to become persons in the image and likeness of the Holy Trinity, for this is what *theosis* is. Created nature will never turn into divine nature, so no human being can become divine in his or her nature, but man can become a person in the image and likeness of the Holy Trinity. Here we can see the decisive contribution that Patristic theology can make to the world. It can replace the psychological conception of the person and teach us the meaning of the person from the doctrine of the Trinity. But this requires that we re-learn the concept of the person from the Cappadocian Fathers. This is the uniquely important task given to Christian theology.

III. Theology and Economy

Now we turn to the relationship of the eternal Trinity and the economic Trinity. The eternal or immanent Trinity, traditionally called the 'theology' proper, refers to how God is in himself. The economic Trinity, traditionally the 'economy', refers to how God is *for us*. The

Greek Fathers insisted that the eternal nature of God is altogether beyond our conception or comprehension and added that we may not participate in the 'substance' of God. So we can have no theology of God's 'nature'.

But although we cannot say anything about God's 'nature' we can speak about the persons of God, and we can even participate in their life. Their life is the life that God intends us to share, so that it becomes our own. We share in the relationship of the Father and the Son in the Spirit. Christ has brought us the relationship he has with the Father, declared that we now belong in this relationship, and that the Father will acknowledge us as his sons. By this event of adoption we enter the life of God, and this participation in the divine life is traditionally called *theosis*. Thus the life of God is the life that is for us, so we are concerned, not with the essence, but with the eternal personal being of God.

It is entirely true that we are always unable to possess and control God, and this is the insight on which apophatic theology insists. To describe the being of God would be to attempt to come up with a totalising and final description and thereby to define and control him. There is always much interest in apophatic theology, but there is also a risk to it. It is true that we may not talk about the 'nature' of God. But we do *know* that God is Father, Son and Holy Spirit. With regard to the persons, we have this positive knowledge; it is not merely logical or intellectual affirmation, but a living participation in the personal relationships of God. We speak about God by talking about his trinitarian life, rather than about his 'nature'. The question is then whether the Trinity reveals God's eternal existence or merely the relationships revealed in the economy of God's relationship with us.

Again we will take Augustine as our example. Augustine ascribes one particular attribute to the Son, that of the knowledge of God. Whenever the Son reveals himself to us, which is to say within the economic Trinity, he does so as this attribute of knowledge. This makes the Son the cognitive means by which we may reach God, which was the position of the Logos theology of the second and third centuries. The relation of the Son to the Logos in the Gospel of John allowed Justin and his contemporaries to find in Christ the cognitive means by which we can reach God. Justin believed that all ancient philosophers participated in what he called this 'seminal' Logos: they all had some share in the knowledge which is Christ. The attribute of communion belongs to the Holy Spirit who reveals God to be communion. The crucial issue is whether the Son and Holy Spirit have these attributes eternally, or whether they take them on in the economy for our sake.

The Greek Fathers avoided giving definite personal attributes to the persons of the Holy Trinity. If they apportioned attributes to each of the persons we would have to say that whatever God is in his eternal being would have to be true of the economy too. In this way we would turn the economy into a necessity to which God was bound, rather than God's own act made in freedom. If the Son were the Logos or knowledge of God, this knowledge must also permeate the economy if we are to have any knowledge of God. He would have been brought into the economy by necessity through the Son. In mediaeval times it was asked whether any person of the Trinity could become incarnate. Some said that there was no logical necessity by which only the Son could become incarnate. In the twentieth century, Karl Rahner argued that only the Son could have become incarnate, because he alone is the Logos who is self-revelation. Within God eternally, God recognises himself in the Son who is his Logos. So if God wants to make himself known to us in the economy, he has to use the Logos who is the instrument of his knowledge of himself. This would mean that only the Logos could become incarnate. But if the incarnation was due to some eternal personal attribute of the Logos, in what sense is the incarnation free?

If we attribute the economy to particular characteristics of the persons of the eternal Trinity, the economy of God becomes logically determined to some degree. Then it would *have* to be the Son who became incarnate or there could be no incarnation. On the other hand, if we avoid ascribing the economy to any specific attributes of the persons, perhaps the Son is not the only one who could become incarnate. We must say that the Son freely said 'yes' to the Father, and took on this mission. If we attribute the incarnation to freedom, it takes the incarnation of the Son out of the realm of necessity and into the realm of freedom.

When it comes to the *Filioque*, we will find that Augustine and Aquinas (*Summa Theol.* Ia 2ae, 4) understood the Son and Logos to be the knowledge of God, and the Spirit to be the love of God. Then the Spirit's origin must be eternally dependent on the Son because, Augustine believes, we cannot love what we do not know, so knowledge must be prior to love (*On the Trinity* 10,1). In his view, God cannot love himself without prior knowledge of himself in the Son. This is the consequence of his association of memory and knowledge, and of the assumption that the mind cannot help but express what it knows. When we ascribe particular attributes to the persons we end up defining logical necessities. By not setting out attributes in this way, the Greek

Fathers brought the issue of freedom to bear on the question of why the Son, rather than the Spirit, becomes incarnate.

Here we must exercise some caution. In the axiom expressed by Rahner, the immanent Trinity *is* the economic Trinity and vice versa. But we cannot make the economic Trinity and eternal Trinity entirely equivalent, and equally, we cannot say that the immanent Trinity is one thing and the economic Trinity is entirely another. Then God would seem to be withholding something of himself from us, or even to become entirely unknowable. So what is the distinction between the immanent and economic Trinity?

The difference we can identify is that for the immanent Trinity we cannot say anything definitive about the attributes of the persons. Here there must be a proper element of apophaticism. In the economic Trinity we can say specific things about the attributes of the persons, because these persons have taken on these particular tasks and characteristics freely for us. Though the Son is the revelation of the Father ('He who has seen me has seen the Father') this does not necessarily mean that the Son has this function and attribute in the eternal Trinity. If the Spirit signifies love and creates communion for us, this does not mean this is due to a specific attribute of the Spirit in the eternal Trinity. The persons take on these attributes freely for our sake, so they relate to the economy, the way God is for us. The differentiation of attributes must be limited to the economy. When it comes to the immanent Trinity, the 'theology' proper, we cannot say that one person is love and the other is knowledge. They are not attributes but the operations of persons acting together in freedom, and all the operations of the eternal Trinity are one.

This is equally important with regard to the unity of God. In the immanent Trinity all action is one and eternal. This united action is expressed in different ways within the economy, so the persons do not all do the same thing, although they always act in unison. Where the Father is, there the Son and the Spirit are; where the Son is, there the Father and the Spirit are. But the Son does not perform the work that the Father performs. Whatever the differentiated actions of God in the economy, they are not extensions of differentiations within the eternal Trinity. Western theology, however, has often turned distinctions in the economy into differentiations within the eternal Trinity, which is one reason why it became trapped in the *Filioque*.

The Greek Fathers' distinction between theology and economy was most clearly expressed by Saint Basil. In '*On the Holy Spirit*', Basil defends a doxology of Alexandrian origin which he had introduced to the liturgy in his diocese. The doxology Basil had inherited took the form 'Glory to the Father, *through* the Son, *in* the Holy Spirit'. Basil's doxology was 'Glory to the Father, *and* to the Son, *with* to the Holy Spirit'. He replaced the *through* (the Son) and *in* (the Holy Spirit), with '*and* the Son *with* the Spirit'. Basil's reason was that the first, Alexandrian, doxology with its use of 'through the Son' and 'in the Holy Spirit', relates to the economy in which we come to know God through the Son and in the Holy Spirit. There is an order and even a hierarchy here, because the Spirit follows the Son. Basil explained that the 'Pneumatom-achians' ('Resistors of the Spirit'), who refused to accept the divinity of the Spirit, used the doxology with '*in*' the Spirit. They thought that 'in' denoted space, which seemed to them to indicate that the Spirit was contained by space, which meant that he was a creature.

Next we must set out the significance of these developments. What purposes does the doctrine of God have? What would change for us if God were not as the Church has taught? Let us begin with the rela-tionship between the being of God and his personal existence.

When a young person says 'no one asked me whether I wanted to be born', they are raising the question of freedom. Since they were not asked about it, they see their existence as an imposition on them. This is not such a strange thought, for there is no greater restraint than existence itself. We are fascinated by the moral concept of freedom: we believe that we must be able to choose between two or more options, and we must have our say at every step of our life. We understand free-dom as the ability to say 'yes' or 'no'. But this overlooks the much bigger challenge to our freedom represented by the fact that you cannot say 'no' to your own existence, or if you could, you would cease to exist and your freedom would disappear with you.

There is a degree of absurdity about challenging our own existence, of course. We want to ignore or overcome the objectivity of life, but we are unable to do so. But however much we may find it painful to pro-test against the phenomena forced on us by life, we must not give up the hope of freedom. The reason my freedom appears to cancel itself out is that my existence comes before my freedom. If we said the same of God, we would be creating a theology in which the being comes before the person of God which would make God the least free being of all. But if God is not free to *be*, how can we hope to be *free*? If God himself is not free, all freedom is surely an illusion. Whatever we do we should not give up our hope for freedom.

We express our freedom by creating new identities for ourselves. When the teenager protests that he was not asked whether he wanted to come into this world, he is tearing himself free of the identity that he received from his family and his education in order to define himself on the basis of new relationships that represent no restriction on him. Consequently, freedom, by which we identify ourselves with what we ourselves desire, and in which we exist for whatever we desire, is absolutely fundamental. We have been created to be free: freedom is what will finally establish us in the likeness of God. We have to know whether the God in whom we believe, and whose likeness we desire to be, is tied to his existence. Does he exist because he has to exist and cannot but exist? This is what is at stake in theology in the issue of the priority of the persons over 'nature'.

God is free if it is not 'nature' that makes him exist, but he himself as a person. God is free if it is the person of the Father who makes God exist. If the Father wills to be, then God does not exist because he has to, but because he is willing to. This absolute freedom of God is expressed in the specific way of the relationships of the Trinity. If God exists because the Father is willing, we can hope that this freedom is not as impossible as it seems but may turn out to be possible for us too. The logic of theology therefore, overcomes the illogic and absurdity of the only way we know how to exercise our desire for freedom, which is by refusing anything and everything that we are confronted by. Because, for us, existence is a given and therefore a necessary thing, our freedom is exercised only by accepting the existence imposed on us or rejecting it and so denying our own selves. For us there is the possibility, or temptation, of exercising our freedom by saying 'no'.

Since his existence is not a given thing, God is not obliged to choose whether to say 'yes' or 'no' to it. For him, there is only one way to exercise freedom, and that is affirmatively. What is there for him to say 'no' to? God has the freedom to say 'yes'. The Father's freedom is expressed by saying 'yes' to the Son, and the freedom of the Son is expressed in saying 'yes' to the Father. This is the 'yes' and 'yes' again, that the Apostle Paul says (2 Corinthians 1.19) has come to us in Christ. Since for God nothing is given, there is nothing which he has to refuse. For God, the exercise of freedom does not take the form of a choice, but it is exercised voluntarily, in the form of love, expressed in his trinitarian life. If we apply this to human existence, freedom is not sometimes 'yes' and sometimes 'no', but only ever 'yes'. The only way to exercise freedom that demonstrates its freedom, is in *love*, which is to say, by affirming beings other than yourself. Our freedom therefore consists in saying that we acknowledge that this person exists for us, that we desire them and intend that they become part of our very being. The

Apostle Paul tell us that 'Jesus Christ who was preached among you, was not 'yes' and 'no', but in him it has always been 'yes' (2 Corinthians 1.19). God's 'yes' and Christ's 'yes' is the freedom of affirmation, demonstrated in love.

This Trinity of persons is the way God is who he is. The Father freely consents to this Son, wills him and acknowledges him as his Son, freely. God exercises his freedom in love and affirmation when the Father begets the Son, and when he sends the Holy Spirit. This opens up the possibility that we can also exercise freedom, affirmatively, as love. This exercise of freedom transforms us into the likeness of God. The image of God is fulfilled in the self-government of man who, though he is able to say 'no', says 'yes', as God does. This is how we may join those great lovers of God and of man, the holy spiritual Fathers, who have learned to pass beyond their own individual will through submitting themselves to another.

These considerations of human freedom are raised by the Christian doctrine of the Trinity. I hope we can see that, though we have to wrestle with these conceptual complexities in order to set out the teaching of the Church, the subject of theology is straightforward, for it is simply that life with God which is the fundamental experience of the Christian. The whole outworking of the doctrine of the Trinity is comprehended in the experience of the one who is learning the freedom of love that belongs to God.

IV. *FILIOQUE*

The *Filioque* – 'and from the Son' – is a clause inserted into the Creed by the Western Church. It declares that the Holy Spirit proceeds not only from the Father, but also from the Son.

There are two aspects to the *Filioque*. The first is the canonical, which relates to the way the doctrine was advanced in the course of the Church's history, and the second is the issue of the truth which means that we need to investigate whether this doctrine has a place in the Christian doctrine of God. To comprehend what is at stake theologically, we will again compare the theology of Augustine and the Cappadocians, for the West used Augustine to defend the *Filioque*, while the Eastern Orthodox used the Cappadocians to reject it.

Let us start with the canonical issue and the history of this clause. The idea that the Spirit proceeds from the Son as well as the Father existed in the West even in the fourth century. We find it in Ambrose in a form that created no theological problems. Maximus (*Letter to*

Marinus) in the seventh century found that this term *Filioque* was employed in Rome, but in a way that was entirely orthodox. So no theological controversy was attached to this phrase before the seventh century, and then it was for reasons of politics that the term became the focus of controversy.

The *Filioque* was first inserted into the Creed in sixth-century Spain, at the Council of Toledo. King Requarerdos, newly converted from Arianism to the orthodox faith, was looking for ways to reinforce the divinity of the Son against the Arian position. He found the means of doing this in the *Filioque*, and persuaded the council to insert the phrase into the Creed, in order to strengthen the confession that the Son is equal to the Father. So far, things were more or less innocuous.

The rise of the Franks under Charlemagne created a new political climate. Charlemagne wanted to establish himself at the head of new Roman empire. Of course, the Byzantine emperor regarded Constantinople as the continuation of Rome, and himself as the leader of the Roman empire. Intending to launch a military campaign against Byzantium, Charlemagne adopted the *Filioque* and declared the Byzantines heretics in order to give his troops a cause to rally to. This borrowed theological term became the focus of a political struggle between the Western and Eastern ends of the Mediterranean.

Charlemagne was also regarded as a threat in Rome itself. Pope Leo III opposed the introduction of the *Filioque* to the Creed and so found himself on the same side as the Byzantines. Leo had the Creed, without the *Filioque*, inscribed on two plaques and placed in Saint Peter's Basilica. Later these plaques were taken down, of course. In a theological conference in Rome on the Council of Constantinople in 1982, a Roman Catholic theologian, Father Yves Congar, suggested that these plaques of the Creed without the *Filioque* should be restored to their original prominent position, though no such action has yet been taken.

Up until that time, the *Filioque* had been a purely Frankish cause. But Rome's advances in Bulgaria had created growing antagonism with Constantinople. In the year 1014, it was agreed that the coronation of emperor Frederick IV take place in Rome on the condition that the *Filioque* was included in the Creed. For reasons of political expediency Rome conceded to this demand, the *Filioque* became part of the Creed in Rome and the Western Church has defended it ever since. In 1054, the year of the schism between Rome and Constantinople, the Pope's anathema, deposited by Umberto in the Church of Hagia Sophia, made the charge that, far from being a Western introduction, it had been the Easterners who had removed the *Filioque* from the Creed!

In subsequent centuries, Westerners continued to level this charge against the Eastern Church, so the truth of its insertion of *Filioque* was forgotten in the West. The fight for the justification of the *Filioque* was now under way. The West drew arguments from Augustine, developed with the aid of Thomas Aquinas, for regarding those who did not accept the *Filioque* as heretics, and an equally recalcitrant anti-*Filioque* theology developed in the East, each side throwing the charge of heresy in polemics that endured over centuries.

As a theological issue the *Filioque* came to the fore in the twentieth century as Russian émigrés in France brought the theology of Slavophiles to the West. The chief representative of this theology, Vladimir Lossky, brought the *Filioque* back into the centre of debate and this has served to renew the controversy. When we ask about the differences between East and West, the *Filioque* is usually the first answer given. The canonical issue remains a problem. Does any one Church have the right to insert a new wording in the Creed? The Creed was produced by an ecumenical council, that is a council of the whole Church. No part of the Church can make a unilateral alteration to the Church's teaching, without the consent of the whole Church. We will come back to this issue.

Having examined the history we must now turn to theological issues around the *Filioque*. Theological justification of the *Filioque* began from Augustine's position that, in the Trinity, as the Logos, the Son represents the knowledge of God, while the Spirit is the love of God. As knowledge comes before love, the reasoning went, the Son comes before the Spirit. On this basis Augustine attributed priority to the Son over the Spirit, and made the Son a source of the Spirit alongside the Father.

A second justification given for the *Filioque* was that, according to Augustine, the 'substance' is prior to the persons of God. One God means the essence within which three relationships subsist, the Father (memory), the Son (knowledge) and the Spirit (love). But, medieval Scholastic theologians would argue, relationships that are complete must be reciprocal, so relationships must come in pairs. The Spirit must originate, not from one person, but from a relationship of two persons. Given that the Son is the only other person, the *Filioque* is required.

The Reformation brought a different approach. Protestants condemned as metaphysics any theology that speaks of the 'being' of God, insisting that we know God solely through his works in history and therefore through the economy. The historical acts of God are the sole source for theology. Their claim was that since the Holy Trinity appears in history in the economy because the Father sends his Son, and the Son sends the Spirit, the Spirit is therefore given to us by the Son. Given that everything we know and can say about God is dependent on what happens in the economy we have to concede that the Spirit is also dependent on the Son, not on the Father alone. The outcome was that Protestants found continuing grounds to support the *Filioque*.

Protestants found themselves in the same confusion as those fourth-century theologians who were unable to distinguish between the two sorts of procession, 'proceeding from' and 'sent by'. 'Proceeding from' relates to the eternal relationship of Father, Son and Spirit. The Spirit *proceeds* eternally and directly from the Father. But in the economy the Son *sends* the eternal Spirit to us; the Son gives us the Spirit. The Son clearly has something to do with the appearance of the Holy Spirit in the economy.

The Greek-speaking East had used 'proceeding from' (ἐκπορεύεται) only within the immanent and eternal Trinity. But Latin did not make it easy to distinguish between the two. From the fourth century the Greek *Ekporeuetai* (proceeding from) and *pempetai* (sent by) were translated into Latin simply as 'procedere'. From the very beginning, the West used *Filioque* of both theology and economy and from this came the mutual incomprehension that drove the controversy. When saying that the Spirit originates from the Father and the Son, are we referring simply to the economy, where the Spirit is indeed given by the Son, or is this being projected back into the eternal being of God?

A second area of difficulty lies in the analogies Augustine used to describe the Trinity. To say that the Father is memory, the Son is knowledge and the Spirit is love, is to project onto God from the economy. In the view of the Greek Fathers such arguments give no support to the *Filioque*. The only thing we can say about the Father, the Son and the Spirit is that the Father is Unbegotten and that he is the Father of the Son; the Son is begotten and is the Son of the Father; and the Spirit 'proceeds from' the Father and that he is the Spirit, not the Son. These characteristics, which derive from the very being of these persons, tell us *how* they are and thus *who* they are. We cannot say anything about the other characteristics that belong to each of the persons.

We have seen that the East did not set the nature of God before or above the persons. If the Father is God, to make the Son equally the source of the Holy Spirit would be to acknowledge two ontological origins in the Trinity, and thus two Gods. The oneness of God is secured by the Father: he is the only source and cause, from whom God's entire life and being comes. The Father secures the unity of God. The absolute sovereignty of God is safeguarded by the sole principle (*monarchia*) of the Father. The *Filioque* would then represent the introduction of a second source (*archê*) beside the Father.

How can three persons not be three separate Gods? The answer is that the Son and the Spirit come from the Father and orient themselves entirely to him. He is the source of their being and thus of the existence of the Trinity. The sovereignty of the Father secures the unity and oneness of God. If the Son is a second principle alongside the Father, the sovereignty of the Father would be gone and we would have two Gods.

We have a similar difficulty when we imagine that knowledge comes before love. Here we need to remember what we said about knowledge of persons and knowledge of things. In order to know someone, I need to be in some sort of relationship with them, and every relationship is informed to some degree by love. Augustine's argument that knowledge comes before love is unfounded. This means that if we are maintaining that the Son is knowledge and the Spirit is love, the Spirit cannot be subsequent to the Son. Knowledge is intrinsically related to love and communion, because we know persons only to the degree that we are in communion with them, which is to say, we love them.

Is there any degree to which we accept the *Filioque*? Understood in the right way, we may indeed accept the *Filioque*. The first consideration is to be clear about the difference between 'proceeding from' and 'sent by' and so maintain the distinction between the eternal and the economic Trinity. It is fine to say that the Spirit depends on the Son in the economy, but it is an entirely different thing to maintain that this relates to the eternal life of God. We cannot talk about any *Filioque* in the eternal Trinity because the Father is the sole cause of the Spirit. Nonetheless, the Greek Fathers make a distinction that allows a role for the Son in the eternal procession of the Holy Spirit.

In '*That There are not Three Gods*', Saint Gregory of Nyssa says:

> We do not deny the difference between Him (the Father), who exists as the causer, and he who is from this causer.

We may get a better idea of how the persons are distinct by agreeing that there is a difference between a cause, and what it causes. The difference between the Father and the Son and Spirit, is that the Father is the cause while the Son and the Spirit are caused by him. The cause is a person, an agent who freely initiates. The distinction between the cause and what he causes is all-important. Gregory continues:

> As for that which is caused (the Son), we recognise a further difference. The Son comes immediately and directly from the Cause, whereas the Spirit

comes through the one who comes directly from the Cause, that is, through the mediation of the Son.

The mediation of the Son in the procession of the Spirit safeguards the fact that the Son is the only-begotten, that is, that he is the only Son and the Spirit is not another Son beside him. The mediation of the Son does not change the fact that the Spirit has a direct relationship with the Father. Gregory insists that it is this mediatory role of the Son in the procession of the Spirit that preserves the immediate relationship of the Spirit to the Father. As long as we are clear that the Son is not the cause, other roles for the Son in the procession of the Spirit are admissible.

So we have seen that Orthodox theology makes some careful distinctions between the doctrine of the eternal God and the economy of God for man in creation and history.

Within the eternal God, however, the Spirit does not proceed from the Son. In the immanent Trinity we have relationships that are entirely ontological, so the only cause or agent must be the Father. 'Proceeding from' (*ekporeuetai*) relates to the Spirit's ontological dependence on the Father within the eternal Trinity. To talk about a second cause or agent would be to introduce a second God.

In the economy, it is right to say that the Spirit depends on the Son, is sent by the Son and given by him to the Church. When dealing with the economy, we are not dealing with the eternal relationships of the persons of the Trinity in themselves, but only those relationships that relate to the acts of God for us, and so to the Son's action of sending the Spirit. So within the economy the term *Filioque*, by the Father *and the Son*, cannot be faulted.

We have seen that in part the *Filioque* controversy was caused by the confusion in the West about two terms, one of which refers to the immanent Trinity and one to the economic Trinity. For the East, this distinction is imperative; if we make this distinction, we are able to accept that the *Filioque* is true in the *economy*.

But as the West defined it, the *Filioque* relates equally to the eternal and the economic Trinity. Can the *Filioque* not be applied at all to the eternal Trinity? Let us take a look at the issue as it was encountered by patristic theology. In the seventh century, as word was getting around that the *Filioque* was being used in the West, Saint Maximus was asked for his opinion on this matter. He replied that he had looked into it, and found that the Latin-speaking Romans did not have respective words for expressing the two notions of *proceeding from* and *sent out by* (*ekporeuetai* and *pempetai*), so they used only one word, *proceeds* and this gave rise to confusion. In the same letter to Marinus, Saint Maximus noticed that Roman Christians referred to Saint Cyril of Alexandria, whose writings seemed to give the *Filioque* some support in the eternal Trinity. Theodoretus of Cyrrhus responded by saying that if Cyril was talking about the economy, all was well; if not, Cyril was in error.

Cyril did not confine what he said about the *Filioque* to the economy, but made inferences for the eternal Trinity. He did not use the term 'proceeds from', but he did say that the Spirit is eternally manifested by the Son also. Given that the 'essence' is common to all three persons, the Son can be said to manifest the Spirit in the being of God. But, in the personal relationship of Spirit to the other two persons, there can be no *Filioque*, because the person of the Father alone is the cause of the Trinity. At first glance, this appears ambiguous, but as we have seen, Saint Gregory of Nyssa pointed out that a cause is one thing, and whoever is *from* that cause is another.

Only when person *is* the cause and the other is *from* that cause, can we perceive that one person is distinct from another. Gregory says that the only way to distinguish between the persons of the Trinity is by this concept of agency or cause. He continues:

> With regard to the person who is *from* the Cause, we have in there another distinction, whereas with regard to the Cause, it is clear that it is only the Father. When referring to '*from* the cause', we can recognise a further difference: one of the two originates without mediation from the first, while the other originates with the mediation of the one who originates directly from the Cause. (*To Ablabius: 'That There Are Not Three Gods'*)

The difference between the Son and the Spirit is that the Son comes directly from the Father, while the Spirit comes through the mediation of the Son. Gregory explains that with this mediation of the Son

> The attribute of being only-begotten abides without doubt in the Son, and the mediation of the Son, while it guards his attribute of being only-begotten, does not shut out the Spirit from his relation by way of nature to the Father.

This mediation does not remove the direct and immediate relationship of the Spirit with the Father, but we have to identify this mediation so that we do not see the Spirit as a second Son. This does look like a kind of *Filioque* in the eternal God. Nevertheless, the cause of the Holy Spirit is always the Father for, though the Son mediates, he is no second cause. These nuances maintain the rule of faith that the Father alone is the cause.

In his letter to Marinus, Saint Maximus said he discussed the issue with Christians in Rome and concluded that they did not mean that the Son is the cause, so Maximus said that there was no heresy involved. That was how the situation was left in the seventh century. In later centuries as the *Filioque* was used by the West as a slogan aimed at the Byzantines, the issue became polarised. The Westerners were no longer ready to concede that the Son is not a cause, with the Father, of the procession of the Holy Spirit and their refusal eventually turned into defiance.

The Council of Florence (1438–39) attempted to heal the division of the Church on this issue. If the two sides had been willing to adopt the term 'through the Son' rather than 'from the Son', that might have been a basis for agreement. 'Through the Son' would have indicated the mediation of the Son that Gregory of Nyssa was looking for. But neither side was willing to make any decisive theological step. The West had already stabilised its own position with the expression 'from the Father *and* the Son', and was not willing to retract it or replace it with '*through* the Son'.

I believe that the *Filioque* is a matter that the Churches of East and West can resolve. Fresh attempts are now under way, and it will be very interesting to see what progress they make. All we have to do is avoid anything that obscures the principle that, within the Trinity, the Father alone is cause and agent. We can all make our case for our understanding of the place of the *Filioque* in the doctrine of God, just as the Church did in the age of Maximus.

Chapter 3

Creation and Salvation

I. THE DOCTRINE OF CREATION

The doctrine of creation can be found in the Creed of the Church from the earliest times. The first article states: 'I believe in one God, Father Almighty, Creator of heaven and earth, of all things visible and invisible.' Historically, the reference to creation is an addition to the first Creed, which was first a confession of faith in the three persons of Father, Son and Holy Spirit. Reference to creation was added because the Church had to show how the Christian doctrine of creation was distinct from other views of the cosmos. As usual, we not only have to say how the doctrine came to be articulated, but also what its significance is for us today.

To examine the development of the doctrine within the early Church, we need to give some account of the rival theories of creation in that period. Gnosticism was the first theory in broad circulation to which the Church had to respond. Gnosticism began from the premise that the world we know is fraught with evil, which reflected the widespread pessimism of the time. The question asked was whether, if the world is full of evil, it really could have been God who created it. Concerned to preserve God's purity and transcendence, Gnosticism denied that God was directly responsible for the creation of this world. Instead, the world was the creation of another being, which it called not 'God' but simply the 'Creator', the lowest of the eons that made up a long hierarchy that separated God from the world. The Church declared that the very opposite was true: it was God himself who had created the world. The Church declared in its creed that the one God, the Father Almighty, was 'Creator of all things visible and invisible.' The Father, God himself, is the Creator. The Church responded to Gnosticism by saying that the relationship that God has with the world is direct and immediate.

Gnosticism isolated God from the world. If the Church had conceded that God had had no involvement in the creation of the world this would put God's omnipotence in doubt. It would also have cast doubt over the love of God, because it would mean that God has no personal relationship with the world. Then there would be the issue of whether the world would ever be rid of evil, or whether evil was an inseparable part of creation. However, since the Church upheld the view that God Himself created the world, it insisted that evil is therefore not part of creation's true nature. To Gnosticism's question about how evil appeared in the world, the Church said that evil was one outcome of the freedom given to man. The world is not intrinsically evil. God has an immediate concern for it and has the power to come to creation's aid: God is Almighty, as the Creed puts it, with power and authority over all things. God creates something outside himself and sustains the world in its relationship with himself.

The next question was whether the world can be perceived as an extension of God, or as something which God simply formed and shaped. This theory originated with Plato, although it had undergone considerable development, principally at the hands of Philo, by the time that the creed was being formulated. Plato dedicated a dialogue, the 'Timaeus', to the issue of creation. Plato was himself responding to the view that the world was not created by anyone but was simply a random occurrence, either in the sense of being a function of chance as the Epicureans understood it, or in the sense that God is identified with the laws of nature. God would then be the logical and cohesive force contained within nature. Plato believed that the world was created by someone whom he named 'Father'. In 'The Laws' he set out severe penalties for atheists, by which he had in mind those philosophers of nature who were his contemporaries. Because Plato insisted that the world was created by God, Christians came to regard him as a believer amongst the pagans and a theologian before Christ.

However, the Christian doctrine of creation is very different from the account of the world presented by the 'Timaeus'. Although he claimed that the world was created by God, what Plato meant was that God created in the sense that an artist creates. He has ideas and, with the materials available to him, he portrays the form he has in mind. The 'Timaeus' portrayed God, whom Plato referred to as 'Mind' (*Nous*), as taking existing matter and ideas and then situated the world in the void as though on a kind of canvas, and giving the world all the beauty and harmony that belongs to it. Thus the God of the Timaeus creates out of elements already in existence. Plato believed that this explains why, though not perfect, this world is the best that could have been made of the material. The laws of space and matter resist the Creator's efforts to conform them completely to the perfect forms. Perfection remained with the ideas, in the realm above creation.

Plato and the ancient Greeks regarded the world as fundamentally good but they did assume that a tendency to evil could be attributed to matter. The more we descend towards matter, the more we distance ourselves from the perfection that the artist Creator was aiming for.

In the first century, Philo attempted to synthesise Plato's insights with the cosmology of the Scriptures of Israel. Philo realised that there were problems with Plato's account because it assumed that God was confronted by the existence of matter as by a given. Who created matter? Philo took the step of declaring matter to be a creation of God, in this way securing God's independence of it. But there was also the problem of ideas. For Plato, ideas also just existed, so God found them ready-made. Philo's solution was to turn the ideas into the thoughts of God. The ideas were not above God but within him.

The ancient Greeks longed to get beyond the changes and decay of this world and so they attributed stability to the realm of ideas, which represents the truth and the unity above all this chaos. The objects we see may change too slowly for us to perceive, but they change nonetheless and one day they will exist no more. So, for example, the table we see before us is in process of decay. We are only able to refer to it as a table because somewhere above there is the true and unchanging table, from which all the tables we see source their existence. If this constant and ideal table is not real, no table can truly exist. The ideas are the source of all that we experience and they secure the identity and truth of all the fragmentary things that we can name. Every entity exists because of its connection to its idea, its rationality or *logos*. According to Plato, God found the ideas and made use of them, so the ideas of things were independent of God. In the 'Timaeus' the Creator did whatever the ideas directed him to; they dictated the form of creation, although matter prevented creation from achieving a perfect correspondence with the ideas.

Philo realised that these theories were not suited to the freedom of God, so he modified Platonism by transferring these ideas into the mind of God. He decided that the entire world, inclusive of all the ideas, and the purposes of things, had its existence and stability within the mind (*Nous*) of God. In this way Philo believed that he had solved the problem of God's freedom with respect to the ideas. In fact, he had created another problem.

The neo-platonist worldview of the second and third centuries regarded the world as an emanation of God or an expression of the thoughts of God in the multiplicity of the world. Origen also linked the *logoi* of beings within God to the world of created beings. The ancient Greeks had believed that the world was eternal, as were the *logoi*, which were the source of each thing that came into existence and gave that thing its shape and purpose. The ideal form from which the world came was understood to be eternal.

Origen believed that there were two aspects to creation. One form was eternal creation, where God eternally thought of this world, and his thoughts were then the rationality (*logoi*) of those beings, which come together in the one Logos, who is the Son. With the Logos of all beings, with the one Logos, God created the world at the level of eternity. Then over time a second stage occurred in which a subordinate creation, the material world that we experience, came into being, this second creation representing a falling away from the perfection of the first. The souls were created in the original eternal creation, so Origen considered the souls to be eternal and linked them with the incorporeal spirits, the angels, and with the ideas. However, a deterioration and decline took place when the souls in this incorporeal, ideal creation took on materiality and flesh. The materiality of the world represents a fall. The spiritual world of angels and souls is eternal, the material world is perishable; the spiritual is superior, the material world inferior.

Origen's doctrine of creation brings with it a whole spirituality. Creation needed to be purged of its materiality. The material body is the prison of the soul, so souls have to be released from the body. Salvation was thus a return to the initial state in which souls and spirits were devoid of corruption and matter. Man can only approach God when he has rid himself of all matter and become as incorporeal as the angels.

We saw that although Philo had tried to free God from creation, he had actually confined him to it. Philo made the world necessarily present to God, ever-present within him in the form of the *logoi*, the thoughts of God. If God creates eternally, beside or within God there is something else, a second self of God, which determines God's existence. The result is simply that God cannot be imagined without the world. It is impossible to speak of God without speaking of the world at the same time. It is impossible for God to exist, without the world existing along with him. This is not very different from the theory of the world of ideas of Plato's 'eternal creation'. In their different ways Plato and Origen had confined the freedom of God. What was needed was a way to show that God's relationship to creation is not binding on God. The existence of the world had to be understood as the result of his own freely-willed decision to create. This was what the Fathers expressed by their opposition to Plato. To distinguish the teaching of the Church from that of the gnostics, it is not enough simply to say that the world is the creation of God. We must go on to say that it is created *ex nihilo*, from nothing.

The idea of the world being created from nothing was developed by Irenaeus and Theophilos of Antioch. In his 'Letter to Autolykos' (2.4), Theophilos says that God created what he wanted out of nothing and so created it as he wished it to be. We have said that if ideas were thoughts in the mind (*nous*) of God, the world would always have existed in God's thoughts. If the thoughts of God are eternal, and the world exists as the thoughts of God, this makes the world eternal too.

To this Saint Maximus in the seventh century gave a comprehensive reply ('Ad Thalassium' 60). God had eternally willed the world and for God, notions of 'before' and 'after' have no significance. However, to have willed it eternally does not mean that God instantly brought it into existence. We should distinguish between 'will' and 'existence': God may have willed the existence of the world eternally, but when the world was created, that act of creation was no necessary extension of God's eternal will. This eternal will did not make creation inevitable. The Logos through whom God created the world is the Logos with whom God has the eternal loving relationship of Father to Son. The existence of the world was not a necessary outcome of this love of Father for Son, even if the will to create the world was eternal. Maximus' distinction between God's will and its realisation means that we do not have to conclude that the world had some eternal existence in the thoughts of God.

Maximus insisted that, because it was the outcome of God's will, the world was not eternal. To establish this, Maximus made bold use of the concept of the Logos, with all its very ambiguous history. There is a relationship of love between God and his Word, the Father and his Son, and the world is created in and through this Word. The relationship between God and the world is now freely willed. God's will is eternal, but this does not mean that God's thought is instantly extended. Maximus refers to the *logoi* as the *wills* of God, not the *thoughts* of God. God exercises his will in deciding to create the world at the time of his choosing.

This is a revolution. It prevents us from imagining that existence is an extension of the thoughts of God. A will may be realised or it may not. This is the fundamental difference between a thought, which is realised in being thought, and a will, which, precisely because it is a will, is not the necessary consequence of a thought. Even a will that is realised is not realised by necessity.

By relating the *logoi*, the reasons for things, to wills, Maximus managed to separate creation from necessity. Creation is brought into being because God has willed it, not because he has thought it. Because it comes from a free decision it is not a matter of necessity.

The Christian doctrine of creation began in response to Gnosticism and Platonism. To Gnosticism, the Church responded by linking the 'Creator' to the 'Father' to stress the direct involvement of God in creation. The Church responded to Platonism with the expression 'creation from nil' meaning from no existing material or ideas. It responded to middle Platonism and neo-platonism by stating that the world did not eternally exist as a thought of the mind (*nous*) of God, but that its existence was the result of the will of God. Because this will was related to the Son of God, the Logos, creation took place and the world became a real entity through a relationship of love, without ever constituting a necessity for God.

Saint Athanasius taught that the Son exists from the substance of the Father, while the existence of the world is owed to the Father's will. Maximus gave a philosophical account of what had until then been merely an intuition. Things exist because God wills that they do.

II. CREATION *EX NIHILO*

Christian doctrine is formulated in response to the challenges other worldviews make to the teaching of the Church. The doctrine of creation was the response the Church made to the Platonist account of creation. Let us review what the Church meant by creation *ex nihilo*, from nothing.

The first thing this doctrine tells us is that the world is not eternal. If it was eternal it would not need to be created. If it were not created from nothing, this would mean that it was created from something that had some other existence. If this something had already been in existence it must have done so prior to the creation of the world, in which case this something could not be within the limits of time or truly *created*. It would have to be an eternal creation which would make the world necessarily eternal, as Origen believed, and ancient Greeks had believed long before him.

But the Christian Church rejected these ideas. It taught that the world is not eternal, but that 'there was a time when it was not' (*Hv ποτέ* ὅτε οὐκ ἦν). If the world 'was not', had no existence, what was there? God was there. There was nothing other than God. This is the first consequence of the term *ex nihilo*.

A second consequence is that if the world was created from nothing, it is also possible that it will return to nothing. If something is not eternal, it cannot live eternally. The world always exists in some relation to this nothing, remains exposed to it and liable to revert to nothing. Athanasius says in 'On Incarnation' that the nature of every creature has within it this nothingness that can bring about its own termination. Since nothing eternal can be created, creation must be mortal and its own dissolution is latent everywhere within it.

If the world came out of nowhere and is destined to disappear back into nothingness again, what real existence does it have? Can this disappearance and death be avoided? If God created a world out of nothing, that world is liable to return to nothing. But God did not make the world with the intention that it would disappear, but that it should have life. Its own nature does not enable the world to survive. When God created the world for life and with the intention that it would transcend nothingness, he did not give its nature the means to secure its immortality. That would have rendered the world eternal, which would mean that it was no longer creation, but immortal and thus a god in its own right. If God had given creation the power to ensure its own survival, though it began in nothing, the world would be able to become eternal by nature. This would mean that God would have created another, eternal, god.

On the one hand we have God, who is alive in himself eternally. On the other we have a world that is without its own means of life, and so without eternity. Nothing within it can enable its permanent survival. The processes of our dissolution and death begin at the moment we are born. All the laws of life and nature are also laws of death. Life and death run in parallel. The only way that something created can transcend death and deterioration is to remain in constant communion with the eternal God. God and the world have to be in communion, and the means chosen for this communion is mankind.

Communion with God is the purpose of man's creation. Why did God choose man rather than any other being for this communion? Since his body is made up of all material elements, man is linked to all creation, and all creation has a share in man. Because of the bond represented by man's body, the entire created world can come into communion with God and receive life from that communion. If God had chosen incorporeal powers, angels, there would have been no place in this communion for the material world.

Man was created at the end of all creation so that he would bring all that is created to the uncreated God and unite them in permanent relationship. When the created world is in relationship with the uncreated, eternal God, its life will not come to an end; this relationship will not allow it to die. The creation of man gives creation its meaning. In 'On the incarnation of the Word', Athanasius showed that God chose this form of incarnation for the Logos so the world would always overcome nothingness and have life without end. Man is the only creature who both includes the material world and also exceeds it. Angels have no link to the materiality of creation. We share creation's mortality: since death is transmitted by our own bodies we die just as every other living creature does, and so we share in the created world's experience of death.

Man was created to unite all nature to God, but man refused to accept that this was his purpose. He decided not to follow this plan, but to make another in which he would become God himself. Adam believed that by becoming God, the world would be able to surmount the nothingness and live on without limit, and that he would live forever too. This is what we know as 'the Fall'. Adam had been given freedom and with it the ability to say 'no'. So Adam said 'no' simply because he could, and this was the way in which Adam exercised his freedom.

The doctrine of creation brings the question of why man has freedom. Why did God not make things in such a way that this project could not fail? Perhaps we cannot ask God why he did things one way rather than another, but we can recognise what would have happened if God had done things differently. If man had been created without the freedom to choose or refuse, this union would have taken place because the world would have been unable to avoid it. But God did not intend for the world a relationship that made freedom impossible. He made the world an entity utterly distinct from himself, not so that it could function as a mechanism driven by its own necessity, but so that it would have its own real independence and function of its own free will, just as God does.

God did not intend a world that had no will to exist. It is no act of love to force a relationship on someone who does not want that relationship. God desired to create a world that would want to exist, and this is the reason why he gave man the freedom to say 'yes' or 'no' to this project. The fact that man chose 'no', and continues to choose 'no' even when he is fully aware that it will lead to his death, tells us that God did not want a world that would exist without freedom. The world has the freedom to decide against its own life. So it seemed that Adam's choice was not to take up this relationship and so to turn down life.

The world was allowed to exist, without any further intervention by God. But it is important to realise that if creation had been abandoned to the form of freedom that Adam chose that the world would come to an end. Adam's choice was respected by God, but God never ceased to work to help the world to live, and this is where the doctrines of providence and salvation come in. God deals with the consequences of Adam's choice, so that the whole world will not unravel as a result of it.

III. THE SIGNIFICANCE OF THE DOCTRINE OF CREATION

We have looked at two approaches to the doctrine of creation. We have seen that the gnostic view isolated God from the world, but when the gnostic view is reversed, the world is turned into an eternal creation of God. If creation is an emanation of him it would mean that God creates because he cannot *not* create.

The Church was determined to remove all sense of necessity from the doctrine of creation, and it did so by insisting that the world was created from nothing. Creation is not an extension of God and it was not created either from existing matter or from ideas with an eternal existence in the mind of God. The world had no form of previous existence whatsoever, not even as the thoughts of God. The world could just as easily not have come into being. The fact that it does exist, is the result of God's good and free will.

The idea that the world might never have come into existence was incomprehensible to the ancient Greeks. In their view, if the world did not exist, something else must have existed in its place, and this something must have had some relation to God. There are therefore two ways of talking about what existence creation has. In one, creation must always have existed, no matter what. In the other, creation had no existence of its own, so it owes its existence to a will that was entirely free. Everything that exists because it is called into existence by will, the Fathers referred to as 'created'. They called the one who always existed, no matter what, and who does not owe his existence to any other will, the 'Uncreated'.

Everything that exists is either created or uncreated. There is no intermediate category. Something either exists because someone willed it to exist, which means that it could also cease to be willed, and as a consequence it would cease to exist. Or something exists because it willed itself to exist. The uncreated is that which exists because it decides for itself to do so. It does not exist because nature makes it do so, or because someone else decides that it should do so. We exist because someone other than ourselves has decided that we should exist: our existence is the outcome of their will, not our own. But God does not exist because someone or something else obliges him to do so. In our case existence is forced on us. It is easy to assume that if it is necessary for us, existence must be necessary for the one who has brought us into existence, but we cannot infer one from the other. Because we received it, from God who preceded us, existence is a given for us. But God exists freely, he did not receive his existence from anyone, there being no one before him. These two categories of the created and the uncreated enable us to set out the doctrine of creation.

We said that the ancient Greeks believed that the world was eternal. They made no radical distinction between created and uncreated. When they talked about the creation of a thing, they meant only that it used to exist in a form different from its present form. An ancient Greek could accept that this table had a beginning, and that someone made it, but before this table had the form we see today, it existed in some other form. There was the timber, and before it was timber, it was a tree, and before it was a tree, it was a seed, and all the other inputs of sun, water and minerals. It is part of a transmutation of elements without beginning or end.

But it is the Church's doctrine that before creation there was absolutely nothing: no existent thing had any previous existence. This view confounds our own familiar logic so it appears very strange to us. How can what exists now have had no previous existence at all? This is a difficult thought even for contemporary science, though contemporary cosmology, with its Big Bang theories of the origin of the universe, no longer finds it unthinkable that there was indeed nothing before the universe.

The universe must not in any way be viewed as an extension of God himself. Our world is created because someone wills it to exist, so its existence is not free. God, the uncreated, is not the result of any other will, so he exists freely, solely because he wills to do so. The necessity of existence is a function of the actual event of existence and of the fact that something exists at this moment. But it is not necessary that anything exists at all.

Since what is created has come out of nothing, nothingness will always be lurking behind it. If the created world could just as easily not exist, what prevents it from disappearing right now? It is only the goodwill of God that keeps it in existence. What is created has a dependent existence and must remain in relationship with the uncreated if it is to survive. If the relationship is severed, the world returns to nothingness. Whatever is created lives under the permanent threat of non-existence. When it severs its bond with the uncreated, turns towards itself and seeks to draw its powers of survival from its own self, it is deceived and its dissolution begins.

We can perhaps imagine a bond between the created and the uncreated which could never be severed in any way. God could have created a world with no desire for any relationship with God, but this would mean that its relationship with God would be one of necessity, not of freedom. This would mean that God had created another 'God', one that would live eternally because it would have an eternal and necessary relationship with the uncreated. But to talk about God creating another 'God' who did not start out as a 'God' makes no sense. The eternity of this 'God' would have been created by time, since he first was not eternal, and then was eternal after all. The word 'God' would apply both to a being that exists without having being created by someone else, and to a being that was created by someone else. Then we would need another word to describe that being who is God without having been created by someone else.

When we accept that this creation was created by someone and that that someone in fact exists, we need to find two different words to describe these two things. We cannot refer to the created being as 'god', and the uncreated also 'God'. We cannot say that a created thing is made eternal by God: what is created does not have eternity, so it is cut off from God, it would relapse into non-being. Only an unbroken relationship with God sustains the world and prevents it from reverting back to nothing. But in this relationship with God that allows it to endure, creation must also have freedom. The doctrine of creation is not only about the world, but also about freedom, and therefore about the role of man within the world. We must examine the possibility of beings within creation that are free.

The relationship with the uncreated God must be a voluntary, freely willed relationship. A relationship that was necessary would turn creation into a second 'God'. But if this relationship is to be freely willed, there must be free beings in creation. For its continued existence the created world needs beings who can affirm their relationship with God in freedom. Creation does not consist of material creatures only. The doctrine of creation refers to two sorts of creature that are free, those with, and those without, a material body. Those who possess a material hypostasis are ourselves, while those without material hypostasis are those incorporeal beings we know as angels, who exist in blessedness that they receive through their relationship with God. They are creatures, and subject to the same conditions as material bodies. To be subject to death is not a consequence of materiality, for it is our createdness, not our materiality, which makes us subject to death. Just as it is not evil, materiality is not the cause of death. It is because they had a beginning, and came out of nothing, that death is always a possibility for creatures.

So far we have said that the purpose for which free beings were brought into existence was to unite the created with the uncreated, willingly and freely. The created cannot be united with the uncreated by force but without this union, creation will eventually disappear. It is the vocation of free beings to allow creation to survive. All creation hangs on their exercise of freedom on its behalf. If they do so in the manner that brings the created into relationship and union with the uncreated, all that is created will live. If they exercise their freedom in any other way, catastrophe threatens. Though free, the angels cannot fulfil this role because they do not have our materiality and so cannot bring the material creation into relationship with God. But because he has a body, man participates in the materiality of creation and so he is able to bring about this relationship of the created with the uncreated. Only through man can creation survive.

It should be clear now why 'all creation groans and suffers' (Romans 8.22) as it looks forward to man's reconciliation with the uncreated. Creation needs beings who can turn freely towards God, accept their existence from him and enter relationship with him. This immense mission belongs to man.

Man appears for the first time at the end of creation. This is a fundamental difference between Christianity and the philosophical and gnostic systems of the period when the Christian doctrine of creation was being articulated. Gnostic systems begin with the creation of man and end with the creation of matter and other inferior beings, believing that creation began with higher beings and that all subsequent movement represent deterioration into inferior and more material forms of being.

But in the biblical view we find no such contempt for the material world. The appearance of man at the end of creation indicates that man is the highest of all creatures and that God intended the material world for him. He is the creature who is to bring the entire material world into communion with God. The position of man at the end of creation also points to his exercise of freedom on behalf of the material world. Because he is created with freedom, man may set himself for the world or against it. He can either receive it as good, or he can decide that he does not want to receive it at all. Man is the 'crowning glory' of creation, as some of the Fathers put it: endowed with the freedom that no other creature possesses, he can rule over the entire material world and use it in whatever way he desires. Man is created to fulfil the destiny of the created world, and he does this both by giving his consent on behalf of creation and by the authority he has to make use of creation. 'Dominion over the earth' means he is made responsible for it.

We have spoken about the mission of man in creation and high-lighted the difference between man and the rest of the created order. Now we take up the concept of the 'image', for man was created 'in the image and likeness of God' (Genesis 1.26). Though they display a range of views, the Fathers often suggest that 'in the image' expresses the per-fect state of man at the beginning of creation, the way he was created by God, while 'in the likeness' refers to the state that man will achieve at the end of time, when he finally looks upon God face to face and the communion of created and uncreated is complete. Then, in the escha-ton, man will also be 'likeness' of God, for he will be free, like God.

Some Fathers considered that man is already the 'image' of God and understood 'likeness' to refer to the end of times, while for others 'image' refers to the rationality of man. Gregory of Nyssa used it to refer to the human capacity of self-government. The difference is not hugely significant because those Fathers who relate the 'image' to the *logos* and rationality of man understand that the *logos* of man is his freedom, which is what self-government is. So we fairly represent the Patristic tradition as a whole when we see the element of freedom or self-government as the difference between man and the rest of the material creation.

We must see what constitutes this freedom of man, and how it serves creation. Freedom is the prospect open to creatures. When they have freedom, they will be like God. Our existence is not free, because for us existence is a given fact. This is the supreme challenge that creatures are faced with. We exist necessarily. But the 'image' means that we may have our existence, not because we are obliged to by the ways things are, but because we are able to receive it for ourselves willingly and freely.

Man's freedom can be exercised in two ways. It can be exercised neg-atively, when man decides to despise creation and disdain its Creator. Man can say that he does not acknowledge God as Creator, and that he does not consider this creation to be any concern of his. But equally there is the possibility that man will not reject creation.

Man will of course wish to create his own world, analogous to the way that God creates. This impulse of man is the only determinant difference between him and every other animal. We cannot talk about the doctrine of creation without some reference to biology and evolution. Darwin's account of evolution prevails in biology. His theory caused panic among theologians of the nineteenth century, because up until that time, and even to this day for many people, what distinguished man from all other animals was his rationality and self-awareness. In *The Origin of Species*, Darwin very convincingly demonstrated that these characteristics are found in other animals too. Other animals possess them to a lesser degree, but this means that the difference between man and the other animals is a difference of degree. Darwin demonstrated that animals have consciousness, are able to achieve some level of organisation, have their own societies and even use instruments. Darwin has us obliged to review the whole question of what makes man distinct from all other animals.

While many continue to see the difference as one of rationality, contemporary anthropology has now described the difference in a way that renders Darwin's theory entirely innocuous to theology. The difference between man and all other animals is freedom. An animal may have the ability to adapt to its environment, but it does not set out to re-create its own environment. An animal cannot create a world of its own: this is only a possibility and a temptation for man. You and your cat see the same tree. As a botanist you can analyse that tree and construct an entire science of ecology that describes it exhaustively, and your knowledge of that tree will still be just of a different degree, not of a different kind, from that of your cat.

But when you decide to draw a tree and so to make your own tree or a world of trees that is all your own creation, you are doing something that makes you utterly different from any animal. An animal cannot be an artist. To reject the existing world and create a world of its own, which will bear its personal stamp, is a characteristic only of man, and it can be observed from man's very first steps.

Contemporary psychology observes that when an infant takes any raw material into its hands, he it will shape it and put his own stamp on it. In this way he shows that he does not have to admit that the world is simply something that he has to adjust to, whether he wants to or not. He wants to make a world of his own. Art creates new worlds, and so art is the practice of man's freedom. There is a tension between man's freedom and his created status: man cannot create from nothing, but is obliged to rely on given images and materials. This is why properly creative art, particularly contemporary art, strives for autonomy and attempts to break up the forms it inherits. Michaelangelo complained that his greatest obstacle was the marble which came between him and his art-work. Picasso and other contemporary artists rebel against all inherited forms because they hinder their freedom. To represent the table as it is, is not a work of creative art, but simply to produce a replica of the object. Art is not about copying the given world, and neither is it about extracting a spirit, or meaning, or essential beauty from nature, as the Romantics believed. Such conceptions are not about freedom or creativity. Art bears a restlessness that is directed towards finding a greater freedom by breaking up forms to find the new thing the artist desires, something so deeply personal that no one else can recognise it. He creates something which he may even call a table, but which looks nothing like a table to the rest of us, and this makes art difficult and sometimes even repellant.

I hope we have established that Christian doctrine is linked to man's search for freedom and that freedom is a central concern of the doctrine of creation. It points towards a creature who, though within God's given world, has no wish to accept it or preserve it as it is delivered to him, but wishes to put his own stamp on it. Man begins by denying the world he finds himself in. To demonstrate his freedom man can either deface the world until perhaps he eventually destroys it, or he can take it and affirm it of his own free will. Though there are many degrees of response, man lives in the space between these two possibilities. Man must never surrender his freedom, for the moment he is tempted to do so, he demotes himself to the status of an animal, and creation's hope of participating in freedom and life through him is lost.

Here lies a problem. If Man's freedom is exercised and respected, creation is in danger. It is particularly crucial to say this, now that we really have become a threat to our natural environment as a whole. The invitation to 'subdue the earth' has allowed us to make a reckless use of the environment. Why have we been entrusted with this dangerous freedom? The answer is that freedom is the one means by which creation can be in communion with God and live on.

Freedom is never simply positive freedom. From the moment it was given, it also means that man has the freedom to bring the world to an end. For God there is only positive freedom. God does not want the destruction of the world. Our whole problem stems from the reality of being created, and the difference between the created and the uncreated.

In the act of creation, God did not have to deal with a given situation. Whatever he had was the result of his will. God affirmed what he made: he gave it his 'yes'. For God 'no' is not the exercise of freedom. There is no choice of 'yes' *or* 'no' for God, because there is no given to which God might say 'no'. There is only a possibility of saying 'no' when there is something to say 'no' to, a situation created by someone else. The freedom God has given to his creature takes the form of a choice between 'yes' and 'no' and the freedom of the creature consists in his being able to decide between 'yes' and 'no' in each situation. The Law given at the moment of man's creation in the Garden of Eden, in the image of the tree, was the means by which man could exercise his freedom. God did not provide the Law in order to take freedom away from man but precisely in order to give him this freedom. Freedom is the law, that is the invitation and command, that God gives man. Now we must examine how this freedom was exercised in man's decision against the world and against God, as we turn to the doctrine of the fall of man.

IV. THE FALL

It was the freedom of man that made the fall possible. Without this freedom there would be no sin and no evil. Man can sin, animals cannot, for it is the exercise of freedom rather than the act itself that makes something sinful.

Man has the freedom which every other created being in the material world lacks, and he exercises it by accepting or rejecting each given event or situation. In order to continue in existence, and overcome his limits and the eventual dissolution that they bring, the creature has to be in relationship with the uncreated God. Although he was created to bring the created into union with the uncreated, man decided to exercise his freedom by saying 'no' to this relationship, and setting out to unite the created, not to the uncreated, but to himself. Adam succumbed to the temptation to declare himself 'God' and set out to redirect creation from the uncreated God to his own, created self. In deciding that everything should refer to him, his fall was also the fall of creation.

Related to God, creation would have life without limit. But man turned creation from God to himself. The first consequence was that man came to believe that he could rule creation as though he had created it himself. He set nature against himself and created a conflict and because man was no longer in harmony with it, nature became a cause of misery to him. Persons were set against nature, so man could survive in this world only by struggling against it.

A second consequence was that man attributed nature with the characteristics that belong to God. Since conflict with nature made man realise how much weaker he is, he began to believe himself to be inferior to nature. Overawed by them, he began to divinise the forces of nature and then to placate them, so that idolatry became another consequence of man's fall. In his conflict with it he regarded nature as a god, or indeed as many gods. When he feared the thunderstorm that he knew was beyond his control, man deified the storm and 'exchanged the Creator for the creatures' (Romans 1.23). The deification of creation is a tragedy for mankind and for nature too. Nature relies on man directing himself to God, because it is only through man that nature can come into communion with God and so preserve its existence. But when man took God's place and turned himself to nature, all creation became victim to man's delusion. Man and creation have together become confined to a life determined by the laws of nature. Though biological life seems to point towards life without limit, it only takes them in the direction of eventual dissolution.

Among our everyday assumptions is the belief that death takes place at the end of life. We say that someone died aged eighty, as though death suddenly made its appearance in his eighty-first year. In reality however man begins to die the moment he is born. Biology sees death as a process that begins at birth, and links ageing to reproduction. The mystery of life and phenomenon of death are bound together, for life bears death within itself. The physical processes are finally all-significant: the organism ages, but because we cannot bring ourselves to think clearly about death, we give only intellectual assent to this fact. The truth of life is that things are beyond our control. We are confined within this counterfeit life and filter out the vastness of the God-determined dimensions of reality. The fall of man threatens to bring about an end to man. Without the relationship with the unconfined and unlimited life found in relationship with the uncreated, nature lost touch with the truth of life. Man is under the impression that he is in possession of life, but what he calls life is in fact no more than a process of dissolution. Death masquerades as life: its claim to be life is a tragic consequence of the fall.

The Gospel points to real life. When the bible talks about eternal life, it does not mean some life other than our present one, but simply the reality of life. The reality of life is 'spiritual', because it is given by the Holy Spirit. This life does not die and does not share in the deception of that life that leads to death. Real life cannot be brought to an end by death and will never prove false. Real life springs from the resurrection, which is to say from Christ who himself transcends biological death. This does not mean that we are trying to ignore biological death or to substitute some other life for it. On the contrary, the afterlife, as it is called, is the truth and fullness of which the life we presently experience is just a part. This counterfeit life with which we are presently content, and which carries death within it, is the outcome of the fall. It is a poor, evil and intolerable form of life. The Christian view is that death is never good; it is always an outrage.

The gospel is the breaching and breaking of death. The resurrection is the promise that the confusion of real life by false life will come to an end and be entirely succeeded by the life that is real. The false life to which we are subject will be removed, to leave only the reality and truth of life. What is true and real can never be delimited, or broken off or brought to an end, nor will we ever run out of it. Life that is real is not finite, but unlimited and eternal.

The New Testament understands eternity simply as life, without death or any other interruption. When the life we already experience now in a fragmentary way is renewed by God so that it continues without limit, life will be eternal. Time, history and the whole course of the material world are positive aspects of creation, and eternity is time, redeemed for us by God. It is Platonism that sets eternity and time in opposition, and regards time as a misfortune. It asserts that we are trapped in time, and must be released from it, and move up to another, timeless, level above. Many Christians think in terms that are more Platonist than Christian. When people commiserate with one another you hear them say, 'Has he passed away? Consider him blessed, since he has left from this poor world of time and gone to eternity.' Such ideas are not Christian. Our hope in the resurrection anticipates that death will be broken, and that life will suffer no further interruption or threat. We must rid ourselves of this concept that time is a misfortune, and grasp the truth, which is that real life, which is what eternity is, is entirely unmixed with death.

There is nothing behind the created world. Since the world is not simply one large thing, but a vast profusion of wonderful entities, nothingness fills the space between each of these entities. Between A and B is space and time, and it is this that gives A and B their individuality and particularity. Space and time both connect them and separate them: the space between us both makes us separate beings and it divides us and makes us subject to dissolution. A and B are composites, made up of smaller elements, so when their dissolution reaches a certain point there is no more connection or communication between them. One form of separation is when A and B lose touch with each other and their relationship ends. The other is when the whole person of A disintegrates into his composite elements, the unity that time and space gave his body is dissolved, and he ceases to exist.

Time and space simultaneously compose and constitute beings, and decompose them and de-constitute them. The life that we know is a mixture of life and death, and a process of composition and dissolution. When our composite world breaks up into its constitutive elements we will disappear again: death is this disintegration. All beings are vulnerable to the nothingness from which they came and which is present in them. In contrast, the real life that comes from the Holy Spirit is entirely free of nothingness, and is unassailable to the forces of dissolution.

When he refused relationship with God, man was left quite helplessly exposed to the processes of dissolution. Man was deceived, and he continues to be deceived, into believing that he is alive when the processes of dissolution are working away within him and will soon make an end of him. Man is tempted to believe that, given more time or more resource, he could establish himself more permanently. But we would be mistaken if we think that eternity can be secured through the processes of history, that given just a little more time we could reach eternity and permanence. We can believe this only by being blind to the processes of death, and ignoring the fact that all beings wear out and pass away. Some try to deal with the problem by transferring the question from the survival of the individual to survival of humanity as a whole. Christian dogmatics however must take the threat to our existence very seriously. It must insist that the death of every single person, even of every single entity, is an outrage, and say clearly that creation has become captive to death.

V. Christology

Creation came from nothing, and since it is permeated with the forces of dissolution, it always faces the prospect of reverting back to nothing. But as long as they are in communion with what is not created, created beings are safe from all such forces. Man was created to provide this communion. He was to be the mediator between the material world and God, and so he was created at the end of creation, when everything else was ready for him. This privilege was given to man rather than to any other free and rational being because as a material being, man is able to unite created materiality with the uncreated, and so to secure the continued life of the material creation. If man is to endure, all creation must endure, for man cannot live without creation. If man is to survive death, all creation has to be transformed so that no part of it succumbs to death.

There are two possible misconceptions here. One is the belief that death entered the world as the punishment for disobedience and the fall, which is to say that God introduced it to creation and imposed it on man. We have seen that death has always been the natural condition of created beings, and since all that is finite has an end, death is inevitable for creation – unless man exercises his freedom positively, for creation and himself. If man does so, the life of creation is sustained endlessly through infinite communion with the infinite God. The fall is the term we give to man's refusal to exercise his freedom in this positive way; the consequence of his refusal is that the death of creation, and of man, remains inevitable. Death is a corollary of finitude, and so is universal for all created things; when we concede the truth of this we are able to come into conversation with biology, which understands that death is a universal natural phenomenon.

A second misconception is that immortality relates chiefly to the soul. Accordingly, when death is abolished at the end of time, it is thought that people's souls will live on, and though the bodies of these souls might live on too, the rest of the world would die. But this view is mistaken too. Death is a biological phenomenon, which if it is to be transcended at all, must be transcended by creation as a whole. The refusal of man to host the meeting of createdness with the uncreated God, makes the continuation and redemption of creation impossible.

The salvation of the world must be salvation from death. Let us start with some general observations. When we diagnose a sick person we identify their disease. The disease here is death, so a cure for death is what we are looking for. Salvation has often been set out in moral and judicial terms, in which death has been caused by man's act of disobedience. But it was not our disobedience that caused this evil; it just made its cure impossible. The problem cannot be put right simply by our obedience. Athanasius pointed out that if the problem could be solved simply by forgiving Adam his sin, God could have done so. Adam could have repented, and indeed he did weep and regret what he had done. God could have forgiven him, and all would have been well. But Athanasius showed that the heart of the problem was not obedience or disobedience, because this was not a moral but an ontological problem. What was required was for the Logos to come to man, and indeed to become man, so that all that has been created can be united to the uncreated. For death to be overcome, the created has to come into relationship with the uncreated, and source its life from it.

Salvation involves a relationship between persons. Man alone was given the privilege of being this bodily and material union of creation with Creator. Man's material body and entire psycho-somatic being have to participate in this union, so that all creation to which we are linked is able to participate in it too. For the world to be saved, man has to mediate between creation and God. No other being could do this, and it could not be done by God simply saying from a distance 'Be saved!' The logic demanded that God become one of us. The inevitable dissolution of creation could not have been averted even if, after his fall, man had been saved and thereafter not fallen again. The incarnation is not simply a response to the fall. Maximus makes it very clear that the incarnation would have taken place, even if man had not fallen. It was inconceivable that this world could endure when nothingness and dissolution are inherent to it. Only when this material creature who unites in himself the material creation to the uncreated God can the uncreated pass life uninterruptedly to the created. The mediation of man is thus the central requirement for the salvation of creation.

A second factor is the fact that man on his own is not capable of transcending death. Transcendence of death cannot be achieved by any creature, and even less so when man fell and became a prisoner of the counterfeit life, which is life permeated by death. From the moment that man became trapped in this cycle of life and death, it was impossible for him to free himself. So the uncreated God took the initiative.

There are two elements that take us to the mystery of the incarnation of Christ. The first is the initiative taken by God, and the second is the need for a union rather than a mere submission or forgiveness, between the creature and his Lord. Christ fulfils the two requirements. The Word became a human being, for Christ must be human rather than an angel or any other creature. Christ is God, and because he is God he is not entangled in this vicious circle of life and death himself. The incarnation of the Word is the salvation of the world, and every creature in it, from death.

The Word becomes incarnate as that creature whose being and identity are primarily determined by his relationship with God, rather than by his relationship with any other creature. The second condition, a consequence of the first, is that this Saviour is not conceived in the way that every other human creature is conceived. The doctrine of the non-biological conception of Christ by the Holy Spirit and the Virgin Mary is essential to the Christian faith. If Christ had been born in the same biological manner that we are, he would have been confined within the same cycles of counterfeit life-in-death that we are, and he could not have been the solution to our problem. The role of the Holy Spirit in Christ's conception is therefore essential. Only the uncreated Spirit could take this initiative; this event could be free because it was not bound by any of the limits that creation represents, because the Son is not created. It had to be free both on the part of the Word who became flesh, and free on the part of created humanity in the person of the Virgin.

God had given Adam the freedom to inaugurate the salvation of the world but, in his freedom, Adam did not do so. Nonetheless, it would have been unthinkable for God to take man's freedom away by intervening and compelling him to do so. Man did not want to preserve the world, but God did not therefore decide to preserve the world, and man himself, despite man. The freedom of man had to be safeguarded by the form that incarnation took. The complete and proper expression of human freedom came at last in the unforced 'yes' given by the Virgin Mary to God's call to carry through this mystery of Christ. Mary could have refused to take part in such a plan that utterly conflicts with our self-directed logic, but her reply was not 'no', but 'yes'. Her consent was the free consent of humankind to the initiative of God.

Adam survives in the person of Christ and, in Christ, Adam is free. Christ has now become the human, Adam, whose creaturely life is no longer constituted solely by his biology and thus by necessity. Though Adam still labours, he is nevertheless a free being now because he originates in this freely-willed human consent. That Christ is born in this manner is the condition by which all that we have said so far about the personal relationship between God and the world holds true. The incarnation of Christ is different from all the various other incarnations and rebirths of gods observed in other religions. All such births and theogonies represent natural phenomena and natural laws, and are the function of necessity, rather than of a free, personal consent on the part of humankind.

Christ is not born the product of natural laws, for this would have signified conformity to the necessary laws of nature which involve death. This would have been a reversion from the initial freedom which God bestowed on humanity, to the life under compulsion brought about by the withholding of Adam's consent. All that God intended had been brought to nothing as a result of Adam's exercise of freedom. But the freedom received in the consent of the Virgin permeates the entire mystery of Christ and of our salvation. This freedom is seen in Christ's incarnation from conception and birth to resurrection and all that happens after it. This freedom that Mary exercised in receiving the incarnate Son in her body is honoured in every phase of the mystery of our salvation.

VI. SALVATION

We have looked at the relationship of the doctrines of the incarnation and creation. God created the world so it would participate in his own glorious life. To bring the world into a living relationship with him, God gave man God's own freedom and self-government, and made him a link between God and the material world which has no self-government and therefore no freedom of its own. Man was the point through which all nature was to participate in God's self-government and life.

But in his freedom, man decided to relate the world to himself instead of God. By his decision to direct nature to himself, man confined himself and nature within the laws that govern creation. Since it came from nothing and nothingness permeates it, the being of every creature is always being worn away. Man was unable to overcome the constraints to which all creatures are subject. It is an extraordinary mystery that by his possession of this God-given freedom, man was able to halt God's plan.

God did not intend this hold-up, but he did not ignore it either. Though his plan had stalled, God's intention remained unaltered. It took a new course to relate to the changed situation. This is the logic Saint Athanasius sets out in his 'On the Incarnation of the Word'.

We would still be talking about the incarnation even without Adam's fall, but Adam's fall determined the form that the incarnation had to take. Had he not fallen, Adam would eventually have brought all creation into this union with God through his own person. This union would have enabled the overcoming of the boundaries of a created being, represented by death: Christology would simply have meant the transformation of man into Christ. By exercising his liberty affirmatively, as Christ, man would have made the existence of the world no longer subject to the constraints of a created entity, decay and death. This Christ would have existed in time and space, as Saint Maximus assures us.

But it was no longer possible for this union between the created and the uncreated to be attained through man, without it passing through the dissolution and death into which man had fallen. Adam's failure obliged God to reach this end by another means, that which involved Christ coming into the broken condition of man, so the incarnation takes the form of this passion which Christ suffers. God never suspended his respect for man's freedom. He chose the Virgin Mary to speak for all mankind, and by giving her assent to it in complete freedom, Mary made possible for Christ to come by this new course that involved taking on our broken condition. Only Mary's freely given 'yes', which affirmed and demonstrated the freedom of mankind, opened this new way by which Christ could come to creation and creation could come to God.

This entrance of God into the world, the penetration of the uncreated into creation to unite the two, was performed by one person of the Trinity. By entering creation, the Son created a bridge between creation and God. The persons of the Trinity are not separated from one another, so through the action of one, the entire Trinity participates in the event of Christ. Each person undertakes a particular role: the Son enters the fallen reality of the created world, taking on its decay and pain, and its sorrow and death. But the Son did this because the Father, in his mercy, made this initiative.

We can only understand the incarnation of Christ by reference to the Father and to the Spirit. It is the Father who initiates the incarnation. It was the error of earlier generations of Christian dogmatics to separate Christology first from the doctrine of God and then from the doctrine of the Spirit. It is the Father from whose will all things come. As the very existence of God comes from the goodwill of the Father, so the whole economy and work of Christ also come from the will of the Father. The Father intends that this incarnation should take place; the Son assents to the Father's will and enters the fallen reality of the creature. In love the Father initiates and participates in this event, while the Son assents and acts. The Holy Spirit carries this plan through, supporting the Son through the pain of this exchange and union, in which the Son takes on the fallen state of creation. The Holy Spirit stands with Christ in all the decisions by which he affirms his freedom, and he liberates the Son from the consequences of his giving of himself to us. The Spirit, who sustains all freedom, ensures that Christ's decisions are free. Wherever the Spirit is, the constrictions of nature are overcome, and so we are liberated from all that confines us. Though he is with Christ throughout his existence, the Holy Spirit is most characteristically present at those moments in which the progress of God's plan for the salvation of the world is decided.

The Spirit is present at every one of the critical points that determine the course of the incarnation. He is present at the Virgin Mary's 'yes' and the conception of the Son of God by the holy Mother of God. The

Holy Virgin conceives through the Holy Spirit. If it were merely a matter of divine intervention the Logos could have inhabited the holy Virgin on his own and there would have been no need for the Spirit. But the Virgin conceived *by the Holy Spirit*, which means that there was no intrusion into the created by the uncreated, so what took place did so in freedom. Any direct intervention by the uncreated would necessarily overcome the created, for wherever one force is much greater than another, the lesser will be overwhelmed. But the presence of the Holy Spirit prevents the lesser force of the creature from being crushed by the greater force of God. The Holy Spirit never makes the creature aware of his presence, so the creature is not overawed, but simply aware that all other pressures are taken off, so that they are able to make a decision that is entirely free. In the presence of the Spirit, the Virgin Mary is able to decide in complete freedom, and thus the incarnation of Christ takes place in true creaturely freedom. The Spirit ensures that what is created is not crushed by the presence of what is uncreated.

The contribution of the Holy Spirit is therefore to allow each agent to act as a person, unconstrained by all limits and pressures. The Holy Spirit frees Christ from the confines of history and is with Christ at every critical juncture. He accompanies Christ in the conflict with Satan in the desert so that, when his preparation and testing are complete, Christ is able to say 'yes' freely to God as a human, and so to act on behalf of all humans. From within them, Christ is able to surmount the bounds of biology and history, and act in freedom. As the title 'Christ' tells us, Jesus is anointed by the Spirit and accompanied by him always.

The Spirit is present at Gethsemane, where the all-important decision to drink down the cup, despite all its horror, is taken. The Spirit enables the Lord's free decision to go to the cross, and the Spirit raises Christ from the confines of death. The resurrection and defeat of death is the Spirit's act in transcending all limits, and all dissolution and death. Though Christian dogmatics have not always been very clear about this, the Bible tells us that it was 'the Spirit who raised Jesus from the dead' (Romans 8.11). Just like the conception and birth, and the ministry, passion and resurrection of Christ take place by the Holy Spirit.

Why is it the Holy Spirit who raises Christ from the dead? Christ is God, so death could never have held him, so why is there this need for the Spirit? The Holy Spirit makes the whole incarnation an expression of the freedom in which, because of Christ, man now participates. The Spirit who liberates all that is created from trials and from deterioration and death, has in Christ passed into humanity. Once dissolution and death are transcended in Christ, the Holy Spirit makes Christ that body within which all mankind begins to experience freedom from death. The Spirit makes Christ's resurrection the liberation from death, not just for Jesus but for all humanity. For Christ's resurrection would make no sense without our resurrection (1 Corinthians 15.13-20).

The Holy Spirit has made Christ the universal being in whom the boundaries of the created are transcended. Christ ceases to be an individual and has become the truth of human existence, so his life has universal reach. He has broken out of the nature-determined constraints that make him merely one person, separated by nature from all other persons. As Christ took on the fate of creation, creation is taking on the fate of Christ, being liberated from its confines and redeemed. Creation is no longer a form of enforced confinement for humanity so each person can receive every other creature in complete freedom.

Christ has broken through these boundaries for created mankind, not as one person alone, but in the Holy Spirit, for all. The Holy Spirit makes Christ *the Christ* by making him inclusive of all humanity, indeed of all creation. The Holy Spirit goes on to make Christ the source of the spiritual gifts so that together mankind is no longer held within those confines but is free to receive the full dimensions of the person of Christ. The role of the Holy Spirit, though all-important, has been so underestimated that we could even say that it has been suppressed. The incarnation requires the whole doctrine of God. Trinity begins with the goodwill of the Father, continues with the Son taking on the fate of fallen creation and ends with Christ gathering us and all creation up by the Holy Spirit. The Holy Spirit always acts *through* Christ, because Christ is the point where all mankind and all creation are gathered up and brought into living communion with God on whom there are no confines. The incarnation is therefore not just about Christ's *receiving* the Holy Spirit, but also about Christ *giving* the Holy Spirit to all mankind, as we shall see as when we come to the subject of ecclesiology.

Salvation is the union of the created with the uncreated. This union is not mechanical or magical; there is no synthesis of these two natures, as though a quantity of divine nature added to a quantity of human nature brings about the admission of man to the communion of God. The role of the Father and of the Holy Spirit are crucial in this union.

The mystery of Christ begins with the Father and ends with the Father, because the Son and Holy Spirit obey the Father in bringing about the whole reality of the union between the created and the uncreated. Considered as a whole, the incarnation is a movement from the Father back to the Father, through Christ in the Holy Spirit. Christology tends to be discussed only in terms of natures, divine and human, but Christology is always a matter of relationships of persons acting in freedom.

The Son of God took on the fallen nature of man. This raises the huge issue of how it is possible for the impassive God to become subject to the consequences of the fall. How should we understand the involvement of God in the suffering, self-emptying and even death of Christ?

The Son, one person of the Trinity, empties himself of glory. His relationship with the Father and Spirit is not broken, but he alone undertakes the fate of the created, making it his own fate. This is uniquely his act, for each of the persons of the Trinity is a complete and free-acting being. As a person complete in himself the Son freely accepted for himself the fate of the world in its fallen form and worked through this world in order to carry through the plan of God the Father. Freely the Son took on all the consequences of entering the fallen reality of the world's existence and, equally freely, the Holy Spirit worked with him so that all three persons participated, each in his own way.

Creation had become trapped within its own boundaries, and was bound for dissolution and death. But as the Word became flesh, becoming a single human being, and taking on the constraints of flesh, he too became subject to hunger and thirst, to tiredness, and so he suffered, until even this life was finally taken away from him. All his suffering was entirely real. For the whole ancient world it was an established principle that God is impassive and cannot suffer pain or death. But the Church dismissed the temptation to regard Christ's sufferings as a matter of mere appearances, that is to say, of illusion or pretence, regarding such a 'docetic' Christology as an evasion of the truth. However difficult and counterintuitive it was to say that it was truly God who suffered all those things, the Church nevertheless insisted that the Son of God was fully involved in this sorrow, suffering and death.

Since the Church was clear that the pain and anguish of the Son were real it had to reconcile them with the impassivity of God. Twentieth-century Christology was inclined to read back into the eternal life and being of God what we see in the economy of God for us. It decided that the passion was directly related to the nature of God and that on account of his love God suffers as soon as he sees mankind suffering and even that he is 'eternally' familiar with sorrow. His love for mankind means that the cross is a part of his eternal existence and that there is no intrinsic conflict between the cross and the nature and being of God. But the Fathers of the Church took quite a different view.

The Fathers insisted that such an understanding cannot fit with God because in his eternal existence he is not bound by the constraints of creaturehood. God is free of the limitations experienced by all created things: this is what it means to be uncreated. If the concept of passion indicates a characteristic of divine nature, this is completely inappropriate here.

The Church teaches us that all that happened to Christ, including the pain, sorrow and death that he underwent, must be understood as an extreme and incomprehensible act of freedom and love. This passion is Christ's action, and a most dynamic and active work. We stand before the mystery of the incarnation and wonder how God could act in this way to become passive to all that man could inflict on him. We cannot explain how Christ could suffer, but must say that it is the love of God that has brought this about and so we can only express our thankfulness. It is extremely important therefore for us to be clear that Christ does not suffer because suffering is part of his divine nature, but that he suffers *despite* his divine nature. He does so because he decides to do so, not because his nature compels him. He freely decided to undergo these things for our sake, and at each moment of his ministry demonstrated his willing engagement in taking on all that belonged to his incarnation among humankind.

Some theologians stress the self-emptying (*kenosis*) involved in the incarnation and suggest that in suffering these things for our sake, Christ gave up his divinity. But his divinity is simply personal relationship with the Father, and the relationship of the Son with the Father is in no way altered by the incarnation. His nature, which is the nature he has with the Father, and which is common to them both, exists without interruption. He suffered because he took human nature and remained obedient to its confines. In Christ we have the whole fullness of God: nothing of his divinity receded or was withdrawn in the incarnation. He was completely human and completely God. We have to affirm this, but beyond a certain point we can offer no further explanations. We can explain it only in terms of the liberty of God who is free to exercise his power and his love and to exercise it in the form of weakness. Thus the Council of Chalcedon (451) stated that in Christ we acknowledge complete divinity and complete humanity, nothing missing in either respect.

That Council went on to say that the union of the divinity and humanity is complete, so Christ's divine and human natures are united indivisibly. This union involved no mixture or synthesis of the two natures; there was no confusion so these natures could always be distinguished, one from the other, 'distinct', as the Council put it. We have two natures, divine and human, joined inseparably while remaining distinct. The third point that the Council made was that the union of these two natures took place in the *person* of the Son of God. There was no creation of a new, human person: we do not have two persons but the one person of Christ. The union of the two natures is personal because it is a person who is this union, the specific person of the Son of the Trinity. The crucial point is that we are not ultimately dealing with natures, but with persons as the focus of unity.

The Church's insistence on the singularity of the person of Christ contrasted with a position advanced by Nestorius. Nestorius wanted to preserve the humanity of Christ in full. He was afraid that if we do not say that the person of Christ is human the humanity of Christ would be diminished. The Church at Chalcedon took the position that we are not dealing with a *human* person but simply with one single person, and that this person is divine. Does this demote the humanity of Christ? We said that Christ is fully God and fully human, so surely it is right to say that his person is a human person?

A person is an identity formed through a relationship. We are persons because our distinct identity is given by our various relationships, biological relationships with our parents, natural relationships with our environment, and a vast complex of other social and political relationships. All these make us the person we are. But each particular person also substantiates these relationships and makes them his own. All we say and do in the course of a lifetime subtly determines the environment which shapes us. Each of us is enabled by the community among which he was born and brought up, but equally through all his life he adds something to that community, by which he alters slightly what those who come after him are able to do. We receive our personhood from the whole vast community around us, and by participating in that community, we contribute to it and in some untraceably small way change it too. So though we receive our personhood from the community, the community also receives its identity from us, so the person has a part in determining the community that determines him.

Each person can assume many relationships and to some degree arbitrate between them. We can decide which relationship is most important and even which is ultimate for us. Only one relationship by definition can finally be the most significant and decisive for us, and this is the relationship that makes me myself rather than someone else. If, for example, I decide that my relationship with my parents is the definitive one, then all of my other natural, social relationships will be mediated through this relationship with my parents. One decisive relationship makes me who I am and is the criterion for all other relationships that contribute to my total identity.

If I do not desire to make the personal relationship with my parents the decisive element for my personal identity, I find others to whom I transfer my affection. And this is something that indeed occurs as we grow: the child gradually transfers its decisive relationship from its mother and family to others, so its personal identity is not longer given entirely by its family, but also by a much wider circle of relationships. If we relate our identity unduly to what we wear, or what we eat or the car we drive, these things will come to determine our entire identity.

Our personal identity is a matter of relationships. When you are in love with someone, this relationship is decisive for the way in which you see the world and all other relationships at that time. So then relationships give us our identity and make us persons. One of these relationships will eventually determine and incorporate all the other relationships. Now what makes Christ a person is the relationship through which all his other relationships pass and by which they are determined. What finally determines the identity of Christ, is his relationship with the Father.

In the incarnation, Christ took on other relationships. He had a relationship with his mother, Mary, with his people, teachers and disciples and with the natural and social environment of Israel. He ate and took his place in the economy and ecology of the land of Israel and had relationships with the entire people of Israel and all those others that shared that land. He takes on all that is common to humanity and nothing that is created is foreign to him. All these relationships belong to his personal identity, and they are all judged by the decisive relationship that Christ has with the Father. When we explain what the Church Fathers achieved by their statement at Chalcedon, we have to show the significance of their statement that Christ is one person with two natures. His divine and human natures, along with all the relationships with the created order, come within the one relationship with the Father that determines Christ's identity. Thus, despite the new relationships that he takes on in his incarnation, he is, and remains, the Son of the Father.

In our case the centre of our identity shifts as we take on new relationships. The 'I' changes, when the 'you' changes. When someone we love dies, we will eventually have to find some other love to replace it. If that love is not replaced through other relationships it will become impossible for us to connect to others, to sustain our other relationships and our identity will be endangered. As long as all our relationships are focused through the love of someone who is no longer alive, all our relationships and our entire identity are threatened.

What should we say about the identity of Christ and about his own understanding of his identity? When Christ says 'I', what does he mean? Where does he get his consciousness of himself from? There was a long discussion, chiefly in Roman Catholic theological circles, of whether Christ had two kinds of consciousness, a divine consciousness and a human one. But we must remember that it is impossible to be conscious, to be a self, without a relationship. I am me because I am related to my brother, my nephew, my neighbour, my employer or whoever. We always are what we are as we relate to someone who is not ourselves. You cannot say 'me', in the complete absence of any 'you'. After many centuries, some twentieth-century philosophers at least have made the discovery that there is no 'I' without a 'you'.

Christ draws his consciousness of himself from his relationship with the Father. This is why the person of Christ has only this single self-consciousness, which is determined by this single relationship. If he had drawn his identity equally primarily from Mary, Christ would have two self-consciousnesses, and thus been two equally fundamental sets of relationships and so would have been two persons. Then Nestorius' position would have been valid: we would have had one human with two persons : one relationship from here, and another relationship from there – equally giving him his identity. Two relationships cannot equally determine an identity: only one relationship can be ultimately determinative.

The truth of this can be seen in iconography. In Western portraits of Christ and the Virgin Mary, Christ is portrayed as a baby alone with his mother. The maternal relationship gives the identity of the baby. But in a Byzantine icon, the painter wants to show us that the child is God, so the baby is not defined by the Virgin. Although the relationship with his mother is real enough, his identity comes from another relationship, the relationship he has with the Father.

What is it that decides our personal identities? They are determined by the attitudes we take through the course of our lives. If the Father were to ask the Son to go the Cross and the holy Mother begged him, as every mother would, not to go, the Son would respond by obeying one of them. Or if he had decided at Gethsemane to follow his own will and not the will of the Father, he would not have gone to the cross. Had he not gone to the cross, the person of Jesus would be defined by his relationship either to himself (self-love) or to his mother and perhaps to the rest of humankind, but not by his relationship to the Father.

Our personal identity is being constantly determined through how we respond and enter relationships. The one who finally determines our personal identity is the one to whom we offer our existence. The saints and martyrs are witnesses to this. A martyr experiences communion with God, *theosis*, because at that moment in which his life is taken from him, he is related single-mindedly to Christ, so all other relationships are subordinated to this one. The martyrs made the relationship with God the relationship that determined their identity, just as Christ had, and so God sees the person of his Son in them. They did what the Son did, and were acknowledged by God as sons, and so they were able to acknowledge God as Father, and attain *theosis*, sealing their lives for eternity.

Christ, however, did not *attain* theosis by transferring his allegiance from human relationships to relationship with God. The relationship with the Father was first: he simply continued to acknowledge the Father as determinative of his identity. Christ does not acquire an identity *from* a created being, though the created element is embodied *within* his identity. He does not allow his own will or interests to become the source of his own identity. In this he was utterly unlike Adam who put himself in God's place and determined his identity from his own self.

Christ subordinated all other relationships to his relationship with the Father, and, being thus included within this relationship, all these other relationships were liberated from the restrictions to which they were subject. They are all set free and are included within his body, as *part* of his identity.

So it is vital that we respect the decision of the Council of Chalcedon that Christ's person is one, the person of the Son of the Father. Only within the Son is mankind brought into all relationships that are made possible when God is God. If a separate human person is attributed to Christ, the definition of man would be restricted to man and remain governed by his biological limitations.

By accepting one person, the divine person of the Son, we allow mankind infinite possibilities, so this is not a reductive view but a very high view of man. We not only have no demotion of mankind but the raising of mankind to life in the Holy Spirit, in free relationship with all humanity and with all creation. The teaching of the Church at

Chalcedon sets out the meaning of the person and so demonstrates that freedom is fundamental to human beings and to creation as a whole.

VII. COMMUNION

We have been asking how Christ can be perfect and at the same time experience suffering? How can he be God who is impassive and Christ who suffers all that we inflict on him? This is the question asked about the Christology of the Council of Chalcedon. We have seen that a person is not confined to, or exhausted by, one nature. We are not defined just by human nature, but since we are animals, by an animal nature too. We are constituted by the whole ecology of the living world, of plant life itself constituted by all the non-living materiality of the minerals that make up our material bodies. We share the whole range of natures of which creation is made up.

If we said that, because Christ possesses a perfect human nature, he must necessarily possess a human person, we would be subordinating the person, Christ, to a nature – human nature. Of course, there can be no nature that does not exist in some specific person. Nature is represented by persons, but a person can represent more than one nature. Nature does not determine the person, but each person lives within a set of relationships.

The Son of God, who is eternally this divine person and an instance of the divine nature, now assumes and represents human nature too. Human nature is not diminished by this, but is elevated to the vastly greater status of life with the persons of God. The human being is raised to participate in the life of God, and to develop the likeness of God and so become God-like. Human nature has no independent definition of its own, for any such definition would prevent it from this participation in the life of God (*theosis*). In all this we are simply saying that without God, there is no creature called man. Man exists truly in unbroken relationship with God. We therefore have here an extremely high view of the human calling. We are not demoting man: this is an anthropological maximalism, not minimalism. The true definition of man is the creature who participates freely in the life of God – not a creature who lives from some resources of his own.

Divine nature did not 'become' human nature, as a result of the hypostatic union. Each of the two natures retained its natural characteristics, but, when the two natures came together in the same person, without undergoing any change or ceasing to be what they are, each nature assumed the characteristics of the other: this is termed the 'communication of attributes', or 'the wonderful exchange'.

The union in the one person of Christ brings this 'exchange of attributes' about. Whatever Christ did, became the reality of his humanity too. Everything he did as a human was equally a divine act, but the divine *nature* was not the agent here. It was this *person* who acted; these were all the acts of the Son. If natures were to impart their particular characteristics to each other, those characteristics or attributes would also be shared by the other persons of the Trinity, the Father and the Spirit – who are one nature with the Son. If it were the natures that were united and exchanged we would be able to make no distinction between what the Son did and what the Father did. So we must be clear that it is not the Father or the Spirit who became incarnate. The deification (*theosis*) of human nature, which is to say of humanity in general, is *not* attributed to man's union with 'God' in general, but only because man becomes united with the Son. In other words, *theosis* is union *in Christ*. All humanity exists in Christ.

Christ is always in relationship with all other humans, and thus to humanity and human nature in general. He is never an individual in isolation who subsequently comes into a variety of relationships. He cannot be known apart from his body, the communion of those made holy in him, so there is no Christ without his Church. He is the head that sustains his body. Christ does not stand at a distance from the Church, so we cannot contrast it with him, but he is the Church's true identity, and the source from which it comes. The Church is therefore nothing other than the kingdom of God in which Christ reigns. The Church is holy because 'One is holy, One is the Lord, Jesus Christ.' Despite all the sinfulness of its members, the Church remains holy because Christ is its 'person' and its identity.

Another consequence is that whoever is brought into relationship with God comes simultaneously into relationship with all humanity. The true form of humanity and the reality of human nature is found in relationship with Christ. Humanity in Christ is the true, and ultimately the only humanity. There is no participation in the communion of God outside the Church, because there is no Church without Christ and no Christ without his Church. Man ultimately exists only within Christ. Christ is the whole territory within which each human being can be distinctly himself or herself, and can receive and give their otherness among all other created persons. Christ is the truth of man, his gathering and redemption. Christology therefore inevitably takes us to communion and ecclesiology, and Christology is always accompanied by ecclesiology. The notion of 'Christ' without the Church is inconceivable, and our understanding of the Church must be shaped by all the Christology we have discussed. The Church is no interim arrangement that is intended to hold good just between the resurrection and the end of time. The Church refers to a Christ-centered reality, the body of Christ, which exists even after the resurrection and will continue to exist, forever.

The distinction between the persons of God is of immense significance for theology. Each of the persons has his own role in the economy and in the Eucharist. The Son presents everything to the Father, while the Father receives and accepts the offering that the Son makes. It was the Father who inaugurated the entire plan of the economy, so the whole economy of our creation and redemption his act of love. The economy began with the 'good pleasure' of the Father and he will receive it again. With the Holy Spirit the Son carries the Father's will forward, and when it is complete he will return all creation to the Father. The Son presents us to the Father together with all creation as his own body. The Eucharist is this presentation and offering of the body of Christ to the Father; the eschatological and final offering is that return to the Father.

The body of Christ is brought into being for us on earth in the Eucharist. It is Christ who prays and worships in the Eucharist. The prayer of the Anaphora that begins with the words 'Let us thank the Lord' is addressed to the Father. In the Divine Liturgy of Basil the Great, it is clear that it is the Father who receives the prayer of offering. The Liturgy of Saint John Chrysostom underwent changes in its offertory prayer after the fourth century, with the addition of: 'Thou (the Father), and Thy Only-begotten Son, and Thy Holy Spirit'. The whole Trinity is named, so the priest should not turn to the icon of Christ when uttering the words 'Let us thank the Lord'. The words 'Let us thank the Lord' which start the Eucharist receive the response: 'Worthy and just' and from then on the words are addressed to the Father. It is Christ who is praying in the Eucharist, and the worshipping Church stands in the person of Christ.

Christ, the head of the Church, prays and presents the whole economy of creation to the Father, and the Church is part of the Son as he prays to the Father. The Son leads us before the throne of God, where God accepts us as members of his Son, and this way we are joined to God. This means that in the Offertory (*Anaphora*) prayer the Church has no separate identity of its own. When the priest sings 'Holy gifts for holy people', the people respond with '*One* is Holy', by which they mean that those who are going to participate in this holy communion are holy, or are to become holy, not because of their personal holiness but because of the holiness of Christ. As we acknowledge that the Son is one with the Father, and holy as the Father is holy, we ourselves are being made holy through him and being made sons of God. In Christ we will be one with God, and holy as he is holy.

The one who is doing the offering in the Eucharist, the bishop in the ancient Church and, in his absence, the priest, is an image of Christ within that liturgical assembly. He brings the entire Church into one body, summing up and recapitulating all creation in this body, which he then presents to the Father. Though the bishop is making the offering in the Eucharist, in prayer before the Offertory he declares 'for it is you, O Christ, our God, who offer and are offered, who receive and are received' (Liturgy of Saint John Chrysostom). Though the people see only the bishop, he declares that it is Christ who is making the offering. Christ, in the Holy Spirit, makes the bishop his own visible form for the sake of the congregation. The bishop who presides at this Eucharist makes visible for us the invisible Christ, even while he is fully conscious that he himself is not Christ. This dialectical relationship between Christ and his icon, the bishop, is intrinsic to the Eucharist in which the whole people are being made one with Christ.

There is no distance between Christ and his body in the Eucharist. All prayers presuppose the unity, or even identity, of the Church with Christ, and are addressed to the Father or to all divine persons together. This unity of head and body generates a dialogue between Christ together with his body and the Father. There was a debate in the twelfth century, led by Nicholaos of Methoni, about whether Christ offers the divine Eucharist to the Father but does not himself receive it. The answer the Church gave was that Christ both offers the divine Eucharist and receives it too. The Father accepts the Eucharist in the presence of the Son and the Spirit, so the Holy Trinity as a whole is involved in the Eucharistic event.

Christ is visible for us therefore only as the Church, and the Church cannot be seen without Christ. The Father accepts the body which Christ offers during the Eucharist. The Son offers this body, as he is united with our humanity, and together with the Father he accepts it. The Church has no other identity than Christ. This means that whatever comes into the Church in the Eucharist becomes *ecclesialised*, rendered 'Church', as it relates to the Father in Christ in the divine Eucharist. By 'Church' we mean that all creation is brought into relationship with God through the human being. So whatever a person brings as his offering, even if simply his own physical presence, he brings the whole created world along with him. He takes it with the bread and wine, and with whatever other offerings there are, and these are all '*Christ-ed*', that is redeemed into the body of Christ. In the Eucharist these offerings, along with those who offer them, are sanctified, so they are no longer constituents that we can investigate sociologically, economically or legally, because they are no longer subject to the principles that govern created nature. They are accepted, sanctified, become holy and in this way come to share in the relationship of Father and Son in the Spirit.

The expression 'One is holy' means that the entire assembly, together with its bishop and its offering, is holy and indivisible. The divine Eucharist unites all these in the person of the Son. All the created elements and persons brought into the divine Eucharist are brought into that new reality and are no longer constituted by any other social or created reality. All created reality is brought into direct relationship with God from whom and through whom it takes its life and will always return thanksgiving and praise to him. The human creature will freely participate in the life of the persons of God and so all creation will be saved in and through man in Christ.

Chapter 4

The Church

I. The Identity of the Church

Now we must turn our attention to the Church. There is no undisputed definition of the Church, and many of the definitions on offer could equally be applied to other institutions. Since the Church is an organised community, many of its characteristics are not very different from those of other organisations that have come and gone in the course of history. What is it that makes the Church distinct from any other institution?

In its Roman Catholic and Protestant forms, the Church was understood as an association (*societas*) with its own organisation. Although it has been dominant for centuries, this view of the Church is beginning to disappear, just as the idea that 'society' means a nation with a unified culture is also receding. This is not simply because the form taken by the Church varies from one country to another but also because national cultures are being dissolved by new social and economic forces.

For the Protestant Churches, the relationship of Church and society, which determines the public aspect of the Church, generally appears in terms that relate to the issue of secularisation. The relationship of the Church to society is not well defined, but it is not very different from the relationship that any other cultural organisation has with society as a whole. Protestant Churches have been profoundly affected by changing views of society, so we can identify communitarian and liberal forms of Church, each denomination with its own definition of the relationship of Church and society. Where the emphasis is on doctrine, as in the Lutheran and Calvinist Churches, it was formulated to create their own particular denominational identity. Protestant Churches in particular are exposed to prevailing secular trends, so their ethics are described in terms of rights and freedoms not very distinct from those held by the population as a whole.

The pressures determining Western ecclesiology have left their mark on Orthodoxy too. When Western denominations appeared in the seventeenth century, the Orthodox were asked which of them they recognised, so they described the teaching of the Orthodox Churches by reference to these denominations. In trying to distinguish themselves from these Western Churches, the Orthodox borrowed arguments from the Roman Catholics in order to reply to the Protestants and vice versa. However, to find a truly Orthodox account of the identity of the Church we have to examine its early history. The Church springs from the relationship of man and the world with God, experienced by the Christian community throughout the centuries.

The Orthodox take their account of the Church from two sources. The first of these is the divine Eucharist, the liturgical experience that all Christians share. The second is the experience of the Christian life and the ascetic tradition of the Church. Roman Catholic and Protestant ecclesiology seems to be informed primarily by the issue of mission. When an Orthodox Christian says that he is going to Church, he does not mean that he is going to hear the gospel of Christ being preached as though for the first time. He means that he is going to worship God in the community of the faithful and particularly to participate in the divine Eucharist. The Church is identified basically by its participation in the worship of God.

However, under the influence of those contemporary Christian movements and organisations that emphasise mission and preaching, a more individual piety has come to affect Orthodox understanding of the liturgy. Some of the clergy promote preaching over worship, to the neglect of the Eucharist, which fundamentally changes the orientation of the Church. Many clergy now read, rather than chant, the gospel in the divine liturgy, in the belief that this makes it more accessible to the laity. The enthusiasm for access and mission has undermined our understanding of the liturgy as participation in the mystery of communion with God.

In Orthodox theology, the Church is not constituted by the task of evangelisation or mission, that is, by its desire to make its faith comprehensible to outsiders. The divine liturgy does not attempt to explain the faith: though there are many accounts of the faith, none of them is central to the life of the Church. At the centre, is the eucharistic worship, and here the only explicit articulation of the faith is the creed, which we share with all other Churches and denominations. At the very beginning of the Church's history, there was worship and the divine Eucharist. In the New Testament and early Fathers, such as Saint Ignatius of Antioch, Saint Irenaeus of Lyons and Justin Martyr, we see the origin of the Church in the celebration of the holy Eucharist. Therefore, it is primarily the divine liturgy that gives the Orthodox tradition its distinctive view of the Church. Monasticism represents another account of the Church. I will examine these two approaches to the identity of the Church, the eucharistic and liturgical on one hand, and the ascetic and monastic on the other, in order to pick out some theological principles.

Monasticism was deeply influenced by Origen, who along with Clement and other Alexandrian theologians of the period, was to some extent informed by the thought of Plato. For Plato the identity of every being is found in that being's original *idea* and its material form was an incomplete if not an unfortunate embodiment of that idea. A thing is not what is it because of its present, material, corruptible and inconstant state, but only because of its relation to its idea that remains constant. We can only identify a thing to the extent it continues to reflect its unchanging archetype. In the view of the theologians of Alexandria, the identity of the Church is given by the same timeless realm of ideas, which is itself given by the Logos of God, which contains the rationality (logos) of all beings. The Church is true to its identity when its members are brought together by participation in this original universal Logos.

Alexandrian theologians responded to the question of the 'being' of the Church with an account of the union of the eternal souls with the eternal Logos. Although Origen's concept of the immortality of souls, which was rejected by the Council of Constantinople (553), was not a decisive influence on monasticism, the union of the soul with the Logos, another essential element of Alexandrian tradition, did play a significant role in asceticism. It was assumed that materiality obstructs the union of the soul with the Logos. The mind (*nous*) had to be cleansed of all that is worldly so it may return to the supreme Logos from which all souls come. The monastery was understood as a kind of rehabilitation centre, in which the souls were stripped of all passion and other impediments to this communion, so that they could return to their pristine state.

From the fourth century, this emphasis on purification began to impact on the Church. Holy communion came to be regarded as a means of carrying on this struggle with the passions. The spread of monasticism made sense within this Alexandrian, or ultimately Platonist, view of the world in which all that was material and tangible was believed to be a corruption of the superior intelligible world. As the influence of this theology of self-purification grew, the significance of the liturgy diminished.

But is the purification of the individual really the fundamental purpose of the Church? Is man being called out of this material world and into a world of beings without material bodies? Is the incarnate Logos simply a means of accessing the disembodied Logos? Is the Church a collection of minds purified of all bodiliness? The Fathers wrestled with these questions, and they continue to be asked today. However, the Church settled on quite a different view of the body and materiality. It decided that in the Church we are being brought together as the recapitulation of the world, body and spirit, in the *incarnate*, materially embodied Logos. Although Origen's views were no longer dominant, they have never entirely disappeared. The individual charismatic holy man, purified of all passion and selfhood, is an important figure for the Church in our age as much as any other, and the hymns and devotional literature of the Church still suggest that individual purification is what the Church is essentially about.

However, when we look at the Eucharist, we see that it is Christ, the incarnate Word, who is the model of man. Christ has taken all material nature into his human nature, and this makes the event of the Eucharist, and is the source of the Church and of all who are made holy within it. It was the achievement of Saint Maximus the Confessor (580–662) to integrate the best insights of asceticism into the eucharistic theology of the Church.

As a monk, Maximus was well acquainted with the views of Origen and the Platonist traditions that underlay them. His use of Plato's conceptuality in his theology made it easy for scholars to align Maximus with Origen and other platonising Fathers. In his 'Cosmic Liturgy' (translated by Brian E. Daley, S.J., San Francisco: Ignatius Press 2003) Hans Urs von Balthasar initially identified Origenist elements everywhere in Maximus' thought, but he was corrected by Polycarp Sherwood, and von Balthasar subsequently rectified his own account. Sherwood showed that Maximus had gone through an 'Origenist crisis' after which Maximus had drastically revised Origen. Maximus had an extensive knowledge of Origen and neo-platonism, as did most of the Eastern monks, but because he conformed his theology to the lived experience of the Church, he came down on the side of a eucharistic ecclesiology.

An extraordinarily creative intellect allowed Maximus to achieve a truly majestic synthesis of these two approaches. He insisted that it is the

Eucharist that most fundamentally expresses the identity of the Church. For him the truth of the ecclesiology of individual purification lies in the transformation and the presentation in Christ of the entire tangible and intelligible world, and of all human relationships. There must be a process of purification by which all negative or worldly elements are driven out, but the purification itself is not the ultimate purpose of the Church. By lifting it and offering it to God, the Eucharist transforms all creation. The Church is the place in which this purification takes place, but rather than producing incorporeal angels, it brings about the salvation of this material world by giving it eternal communion with God. The process of purification must be understood as part of the eucharistic transformation of the world, not as rejecting or devaluing the material and bodily creation. Though at one time or another each of these two aspects has been given greater emphasis, the Church has always held to Maximus' synthesis.

Problems begin when theologians make one aspect bear too much weight. Unbalanced statements can be found in Saint Maximus himself, so some have seen him as a great exponent of the theology of self-purification. Among later Fathers, Saint Gregory Palamas in particular was promoted as a standard-bearer of Orthodoxy and representative of the theology of self-purification. Some scholars believe that there was a tension between those theologians who stressed individual spirituality, the 'Hesychasts', and other, eucharistic, theologians of the fourteenth century, such as Saint Nicholas Cabasilas of Thessaloniki (c.1323–c.1391). Saint Gregory Palamas has been commonly portrayed as representative of the ecclesiology in which the divine Eucharist is less important than individual spirituality. Nonetheless, I believe that, taken together, his treatises, doctrinal essays and sermons show that Palamas is in agreement with Maximus in regarding the Eucharist as central. We are still waiting for studies that will show us where the other significant representatives of the Patristic tradition, in particular Saint Simeon the New Theologian, stand on this issue.

One area in which the tension between the theology of self-purification has vied with eucharistic ecclesiology has been in the relationship of the bishop and the monastic communities. It is the bishop, presiding at the divine Eucharist, who is the head of the Church, so the bishop represents this eucharistic ecclesiology of the entire gathered community. The monk, on the other hand, tends to represent the ascetic self-purification of the individual, even though we should see the monastic communities as essential to the holiness of the whole Church.

Nevertheless, there is always a tension between the eucharistic and monastic ecclesiologies. In the ninth century, councils brought the monasteries under the authority of the local bishop and decided that monks should not exceed their office.

In our day, spiritual elitism and individualism are a very obvious problem for the Church. This spirituality comes in the form of monasticism for Orthodoxy, whilst in the West it takes the form of an amorphous interest in the Spirit and spirituality, which makes little reference to the Church or its teaching. Though it began as a departure from the world, the spirituality of the individual ascetic has now spread everywhere. Spiritual fathers from monasteries want to bring their ascetic spirituality to the lives of people who are married and bringing up families. The notion of obedience as an ascetic ideal that a monk undertakes from the moment of his tonsure, before God and people, promising to uphold it, has come out of the monastery to shape the Christian life. We see lay people struggling to become spiritual disciples without taking the vows of monks, while on the other hand, those who have vowed obedience and lifelong retreat in a monastery, are soon back out again and trying to turn ordinary Christians into followers of some particular spiritual path. Christians are puzzled about who they should obey and need guidance through a range of decisions that they never used to face. Therefore, it is important to cut through some of the confusion. This cannot be achieved by intellectual work alone, of course, but it does require that we find the proper balance between the Eucharist and the search for personal holiness, so that the holiness of individuals serves the whole gathered Church.

Christians have a relationship of direct and personal familiarity with the Church and the saints. The relationship is personal and involves our entire being, not merely our minds or feelings. Yet when someone lights a candle or makes an offering, you will often hear someone remark that such an action is meaningless if that person is not thinking the right set of thoughts or experiencing the right set of feelings. However, we must be clear that it is not our thoughts or feelings that make anything what it is: what is significant is that we have left home and come to Church to be with the saints. The liturgy is simply the realisation of our relationship to God, the whole communion of his saints and the entire world. Its purpose is not simply to grasp something intellectually or emotionally or arrive at some particular state of mind. When the congregation signs themselves with the Cross each time a saint is mentioned, this shows that, even if they are not thinking the right thoughts or experiencing the right emotions, they enjoy a living relationship with that saint simply by being there together with the other members of the community.

II. GATHERED CHURCH

The Church is the people of God assembled together, 'being of the same mind, having the some love, being in full accord and of one mind' (Philippians 2.2). The entire world is represented in this people, united in the person of Christ in the Holy Spirit. This is not only the truth of the Church, it is also the future of the world. In the meanwhile, the Church has to struggle to remain true, to keep itself distinct from all competing influences and identities, and then to allow the rest of the world to move towards this truth and future.

The origin of the Church is in God's election of Abraham and the subsequent formation of the people of Israel as the people of God. Although Clement of Alexandria and Origen spoke of the pre-existence of the Church before the creation of the world, Scripture tells us that the call of Abraham is the origin of the people of God. Israel was created from the seed of Abraham for the specific purpose that 'all nations shall be blessed in you' (Genesis 12.3). This nation is the source of the Messiah and his eschatological community; the first Christians understood this call that created the nation of Israel as the origin of the Church, the 'new Israel'. Then came the Incarnation. Yet the incarnation of the Son of God did not as yet include you, me or anyone else who would subsequently be brought into relationship with Christ, so the incarnation of Christ alone is not the final realisation of the Church. The Church is not simply the single body of Christ, as though Christ were an individual who extends into eternity. A body of Christ that consists of the incarnation of the Son without a subsequent Pentecost, and without our personal incarnation, would not be the Church.

Though the incarnation may at first sight present itself as an isolated event, the incarnation has to be understood as the incarnation of a community. The incarnate Christ takes the form of the community that is the Church. When the Apostle Paul discusses the Body of Christ in 1 Corinthians 12, he says that the members of the Body of Christ are God's people, and the body of Christ exists because the Holy Spirit calls these members together. The members of the Body of Christ are not merely the physical limbs that were crucified, or even the limbs that were resurrected. The members are the *many* joined together in the *one* to become a single whole, so the Body of Christ is the many actual members who make up the Church.

The Church lives in history, but its true identity is to be found in the future. The first Christian communities had a sense of expectation of the risen Christ. They looked forward to the climax of history, and in the expression 'Come, Lord' (*maran atha*) (1 Corinthians 16.22), their anticipation became part of their liturgies. The Church preserved a strong eschatological sense through its hymns, vestments and the iconography of the saints, all of which served to make it clear that the kingdom is imminently present to us in the liturgy.

When the liturgy is allowed to keep this anticipation of the kingdom present to the world, this eschatological dimension has a public outworking. The Church is transcendent of secular institutions, so it does not compete with them. As a sign of the limits and transience of all institutions, the Church prevents every worldly claim from becoming totalitarian. Rather than involving itself in social work, and adopting the administrative systems of secular institutions of social welfare, the ancient Church encouraged unforced person-to-person charity. Love cannot be turned into an institution. This is not to say that the Church could ever be inactive in the world: when someone is hungry, you share food with him. The more of your eschatological identity you carry with you, the more you will love and come to the aid of whoever needs your help, whatever it costs you. Yet the Church can live in the world without becoming absorbed into organised social outreach or into politics, just as it can without retreating into quietism. Its action is personal, rather than institutional, and the same is true of missionary work and every other form of outreach. Today organised social work is the responsibility of the State and is usually performed better by it. If its charity becomes managed and administered, the Church will be driven by secular imperatives and cease to love, for love must always be free. For this reason, social action or activism cannot define the Church. So though the Church serves the mission for which it has been sent to every corner of the world, mission does not constitute the basis of the identity of the Church.

The Church is primarily a foretaste of the eschatological assembly of the Lord, made present in the world. The resurrection of Christ and Pentecost makes the Church and its worship the presence of the future. People go to Church because they want to grasp something of this elusive future, and this indefinable future element can be found in no other institution.

Christian ecclesiology evolved from the expectations of the people of Israel that the scattered people of God would be called together around the Messiah 'on the last day'. This 'Son of God', who was also referred to as the 'Son of Man' in the Book of Daniel and other apocalyptic literature, would take all the sins of the world on himself and bring the kingdom of God in history. Christ confirmed these expectations in his teaching and ministry, using these two titles of the Messiah who would reunite the whole people of God. The Gospel of John tells us that the Son of Man would bring the many into himself, giving his own body for their sustenance and unite them in his eschatological assembly. The Apostle Paul says that all who believe in Christ and who through baptism and the divine Eucharist became incorporated in his Body would be members of the 'people of God'.

From the resurrection of Christ, and even more after Pentecost, the Church declared that the 'last days' were making themselves felt in history, wherever the divine Eucharist assembled the scattered people of God together, incorporating the many into the one Christ. The Church is built on this historical experience of those who, from being scattered and opposed to one another, were brought together, reconciled and united in the person of Christ. For the Apostles John and Paul, and for Saint Ignatius of Antioch, this assembly of God's people in one place and with one mind is the foundation of all ecclesiology.

At the time of the Apostle Paul, the community was loosely structured into those who led the divine Eucharist, and the people as a whole who received the Eucharist with their 'Amen'. Saint Ignatius distinguished between the *episkopos*, one who heads the assembly, and the presbyters or priests who accompany him, and the deacons, who link the people to these ministers. As the officiating clergy assemble around the bishop they are an image of the eschatological assembly of God's people, and this gives the Church its form and structure. The bishop is the centre around whom the people of God unite. In the words of Ignatius, 'Where the bishop is, there let the people gather, just as wherever Christ is, there is the *catholic* (ie the whole) Church' (*Letter to the Smyrnaeans*, 8). Just as all God's people are brought together around Christ, the community of the Church gather around the bishop.

This bishop is surrounded by the 'college' of the presbyters who together represent the Apostles. In the eschatological assembly, the Apostles will be the judges of the tribes of Israel. 'In the last days, you will be seated on twelve thrones, judging the twelve tribes of Israel' (Matthew 19.28). At the completion of all time, Christ will return, accompanied by the twelve who represent this eschatological assembly which will judge first Israel and then the world. The Apostles are represented by the presbyters who stand on either side of the bishop.

The bishop, surrounded by the presbyters, acts as judge of the Church and the world and so represents the Father to us, occupying, as Ignatius tells us, the 'place of God' (*Letter to the Magnesians* 6.1).

This typological ecclesiology gives us a foretaste of the eschatological reality. The reality of the Church comes to it from the eschaton, so the identity of the Church is not limited to its created history. The Church receives its identity from that which is to come, so that the Church is able to make the future present to the world now. This future makes itself present whenever the divine liturgy is performed. The Eucharist requires the physical presence of a figure who represents Christ, surrounded by his Apostles, to stand before us as we will finally stand before the Father. The people gathered by that Eucharist are an instalment of that final assembly. This is the account of the Church that had been established by the second century.

However, the clarity of this view of the Church did not last. With the 'Christian Gnosticism' that appeared at the beginning of the third century in Alexandria, this eschatological account of the Church began to give way to another ecclesiology. For Clement of Alexandria and Origen, its representatives, it is not the future fulfilment but the original existence of the Church that is significant. They regarded the original state of things as perfection, and everything subsequent to this as a falling away, which meant that the future had to be a return to that first state of perfection. In the ecclesiology of Origen and Clement, the gathering, the structure and offices of the Church in the liturgy are of secondary or even of no importance. For them the original perfection of the Church is demonstrated by the 'logos' of the world as a whole. The *logoi* of all separate beings will unite again within the one Logos of God that existed before the creation of the world. In this account the eucharistic gathering and unity of the Church makes no constitutive contribution to bringing all things together in the one eternal Logos.

The 'logos', rather than the liturgy and the offices of the gathered Church, became significant, and not in a merely judicial sense. The specific offices that gave the Church its public structure would have no role because only the union of the soul or the mind with the eternal and pre-eternal Logos is of any significance. Salvation no longer means the hope of a new world, with a new community and structure, for as we have seen, salvation in the Alexandrian account involves purifying the soul so that it may be re-united with the Logos who is before all society and before the created and material world. Consequently, purification means removing ourselves from society, cleansing ourselves of material things, and becoming united to the One who came before the creation of the material world. Perfection will take the form of a reversion. This account sees no significance in the Church as a gathered and ordered community imaging the future kingdom.

Under Cyprian and other Church Fathers, Ignatius' ecclesiology continued to develop, so the two ecclesiologies progressed in parallel, and even interacted constructively. However, as often as they moved towards a degree of integration, tensions would re-merge and they would diverge again. Which is the right account of the Church? Where does the true identity of the Church become visible? Is it in the monastery, in the cell of the individual who removes himself from society in order to free himself of all passions by removing himself from the world and matter? Or is it in the community of all disparate persons gathered together by the Eucharist? This was the question that came up repeatedly through the history of the Church.

The Church has the resources to answer this question, but the readiness of any generation to receive these answers is another matter. The problem represented by this dichotomy is at heart a spiritual one. That the Church offers therapy for our passions is beyond any doubt, but there is no more difficult thing than to give up our passions and finally leave them behind. As soon as anyone begins to believe that he has had some success in this spiritual struggle, pride comes creeping back again, and then we are tempted to despise the Church and undermine its ministers.

If we truly have some control over our passions, our pride will be brought under control too, and we will not be tempted to sit in judgment on the gathered Church or its ministers. The person who has learned to control his passions will regard the bishop with respect, and gladly receive the teaching and instruction of their bishop. Those who have not achieved such self-control will of course ask what authority bishops and priests have. If we do not exercise the proper control over our passions, especially self-love and pride, we will come to believe that the spirituality of the bishop is no greater than our own, and thus undermine his authority over the Church. Those who go this way tend to make their own spiritual disciples and gather their own community, criticising the institutional Church and creating a contradiction between institution and charisma.

The religious individualism of such an ecclesiology constitutes a serious problem. It allows us to believe that we are not in need of the institutional community of the Church. This notion of salvation is without love, so rather than bringing us towards one another, it leads us away from one another. Though it talks about overcoming passions, it allows our passions to serve our own elitism.

In itself, this ecclesiology of personal spirituality or piety is not absent from the tradition of the Orthodox Church. But the main source of Orthodox ecclesiology is to be found in the eucharistic communion, headed by the bishop, who unites it in one body and lifts up its offerings to God, and with it the daily needs and hopes of mankind and all creation. All these are brought together as a foretaste and image of the eschatological kingdom of God.

The relations of the bishops and these other individualistic spiritual and charismatic leaders is a perennial problem. We must conclude that the true ecclesiology is the one that relates to the structure of the eucharistic community which portrays the eschatological assembly that is called into being by Christ. So it would be a mistake to look for the essence of the Church either in individual spirituality or through the cosmological approach that relates the Church to the beginning, rather than to the future recapitulation of human history. Perhaps it is no coincidence that Origen, and to a lesser extent Clement, finally diverged from the faith of the Church.

Saint Maximus the Confessor offers us the proper solution. Maximus succeeded in combining the two trends by integrating the cosmological approach, which refers creation to its origins, into the eschatological approach, which looks forward to the future kingdom of God. Maximus took the cosmology of Origen and made it eschatological, transferring its reference from the beginning to the end, so dethroning Plato. He turns us around from the past to the future so that the eschatological community became the centre of ecclesiology again. When cosmology is reconciled with eschatology, we get the eschatological community in the divine Eucharist and the body of the Church. This single eschatological community incorporates the logos of beings, the world, as realities that come to us from the future. The events of the end which the Church portrays are not about this people only, but about creation as a whole. Just as each Christian represents in his own body the gathering and redemption of material creation, so the whole Church is the assembling of all creation in Christ, who is himself the final truth of all things. This ecclesiology gives us an account of mankind in which the new Adam recapitulates all things, and so it overcomes the dichotomy of individual and eucharistic ecclesiologies.

We have seen how two accounts of ecclesiology sometimes competed and at other times combined to make a robust single ecclesiology. We have seen that Saint Maximus brought the two streams together to show that the divine Eucharist creates the Church as the foretaste of the eschaton. Though he is concerned with our spiritual life and purification, Saint Maximus is confident that the Logos has taken our flesh so he can enable us, with all our materiality, to take our place within him in the communion of God.

III. The Church of God

We must now turn from history to examine the issues this double approach creates for ecclesiology. Let us start by setting ecclesiology into its broader theological framework. Few will deny that the division of ecclesiology from theology and its relegation to a separate chapter of dogmatics has not been a helpful development. We cannot discuss ecclesiology in isolation from theology, because the Church is a reality that springs from God himself. The Church is the outcome of the Father's will, a will he shares with the Son and the Holy Spirit, and which is realised through the economy in which each of the persons of God is engaged.

What is the distinct contribution of each member of the Trinity in the realisation of the Church? Every event of the economy begins from the Father and returns to the Father. The Father wills and brings everything to its beginning, and it was by his 'good pleasure' that the communion of God should extend into creation through the Church. The Father intended the world to come into eternal communion with God, the created with the uncreated, and so receive true life.

The Father initiated, and the Son and the Holy Spirit accepted and realised the Father's 'good will'. These distinct acts oblige us to distinguish between the divine persons, and to observe that a certain movement takes place in the Holy Trinity. The life of the Trinity is not static, but as the persons relate in love to one another so their will is ordered by reference to one another so that the Trinity has its own intrinsic order. The Father initiates, and the Son and the Spirit execute the initiative of the Father in the economy.

The particular role of the Son is to carry out freely the Father's 'good pleasure' and become the person in whom this union of created and uncreated is realised. The salvation of creation will take place in the Son, and then be presented to the Father by the Son. The Holy Spirit has his own contribution to this plan. He makes the incorporation of creation in the Son possible by enabling creation to open to its incorporation in the Son. Its natural limitations mean that, left to itself, creation cannot sustain any relationship with God, while the fall puts a further barrier to creation's openness. However, through intervention of the Spirit this openness becomes possible and thus the incorporation of creation in the Son can be accomplished as the work of all three persons of the Trinity, Father, Son and Holy Spirit.

The Church is brought into being within this triune 'economy' in which the Father initiates, the Son undertakes to incorporate creation and bring it to the Father, and the Holy Spirit liberates the world from the limitations of its createdness. Through his incarnation the Son is the centre of this event, so the Church is described as the Body of Christ, rather than as the body of the Father or of the Holy Spirit. The distinction between the activities of the persons is crucial. It is the initiative of the Father that creation should be embodied and united in the Son that explains why this incorporation became reality. The Father created the world in order that it become the Church, and so made the plurality given in the Church the whole purpose of creation. However, in order that there could be this incorporation of creation in the Son and the arrival of the Church, mankind's free consent had to be secured. Mankind is able to represent creation because he is the one free being within material creation who is able to give consent so that creation can be brought into relationship with God in freedom. For this reason Mary's free 'yes' to the incarnation of the Son is crucial to the economy of our salvation.

We saw that, rather than representing creation and bringing it into this union with God, mankind freely decided to refer creation to itself and so make death part of its predicament. He deified himself and deified nature, and consequently he and nature fell into a closed relationship that condemned them both. God's hope for the conversion of the world into the Church stumbled on man's free denial, so God then had to find another way to bring the world into this relationship which would ensure its survival. This other way was the incarnation of the Son in the now fallen creation, something which required the Son, mankind, and all creation to pass through death and emerge from it in order to reach that union.

Although the Church and the whole economy now took a path that passed through the cross, the end of that path remained as it had been from the beginning, the union of the created with the uncreated God. The Church goes through the cross and travels on until all the discipline of the cross is transformed into the attributes of the eschaton, the resurrection.

This is where ecclesiological differences are crucial. For Western theologians, the passage through the cross gives the Church the wounds which evil and history deal out to the Body of Christ. Many stop at this point and assert that the Church is finally scarred by the cross and therefore by evil, thus Western theologians are inclined to begin with history and to end up with evil, thus even attributing it with some ultimate ontological status. Much of the music, art and literature informed by this theology is preoccupied by the cross and suffering, and never moves on to the kingdom of God.

The result is an ecclesiology that stops with Calvary and the crucifixion. It conceives of the Church as the body of the one sacrificed, and who ministers to the world through his suffering. Although this ecclesiology is often successful in eliciting an emotional response, it incarcerates the Church within the world, with the result that the Church's activity in the world becomes important to the exclusion of all else. What can the Church be in the face of evil and human suffering? What consolation and recompense can it offer, and how much must it minister to mankind to ease this suffering? Thus the Church is motivated by the desire to relieve this endless pain and need, so it is driven by social and ethical concerns. By identifying itself exclusively with those who suffer it makes itself powerless to help them by offering them the truth of the redemption of creation that comes with an eschatological perspective.

The Son is crucified, and the event of the cross and its suffering is transferred into the eternal life of the triune God. This theology was advocated by some Lutherans, though the same sentimentality can be observed in those Russian theologians who also see the life of the eternal as bound to suffering and the cross. The sacraments and in particular the Eucharist are understood as the perpetual presence of Christ's death. Even in many Orthodox Churches today, the crucifix is now set at the centre of the Eucharist, a trend which prevents us from receiving the truth of the Church's liturgical experience. The truth of the Eucharist is that it does not take us to Calvary in order to leave us there, but brings us through it and beyond to the communion of the saints and the glory of the kingdom of God. This glory is made visible to us by the icons, vestments, and the chanting of the psalms, all of which point to transcendence of the cross. Our understanding of the Church must start from Father's good will, which has brought about the whole economy of God for man and the unity of the created with the uncreated which is the true purpose of creation.

The Church is the foretaste and realisation of the kingdom of God, so the spiritual and ascetic life by which we participate in suffering and the cross do not represent the ultimate purpose of the Church. The ascetic life is part of the Church, and the Christian who bears the marks of his participation in the cross of Christ on his person is assuredly a part of the life of the Church. However, when we put on the gold vestments of the eucharistic liturgy, we are looking forward to the kingdom of God. The Church is constituted by the resurrection and so has travelled past the cross and broken through into that new creation which is filled with the uncreated light of God.

The experience of the resurrection and new creation can be found in each individual who radiates sanctity, but this experience cannot simply be related to individuals. It is the Church that reflects the transformation of the entire material world and with it all human society and community. We have the Church only when we have a community. The Christian who hopes to radiate sanctity *must become Church* so he can participate in the community of the end of times.

We have come to the conclusion that it is the good will of the Father that the entire material world should become the Church, the body of the Son in the Holy Spirit. The Father does not desire mankind only, or only a certain number from among mankind, but all creation. However, because of man's fall, the incorporation of the world in the Son must pass through the cross, and through the costly experience of the disciple and the ascetic, through a profound and consuming struggle against evil finally to gain the victory. The Christian goes through the narrow gate and along the narrow path set out by the Father's good will, but his destination lies beyond that gate, at the end of that path, in the kingdom. The kingdom is being realised in the Church, and the Church is being fulfilled, by its progress along this narrow path. The Church that focuses on history and on Calvary will come to a halt before it reaches the end of that path. The overcoming of evil and defeat of the devil is not our final destination. A healthy ecclesiology will lead us on beyond the struggle with evil and into the light, to gain in the divine Eucharist our first experience of the kingdom of God. In this experience, a community of people portrays the future of the world, in which both society and all material creation overcome corruption. Such an ecclesiology will have profoundly positive consequences for the Christian life, the organisation of the Church, the sacraments, and for every aspect of the Church's witness to the world.

IV. THE CHURCH AS IMAGE OF THE FUTURE

The Church is rooted in the being and life of the Holy Trinity. God's purpose in creating the world is that it attain communion with him and share his life. The Church is the future of the world in this communion, so we must look for the origins of ecclesiology and its destination in eternity.

We have said that the Holy Trinity is the communion in which the Church participates and that the Father loves and wills that creation come into communion with God. It is the Father who intends this and to whom we must attribute all that follows. The Son undertakes to carry out and personally substantiate this union of the created to the uncreated. The Holy Spirit enables the transcendence of the limitations between the created and the uncreated. He is the Spirit of communion, of power and of life, who tears down the barriers that separate beings; he enables creation to surmount the physical impossibility of communion of created and uncreated. The three persons act and are present in the Church, and so the Church is the product of their unity, but it is the Son who is the mediation of created and uncreated, and for this reason the Church is called the Body of Christ.

The Church is the image or 'icon' of the kingdom of God. In the Church all things are brought together, included and recapitulated so they will continue in life forever. The Church depicts the end time in history. I choose the term 'depict' in order to avoid some of the problems that the word 'identify' would cause us. The Church in history is clearly not identical with the kingdom of God. The trauma of history means that along with the rest of the world, Christians struggle with evil, and the way of the cross is this struggle. The Church is not the society of those who have overcome evil but of those who are struggling against evil. The holy Church is full of sinners, being made holy. Therefore, we must say that the kingdom of God is *depicted* in the Church. This iconological ontology is key.

The Church is presently only a depiction of the end times, not the end times themselves. However, we need to clarify this distinction. The relation of a photograph and its object is dependent on the imagination of those who look at the photo: the resemblance they see comes from their ability to find likenesses. The photograph has no ontological continuity with that person: it is not a collage of items belonging to him, and if we disposed of this photograph this would not hurt the person portrayed in it.

However, an icon does have an ontological share in the original, so we honour the icon because we honour the saint whose image it is. There is an ontological continuity between the saint and their image, even though there is no continuity of material between them. The honour given on an icon 'passes to the original', in the words of Saint Basil the Great.

The distinction between image and truth that Maximus uses to express this iconological ontology comes from the distinction that the Letter to the Hebrews makes between shadow and reality (Hebrews 10.1). Maximus says that the 'shadow' refers to the Old Testament, while the

New Testament gives us the 'image', but the reality itself, Christ and his kingdom, is still to come (*Scholia on Dionysius' Ecclesiastical Hierarchy* 3.3.2). The reality, which is what the eschaton is, continually projects itself into our history to reveal itself to us.

The eschaton projects an image of itself backwards to create the experience of the Apostles which then constitutes the realities of the New Testament. The New Testament is the 'image' of the eschaton, the truth, and possesses something of it. The New Testament is the present image of future things. This distinction between image and the truth allows us to talk about the holiness of the Church, and even the holiness of Christians, even while Christians are still struggling with sin. Christians already participate in the truth, and this truth will become the whole truth about them. The Church is not simply what it is now, but what it will be. Its identity is given to us in 'earthen vessels'. The Church is *mystery*. The term 'mystery' indicates that the Church is 'revealed', and thus no complete definition of it is possible. Although the Church comes to us, it comes from the place that we cannot access, so we are unable to take final possession of it.

The Church can truly be known but, because it is sourced from Christ and his kingdom, it is inexhaustible, and cannot be known exhaustively and finally. The identity of the Church has to be set out by examining the mysteries and sacraments that make the Church present within our historical experience. The sacraments are images of the truth arriving from the end times so that they become the experienced reality of the Church. The sacraments transform sinners into saints so Church is not only revealed in them but constituted by them. A sacrament enables the Christian freely to take their place in the complete reality in which all creatures will share. The sacraments witness to the indivisible and inexhaustible mystery of Christ, and cannot therefore be regarded as an individual topic, but rather as the hermeneutic by which we can approach ecclesiology as a whole.

The divine Eucharist is the revelation of the kingdom of God and so quite simply the revelation of ultimate reality. The Eucharist reveals this reality which is future to us in the form of the present. The origins of this iconological ontology are found in the prophetic books of Scripture, in the apocalypses or revelations of heaven that we see in Isaiah, Daniel and the Book of Revelation. The prophet sees the completion of all time entering our still partial history and giving judgment on it before the whole assembly of heaven and earth.

In the form of the Eucharist all creatures are brought together and recapitulated in Christ. The Eucharist manifests and substantiates within time the identity of this assembly in the form of the Church. When we want to speak of the actual lived experience of the Church we have to start from the Eucharist, for this is where the Church appears. The Eucharist is the free coming together of all parts into their proper relationships and so into the good order of the whole in which each creature is liberated from the limits given by its own nature. This liberation is the eternal will of the Father which the Son has substantiated and which the Spirit now makes possible for us to share.

The sacraments that we regard as separate today all took place in the context of the Eucharist of the ancient Church, as is still clear from the liturgical structure in which these sacraments appear. This is the case for example with baptism.

As long as theology has been dominated by Scholasticism, it has tended to divide the indivisible mystery of the Church into separate sacraments which can be enumerated. Though the number seven was formalised in the twelfth century it had gone through a series of fluctuations: in one period the funeral service, and even the tonsure of a monk, were regarded as sacraments. In the scholastic understanding the Eucharist is just one particular sacrament, the one that perpetuates Christ's passion through history. This division into separate sacraments should not prevent us from understanding all sacraments as aspects of the divine Eucharist. We must learn to see the Eucharist as the focus of all sacramental life in the Church.

If we want to see the unity and good order of the Church, we should look for it in the structure of the Eucharist. There we will find it exactly as it was shaped in the ancient Church, verified by the Church as a whole, and articulated by the canons given by the councils. The kingdom of God is well ordered, and the canonical structure of the Church is a manifestation of this good order, not simply an accommodation to those contingent organisational requirements by which the Church relates to the world. Therefore, we cannot say that some canons are essential and dogmatic while others are merely contingent and administrative. All the canons are ecclesiologically and ontologically significant.

The real danger of altering the image of the Church is that, rather than an image of the completion of history by the kingdom of God, it becomes a picture of hell. Those distortions of its teaching that the Church refers to as 'heresy' are not limited to dogmatic formulations, but also include liturgical and canonical matters: they are the result of introducing imagery that does not come from the eschaton. Those images that do not come from the kingdom of God, come from that other kingdom which loves disorder and hates and opposes the kingdom of God. For example, if we were to perform a eucharistic service for white people but not black people, or for men but not women, or for the educated but not the illiterate, or the rich but not the poor, or just for students, or just for lawyers or any other group, then that service would be the very opposite of the Eucharist. Every time we segregate ourselves from our neighbour through criteria of this kind, we receive a foretaste of hell. The Church can very easily be turned into the image of hell without even noticing that this has happened.

V. THE CHURCH AND THE CHURCHES

So far I have talked about the identity of the Church. Now we must say something about the form of the Church. The form of the Church relates directly to the Church's very being, for there can be no gap between *what* the Church is and *how* the Church is. The way the Church is structured and arrayed is determined by what the Church is, for the Church must be truly itself even in its outward form.

Our first principle is that the Church is the mystery of God's dealings with man. The Church is the purpose and culmination of the whole work of God for man and the recapitulation of all creation. It is the form in which the love of God is present to the world, and so manifests the world's own origins to it. The Father initiates the whole economy of God for man and brings the Church into existence. Jesus Christ, the Son of God, provides the body that is the literal embodiment of the communion and love of God, while the Holy Spirit enables the communion of the created with the uncreated so this body can enable the communion of every being with every other.

The Church has its basis in the trinitarian life of God, that is to say, in 'the grace of our Lord Jesus Christ, the love of God and the fellowship of the Holy Spirit' (2 Corinthians 13.14). Grace means that Jesus Christ is the gift of God, while the Holy Spirit enables us to exceed the limits of our creaturely being and enter that communion with God which is God's love. Beings must have boundaries so that they can be acknowledged as distinct, but they must surmount these boundaries in order to come into communion with one another and so live as a society. Creatures must be able to distinguish themselves from God who is the source of their communion. The Holy Spirit enables both this demarcation and its transcendence and so makes all community possible. We have to bear in mind this trinitarian account of the Church as we consider its form and structure.

Our second basic ecclesiological principle is that the Church arises from the kingdom of God. The Church's being does not come from within the history in which the Church presently exists, but from that which is to be revealed. The real identity of the Church is the community of the future, so the structure of the Church must reveal the eschaton out of which the Church comes. The third basic ecclesiological principle is that in history the Church is an image of the kingdom of God, created by the kingdom itself. It portrays the kingdom that prevails against all other kingdoms. Because it represents God's judgment of history, the Church holds out against all secular, historical realities, and against the current of history itself. The Church fits no particular social forms, it cannot be represented by a political party or be absorbed into the state. The Church remains a stranger in the world, always at odds with it, while it looks forward to the fulfilment of time. The Church cannot be content to be identified with the partial historical realities or partial and antagonistic communities of this world. Our final ecclesiological principle is that the Church substantiates the fulfilment of time through the divine Eucharist. With these basic ecclesiological premises, we can now see how the function of the Church is structured, assembled and organised.

First of all, let us take a look at the Church as a whole. The Lord founded one single Church which we identify as the Body of Christ. This one Church is expressed and realised in a single community which necessarily appears in the world as many communities or Churches. It is for the sake of the world that this eucharistic community exists in many places. Wherever the faithful assemble, the complete Body of Christ is present, and the whole work of God for man is made known and the kingdom revealed. The one Church therefore consists of many local Churches, each of which is the image of the eschatological community. From its very earliest times the Church was called 'the catholic Church', by which the Fathers meant that each local Church represents the whole eucharistic assembly and the recapitulation of all things, in each particular place.

The Church consists of many catholic Churches. In his attempts to defeat the Donatists, Augustine emphasised the universality of the Church against the particularisms of the Donatist communities, so that after him, the term 'catholic' began to refer to the one worldwide Church. The Church in the West was constituted as a single organisation, with a single head in the bishop of Rome. In the East by contrast, the Church was not regarded as a single organisation with a universal reach that required a single figurehead. It is chiefly this understanding of the Church as the image of the end times, realised in the divine Eucharist, that differentiates the East from the West. We regard every assembly that performs the divine Eucharist as the presence of the whole Church, for the presence of the whole Christ in the Eucharist takes precedence over all considerations of history or distance. Christ is not divided by geography, for he unites all places in himself. The Eucharist is celebrated in cities separated by distance, but this does not make them two Eucharists, so these two eucharistic assemblies do not need the extrinsic form of a unitary administration to bridge the distance between them. The Eucharist provides the Church with unity, for unity is what the Eucharist is. Each of the Churches that celebrate the Eucharist has the whole presence of Christ, indeed each of them is the whole presence of Christ, for that place. Each place in which the Eucharist is celebrated, participates in the future unity of all time and place. We do not therefore see individual Churches as fractions of Christ, for every Church is the indivisible presence of Christ that unites and recapitulates all things.

We turn now to the account of the Church given by Western theology. We have seen that Western theology characteristically attributes priority to *being*, making particular realities less important than what is general and universal. The Church is one, but this indivisible Church is made up of many Churches. So which comes first, the particular Churches that gather in each particular place, or the universal Church? Western theology has taken the view that it is the one universal Church which comes first, and that each individual Church is consequent on it. It defines 'catholic' as worldwide, and attributes the worldwide Church with a structure that is independent of all local Churches. The one Church stands over all the many Churches, and the papacy over all other bishops. Just as this theology gives priority to the essence over the persons, Western ecclesiology gives precedence to the worldwide, 'ecumenical' Church over the many, actual Churches. Karl Rahner and Joseph Ratzinger used the standard distinction between essence and existence to assert this: Rahner subsequently pointed out that the one Church cannot exist without local Churches. Nonetheless the single worldwide Church was assumed to be prior to the local Churches. This was given expression by the First Vatican Council (1870) with the ruling that the Pope is infallible, and that all other bishops must be obedient to him. This is not simply a judicial matter, but a consequence of placing essence before existence, the one before the many.

The Second Vatican Council introduced a new ecclesiology, announcing that each local Church is the whole Church in each that place. Each local Church is 'catholic' and complete in itself, under its bishop. Orthodox theologians had clearly had some influence on Roman Catholic ecclesiology. However, the newly acknowledged catholicity of the local

Church was in conflict with the older view that catholicity meant the unity of the whole Church (*ecumene*) above all particular Churches.

Vatican II did not formally overturn Vatican I but simply asserted that the new ecclesiology was fully in keeping with that of the previous council. However, far from being complementary, the decisions of these two councils seem to be contradictory, so Roman Catholic ecclesiology has to clarify this. Its concessions to the Orthodox Churches have opened new possibilities but they have also put Roman Catholic ecclesiology in a dilemma. It must either move towards conceding the catholicity of each local Church, or it can ignore other Churches and continue to insist that the authority of the Pope prevails over the local bishops, in which case Vatican I will continue to represent the real logic of Roman Catholic ecclesiology.

If we do not want to understand 'catholic' in the sense of a single worldwide Church united by a single organisation, what is the relationship between the particular Churches? How can we find the right balance between an ecclesiology that shows the fullness and catholicity of each local Church, and an ecclesiology that understands catholicity only as universality?

Each local Church is fundamentally related to every other. This unity consists in the councils of the Church which express the teaching of all the Churches that together constitute the one Church worldwide. The balance between the Churches and the councils is not easy to get right, for the council must not be allowed to become an autonomous institution suspended over all Churches together.

In the West the idea that councils express the supreme authority of the Church has been termed 'conciliarism'. Both before and after papal infallibility was made an explicit doctrine by the First Vatican Council in 1870, Western Catholics argued for councils and hoped to establish limits to papal authority. It is a common assumption that the Orthodox have councils in the same way that Roman Catholics have the Pope, but the council does not stand above the local Churches in this way. No council is allowed to intervene in the internal issues of a local Church. In the third century Saint Cyprian set down the principle that every bishop is to lead his own diocese, ordain whomever he wishes, and be responsible directly to God. However, ignorance of ecclesiology has produced many anomalies, so we often hear demands for a council to intervene in issues of a local Church. Orthodox ecclesiology provides no justification for such intervention because this would create a single universal authority over all Churches.

However, many issues are common to more than one Church. A bishop can only make a decision for his Church if it will not affect another Church. If the issue within his own diocese has wider implications it requires a council which can then make the decision for all the Churches involved. Every bishop has to ordain, and this does not need the mediation of other Churches. However, what about the case of someone who is excommunicated from holy communion in one Church who then goes to another Church to receive communion? This was the issue that the Fifth Canon of the Council of Nicaea (325) ruled on. Having been denied communion by their own Churches, many people were going to other Churches to receive communion and complaining that the reasons for these excommunications were not being made clear. Bishops therefore took the decision to meet twice a year, in Lent and in the autumn, to examine cases of exclusion from communion. The right to exclude someone from communion was transferred from the local Church to a council. Whenever the issues are common, a council is required, the authority of which is limited to that issue. A council cannot impose anything on a Church, unless other Churches are affected by the consequences of its actions. This principle is basic to conciliarism.

The other basic rule that maintains the balance between any particular Church and the worldwide Church is that the councils that decide on issues in common, must be comprised of bishops, and all bishops must be allowed to take part in them. If bishops are excluded from a council, the council becomes an authority that is imposed on the Churches. If a bishop is excluded from a council, whatever decisions that council takes would simply be imposed on the Church led by the excluded bishop. When its bishop participates in that council, that Church shares in the decisions taken by that council, so they cannot be said to be imposed on it from outside. The Church maintained the balance between the local and the universal, by making the council the means of expressing the consensus of Churches, and not allowing it to become an authority above them. As Saint Ignatius says, bishops 'throughout the world have the mind of Christ' (Magnesians 7). They agree in Christ, and they come to agreement on each issue by means of a council which expresses their unity in Christ.

Any council that does not invite or include all bishops, is seriously at fault. Such is the pressure towards centralising authority that there have been, and indeed still are, many such failures in the proper exercise of conciliarity. If national governments prevent bishops from travelling, as the Ecumenical Patriarch has often been prevented from travelling to the Churches of his patriarchate, there is nothing that anyone can do. However, when all bishops are able to be present at a council, yet some of them stay away, or some are allowed to dominate the proceedings, creating anomalies, the foundations of the Church are threatened. Of course there is always the issue of whether all representatives of all Churches can be present, without the numbers making the council unwieldy, which is why the practice of alternating which bishop is to participate was established. The alternating participation of bishops in order of seniority of ordination ensures that all bishops participate in the council at some time.

Naturally, the ideal situation is that all bishops participate, which is why, as often as the Church was able and it was judged necessary, the Church would convene an *ecumenical* council, which for this reason acquired a prestige and authority greater than that of any local synod. However, the essence of a council, whether or not it is ecumenical, is to express the unity and consensus of the Churches.

To some it may seem as if the Church has two heads, the Pope for the Catholics and the Ecumenical Patriarch for the Orthodox. However, this is not how it is. The patriarchates and autocephalous Churches developed as expressions of the conciliarity of the Church, not as institutions positioned above the Church. The five patriarchates were the synods of their five respective territories, as are the autocephalous Churches, that do not belong to any of the patriarchates. Their status is governed by the Thirty-Fourth Apostolic Canon, according to which all bishops in one territory have to acknowledge a single head. It was the need to meet in councils that brought these primacies into being, because it requires a primatial bishop to convene a council and take the chair. The Canon goes on to say that the bishops must act with the primate, and he must act with them. This was the spirit in which the Patriarchates and the self-governing Churches developed, and the result is that we have a primate and a synod in every territory. If this pattern is abused, either because a primate or the bishops have excessive power, this is not a structural fault but a matter to be put right by those involved.

Each of these local Churches is lead by a primate. If a synod has to be called because joint action is required, someone has to preside. For the greater part of Christian history the Bishop of Constantinople has been acknowledged as this primate. If the Bishop of Constantinople acts within the spirit of this Canon, doing nothing without taking the others into account, and they do nothing without taking him into account, the institution remains healthy and we have no problem. The Pope has assumed the right to intervene in any local Church, without consultation of primates, and even when he does consult them, the Pope makes a final decision alone. Now if, out of courtesy or any other reason, the bishops make this concession to the Ecumenical Patriarch as their primate and allow him to officiate wherever he wants, this is their own decision, but there is no papal element to the institution of the Ecumenical Patriarch. This is what has to be said about the particularity and universality of the Church.

VI. THE CHURCH AROUND THE BISHOP

Let us now take a look at the local Church. How can a Church be organised on the basis that we have set out? The structure of each Church comes from the performance of the divine Eucharist, in which the good order of the Church depicts the good order of the eschatological communion that will be revealed at the end times. The offices cannot be altered without distorting the image of this eschatological communion. We have to distinguish between the offices that can be altered to respond to historical contingencies, and that essential form which cannot be changed.

Let us start with the elements which relate to the eschatological community, and which represent what is constant in the structure of the Church. The prayer of the preparation of gifts (*proskomide*) says that at the fulfilment of time, as the kingdom of God begins to break in, the scattered people of God will assemble together 'with one mind'. A Church whose members do not come together with one mind but remain divided and disordered, cannot depict the fulfilment of time, and so cannot be the Church, for which the orderly and united assembly of God's people is essential.

The second element, which also comes from the kingdom of God, which is to say, from the community made complete at the eschaton, is that the centre of this assembly is Christ. It is not enough for God's people simply to assemble, but they must do so around the bishop.

The third element is that Christ is surrounded by the twelve Apostles. They must be present to identify the true Christ who is the fulfilment of history. The Gospels say that there will be great confusion about who the real Christ is; there will be many making claims that identify Christ here or there. Many Christians will be misled because they will not know which is truly the gathering point around which the scattered people of God are to assemble. But the twelve Apostles, as the ones who actually saw the risen Lord, will recognise Christ and be able to verify that this really is the one who rose from the dead, and that he really is the one appointed by God to be the 'Son of Man' who will judge the world. Because it relies on the Apostles to identify him, the Church is termed 'apostolic.'

This why it is not enough to say that Christ is our focal point at the eschaton. We also need the Apostles to corroborate that this is indeed Jesus Christ, the genuine identity of Christ. Their presence around Christ is also essential for the image of the fulfilment of history. These are the elements of the eschatological community, without which there can be no Church or kingdom of God.

In the Eucharist the Church is becoming the image of the communion of God on Earth. In the Church this image is being realised here on earth in advance of the Lord's return. In the divine Eucharist, all the scattered people of God assemble together, with one mind, who is Christ, the head of the body and the summation of all creation offered to the Father. The bishop depicts Christ for us in each place, so the bishop is head and focus of the Eucharist and we gather around him. The bishop lifts all creation to the throne of God, praying: 'We offer to you these gifts from your own gifts in all and for all'. In the person of the bishop, Christ's recapitulation of all things to the Father is brought within our hearing.

We said that Christ will not return alone, but surrounded by his apostles. Saint Ignatius saw the image of the twelve Apostles in the divine Eucharist of the local Church, in the persons of the presbyters who surround the bishop. The ancient Church had a set of thrones, a 'synthronon', at the centre of which sat the bishop, and around him sat his presbyters in a clearly eschatological image that recalls Christ's promise to the twelve, that 'you shall be seated on twelve thrones, judging the twelve tribes of Israel.' The Apostles point us towards Christ.

Gathered around the bishop the presbyters are the image of the Apostles, pointing us to Christ. The presbyters' first task therefore was teaching, convening assemblies, preaching and catechizing. Saint John Chrysostom and Origen have left us the homilies they preached as presbyters. While bishops gave us our liturgies and in particular the *anaphoras*, the eucharistic prayers of offering, presbyters taught, preached and looked after the administration of the Church, and together with the bishop, were members of the synod of the Church in that place.

However, this arrangement did not last long. By the third century the Church was beginning to take a different course, particularly in the West, as evidenced by Cyprian. The notion of the bishops as the image of Christ changed in favour of the idea that they were the image of the Apostles. Nowadays a bishop is regarded as a successor to the Apostles, so his primary responsibility is to teach. However, Saint Ignatius says that it is not the bishop who does the teaching and that we should respect the silence, which according to his understanding, the bishop may maintain for everything, apart from the *anaphora* of the divine Eucharist, which is his responsibility solely.

The contemporary view that the primary role of the bishop is teaching and only secondarily the Eucharist, is a clear divergence from the early understanding of the Church. In the Middle Ages, teaching became the bishop's chief role, while the celebrating the liturgy was handed over to the presbyters. Thus the priest performs the liturgy, while the bishop is primarily a manager, who exhausts himself in the administration of the Church. Here is a very significant divergence from the eschatological understanding of the bishop.

Quite early a fourth element was introduced into the Church. This is the role of the deacon as a link between those who preside at the Eucharist and the people as whole. Deacons are clergy, but they are not priests, so they cannot lead the liturgy or be seated. They go back and forth between people and their ministers, bringing the gifts from the people to the bishop who presides at the Eucharist, passing on to the priests the names of those who are to be prayed for in the liturgy, and giving the sanctified gifts to the people. The deacon receives the gifts that the people bring, and when they have been sanctified he distributes them to the people as the body and blood of Christ. He is the dynamic link between ministers and people that is crucial to the unity of the Church.

These offices must all be present in order to represent the eschatological image of the Church as the assembly of God's people, gathered around the bishop, who is flanked by presbyters or priests, with the deacons forming the dynamic link between the people and the ministers. Saint Ignatius insisted that it is four offices, of people, deacons, presbyters and bishop, which makes this assembly the Church.

The Church has a variety of functions and relationships that are not provided by this structure of offices, such as teaching, missionary work, charity and spiritual direction. However, these will not pass over into the eschaton. There will be no evangelists at the fulfilment of time, because the need for evangelism and conversion will be over. Bishops and deacons will give way to the original, Christ with his apostles. These realities are essential components of the kingdom which is made up of Christ with his apostles and all the children of God gathered around him. Though there are other functions that are essential to us today they make no direct contribution in the public formation of the image of the kingdom of God.

VII. SON AND SPIRIT

Now we must turn to the relationship of Christ and the Holy Spirit in order to make clear the issue of the one and the many in the Church. We have to find an ecclesiology that is shaped by the right doctrine of God and so able to hold Christology and pneumatology in their proper relationship.

We have said that Western theology tends to emphasise Christology at the expense of pneumatology. Western theology is largely concerned with history, the incarnation and the life of Christ. The Holy Spirit however liberates the Son from history, because the incarnate Son took on himself the consequences of man's refusal and fall. He became a man, taking on the constraints of time and space, along with all the consequences of our fallen history, being born at a specific moment of history, in Palestine under the rule of Caesar Augustus, and crucified under Pontius Pilate.

Our history carries death within it. To take the example of our own individual life-stories, the way in which we live in history and experience history relates to the fact that there was a time that we did not exist and there will come a time when we shall no longer exist. Our historical existence is interwoven with death: it is a thing of gaps and holes, and one of these gaps will turn out to be an end, after which life will be over for us.

This was the life that the Son entered in the incarnation. Since it was the Son rather than the Spirit who entered our life and became incarnate, it is he rather than the Spirit who bears the dissolution and death that are the outcome of our history. The Spirit stands by the Son and finally sustains him through all the trauma that comes with his involvement in fallen creation.

In taking on human flesh, the Son took on death and suffered the pain of the cross and death. However, death did not succeed in holding on to him so he was not finally overcome by it. He was raised from the dead by the Holy Spirit. The biblical witness is clear that it was the Father who raised the Son through the Holy Spirit. Whatever occurs in Christology is a matter of persons, not of natures, so the Spirit is crucial to all Christology. It is not enough to say that it was Christ's divine nature that overcame death. The idea that it was by his divine nature that Christ overcame death was introduced by Pope Leo I in the council of Chalcedon, against Cyril's insistence that agency can be attributed only to persons, not to natures.

Western theology tends to emphasise Christology at the expense of the Holy Spirit. When the Western Churches did eventually develop a pneumatology, it was not integrated into its ecclesiology, so the Church was regarded as primarily an historical reality, to which the Spirit brings an additional and almost cosmetic element. For Western theology, the Church was built solely from the material of history, so this community is given its form by the past, and then the Holy Spirit is allowed to animate it. However, the truth is that the Holy Spirit builds the Church together with the Son and is present at the foundations with the Son: the Spirit does not arrive when the Church is complete.

The Church is the indivisible act of the triune God in which all the persons of the Trinity are involved so we must allow no sense of competition between the persons of God to creep into our account of the Church. The 'christo-monism' of Western ecclesiology tends to assume that the Church began at creation, or perhaps with the incarnation, and that it will end with the coming of Christ, making the Church a kind of interim measure.

The East responded by over-emphasising the role of the Holy Spirit. In order to demonstrate his difference from the West, Alexis Khomiakov declared that the Church is the communion of the Holy Spirit, and so omitted its foundation in Christ entirely. Khomiakov declared that the Orthodox must regard the Church as the communion of the Holy Spirit, and *not* as the Body of the historical Christ. This immediately introduces an opposition between the Spirit and the Son, which represents an inadmissible division in God. Sadly we see this division often enough in the assertion that the Holy Spirit has nothing to do with the traditional institution of the Church, or that the gospel cannot be confined within institutional frameworks. We see it in the contrast between the supposed freedom of charismatic ecclesial communities, and the Churches with 'institutional' apostolic and episcopal ministry. This contrast is the disastrous outcome of emphasising pneumatology at the expense of Christology.

Whenever a new charismatic leader starts a new and more 'spiritual' community, they have divided the body of Christ into spiritual and non-spiritual, or charismatic and non-charismatic, and decided that they do not need half of the body of Christ. Such a distinction between the 'spiritual' and the 'institutional' Church means the abandonment of ordinary Christians, if we may call them that. Are not all Christians members of the body of Christ? Has the Spirit abandoned them? Charismatic leaders who separate themselves from the order and offices of the Church claim that baptism does not transmit the Spirit. But how can the Spirit not be given in baptism when it is the Spirit who baptises us, and who gives us all the sacraments by which we are to be made holy? It is the Spirit who gathers us all in Christ.

Some generations later George Florovsky very justifiably corrected Khomiakov, but he did so equally without nuance, by insisting that ecclesiology should be understood merely as a sub-section of Christology. The emphasis returned to the history of Jesus Christ, again conceived as confined by history as much as any other individual. Others like Lossky, Nissiotes and Bobrinskoy responded to Florovsky by placing all the emphasis back on the Spirit again. However, ecclesiology is not a matter of either Christ or the Spirit, but of all the persons of the Trinity in indivisible unity. When we emphasise the Spirit we must be clear that that we are speaking of the realisation of that recapitulation of all things *in the Son.* The choice is not between a christological ecclesiology on one hand and a pneumatological ecclesiology on the other, but between a christo-*monist* ecclesiology and a fully *trinitarian* ecclesiology in which all the persons of God are at work. The proper basis of ecclesiology is the trinitarian doctrine of God. The role of the Holy Spirit should never lead us into an ecclesiology not founded in Christ: ecclesiology cannot be *Spirit*-centred because the Church is the recapitulation of everything *in Christ.* Christ is the head that this recapitulation refers to. Christ redeems each being, and makes every creature present, both to the Father, and to every other creature.

Having established that all things are recapitulated and made present in Christ, we have to ask whether the Father alone accepts the offering, or whether the Son receives it too. The tradition tells us that the Son receives it too, which is why in the liturgy, the priest prays: 'You are the one who offers and the one who is being offered; the one who accepts and the one who is being given'. Liturgists agree that the Liturgy of Saint Basil is older than that of Saint John Chrysostom. In the *anaphora* of the Liturgy of Saint Basil, the Eucharist is offered to the Father alone, and this comes straight from the earliest tradition. In the prayer, 'Worthy and just it is, to offer songs to You, to offer praise to You, to exalt You, to thank You, to worship You, in every place of Your dominion', we can see who 'you' refers to, from the words that follow. 'For you are the inexpressible, the unimaginable, the invisible, the incomprehensible, the inapprehensible God; the one who always is, and thus is;

you and your only-begotten Son, and your Holy Spirit.' The 'you' refers to the Father.

In the Liturgy of Saint John Chrysostom however, the *anaphora* is offered to the Father and to the Son and to the Spirit. Mention of the Son and Spirit was added to avoid any sense that the Father works without them and so to remove any suspicion of division in the persons of the Trinity. When the Father receives the offering, the Son is with him: 'You, and your Son, and your Holy Spirit.' Nonetheless we cannot say that it does not matter whether we are praying to the Son or to the Spirit. We always address specific persons, for the relationships in which we participate are personal and therefore non-transferable.

So, along with its over-accentuation of history, theology has often been tempted to state Christology at the expense of pneumatology, and allow the Spirit only a secondary and non-constitutive role. In Roman Catholic ecclesiology this takes the form of emphasising the historical succession and historical privileges of the clerical hierarchy. Such an ecclesiology gives the impression of only ever looking for the definitive demonstration of historical succession back to Saint Peter, as though proof of this would be decisive for all questions of the Church. Yet we must say that the Church is not simply an organisation that is created by its *history*, but that it is always constituted by the Spirit, so 'spiritual' and 'charismatic' elements are as fundamental as its history. The Holy Spirit was present from the very first to liberate beings from confinement within their own individuality and so create this communion that is the Church.

For Protestant Christians, the Church is chiefly the community that hears Christ's word and follows his teaching. In coming after Christ in this way, the Christian body does not appear to be fully connected to its head. Only when pneumatology is allowed to be as foundational as Christology, can we see that Christ embraces all of us within him and that Christ is the community of which we are members. The identity of the Church springs from Christ, and we cannot refer to it without referring to him.

Thus the holiness of the Church is fundamental. The Church draws its holiness from Christ as much as it draws its being from him. Where does this holiness come from? The answer is given by the divine liturgy: 'The holy things unto the holy. One only is holy, One only is the Lord, Jesus Christ, to the glory of God the Father'. The 'holy' are the 'saints' that is, the members of the community – to whom the sanctified gifts are given, and who are made holy by those gifts. Though the members of the community are sinful, they are addressed as 'saints' because this is what they will be in that kingdom. Because they are fully conscious that they are not yet holy, they respond by saying 'One only is holy. One only is the Lord, Jesus Christ'.

If the identity of the Church is derived from the community itself, rather than from Christ, it would of course be scandalous to say that the Church is holy. This issue comes up regularly in ecumenical talks. The first thing that Protestants tend to say about the Church is that it is sinful, as though it were *sin* that most fundamentally constitutes the being of the Church.

Some Orthodox suggest that the identity of the Church comes from the saints, regarded as that tiny minority formally designated as such. They believe that when we say that the Church is holy, we are referring to these exceptionally spiritual disciples, marked out by unusual asceticism. However, this is not the answer that we find in the liturgy. There we say, 'The holy things unto the holy', because the gifts of the Spirit are given to the saints. They are not given to *some* saints, who set the standard for the rest of us: Christ is the one standard we have been given. We respond, 'One is holy', that is, Christ is holy and no one is holy beside him. All the saints put together before Christ are sinful, for nothing in all creation can sustain any comparison with him.

So when we are asked how, with so much sin, the Church can be regarded as holy, we must simply reply, with Saint John Chrysostom, that the head always lives to give life to the body. Christ is the head and the source of all that body's life and holiness. The union of this head and body is utterly indissoluble. Any time we start to make a distinction between them it starts to turn into a separation, which is the beginning of the death of the body.

Everything depends on the correct relationship that we give to Christology and pneumatology. In the mediaeval era it was thought that the Holy Spirit just plucked a few saints from history, and concerned himself solely with these isolated cases, leaving the rest of us to Christ and to secular history. Pneumatology thus meant a preoccupation with saints, while Christology was about the main body of the Church in history. However, when we bring pneumatology into its proper relationship to Christology, we no longer have to see the saints as a small elite of Spirit-bearers. Linked to Christology, pneumatology does not refer merely to certain individuals but to the entire body.

The specific question for Western theology that derives from this separation between Christology and pneumatology, is whether the Church is the historical community *primarily*. Roman Catholics insisted on the historical continuity of this community, while Protestants have responded with the notion of the invisible Church, thereby suggesting that the actual historical community is not the true being of the Church.

For the Orthodox, the historical reality of the Church relates to the Eucharist and so to that reality which comes to us from the eschaton. This eschatological reality reveals itself to us by means of sacraments and icons, which must be described in terms of an eschatological and iconological ontology. These sacraments and images are created as the Holy Spirit draws us and all our history into relationship with the end time, the reconciliation of all partial kingdoms in the true history of the kingdom of God. To ask whether the true Church is the *historical* or the *eschatological* Church is to fail to grasp that the eschaton is the reconciliation and integration of all history and therefore the truth of history. The eschaton is the summation and truth of all time and all kingdoms, and thus the eschaton is the truth of the world, of which the Church is the foretaste.

For this reason we must not isolate history from eschatology. The liturgy shows that the divine Eucharist is both a historical *and* an eschatological event. Remembrance does not mean recalling an event that is simply past, an event borne away from us by the stream of time. It requires a conceptual revolution to grasp that the liturgy is both an eschatological and historical event, and that it is a historical event *because* it is first the eschatological event in which all histories are called into being and gathered up into one.

VIII. Eschatology and History

We have said that the liturgy is an eschatological and historical event. However, how can it be both at once? In the Western intellectual tradition we remember what is past, not what is still future to us.

The Western tradition is constituted by its historical awareness, since it assumes that specific historical events are what is most fundamentally true, so all its scholarly efforts are directed to capturing or recovering the truth of historical events. This means for instance that when we ask about the authority of the councils, and want to identify where this authority begins and ends, we have to say that the authority of that council cannot be sourced merely in the event of that council, but also over the much longer event of the reception and acceptance of that council. Each conciliar decision is accepted in the fullness of the Church and so over time. Of course, it is not easy to accept such a degree of indeterminacy, for we want to identify an unchanging principle or institution or particular historical moment that we can date. This preoccupation with the givens of history is part of a larger yearning for security. Objective data takes the element of the unknown, and with it, the burden of responsibility away from us. It is important to seek the truth of events and to record them in the way that they occurred, but such scholarship is not only historical but also historicist, in that it claims such 'historical' knowledge precisely by divorcing events from their meanings.

The historical event is one apprehended by the mind and so constrained by the boundaries of the mind. When this is the case, what role is there for the Holy Spirit? We have a Christology at work here, because it is understood that we are in search of a series of past events, the cross, tomb, resurrection, ascension which fit into a timeframe, 'under Pontius Pilate', 'on the third day' and so on.

Yet we also have to come to terms with the thought that the liturgy also remembers what has not yet taken place. In the prayer 'We offer unto thee in all and for all' of the Liturgy attributed to St. John Chrysostom we read the words:

> Remembering, therefore, this commandment of salvation, and all those things which came to pass for our sakes: the cross, the tomb, the resurrection of the third day, the ascension into heaven, the sitting on the right hand, *the coming again a second time in glory*, Thine own, of thine own, we offer unto thee in all and for all.

This is the commandment of Jesus to his disciples to take and eat from his body and drink from his blood, in remembrance of him. However, it is perhaps not easy to see why we say that we are *remembering* his coming again in glory. How can we remember an event that has not yet taken place?

When we refer to remembering the future we part ways with the main Western intellectual tradition. The Church confesses that the Holy Spirit brings the future into history. Our kingdoms are founded on opposition to one another, each kingdom is in competition with every other. The peace of God, sustained by the rule of God, brings to an end this conflict between all partial kingdoms. The Holy Spirit invades the territory we hold against all others, and brings us into the rule and the peace of God, 'In these last days, I shall pour forth from My Spirit, on all flesh' (Acts 2.17). The Spirit brings all other rules and kingdoms, under the rule of Christ, bringing about the peace of Christ by which all things are reconciled and made peaceful. Christ brings the rule and peace of God into history.

Pentecost is the fulfilment of all times. Though many Christians assume that Pentecost and the Holy Spirit illuminate them personally, enabling them to grasp the events of history and so to grow in the knowledge of Christ, this is only a partial understanding. The Holy Spirit frees us of all the various confinements that hold us within our individual histories or the histories of our nation or social group. The Spirit draws us into the vastly larger dimensions given by the future, in which we are free to be fully present to one another, each of us to all others without limit. The life the Holy Spirit gives us is not divided, but all at once, so for the first time we may live knowing that all Christians, past, present and future are present to us, in a communion not delimited by space or time.

What we experience in the divine Eucharist is the end times making itself present to us now. The Eucharist is not a repetition or continuation of the past, or just one event amongst others, but it is the penetration of the future into time. The Eucharist is entirely live, and utterly new; there is no element of the past about it. The Eucharist is the incarnation live, the crucifixion live, the resurrection live, the ascension live, the Lord's coming again and the day of judgment, live. We cannot go to it casually or without repentance for it is the event in which all events are laid out and examined. 'Now is the judgment of the world' (John 12.31). This 'now' of the Fourth Gospel refers to the Eucharist, in which all these events represent themselves immediately to us, without any gaps of history between them.

The whole force of the Western intellectual tradition attempts to separate history and eschatology and fit Christian doctrine into its historicist and immanent mentality. Either the end times is a separate chapter that will take place 'afterwards', or it is the charismatic experience of a select few, set apart from the historical community. However, the eschaton means the end of all separate, disconnected times, the reconnection and reconciliation of our separate histories and the arrival of their future and fulfilment. All the continuity of our histories come from outside them, from the end times, so there cannot be any final reckoning of our history apart from the eschaton which gives it its coherence and future.

The Eucharist is the communion of all things penetrating into our presently mutually antagonistic 'communions'. The fulfilled communion that is the Church is brought into being for us now by the entrance of the future reality of communion into our presently divided communities. Only a properly *pneumatological* Christology can give us the ecclesiology that understands the Church as the witness of the future.

Next we must consider how neglect of the role of the Holy Spirit in theology has impoverished the Church.

When Christology provides the sole foundation of ecclesiology, the Holy Spirit has only a subsidiary role. For some it is important that Christ founded the institution of the Church, because it is the institutions which have allowed the Church to persist through history. For others the primary reality is the historical events of the incarnation, recorded in the bible. Both these views are based on a Christology without pneumatology: Christ constructs the body, which the Holy Spirit subsequently enters and brings to life as a soul animates a body. Protestants have not had much interest in the institution of the Church, some even doubting whether Christ intended to found the Church at all. The Holy Spirit is regarded as the inspirer, who assists every person individually, and the community generally, to receive the word of God. The Spirit is subordinate to Christ, who either founded the Church, as Roman Catholics have it, or provided the word which the Spirit reveals to us, as Protestants have it.

However, Christ does not form the Church without the Spirit, and the Spirit does not arrive later to fill a Church that is already in existence. The Holy Spirit 'composes the entire institution' of the Church, as one Vespers hymn puts it at Pentecost. The institution of the Church was not founded once and for all at one point in history, but is perpetually constituted and renewed through history by the Spirit. Every time that the Church congregates, it becomes the Church anew. The Spirit therefore makes the Church gather around the Son, giving it its basic structures and offices, the people through baptism and chrismation, and their ministers through ordination. The ordination of a bishop is a manifestation of the Spirit's foundation of the Church, and a renewal of Pentecost, for the gathering of the Church will be renewed around him. The Spirit constitutes and re-constitutes the Church with the Son and thus it receives its continuity, historically, from the eschaton.

The Church is always the creation by the Spirit in one place in time of the coming events of the eschaton. The Church is the summation and recapitulation of the world, so it is only through its continued incorporation in the Church that the world survives. The being of the Church is the outcome of the present work of the Holy Spirit, who enacts the labour of Christ, rendering the whole body of Christ alive and present for this specific time and place. The particular Church that is here in this specific place is of primary importance. Each of the Churches that represent each geographical location is a faithful image because it points towards that single eschatological community. By enacting this image of the end times each time we gather at the Eucharist, we reveal the risen body of Christ, in whom the whole world is hidden.

The consequences of this go very deep. Ecclesiology requires more than finding the right balance between institution and charisma. The Roman Catholic inclination to make the Church the institution that Christ created imposes an institution above human freedom, while the Protestant insistence on fidelity towards the Word of God in the bible imposes the institution of the bible over human freedom. An ecclesiology constructed prior to the Spirit will always struggle because the institution of the Church and the Church's history will appear as limits on freedom.

The Church is that congregation which is created by the Spirit as a portrayal of eschatological events, every time, in every place and whenever the divine Eucharist is performed. The Church is formed by the freely-willed gathering of Christians. We say, 'I'm going to Church'. The structure, the institution of the Church is not something that is imposed by someone for we ourselves compose and constitute it. The Holy Spirit makes us all its founding members as he gathers us together as the Church, so the Church does not come into existence without us. In this way, we do not have problems of clericalism, or of the secularism which is a reaction against it. Clericalism results from the perception that the institution of the Church and its officiators, the clergy, exist independently of the event of the gathering of the Church.

This brings us to the role of the whole people (*laos*) in the Church. The people must be present in order that the clergy celebrate the Eucharist, or even exist as clergy. It is the people who allow the clergy not merely to perform this as a ritual, but really to act with authority and be effective. The charismatic action and authority of the clergy depends on the presence of the whole people who lend them that authority and receive and acknowledge their action. Ordination is no separate ritual but takes place within the divine Eucharist, so it is the act of the whole Christian people, for we participate in the act by which the Holy Spirit makes these ministers our servants. There can be no 'private' or clerical liturgies for which the laity is not present. The Church is constituted by the people and presupposes their presence and willingness in order to exist. The people's 'Amen' is required to validate the clergy's words and acts, and make them the words and acts of the people of God. So when the priest says 'Peace to all', the response 'And to your spirit also' must come from someone who is not the priest: people and priest are in dialogue. The people must actively confirm with their 'Amen' that these prayers are their prayers.

The authority of the bible is always one of the most pressing concerns for Western theology. For Roman Catholics, the bible is interpreted authentically by the ministers appointed by the 'Magisterium', that received its own authority from Christ and which as successor to the Apostles, continues to represent him. For Roman Catholics, the word of God is authentically interpreted by a priest, under the authority of a bishop, and finally the pope, in their own individual authority.

The Protestant approach is to interpret the Word of God by the Word of God, so Scripture is interpreted *through* Scripture. This makes the interpretation of Scripture an autonomous field of academic research. This is why, in order to become a minister, which essentially means someone who expounds the Word of God for Protestants, you must be trained in historical scholarship, for this is the means by which the authority of the bible is explained.

Protestants look to the historians to tell them what in any passage of Scripture is essential and what is merely contingent to the present expression of the Christian faith. Biblical scholarship has to identify which things are purely cultural and historical and no longer directly relevant to us today. When for example, Paul tells us that it is wrong for a man to grow his hair long, or that the world consists of sky, earth and the underworld, we have to recognise these as part of the cosmo-logy of previous generations which is not binding on us. We then set out to establish a canon within the canon, and for criteria on the basis of which we can decide whether something in the bible is authentic or authoritative for the contemporary Church. The result is that historical critical studies tells the Church what it can and cannot find in the bible. The bible is re-interrogated with new categories and new charges laid against it as each generation discovers a new set of anxieties. However, this leads to a crisis in the authority of the bible. Those who decide not to accept the authority of Scripture are the intellectual heirs of those who proclaimed 'sola scriptura'. By insisting on the bible only, they have ended up without the bible altogether.

These are the consequences of the desire to fit the truth, and the identity of the Church, into forms shaped solely by the past, forms which each generation then reacts against and struggles to escape. All the issues of authority, whether of the councils, bishops, the pope or the bible are related to the deep assumption that the past alone determines the forms and authority for the Church.

However, the Church that teaches a properly *pneumatological* Chri-stology will not privilege the past over the future, with the result that it will not be so perplexed by these issues. It is for the Church to interpret her own Scriptures. However, even for Orthodox Churches there has been a trend towards reading in narrative or realist style instead of chanting the gospel. The gospel is often now read rather than chanted in the belief that this will make its meaning accessible for, it is believed, its historical meaning is what has to be grasped. The assumption is that the bible is like an educational textbook, which brings to the surface of the mind memories out of the past; so we are to read the Sermon on the Mount, for instance, as we imagine that Christ first gave it, so we may experience the events just as they took place then. However, this is a misapprehension for it is not just how things happened back then, but the way things *will happen* that is significant. The word of God shows us the future because it comes from the future and it brings the future to us.

It is within the framework of worship and the divine Eucharist that we find the reason and meaning of the gospel we chant. Saint John Chrysostom says that through chanting, the word of God 'opens' and incorporates us. We all experience the desire to grasp knowledge and land it in our net. The Word of God can never be grasped: all our concepts and conceptualising must wait for the Word of God to grasp us. It is our desire to take control of the truth of God which is driving the demand to replace chanting with reading in order to make the Scriptural readings instantly and universally comprehensible. However, even the word 'comprehensible' is telling: who believes that he can comprehend or apprehend these readings from the Word of God? The gospel cannot be laid open by any scholar, regardless of how great their grasp of these texts as documents of history. The chanting of the liturgy is not about some secret or exotic mystery, but simply the form of knowledge that is based in the communion of persons that is the Church, rather than simply in the intellectual achievement of the individual scholar or even of historical scholarship as a whole when they are not formed by the life and worship of the Church.

The Gospel is not just another book. If we study the bible outside the gathered congregation, in Western-style bible studies, we will only gain what Protestants have been gained by this method. We must move away from our preoccupation with hermeneutics and instead understand words as summonses, and as icons that open us up to reality. The bible speaks to us in quite a different manner when we hear it read in Church than when we read it at home. When the Gospel enters the Church we make the sign of the Cross and kiss it, welcoming it as Christ himself. The sermon should immediately follow the reading of the Gospel, and expound the text of the Gospel with reference to the liturgy as a whole. The preacher who suddenly appears with a sermon in the middle of holy communion upsets the logic of the liturgy. The sermon is as much a liturgical and sacramental event as the gospel itself, for together they are the Word addressing us from the end of time. We cannot introduce changes without risk to the image of the eschaton, which is what this gathering is. The very fact that you go to Church, and take your place in this assembly, means that you are part of this image of the end times, which the whole Church presents to the world.

The Eucharist realises and reveals the Church as a *community*. If the Christian people do not gather, or do not participate in the worship or do not affirm the decisions and teaching with their 'Amen', the identity of the Church is lost. Then we do indeed start to refer to the clergy as though they were the Church, as the media do every time they say that 'the Church has announced', with all the resulting division and confusion that we see around us. Without a theology of Christ and Spirit, and head and body, we are of course only able to pit clergy and people against one another, so every news story about the Church is about the individual opposing the hierarchy. But is by their being gathered together into one that the people of God are brought into being.

People often ask how we should prepare ourselves for the divine Eucharist. Should we avoid going if we are angry or tired? Let us not allow this deep assumption that everything is merely cognitive or a matter of psychology to affect our understanding of the Church. Does our resentment change the grace of God? All that counts is that we go. However, we must patiently insist that when the whole people freely gather around the bishop in the Eucharist, it demonstrates the indissoluble unity of the body of Christ.

When our bishops meet together in synods they are also part of a larger whole, the fellowship which is constituted by the Holy Spirit. Authority emerges finally from that complete event in which Spirit moves through all members of the Church. A decision or an interpretation by bishops can prove to be mistaken, just as we understand that academic historical scholarship can be mistaken. It is the whole Church expressed over the long term, through all its councils and through the worship of the whole Christian people, which gives us the truth of God.

The Church is the gathering of God's people in a specific place and time, which portrays the complete assembly of all created things. It is summoned by the Holy Spirit who makes the Church new every time it gathers, and so sustains the constantly life-renewing body of Christ on earth. In this way, we are neither defined by history nor in denial about it. The Eucharist is the inaugural event of freedom and the moment in which eschatological reality becomes the actual presence of this assembly brought together by the Holy Spirit. This is the work of the Holy Spirit, which is why the invocation (*epiclesis*) of the Holy Spirit is fundamental. The gifts that bear the body and blood of Christ bring us into increasing participation in that body. This event of person-to-person relationship takes place in the Spirit, between each of us and Christ. These eschatological events are seen, felt and tasted in the gathering of the Church. This gathering is the event in which the Holy Spirit opens us to life together in freedom.

IX. RECEPTION

Finally, we must return to the issue of the many Churches and the one Church. The idea of reception is deeply rooted in the history and being of the Church. The Church was born out of a process of reception and has grown and existed through reception. First the Church *receives*: she receives from God through Christ in the Holy Spirit. However, the Church also receives from the world, its history, its culture, even its tragic and sinful experiences and failures, for it is the body of the Lord who takes upon himself the sins of the world. Second, the Church itself is received. The Church as a distinct community within the world exists in constant dialogue with whatever constitutes the 'non-ecclesial' realm, in an attempt to make herself acceptable to the world. What we used to call 'mission' is better rendered with the notion of reception, because the Church should be offering itself to the world rather than imposing itself on it. In the prologue of the Fourth Gospel the Son of God is spoken of as not having been *received* by the world: 'his own did not *receive* him'. The other point in the Church's being received is that each Church is received by another Church. The most important aspect of reception, stems from the basic ecclesiological fact that the Church, although one, exists as *Churches*, in the plural, and these Churches exist as one Church by constantly receiving one another as sister Churches. But what is it that is being received?

What is received is, as we have seen, the love of God the Father incarnate in his own beloved Son, who is given to us in the Holy Spirit. The Church exists in order to give what she has received as the love of God for the world. Because the content of reception is this love of God for the world incarnate in Christ, the Apostle Paul uses the terms *parelabon* and *paralabete* with reference to the *person* of Christ. He writes, 'as you have received Christ' (Colossians 2.6) and in Hebrews the verb 'to receive' is used in the sense of 'receiving the kingdom' (Hebrews 12.28).

The Church received the *gospel* which is the good news of God's love to the world in Christ, and it is given in the concrete form of the teaching and of creed that give the historical facts of the coming of the communion of God to us. Thus, the Church receives also the historical facts, that Jesus Christ died and was raised from the dead , which are essential to the history of the people of God. The Church receives in this way a confession which it offers as a true statement of the acts of God in the history of mankind.

What is received is therefore the person of the Son. The fact that the Church receives a person, rather than simply information, underlies Paul's use of 'hand on' (*paralambanein*) for the Eucharist, which the Apostle tells us (1 Corinthians 11.23) is both received and handed on.

Attempts to maintain the truth of the facts of the gospel through which the love of God is received led the Church to develop a teaching authority which is responsible for protecting this gospel from distortions. The decisions and pronouncements of the councils are an essential part of the *what* of reception. The Church does not receive and perpetuate ideas or doctrines as such, but life and love, the very life and love of God for humanity. Dogmatic formulations which have no bearing on the life that the Church cannot claim to be part of the deposit of faith received by the Church.

The Church is itself also the object of reception, in two senses. The Church is received and accepted by the world. In addition, each Church receives and recognises each other Church in the communion of the *one Church*, which is the indivisible body of Christ that makes itself present to the world in each place. As long as the world rejects the Church, or the Churches reject one another, the need for reception continues. There is no full catholicity of the Church in such a state of division. How does this reception take places?

The form of reception is the most difficult thing to agree upon in our present ecumenical situation. However, with the help of some theological principles we can make the following points. God's giving of his Son to us took and takes place, we all confess, *in the Holy Spirit* and thus in an event of communion. By giving his Son as his own very love, God does not impose the reception of this gift upon us. The Spirit is freedom, and reception of anything that is the content (the *what*) of reception cannot be imposed, on anyone by anyone. Truth is authoritative, but it is not authoritarian, because it comes to us through this event of communion.

Communion means *community*. Communion must come through the concrete communities of the Church. However, not any and every ecclesial community is a Church. No community can hold itself in isolation from the whole Church, for a Church is always structured in a particular way in an event of communion. No matter how widely something is received in the Churches, unless it is received by one Church from another, and this means that it must be received in the context of the Eucharist. All creedal and conciliar formulations meet their final purpose only when they become integral parts of the eucharistic community.

Reception is not just about individuals, but about communities, being in communication with each other. Because the Churches receive the gospel and the creeds as communities, we need a particular ministry that expresses and confirms the unity of the community. This ministry of *episcope* is the function of the bishop. Each bishop ensures that what his Church receives is faithful to all previous communities going back to the first apostolic communities, and that what that Church receives sustains it in communion with all other Churches worldwide, which is achieved through conciliar gatherings and decisions. Therefore, the oversight of a bishop is essential to reception.

In the Holy Spirit everything takes place as an event of communion. Every decision taken by a bishop or by the bishops in council has to be *received* by the community. Therefore, there is an element of reciprocity: the community could do nothing without the bishop, who had to receive the 'Amen' of the community in all he did.

Reception cannot be limited to the local level, rather it also has to be universal. We need a ministry of universal reception that meets these requirements. This ministry should be *episcopal*, exercised by the head of a local Church, for this ensures that universal catholicity does not bypass or contradict the catholicity of the local Church. The consensus of the faithful should be obtained in every case of reception and this should go through the local bishops and not be delegated to individuals.

Since different people receive the gospel and Christ himself in different ways, reception involves the proper inculturation of the gospel. There should be room for freedom of expression and variety of cultural forms in reception, and this is why the reception of the gospel takes place in the local Church. Each local Church receives the gospel and re-receives it constantly, with the bishop supervising, in communion with the faithful and with other local Churches in conciliar decisions through a universal ministry. In the very act of responding to documents the Churches receive one another as Churches. All Churches constantly need to re-receive their own tradition and through such ecumenical encounters and re-orient themselves to the original apostolic community.

Two hopeful signs are emerging. The Churches which have always had bishops are beginning to realise that the office of bishop must be exercised as episcopal oversight in unity with the whole Christian community. Second, the Churches which have traditionally rejected episcopacy are beginning to see the need for such oversight as an essential part of ecclesial unity. With this issue of *episcope*, the thorny issue of the ministry of the Pope will have to be tackled sooner or later, but if it is put in its proper theological perspective, perhaps even this issue can be resolved.

Index

Abraham 8, 40, 126
Adam 52, 90–1, 102, 104–5, 131
Anaphora 117, 146, 147
   see also offering
Apostles 9, 13, 128–9, 145–7
asceticism 122–5, 134–5
Athanasius 23–4, 59–60, 89–90, 102,
   105
Augustine 65–8, 70–1,
   77–8, 140

Baptism 2, 33–6, 45, 150
Basil, Saint, of Caesarea 6, 52, 55,
   58, 62, 72–3
Bible 157–9 *see also* Scripture
bishop 2, 13–14, 118–19, 123–4,
   128–31, 141–7, 156, 160,
   163–4
body 86, 89, 93, 123
Body of Christ 13, 31–2, 116–19,
   126–8, 133, 139–40, 149–52, 156,
   160–1

catholicity 13–15, 128, 140–2,
   162–3
cause (agency in God) 53, 59–61
Chalcedon, Council of 110, 111,
   112, 114–15, 149
charism, charismatic 11–12, 130–1,
   149
Christ, Jesus 8–9, 13, 40, 43–5,
   103–14, 116–18, 126, 148–50,
   156

Clement of Alexandria 129
communion 7–8, 11–13, 45, 53, 58,
   89, 94, 108, 116–18, 125, 135–6,
   139, 143, 155, 163
cosmos 29, 41–2, 48
   see also creation
Councils of the Church 2, 9, 17,
   13–15, 77, 142–4, 153, 162
creation 42–3, 46, 83–108, 132–3
creeds 2, 4, 33, 61, 75–7, 121
cross 110, 114, 134–6
Cyril of Alexandria 64, 81, 149

death 53, 56, 63, 133–4, 148
Dionysius, Ps-Areopagite 21–2
doctrine 1–9, 12–15
dogma 5–6, 9, 14–15, 138

economy 69–73, 77–81
eschatology 127–31, 137–40,
   145–7, 153–7, 160–1
Eucharist 8–9, 14, 117–19, 122–5,
   128–31, 137–41, 146–7, 155, 157
Eunomius 57, 59, 61, 64

faith 33–9
fall 86, 90, 98–109
Filioque 71, 72, 75–82
freedom 20, 23, 26–9, 38, 61,
   73–5, 85–6, 90–8, 104–9, 157

gifts 11–12, 147, 162
Gnosticism 83–4, 88, 94

God, the Father 23–4, 26, 31, 43, 53, 57–61, 64, 68, 88, 106, 114, 117
Gregory of Nazianzus 11–12, 56–7, 61
Gregory of Nyssa 6, 79–82

heart 36–7
heaven 36–7
hell 136
history 37, 101, 107, 139–41, 148–61
holiness 36, 118, 124–5, 137, 151
hypostasis 34, 49–50, 61
    see also person

icons 9, 113, 127, 134, 136
    see also image
Ignatius, Saint 13, 122, 128–30, 146–7
image 8, 10, 13, 24, 64, 67, 69, 95, 118, 137–9, 145–6, 160
incarnation 8, 148, 156
infallibility 15–16, 141–2

John Chrysostom 55, 159
judgment 18, 35, 43–4, 137, 140

kingdom of God 36, 130–1, 140, 153–4, 157, 159–60

liturgy 127, 134, 146–7, 150–3
Logos 22–4, 46–8, 66, 70–1, 86–8, 95, 122–3, 129
Lossky, Vladimir 22, 77, 150
love 23–33, 35, 53–4, 66, 71, 75, 79, 110, 112–14

Mary 103–7, 113
materiality 58, 90, 94, 101, 103, 115, 122–3, 135
memory 65–7, 71, 159

mind 22, 24, 58, 65–8, 85, 122–3
monasticism 122–5, 130

nature 27–9, 89–92, 98–9, 105, 108, 110, 115
    divine nature 53, 61, 70, 110–12, 115–16
    human nature 51–2, 59, 63, 115
Nicaea, Council of 2, 9, 15, 59, 61–2, 143

offering 117–19, 124, 146, 150
Origen 22–4, 86, 122–3, 131

Pentecost 11, 126–8, 155–6
person 8, 23–4, 25–9, 42, 46–51, 54–66, 62–4, 67–70, 106–7, 111–14
Philo of Alexandria 49, 85–6
Pope 141–2, 144–5
Presbyters, Priests 128–9, 146–7

resurrection 44, 99–100, 108, 117, 134–5
Roman Catholicism 7, 120–1, 142, 151–2, 158

Sabellius 47–8, 50–1, 62
sacraments 38, 134, 137–8, 153
Saints, Christians 15, 38–9, 125, 151–2
salvation 102–4, 105–15, 124, 129
Scripture 3–10, 158–9
sin 98, 102, 152, 161
space 16–17, 51, 100–1
suffering 109–10, 115, 134

time 17, 51, 100, 153–5

worship 44, 46, 68, 117, 159

The New Oxford World History

The Atlantic in World History

Karen Ordahl Kupperman

OXFORD

UNIVERSITY PRESS

OXFORD
UNIVERSITY PRESS

Oxford University Press is a department of the University of Oxford.
It furthers the University's objective of excellence in research,
scholarship, and education by publishing worldwide.

Oxford   New York
Auckland   Cape Town   Dar es Salaam   Hong Kong   Karachi
Kuala Lumpur   Madrid   Melbourne   Mexico City   Nairobi
New Delhi   Shanghai   Taipei   Toronto

With offices in
Argentina   Austria   Brazil   Chile   Czech Republic   France   Greece
Guatemala   Hungary   Italy   Japan   Poland   Portugal   Singapore
South Korea   Switzerland   Thailand   Turkey   Ukraine   Vietnam

Oxford is a registered trade mark of Oxford University Press in the UK and certain other countries.

Published in the United States of America by Oxford University Press
198 Madison Avenue, New York, NY 10016

© Oxford University Press 2012

Library of Congress Cataloging-in-Publication Data
Kupperman, Karen Ordahl
The Atlantic in world history / by Karen Ordahl Kupperman.
p.   cm. — (New Oxford world history)
Includes bibliographical references and index.
ISBN 978-0-19-516074-1 (hardcover : acid-free paper) — ISBN 978-0-19-533809-6 (pbk. : acid-free
paper) 1. Atlantic Ocean Region—History—To 1500. 2. Atlantic Ocean Region—History—16th century.
3. Atlantic Ocean Region—History—17th century. 4. Atlantic Ocean Region—History—18th century.
5. Social history. 6. Atlantic Ocean Region—Civilization. I. Title.
D210.K84   2012
909'.09821—dc23   2012006933

3 5 7 9 8 6 4 2

Printed in the United States of America
on acid-free paper

Frontispiece: *Native American life in seventeenth-century Canada.* Courtesy of the John
Carter Brown Library at Brown University

For Ulysses, intrepid explorer

Contents

Editors' Preface ix

INTRODUCTION Thinking Atlantically 1

CHAPTER 1 Atlantic Memories 3

CHAPTER 2 Atlantic Beginnings 20

CHAPTER 3 Atlantic People 44

CHAPTER 4 Commodities: Foods, Drugs, and Dyes 72

CHAPTER 5 Eighteenth-Century Realities 98

EPILOGUE The Atlantic 122

Chronology 125

Notes 127

Further Reading 133

Websites 139

Acknowledgments 141

Index 147

Editors' Preface

This book is part of the New Oxford World History, an innovative series that offers readers an informed, lively, and up-to-date history of the world and its people that represents a signifi cant change from the "old" world history. Only a few years ago, world history generally amounted to a history of the West—Europe and the United States—with small amounts of information from the rest of the world. Some versions of the "old" world history drew attention to every part of the world *except* Europe and the United States. Readers of that kind of world history could get the impression that somehow the rest of the world was made up of exotic people who had strange customs and spoke difficult languages. Still another kind of "old" world history presented the story of areas or peoples of the world by focusing primarily on the achievements of great civilizations. One learned of great buildings, influential world religions, and mighty rulers but little of ordinary people or more general economic and social patterns. Interactions among the world's peoples were often told from only one perspective.

This series tells world history differently. First, it is comprehensive, covering all countries and regions of the world and investigating the total human experience—even those of so-called peoples without histories living far from the great civilizations. "New" world historians thus share in common an interest in all of human history, even going back millions of years before there were written human records. A few "new" world histories even extend their focus to the entire universe, a "big history" perspective that dramatically shifts the beginning of the story back to the big bang. Some see the "new" global framework of world history today as viewing the world from the vantage point of the Moon, as one scholar put it. We agree. But we also want to take a close-up view, analyzing and reconstructing the significant experiences of all of humanity.

This is not to say that everything that has happened everywhere and in all time periods can be recovered or is worth knowing, but that there is much to be gained by considering both the separate and interrelated stories of different societies and cultures. Making these connections is still another crucial ingredient of the "new" world history. It emphasizes connectedness and interactions of all kinds—cultural, economic, political, religious, and social—involving peoples, places, and processes. It makes comparisons and finds similarities. Emphasizing both the comparisons and interactions is critical to developing a global framework that can deepen and broaden historical understanding, whether the focus is on a specific country or region or on the whole world.

The rise of the new world history as a discipline comes at an opportune time. The interest in world history in schools and among the general public is vast. We travel to one another's nations, converse and work with people around the world, and are changed by global events. War and peace affect populations worldwide as do economic conditions and the state of our environment, communications, and health and medicine. The New Oxford World History presents local histories in a global context and gives an overview of world events seen through the eyes of ordinary people. This combination of the local and the global further defines the new world history. Understanding the workings of global and local conditions in the past gives us tools for examining our own world and for envisioning the interconnected future that is in the making.

Bonnie G. Smith

Anand Yang

Thinking Atlantically

What difference does an Atlantic approach make? It allows us to understand the lives of people who were part of the Atlantic in ways that are truer to their actual experience. Older approaches formulated history in terms of European empires and followed transatlantic links between centers in the Old World and colonies or stations in Africa and America. Each colony or station was an isolated island that communicated only with the parent country. These were stories in which conflict and rivalry between empires loomed largest and which always distinguished between legitimate trade (within empires) and smuggling or piracy.

If, by contrast, we approach the several hundred years following Columbus's first voyage through an Atlantic lens, we see that the links and exchanges were as often between people of many different origins as they were within strictly imperial lines. One could go so far as to say that no colony or venture could have survived if its people had not exchanged and traded with all comers, whether they were from supposedly enemy empires or from indigenous people. African and Indian leaders judged the new opportunities and risks for themselves and chose to participate in Atlantic enterprises. Some ordinary people also chose to throw themselves into the Atlantic maelstrom to test their chances. The possibility of miscalculation was ever present, and many came to regret their choices. Conflict was always possible and often occurred, but practicality dictated a pragmatic approach that sometimes recognized mutual support as well. This means that much of the trading and exchange was along the coasts, as circum-Atlantic enterprises came to be as important as trans-Atlantic ones. In short, Atlantic people were caught in webs of interdependence. If they survived, they had recognized this fact.

The older imperial approach made the nineteenth-century outcome, the emergence of creole nation-states in America and colonial states in Africa, seem overdetermined. Anything that did not contribute to that outcome was ignored on the grounds that those people or ventures could not have been important or that they were obviously doomed to failure. Looking at the early modern period Atlantically allows us to see that many of these supposed dead ends actually were essential to the evolution of relationships. For example, Dutch traders knitted together the activities of people from all over Europe and West Africa in the Americas, and their role as knowledge brokers was essential, yet the Netherlands did not have long-lasting and large land-based empires in the Atlantic.

Atlantic history involves decentering the narrative away from capital cities to the places on the margins where the trade and exchange actually took place. The people who traveled around the margins, either on the ocean or on land, were at least as important as the governors and directors. And their influence was cultural as well as economic. Exchange of news and views, the emergence of new religious groups that cut across older lines, and the spread of new ideas all were owing to their activities. So Atlantic history means a whole new cast of characters, people who may not appear in national stories, but who were the most important actors in creating a new historical reality.

Finally, looking Atlantically means recognizing the high degree of uncertainty and the ever-present specter of failure that everyone lived with in the early modern period. Carefully constructed relationships could crumble without warning because of changed policies or personnel in places thousands of miles away. Epidemic disease made all plans vulnerable, as did the presence of pirates. The whole construct ran on trust: every merchant who sent out a cargo and everyone who adventured her or his own person was forced to trust in the many people who would play a role in deciding where and how that person or cargo ended up. Those who entered into such relationships often had no knowledge of who the various people determining their fate would be, so the level of trust is remarkable. The identity of almost everyone who entered into this Atlantic world in some way is lost to us; only the handful of personal stories that survive, often by accident, allow us to imagine the experiences of the rest.

CHAPTER I

Atlantic Memories

In the beginning there was no Atlantic Ocean. People who lived on the four continents bordering the great sea looked inward toward the land and the inland thoroughfares along which goods and people traveled. Great rivers—the Rhine, the Mississippi, the Amazon, and the Orinoco—and a network of smaller rivers accommodated the traffic that knitted the regions of each continent together. In the case of Africa, the Sahara desert, which has been likened to a sea of sand, linked north and south in trade.

Europeans centered their attention on the Mediterranean, the body of water whose name conveys its ancient status at the center of their known world, where it separated Europe from Africa and bordered on the Levant, the land to the east where the sun rose, and through which spices, silk, and other rich products came into Europe and Africa from Asia. African gold also entered Europe through the Mediterranean. In the west, the Caribbean similarly separated and linked continents. Those who lived on the Atlantic coasts with the ocean at their backs were marginal in their own worlds, as they were farthest and most cut off from the centers of trade and ideas.

Looking backward we can see that all this began to change after Christopher Columbus and his sailors traveled across the Atlantic in 1492, but no one at the time would have described the voyage as crossing an ocean. The name Atlantic Ocean as we use it today would have been meaningless to people in the early centuries of regular transatlantic crossings. In fact, they did not think of the Atlantic as a separate body of water. Columbus's title was Admiral of the Ocean Sea, indicating the assumption that one great ocean system flowed around the known land. Geographers even in ancient times had known that Europe, Asia, and Africa were all connected in one enormous land mass. It was natural to assume that the sea they saw stretching to the horizon surrounded the land and that that was all there was. They knew there were islands in the sea and they assumed that Columbus had found yet more islands. It would be a long time before those from the ocean's eastern shores would understand the full extent of the lands that split the Ocean Sea.

Even after the continents on the sea's western side were recognized as such by Europeans, there still was no Atlantic Ocean. As the lands around the ocean began to be mapped, cartographers divided the single world ocean up into bands of seas. The Ethiopian Sea appeared on many maps as the southern part of the ocean between Africa and South America. Often the ocean between Europe and America was labeled the Mar del Nort, or Northern Sea, and sometimes part of this was named the Atlantic Sea. Sometimes the ocean was subdivided into as many as five bands, and it did not become customary to refer to a single Atlantic Ocean until the nineteenth century.[1]

Columbus's voyage opened an age of countless crossings and recrossings and inaugurated the Atlantic as an integrated system of exchange for people, commodities, and ideas. The Atlantic was marked by great opportunities and also great loss and suffering. Modernity was born there.

Atlantic travel did not begin in 1492, however. Long before Columbus, African mariners had begun venturing out into the Atlantic. Phoenician sailors from Carthage in North Africa established forts on Africa's Atlantic coast thousands of years ago, and Herodotus, the ancient Greek historian, wrote that Phoenicians had navigated through the Red Sea around Africa and back into the Mediterranean, an exceptionally difficult feat. Carthaginians also traveled regularly to the Purple Islands (modern Madeira), and to the Canaries, which were known to the ancient world as the Fortunate Islands. In fact, the Canary Islands had long been inhabited by people with North African roots.

Crossing the ocean was not the goal of early ventures as Europeans began to sail along these routes in the 1300s. In fact, they initiated voyages into the Atlantic and sought to control islands as a way of getting to the lucrative trades, first in gold and then in pepper, with West Africa. Sailing along the African coast was so difficult that it was actually easier to swing out into the Atlantic and then back to the shore, and island bases enhanced this endeavor.

A joint Portuguese-Italian venture encountered the Canary Islands, and their populations, at the beginning of the 1340s. The Italian poets Petrarch and Giovanni Boccaccio wrote about the Canaries soon after, and Spain sent ships there looking for seal skins, dyes, and slaves. An expedition from Normandy created a settlement in the islands at the start of the fifteenth century. At about the same time, Spanish expeditions arrived in the Canaries and inaugurated a long process of conquest. Over the course of the century, the Norman settlement slowly became more Spanish than French. Columbus stopped at the Canaries on his first westward journey and compared the Indians he encountered in the Caribbean to the Canarians; the Spanish conquest culminated in victory over the islands four years later, in 1496.

Under the influence of Prince Henry (called the Navigator), Madeira became a site for settlement by Portuguese adventurers early in the fifteenth century, and settlers quickly began to filter into the islands where they established sugar production. Around the same time, Portuguese mariners found the Azores. In Madeira, the European population included many Italians, and the Azores had so many Flemish people from the southern Netherlands that they became known as the Flemish Islands. The Portuguese also built bases on the Cape Verde Islands off the coast of Africa, and on the island of São Tomé. Madeira, the Cape Verdes, and the Azores had all been uninhabited at the time the Portuguese contacted them.

Islands in the North Atlantic had also been occupied long before Columbus. Norwegian ships made many visits to Iceland during the Middle Ages, and permanent settlement began there in the tenth century, at a time when the northern hemisphere experienced a period of relative warmth. Greenland, to Iceland's west, had been inhabited in ancient times by people related to the Inuit of North America's far north, but those communities had died out. Then, near the end of the tenth century, in 985, Norse adventurers led by Erik the Red began settlements there. Expeditions continued across the ocean and Norse families led by Leif Erikson and Karlsefni Thorfinn created outposts in Newfoundland, the land they called Vinland, and they even ventured into modern Maine. Their presence in Newfoundland has been documented by recent archaeological investigation, so the Norse sagas that talk of experiences across the ocean are the first authenticated written descriptions of transatlantic voyages.

The story as told in Erik the Red's Saga recorded a land with "wild wheat growing in fields on all the low ground and grape vines on all the higher ground. Every stream was teeming with fish." Only after several weeks did they see any of the native people, who approached the settlement in boats covered with skins. Those first people soon left, but then a "great horde" of boats approached and in every boat native people were waving sticks. The Vikings and the Indians were soon engaged in trade, with the Indians offering pelts in exchange for red cloth, exchange that ended when one of the Vikings' bulls came raging out of the woods and frightened the Indians. A few weeks later the Norsemen again saw

the approach of Indians in skin-covered boats but these were intent on attack. The Vikings were frightened and ran away until a pregnant woman named Freydis came out of the refuge shouting, "Why do you flee from such pitiful wretches, brave men like you? You should be able to slaughter them like cattle. If I had weapons, I am sure I could fight better than any of you." She picked up the sword of a dead Viking and slapped it against her bare breast while running toward the amazed Indians, who abandoned their attack.[2]

The Norse venturers gave up all their Atlantic settlements in the colder temperatures of what is termed the Little Ice Age, but European fishermen began visiting the rich fishing grounds off the Newfoundland Banks, and there is some evidence that these voyages began in the fifteenth century before Columbus sailed. Although they processed their fish on land over the summer, no one at this early date would have assumed they were actually on the edge of a vast continent.

Ancient traditions came to mind as those who lived on the Atlantic's eastern shores in the fifteenth and sixteenth centuries looked out into the vast sea. Many stories told of a lost civilization that had disappeared beneath the ocean's waters as the great island continent of Atlantis had sunk. The name Atlantis came from the Greek mythological figure Atlas, the Titan who, as punishment for joining a rebellion against the gods of Mount Olympus, was sentenced to stand on the western shore of the known world and hold up the sky. The Greek philosopher Plato told the story of Atlantis and its disappearance, which he placed almost 10,000 years in the past when he wrote in 360 BCE, and he said that its king, like the Titan, was also named Atlas. Atlantis had been located, according to Plato, beyond the Pillars of Hercules, which marked the strait where the Mediterranean Sea linked to the great ocean beyond. Atlantis had been a rich and powerful kingdom advancing aggressively against Europe when suddenly a great earthquake and attendant floods overwhelmed it and the entire land was swallowed up by the sea.

Was it possible that Atlantis had not actually sunk, but that the ancients had merely lost contact with it? As mariners who ventured westward during the fifteenth century encountered more and more islands in the vast ocean, it seemed reasonable that perhaps Atlantis remained to be rediscovered. The lost continent even appeared on some European maps in this period. Could the American lands that Europeans had come to know only at the end of the fifteenth century actually be the site of that vanished culture? Gonzalo Fernandez de Oviedo y Valdes, who wrote one of the earliest histories of the Indies, connected the newly discovered lands to Atlantis in the 1530s. The Reverend Richard Hakluyt, who collected travel accounts and was one of the first great promoters of English colonization, wrote that the ancients had had some knowledge of America and referred to "my Westerne Atlantis or America."[3] In 1607 a Spanish Dominican priest, Gregorio García, pointed to the many Mexican words containing the letters "atl" in combination, particularly in religious language, and argued that this linguistic evidence proved a connection to Atlantis.

Others denied that the Americas could be Atlantis. The Spanish Jesuit scholar and natural historian José de Acosta rejected the Platonic association in his *Historia Natural y Moral de las Indias* in 1590. The French essayist Michel de Montaigne denied that the Americas could be the lost Atlantis because they were so far across the ocean, whereas Atlantis "well-nigh touched Spaine. . . . Besides, our moderne Navigators have now almost discovered, that it is not an Iland, bur rather firme land, and a continent." Samuel Purchas, Hakluyt's successor as a compiler and publisher of travel accounts, agreed that America was too distant to be Atlantis and, like Acosta, argued that Plato's work had been an allegory, not a history. He refuted the idea that ancient writers had actually known about the Americas by pointing out that they had said that human beings could not live near the "burning zone" of the equator. Now experience had proved them wrong, and showed that their statements were mere conjecture.[4]

People on the Atlantic's western shores also told ancient stories of great islands as cradles of civilization. The Huron people of northern North America believed human life on earth began when a supernatural being called Aataentsic fell through a rip in the sky. Turtle saw her falling and called on the other sea animals to dive down and scoop up earth. The earth, piled on his shell, became the land on which Aetaentsic landed. She was pregnant when she fell, and her daughter, born on the new earth, later gave birth to twin sons. As in the biblical story of Cain and Abel, these sons quarreled, and one, Iouskeha, killed his brother, Tawiscaron, whose blood turned into flint as he died. Ultimately Aetaentsic and Iouskeha became the moon and the sun. The island earth on turtle's back supported human life from then on.

Europeans thought of other stories from ancient lore as they gathered reports of new people in the Americas. Although he did not personally encounter them, Columbus and his men heard stories that they connected with archaic legends of the Amazons; their interest was intensified by rumors that these women had large amounts of gold. Other Spaniards collected accounts of warrior women who lived without men, but never saw them.

These early reports soon entered popular culture back in Spain in the form of chivalric romances. One, *Las Sergas del Muy Virtuoso Caballero Esplandián* (The Deeds of the Very Virtuous Knight Esplandián) by Garci-Rodriguez de Montalvo, published in Seville in 1510, told the story of Calafía, queen of the Amazons, who lived on an island called California located "on the right hand of the Indies . . . very close to the earthly paradise." Calafía and her followers also figured in a second romance, *Lisuarte de Grecia y Perión de Gaula* (Lisuarte of Greece and Perión of Gaul) by Feliciano de Silva, published about 1514. Both were continuations of the medieval romance *Amadis of Gaule*, which Montalvo had presented in a modern edition; Esplandián and Lisuarte were presented as the son and grandson of Amadis. Hernan Cortés, a voracious consumer of chivalric fiction, applied the name California to the peninsula north of New Spain that he thought was an island.[5]

The Spanish explorer Francisco de Orellana led an expedition between 1539 and 1542 that actually encountered women warriors. The party set out from Quito, traveled across the Andes to the headwaters of the Amazon, and were the first Europeans to descend the full length of the river. Orellana and his men were attacked by a party of warriors led by ten or twelve very strong women under the command of their leader, Coñori. The Spanish explorers were convinced these were the Amazons, and it was from this connection that the river got its name.

Sir Walter Raleigh, who was in Guiana in the mid-1590s, interviewed "the most ancient and best traveled Orenoqueponi"; he was "very desirous to understand the truth of those warlike women because of some it is beleeved and of others not." What he learned caused him, like Orellana, to think of Old World stories:

> The memories of the like women are very ancient as well in Africa as in Asia. In Africa those that had Medusa for Queene: others in Scithia neere the rivers of Tanais and Thermadon: we find also that Lampedo and Marthesia were Queenes of the Amazones: in many histories they are verified to have been, and in divers ages and Provinces: But they which are not far from Guiana doe accompanie with men but once in the yeere and for the time of one moneth, which I gather by their relation to be in Aprill. At that time all the Kings of the borders assemble and the Queenes of the Amazones, and after the Queens have chosen, the rest cast lots for their Valentines.

The Amazons kept daughters born of these unions and sent a present to the father. Baby boys were sent to the fathers to be brought up. These fierce women put captives, especially invaders, to death, for "they are said to be very cruell and bloodthirsty." Raleigh also collected reports that they had great wealth.[6]

Fray Cristobal de Acuña, writing forty years after Raleigh, also said that the Amazons were "women of great valour" who welcomed men into their midst once a year for the purpose of procreating. From these unions, they kept and reared the daughters. What happened to their sons, according to Acuña, was unclear. Some said they were given to their fathers; others that they were killed. His conclusion was: "Time will discover the truth."[7]

America evoked other remembered stories. Venturers avidly sought one legendary location, Antilia, as the ocean was explored. Lore said that seven Portuguese and Spanish bishops fled westward across the Atlantic with their congregations as Muslim invaders from North Africa overwhelmed the Iberian peninsula in the eighth century. These refugees founded seven cities in Antilia, and their riches were golden. The Antilles, the name given the islands of the Caribbean on Spanish maps, reflected the hope that Antilia was among them. Although Antilia was not found in the West Indies, reports of Indian pueblos in the American

Southwest and the way the afternoon sun glinted off them kept alive the hope that ancient golden cities founded by Spanish Christians would yet be located. Spanish lore said that the nearest of the seven cities was called Cíbola. English sources claimed similar medieval contacts, as they told the story of the Welsh bishop Madoc, who was reported to have made two trips across the Atlantic bringing settlers fleeing civil war at home.

Other ancient associations rose among the Europeans as they investigated the newly revealed lands. The Italian navigator Giovanni da Verrazano sailed along the east coast of North America on a commission from the king of France in 1524. Block Island, off the New England coast, reminded him of the Isle of Rhodes in the Mediterranean, the site of the vanished ancient Minoan civilization: "We discovered a triangular-shaped island, ten leagues from the mainland, similar in size to the island of Rhodes; it was full of hills, covered in trees, and highly populated to judge by the fires we saw burning continually along the shore."[8] Rhode Island, the name given to the region by Europeans, may reflect Verrazano's identification.

Encounters stirred ancient associations. William Strachey, who came to Virginia in 1610, imagined the first little fleet of English ships in 1607 traveling up the James River engaged in a "weary search" for a proper site "with their barge coasting still before, as Vergil writeth Aeneas did, arriving in the region of Italy called Latium, upon the banks of the river Tiber." When he arrived at Jamestown and first saw the fort, Strachey wrote that its size and shape reminded him of the famous trick associated with the founding of ancient Carthage. Having asked for only as much land as could be covered by the hide of a bull, Queen Dido had the hide cut into one continuous thin strip so that it surrounded a much larger space in which she built her fortress.[9]

Opening the Atlantic and regular contacts also caused Europeans to remember lore about ancient old world relationships. From the twelfth century, rumors told of a fabulous Christian kingdom in India or eastern Africa led by Prester John, a descendant of one of the Three Wise Men who had visited the baby Jesus. Various locations were suggested, but most Europeans had come to concentrate their attention on what they called Ethiopia. Although the existence of a Christian nation in East Africa was known, the extent and location of Ethiopia was unclear. The southern portion of the Atlantic Ocean on maps in the period when transatlantic voyaging became widespread was called the Ethiopian Sea, indicating fond hopes that part of Prester John's country might even border on the Atlantic.

European encounters with previously unknown lands beyond the ocean recalled antique legends, but as those on its eastern shores began to think about venturing into the ocean, the possibilities also stimulated new ways of thinking. Europeans were concerned that their own societies were steadily being transformed by new wealth and changing social relations. Formerly, according to this thinking, all levels of society had played an essential role, and great lords took responsibility for those who lived on their estates. Now, the poor and their needs were ignored by greedy and grasping rich men. Lands in and across the Atlantic became screens on which Europeans could project their ideas about how new societies, untouched by inherited corruption, could be formed.

Sir Thomas More, the scholar-statesman who would be executed by Henry VIII for refusing to compromise his principles, inaugurated a genre with his book *Utopia*, published in Latin in 1516 and posthumously in English in 1551. *Utopia*, which means "no place" in Greek, is a dialogue between a humanist like More and a mythical venturer, Raphael Hythloday, who was said to have sailed to America with Amerigo Vespucci and stayed behind when Vespucci departed for home on his third and last voyage in 1502. Hythloday was thus able to describe intimately the society of the Utopians which, with its disdain for riches and respect for accomplishment and piety, contrasted so vividly with the European societies his readers inhabited. *Utopia* was a huge success and went through many editions; its name became synonymous with the notion of an ideal society.

The great English statesman and scientist Sir Francis Bacon wrote his utopian tract *The New Atlantis* at the end of his life. Although it was left unfinished when he died in 1626, it was published with his essays in the same year. Bacon's book, like More's, began with a fictitious traveler. This migrant was on a voyage in the South Sea, which was the contemporary name for the Pacific Ocean. The travelers stumbled on an island where they found an advanced society. The island's governor told the travelers that their ancient seafarers had frequented all the places that Europeans of his time thought they were just now discovering, including "the great Atlantis (that you call America)," and he added that "the inhabitants of the great Atlantis did flourish" with magnificent cities and landscapes. This civilization was destroyed, not by an earthquake as Plato wrote, but by a great flood. The inundation continued a long time, so most of the people and animals died of hunger; the few survivors lived on barren mountaintops. Thus, wrote Bacon, the American people, plants, and animals were still recovering from this catastrophe; their cultures were younger by at least a thousand years than those

Sir Thomas More's Utopia *included this map of the legendary island. Maps conveyed information about newly discovered places, but could also engage readers in new thinking about society and culture stimulated by the discoveries.* By permission of the Folger Shakespeare Library of other parts of the earth. For their part, the people of his New Atlantis, which they called Bensalem, had an advanced society centered on a sophisticated scientific academy called Salomon's House.[10]

Some Europeans who recorded their American experience thought they had seen evidence confirming that the American continents had been underwater in ancient times. Two such reports came from sixteenth-century Brazil—one from a Calvinist preacher and the other from a Jesuit. Jean de Léry was a French Huguenot minister who went to Brazil as a missionary in the 1550s. He wrote of the Indians that "mingled in their songs there was mention of waters that had once swelled so high above their bounds that all the earth was covered, and all the people in the world were drowned, except for their ancestors, who took refuge in the highest trees." He believed these memories must refer to "the universal flood that occurred in the time of Noah," and that they had been passed from father to son and had been somewhat corrupted in the process, as in the detail of people saving themselves by climbing trees.[11]

Fernão Cardim, a Portuguese Jesuit priest who was in Brazil in the late sixteenth century, wrote extensively about his impressions of the land and people. His manuscript was seized by an English shipmaster, Francis Cooke, who captured the ship on which Cardim sailed in 1601, and Cooke sold Cardim's work to Richard Hakluyt for twenty shillings. Hakluyt had it translated but did not print it in his collections, so the translation was finally published in 1625 by Hakluyt's successor Samuel Purchas. Purchas did not know the identity of the author and remarked that he seemed to have been a "Portugall frier or Jesuite." Cardim wrote that "It seemeth that this people hath no knowledge of the beginning and creation of the world, but of the deluge it seemeth they have some notice."[12]

Such evidence was interpreted by many people as showing that these lands had been affected by Noah's flood in the Bible. Others remembered the huge flood that was said to have destroyed Atlantis in accounts all the way back to Plato. George Sandys published his translation of the ancient Roman poet Ovid's *Metamorphoses* after his years in early Virginia. Ovid wrote of sea shells far from the coast and drew the conclusion that the lands where these were found had once been under water, and Sandys added a note saying "Such have I seene in America."[13]

As the magnitude of the lands across the ocean began to become clear, Europeans' first impulse was to try to fit them into their own established intellectual and legal structures. Portuguese navigators had pioneered the difficult route around Africa—a far more challenging feat

The title page of The Mariners Mirrour, *translated from the Dutch original written by Lucas Jansson Wagenaer, shows the kinds of knowledge and instruments required for Atlantic navigation. The English translation was published in 1588 and all English navigation manuals were called Waggoners for 200 years.* By permission of the Folger Shakespeare Library than sailing to America—and had rediscovered the island groups in the Ocean Sea to the west early in the fifteenth century. Then at the end of the century the Genoese mariner Columbus, sailing for Spain, had stumbled on the Caribbean Islands in his search for a direct sea route to Asia. Shortly after his return, Spain and Portugal appealed to Pope Alexander VI to issue a ruling concerning their rights to newly revealed lands. The pope issued a bull in 1493 creating a division line 100 leagues west of the Cape Verde Islands off the African coast and stipulated that Spain should have rights to all lands not currently in Christian hands lying west of that line. Portuguese dissatisfaction with this settlement led to further negotiations and the Treaty of Tordesillas in 1494 that moved the demarcation line to 370 leagues west of the Cape Verdes. Both the bull and the treaty were based on the notion that non-Christians could not truly possess lands; they could only occupy them. No European at the time would have had any idea how many millions of people could be affected by these negotiations.

European Christians' arrogance in assuming that they could divide up the world's lands among themselves stemmed in part from contemporary Christians' belief that they lived in momentous times, possibly even the culmination of world history foretold in the biblical book of Revelation. Columbus himself observed the earth's tendency to bulge at the equator and he linked the flow of water at the mouth of the Orinoco River with descriptions of the Garden of Eden. He wrote to Ferdinand and Isabella, "I believe that the earthly Paradise lies here, which no one can enter except by God's leave."[14] Jesus had charged his apostles with the task of preaching the Gospel to the whole world, and Christians believed that Christ's second coming and the end of history would occur when that was accomplished and the world was converted. Within their own mental universe, it was logical to assume that God had kept these two huge continents and all their people hidden until it was time for these great culminating events. In accordance with God's will, European Christians would embark on the task of bringing Christianity to the Indians knowing that God had brought them to the point where they would be receptive. Everything was happening in accord with God's unfolding plan.

Europeans' thoughts about the origins of the American people added intensity to this discussion. Orthodoxy demanded a single creation, so the vast populations in the two newly revealed continents must be descended from some past diaspora. Beginning in the sixteenth century, Spanish intellectuals began to argue that the Americans, or some of them, were the descendants of the Ten Lost Tribes of Israel. Diego

Durán, a Dominican priest, proposed this theory in his history of the Aztecs published in the 1580s. Spanish friar Juan de Abreu de Galindo wrote a history of the Canary Islands in the sixteenth century. In it, he denied that the Canarians were the lost Jews and argued that the inhabitants of Mexico actually retained many Jewish practices and were clearly the long-sought lost Jews. In the next century, Manasseh ben Israel published his theory that the Americans were members of the Ten Lost Tribes of Israel; he came from a Portuguese Sephardic family that had moved to the Netherlands. His book, *Mikveh Israel*, first published in Amsterdam in the middle of the seventeenth century, was quickly translated into English as *The Hope of Israel*. He wrote that his theory was based on the report of a Portuguese Jew named Antonio Montezinos who had lived in South America for twenty years and had encountered Indians who maintained their Jewish customs in Ecuador's Quito province.[15] The idea that the Indians were the lost Jews fed Christians' belief that God had revealed America's existence at this time because these were the last days foretold in the biblical book of Revelation. Conversion of the Jews was an essential step toward bringing on the culmination of history.

Celestial signs intensified Christians' belief that they were living in momentous times. In 1572, a supernova appeared in the constellation Cassiopeia. The Danish astronomer Tycho Brahe analyzed this apparition with instruments that he had designed, and then published a book establishing that this was a new star, not a comet. The star that shone at the birth of Jesus was the closest analog, and many assumed this star was similarly momentous in its implications, especially when it was followed by a massive comet five years later. A conjunction of planets that occurred on December 24, 1603, coinciding with the agreed day of Jesus's birth, was also an occasion for prognostication; moreover, there was an eclipse in that same year. Other comets in 1607 and 1618 also provoked speculation.

Naming patterns reflected this sense that Europeans' activities were part of a larger purpose. The first baby boy and girl born among the Portuguese settlers on Madeira were given the names Adam and Eve. Although many ships were named after their owners or reflected other interests, names such as *Buen Jesus, Grâce-de-Dieu, Godspeed, Nuestra Señora de la Anunciada,* and *Virgin God Save Her* predominated in the early years of transatlantic voyages. The first ships sent to the English Roman Catholic colony of Maryland in the 1630s echoed not only Noah's flood but also the belief that America was a place of refuge; they were the *Ark* and the *Dove*.

Just as Europeans viewed their encounter with the Americas as evidence of their momentous assigned role in God's plan, there is evidence that America's peoples interpreted the newcomers in terms of their own religious traditions. From the beginning, Spanish venturers reported that the Indians believed the arrival of Europeans fulfilled ancient prophecies. Some thought the Americans saw the newcomers as gods. Columbus wrote that the first people he met in the Caribbean thought he and his men had come from the sky or the heavens (*cielo*). In their retellings of the story of the conquest of Mexico by Hernan Cortès, European writers asserted that he was taken for Quetzalcoatl, a bearded hero of long ago who had prophesied his own return in triumph, and that he and his men were thought to have supernatural powers. Europeans interpreted these accounts as evidence that they were carrying out God's plan.[16]

English venturers also sometimes reported that the Indians they encountered "thought we were gods." Some of these accounts were written long after the fact; others, such as Thomas Harriot's report from Roanoke in the 1580s, said the Americans viewed the newcomers as "men of an old generation many yeeres past then risen again to immortalitie."[17] As with Columbus's report that the Spanish were believed to have come from the sky, much depends on interpretation. Those, like Harriot, who learned enough of the language in the region where they lived to be able to understand something of the Indians' religion, sometimes reported the belief that when people died they went to a land under this world where they lived before being reborn again in this world. Referring to the Europeans as risen spirits might have meant that they were seen as previously dead people who were resuming life in the human sphere. The dead were dangerous, so their presence would have been spiritually charged until they were fully reintegrated into the present. Seeing the Europeans as risen spirits did not imply that they were gods in the European sense, but, as with the belief that Columbus and his men came from the sky, it might carry overtones of otherworldly meaning. Indians along the coast of North America frequently told the European newcomers that they had had advance warning from God or from their wise men about their coming. Thus, like the venturing Europeans, America's people believed the events in which they were participating might be part of a larger divine plan.

In the early days, as Europeans assimilated information about the unknown lands and peoples across the sea, some were intrigued by hints that not only were these continents populated by species of plants and animals unlike those in the Old World, but that they might be in some ways enchanted lands or at least places whose development had taken a far different course. Reports from many areas seemed to indicate that the lines between the plant and animal kingdoms, so firm in the Old World, were blurred in America. Fernão Cardim sent an observation from Brazil that he wanted European scholars to judge. He had a long and admiring description of the hummingbird, "the finest bird that can bee imagined," and he said that some of them were hatched from eggs like other birds. Others, though, came from "little bubbles." He wrote that it was a "wonderful thing" to watch a bubble being converted into a bird "and unknowne to the Philosophers." Similarly, Robert Harcourt, writing of his experience in Guiana, described the sensitive plant, which, he argued, "had assuredly the sence of feeling." If you touched a leaf, it would curl up and appear dead, but if you "cut off a leafe with a pair of Cizzers," the entire plant would seem to be dead and then fifteen minutes later it was alive again. Harcourt tried to bring some of these plants home in pots, but on the voyage home

The French explorer Samuel de Champlain drew many maps and sketches of the regions he visited. He also included this fanciful picture of a dragon in his portfolio, showing how, even for people with firsthand experience, America continued to be a place of the imagination. Courtesy of the John Carter Brown Library at Brown University "certain Monkeyes that brake loose" destroyed them. Descriptions of opossums, whose babies seemed to go back into the womb at will after birth, were also disturbing, as marsupials were unknown in Europe.[18]

Claims that America might have associations with ancient Old World cultures continued but began to be scrutinized differently in the eighteenth century. Charles-Marie de la Condamine was a mathematician and scientist who went to South America in 1735 as part of a French expedition to measure the length of a degree of latitude near the equator. He became separated from his group and embarked on a voyage down the Amazon River, and on his return to France he published an ethnographic and geographical account of the region. La Condamine referred to his reading in both Orellana and Acuña, and he was determined to find out the truth about the Amazons. He was directed to an old man whose father had actually seen them, but when he arrived, he found that the man had died. La Condamine interviewed his son, "who seem'd to be about seventy, and commanded the other Indians of that district. He assured us that his grandfather had actually seen those females. . . . He added that his grandsire had spoke with four of them." La Condamine elected to "omit certain improbable circumstances, which have no relation to the principal point. Below Coari also, the Indians everywhere gave us the same account, differing only in some few particulars, but all agreeing as to the main article." One Indian even offered to conduct him to where the Amazons lived. La Condamine also interviewed an "old soldier, of the garrison of Cayenne" who had collected accounts of "the women without husbands," and referred to reports by Spanish governors.

Ultimately, La Condamine, after applying all the tests available to him, could not conclude definitely whether Amazons lived in South America or not. One possibility was that such a "female Republick" had existed in the past but had been conquered or absorbed. He also pointed out that Indians apparently had had stories of Amazons before they were interviewed by Spaniards. But many travelers had collected these stories and written about them, so their dissemination might have occurred more recently. He did judge that if they currently existed or had existed anywhere, it would have been in America.[19]

Atlantic crossings and the intensive knowledge of other peoples and lands that followed led participants in all four continents to rethink their inherited lore about the world and its history. After the early Norse voyages, Africans were the first to venture to Atlantic islands, followed by Iberian mariners. Soon ships from all over Europe crossed the ocean, and people moving in both directions assimilated the knowledge newly available to them. The Atlantic was a new world for everyone.

CHAPTER 2

Atlantic Beginnings

B efore people living in the four continents bordering the Atlantic began to reorient their gaze toward the ocean, there was movement within those lands that set the stage for large-scale transoceanic movement. Desire for exotic products fed much of this movement, but it was also driven by religious ideology as peoples worked toward the goals they believed destiny had designed for them.

On the ocean's eastern shores, Africa was the original golden land. Camels and the merchants who drove them began to crisscross the Sahara, Africa's great inland sea of sand, in the fourth century as the Roman Empire was in its final decline in Europe. They carried salt, fruit, and woven cloth inland, and gold, kola nuts, and slaves to North Africa. The Sahara linked the south to the ports of North Africa on the Mediterranean, and to the Atlantic.

Muslim armies conquered North Africa and swept northward into western Europe at the beginning of the eighth century. The invaders from North Africa, including many Sephardic Jews as well as Muslims, overran the Iberian peninsula. After their victory in 718, Iberia became the province of Al-Andaluz. Over the next several centuries, Christian armies pushed the North Africans, whom Europeans called Moors, out of the conquered lands until only the Emirate of Granada remained by the thirteenth century. In the course of this continuing struggle, Portugal achieved recognition of its separate existence as a kingdom; Spain accepted Portugal's independence, and the pope endorsed the agreement.

In 1492, Isabella of Castile and Ferdinand of Aragon, having united their two states by their marriage, completed the Reconquest by winning control of Granada and eliminating the last of Moorish power. Castile and Aragon formed the nucleus of the modern kingdom of Spain, and Ferdinand and Isabella were henceforth known as "The Catholic Monarchs." Coincidentally, in the same year they also initiated the conceptualization of the Atlantic by sending Columbus out into the Ocean Sea in search of the westward passage to Asia.

Islam may have been expelled from Western Europe, but the assurance implied by the Spanish monarchs' title was short-lived. The eastern Christian Byzantine empire had fallen to the Ottomans in 1453. The expansive Ottoman Empire, whose capital was Istanbul, formerly Constantinople, threatened Christian states in Eastern Europe. Events in the East directly affected Europe's Atlantic rim when Ferdinand of Aragon was succeeded by his grandson Charles in 1516. Through his paternal Hapsburg line he became the Holy Roman Emperor Charles V in 1519, and resisting Islamic expansion once again became the concern of a Spanish king.

Tremors of another sort were felt in the Hapsburg realm at the same time. In 1517, Martin Luther, a priest in Wittenberg, distributed his Ninety-Five Theses arguing that Christians should look to the Bible as their sole source of religious authority and denying the validity of the Roman Catholic hierarchy. Although others had presented such ideas earlier, their voices had been silenced. Luther's thinking found a receptive audience and spread rapidly, especially in northern Europe.

Religion was a matter of state in Europe in this period; the people were supposed to follow the religion of the ruler. Many of the German states became officially Lutheran, as did the Scandinavian countries. Protestantism was by definition a movement inclined to splintering as believers interpreted the Bible for themselves, and other competing forms quickly emerged, especially that led by John Calvin. Calvin's Switzerland followed his interpretation, as did Scotland and England. The Low Countries, which were under Hapsburg control, split; the part that remained Roman Catholic would become Belgium and the Calvinist north became the Netherlands. Because religion was a matter of official policy, these categories masked turmoil and uncertainty. Countries such as France, which remained officially Roman Catholic, often had large and dedicated Protestant populations; French Protestants were known as Huguenots. In every Protestant country, many remained faithful to the old religion and practiced their beliefs covertly. Protestant regimes could be threatened not only by those who wanted to go back to the faith that gave them comfort but also by the centrifugal forces within Protestantism.

England saw threats on both sides. It became a Protestant country under Henry VIII in the early sixteenth century, but his daughter Mary restored Roman Catholicism when she came to the throne. His second daughter, Elizabeth, returned the nation to Protestantism, but powerful Catholic nobles saw the possibility of another restoration, especially with Mary Queen of Scots who had a claim to the throne they deemed to rival Elizabeth's. Ordinary people could only lie low and hope for stability. On the other side, many Protestants wanted to push the logic of the Reformation much further. The more extreme among them, called Puritans by their enemies, wanted to abolish the church hierarchy and, following the doctrine of the priesthood of all believers, place all religious interpretation in the hands of individuals.

Persecution and potential civil war always loomed. France was rent by war between religious parties, and the Netherlanders fought for eighty years to free themselves from Hapsburg domination. Every nation sought to control belief and to ferret out hidden pockets of dissension. The Spanish Inquisition was the strongest effort to create ideological uniformity. It sought not only Jews and Muslims, but also those who had, or whose parents had, converted to Christianity. These Conversos, or New Christians, were to be eliminated as unsafe; fleeing Sephardic Jews then went to the Protestant Netherlands and to the Ottoman Empire, the most tolerant countries in Europe. Tensions culminated in a Europe-wide conflict, the Thirty Years' War, between 1618 and 1648. England stayed out of the European war, but that nation was torn by Civil War between the Puritan-controlled parliament and the king in the last years of the continental conflict.

All these tensions and concerns directly affected Europe's engagement with the Atlantic. American treasure allowed countries like Spain to fuel their campaigns in Europe. Relative poverty made Atlantic ventures attractive to other countries who hoped for similar gains that would allow them to rival or stand up to Spain. Religious dissidents of all stripes, when persecution loomed too dangerously, were prepared to pick up stakes and move across the ocean in order to find peace and security in which to establish their own worship. Religion may have been the only thing sufficiently important to provoke ordinary people to give up everything they knew and try again in an unknown land.

The Thirty Years' War made previous refuges in Europe unsafe for dissidents such as the Separatist Puritans, known to Americans as the Pilgrims, who had lived in the Netherlands. As the war began in Europe, they made arrangements to emigrate to New England, which they did in 1620. An even larger number of them went to Virginia at the same time. Also in 1620, George Calvert, Lord Baltimore, was granted a patent for a settlement in Newfoundland where he hoped to create a refuge for English Roman Catholics. Newfoundland's climate proved to be too harsh and in 1634 Baltimore founded the colony of Maryland for his group. English Puritans went to New England in very large numbers in the decade of the 1630s as they increasingly feared persecution at home.

English engagement with America was in large part driven by religious rivalries in Europe.

The Ottoman Empire, expansive in the Old World, disdained interest in the Atlantic. The great seventeenth-century traveler and writer Evliya Çelebi recorded that a Portuguese named Kolon and a Spaniard named Padre had come to Sultan Bayezid II in 1484 and offered the New World, which they had already discovered, to him. He replied that "Mecca and Medina and this Old World are enough to conquer, we don't need to cross the ocean and go tremendous distances." Padre and Kolon then offered America to the king of Spain, according to Çelebi.[1] In that year, 1484, Columbus had reportedly first proposed an expedition to reach Asia by sailing west when he sought funding from the Portuguese king. He also approached the French and English monarchs before winning Spanish support, but Çelebi's account is the only mention of his having spoken with the Ottoman sultan.

The African states on the Mediterranean were Muslim; all, except for Morocco, which bordered on the Atlantic as well as the inland sea, were part of the Ottoman Empire. The trade routes linking West Africa to the Levant at the eastern edge of the Mediterranean brought knowledge as well as products; Islam made its way westward on these routes.

By the time Europeans arrived on West African shores, networks of Muslim merchants operated all along the coast and in the interior; although they spoke different languages, their religious allegiance facilitated sharing of information and products. These merchants were also Islamic scholars devoted to studying the Koran and spreading the teachings of Islam. Because of their learning, they functioned as judges as they traveled.

Among Europeans, the Iberians took the lead in seaborne trade and exploration partly because of their location but also due to their long experience of Muslim presence. North African scholars had preserved much of the ancient learning of the Greeks and Romans that had been lost in Western Europe. They were far advanced in mathematics and philosophy. North Africans, in turn, benefited from their access to the learning of India and, through South Asian sources, to Chinese science. Arabic numerals, which made modern mathematics possible, originated in India. The compass, without which sailing out of sight of land was unthinkable, was invented in China and came to North Africa via South Asia. Gunpowder and printing also came along these routes. Sir Francis Bacon, whose utopian *New Atlantis* fantasized about the possibility of an ideal society, wrote in another work about the three inventions that had "changed the Face and State of affairs of the whole World." They

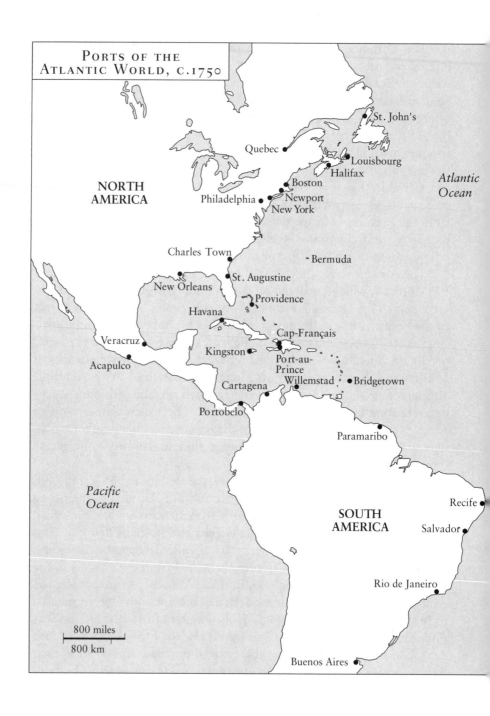

PORTS OF THE
ATLANTIC WORLD, C.1750

NORTH
AMERICA

Atlantic
Ocean

St. John's

Quebec

Louisbourg
Halifax

Boston
Philadelphia   Newport
New York

Charles Town

- Bermuda

St. Augustine
New Orleans

Providence

Havana

Cap-Français

Veracruz

Kingston

Port-au-
Prince

Acapulco

Willemstad   Bridgetown

Cartagena

Portobelo

Paramaribo

Pacific
Ocean

SOUTH
AMERICA

Recife

Salvador

Rio de Janeiro

800 miles

800 km

Buenos Aires

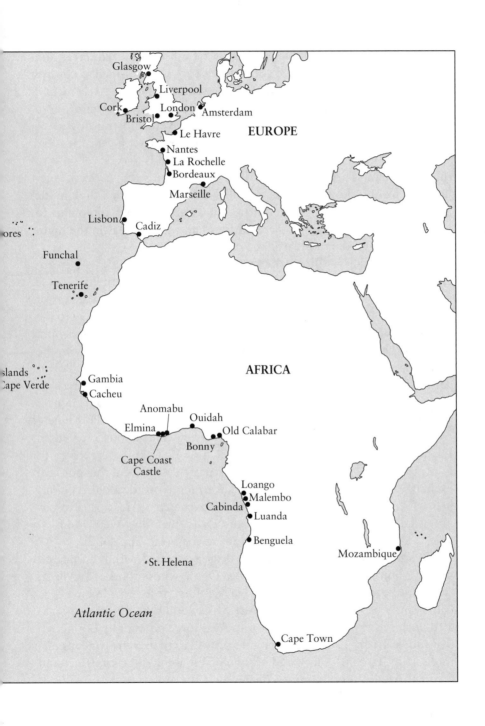

Glasgow

Liverpool

Cork London
Bristol Amsterdam

Le Havre

Nantes
La Rochelle
Bordeaux

Marseille

Lisbon
Cadiz

EUROPE

ores

Funchal

Tenerife

AFRICA

slands
Cape Verde

Gambia
Cacheu

Anomabu
Ouidah
Elmina
Old Calabar
Bonny
Cape Coast
Castle

Loango
Malembo
Cabinda
Luanda

Benguela

Mozambique

St. Helena

Atlantic Ocean

Cape Town

were "the Art of Printing, Gun-powder, and the Sea mens compass"; all three came into Europe from China through Africa.[2]

Portugal was just across the narrow mouth of the Mediterranean; as that nation's leaders looked south to Morocco, they hoped to control the flow of essential salt, the only food preservative known to them, and luxury goods into Europe. Portuguese mariners began to venture into the Atlantic in their fast and lightweight caravels, moving down the coast in search of gold, pepper, and spices in the fifteenth century a few years before Columbus would catch the trade winds and travel west to the Caribbean. Through the sixteenth century, western African kingdoms of Kongo, Loango, Angola, and Ndongo established diplomatic and trading relationships with Portugal and sent their own diplomats to Lisbon. Except for Loanga, these nations had their centers in the highlands away from the more arid coast.

Kongo, which had long dominated the region through its bureaucracy and justice system, shaped the early relationships with Portuguese traders. The Portuguese had hoped to find the Christian descendants of Prester John's people. Instead they met rulers who were receptive to the initiation of diplomatic ties, and who welcomed missionaries and teachers. The Kongolese king, Nzinga a Nkuwu, was baptized with the name João I in 1491. Children of elite families in Kongo went to Portugal for their education. Some Africans who studied in Europe became priests; on their return to Kongo, they worked alongside Portuguese priests. The pope created bishoprics in both Kongo and the Portuguese colony of Angola to the south, and a Jesuit college was created in Luanda to educate African clergy. But although they were open to European influences, Kongo leaders strictly controlled the cultural exchange, adapting Christian categories to match traditional religious beliefs. In the maelstrom of cultural exchange, Africans evolved imported religious practices into forms with which they were comfortable, and these spread through missions to the north and south.

Religious figures such as Ogun, a deity associated with hunting and war, continued to thrive in West Africa. Ogun, whose roots are ancient, came to be linked to iron and blacksmiths. Iron bars as well as Christianity were imported into West Africa, and Ogun became associated with the expanded work in iron. As a force potentially both creative and destructive, Ogun's attributes proved to be extremely adaptable to evolving circumstances and technologies. Religious rituals around Ogun thrived in communities throughout the Americas, especially in Brazil and the Caribbean. In Haiti, Ogou, as the spirit is known there, joined Christian saints as objects of reverence in Vodou.

King Dom Garcia of Kongo, who was known for his Christian piety, welcomes three Capuchin missionaries. This image, showing the humble posture of the Europeans before the royal court, was created in the middle of the seventeenth century by an Italian Capuchin missionary. Giovanni Antonio Cavazzi, *Istorica Descrizione de Tre Regni Congo, Matamba, et Angola* (Milan: Nelle stampe dell'Agnelli, 1690)

Europeans found that the coastal African kingdoms had well-established trade networks with Islamic inland states, initially linking with the empire of Mali, which controlled the headwaters of three great rivers—the Niger, Senegal, and Gambia—that flowed between the West African coast and the interior. In the fifteenth century the great Songhay empire came to power as the Mali kingdom crumbled. These Islamic empires looked to the east more than the west. Mansa Musa, the Mali king who built numerous mosques in his kingdom, made a celebrated pilgrimage to Mecca in 1324, and the Songhay emperors continued these connections. In 1352, the Moroccan legal scholar Ibn Battuta capped a lifetime of travel in North Africa, Asia, and Europe by traversing the Sahara to spend more than a year in Mali on the Niger River before being recalled to Fez by the sultan. He was dismayed by the ways in which practices in Mali, informed by local religious traditions, diverged from what he considered proper Muslim form, but was fascinated by what he saw there and impressed by the people's devotion to Islam, particularly parents' firm insistence on children learning the Koran by heart.[3]

In the early period of regular Portuguese voyages to the African coast, the Europeans learned that the African kingdoms had very sophisticated vessels of their own patrolling the coasts and rivers and they were fully capable of defending against raids from the sea. Some people who lived along the coast of modern Ghana, known as the Gold Coast in the days of the slave trade, ventured out into the ocean in their canoes. Others restricted navigation to the lagoons, and oral tradition records Akans encountering Europeans "at the mouth of the ocean." The newcomers were named "lagoon people," meaning people from beyond the known world.[4]

These newcomers engaged in and added to the existing trades. Horses were an especially prized commodity, and also iron bars and cloth flowed in from Europe. Slaves, gold, beeswax, and hides were taken back to Europe. Portugal traded these commodities from Africa with other European countries in order to gain the grain, textiles, and brass and glass items in demand in Africa. In the sixteenth century, Portuguese resident traders formed enclaves along the coast as Muslim traders had done earlier. Communities inhabited by Africans and Portuguese grew up, and people of mixed African and Portuguese descent soon came to dominate the trades in these settlements. Trade languages, creole versions that mixed simplified European and local languages, evolved, and women were very active in this commerce.

These relationships were carefully formed and required finesse. In 1575, Portugal began to build fortified permanent bases along the coast of Angola. A few years later, in 1579, the Portuguese king invaded Morocco, directly across the Strait of Gilbraltar. Controlling Morocco would have given Portugal command of traffic into and out of the Mediterranean as well as the trade traveling north and south, but the ill-considered invasion ended in disaster at El-Ksar el-Kebir (known in Europe as Alcazarquivir) in 1579, a battle in which the Portuguese king and many of his nobles died; the Moroccan king and his principal rival also died in this Battle of the Three Kings. Philip II of Spain added the Portuguese crown to his own and Morocco soon extended its own influence south, exerting control over the Songhay empire and the entire Sahara at the end of the sixteenth century. The Europeans were kept to the coast. Portuguese historian João de Barros wrote that the very hand of God kept them from the interior: "In all the entrances of this great

The same Italian priest who portrayed Dom Garcia also painted these Kongo ironworkers. Ironworking played an important religious as well as technological role, and the choice to depict men engaged in daily pursuits as well as important leaders shows the range of interests among European consumers anxious to understand other cultures.
Courtesy of the Pitt Rivers Museum at the University of Oxford

Aethiopia, he has placed a striking angel with a flaming sword of deadly fevers, who prevents us from penetrating into the interior to the springs of this garden, whence proceed rivers of gold that flow to the sea."[5]

On the western side of the ocean, movements of people and ideas also preceded the Atlantic connection. Great empires—in the Valley of Mexico, on the Mississippi River, and in the Peruvian highlands—had collapsed or declined in the centuries before 1492; adverse climate conditions, particularly drought, may have hastened these events. The Toltecs had succeeded the great Maya culture in Mexico. In the wake of the Toltec empire's demise, various groups were drawn into the Valley of Mexico, and the Mexica ultimately emerged as the dominant power among them. Mexica wanderings followed the lead of the God Huitzilopochtlli; they knew they had arrived at their intended destination, an island in Lake Texcoco, when they saw an eagle perched atop a prickly

This representation of the founding of Tenochtitlan comes from the Codex Duran, a history of New Spain by a Dominican friar. The Mexica leaders knew they had arrived at their destined location when they saw a prickly pear cactus topped by an eagle with a snake in its beak. Snark/Art Resource, NY, ART167171

pear cactus with a snake in its beak. They named their city Tenochtitlan. As Columbus embarked on his first transatlantic voyage, the Mexica, or Aztecs, were consolidating their position; their city was a center of both trade and military might. Tenochtitlan, with great public buildings around magnificent squares, held 200,000 people, a population greater than in the largest city in contemporary Europe.

In the Andean region to the south, the Incas and their expansive empire were similarly consolidating their power in the century before they encountered the Spanish. Building on earlier systems, the Incas incorporated many different groups into their huge bureaucratic system centered at Cuzco; it was the largest state in the Americas in 1492. They built massive public works, including huge networks of canals that made large-scale agriculture possible. When the Spanish entered the region, they made use of some of the Incas' systems of recruiting labor through tribute from subject peoples. And priests who attempted to convert the Indians were preaching to people whose religion had already been altered by invaders.

Along the Amazon in the territory that became Brazil, there were massive settlements. The expedition of Francisco de Orellana, floating down the Amazon in the early 1540s, came upon a very large urban center where they had a frightening encounter. Their ships were surrounded by more than two hundred boats, each carrying at least twenty Indians; some were so large they had forty men in them. The boats were very colorfully decorated and they carried musicians playing "many trumpets and drums, and pipes on which they play with their mouths, and rebecs, which among these people have three strings; and they came on with so much noise and shouting and in such good order that we were astonished." This musical introduction actually presaged an attack. The Spanish managed to fend off the Indians with their guns and crossbows and noted huge squadrons of men on the riverbank who were "playing on instruments and dancing about, [each man] with a pair of palm leaves in his hands, manifesting very great joy upon seeing that we were passing beyond their villages." The chronicler, Fray Gaspar de Carvajal, considered the sight very impressive, "a marvelous thing to see."[6] Modern archaeological investigation has found evidence of such massive settlements supported by fields of earth that was artificially enriched so as to support agriculture; archaeologists have also uncovered evidence of large human-made reservoirs.

North of the Rio Grande River, the Mississippian culture spread east and west from its center, the city of Cahokia, on the Mississippi River near the site of modern St. Louis. It was a successor to earlier cultures, evidence of which can been be seen in the great ceremonial mounds they built. Cahokia declined and was ultimately abandoned completely in the later thirteenth century, possibly in response to changing environmental conditions. The meandering expedition of the Spanish explorer Hernando de Soto through the southeastern part of the future United States in the 1540s encountered many satellite mound-building centers, including those of the well-documented Natchez Indians. Throughout the Southeast, smaller mound-building centers continued.

Farther north, five Iroquoian-speaking tribes—the Senecas, Onondagas, Cayugas, Oneidas, and Mohawks—joined together to form the Haudenosaunee, the Great League of Peace, in the same period when the Mexica and the Incas were consolidating their empires. The league was founded in response to the teachings of Deganawidah, the Heavenly Messenger, who had been sent to stop the cycle of war that was destroying the people. His first disciple was Hiawatha, who became his spokesman. Deganawidah won support by performing a series of miracles, one of which, blotting out the sun, may have coincided with a complete solar eclipse in 1451.

Paul LeJeune, a Jesuit missionary in Canada, recorded Deganawidah's message as he heard it from league emissaries: "The land shall be beautiful, the river shall have no more waves, one may go everywhere without fear."[7] The creation of the league meant that the five nations would not make war on each other, and it was maintained by a council that determined the rules of conduct among the nations and oversaw elaborate rituals of reconciliation. This unified group emerged as the most powerful in the Northeast.

Political and religious change was taking place all around the Atlantic, but even more fundamental conditions affected both sides of the ocean at the time when their inhabitants became aware of the others. These physical phenomena united the Atlantic world before human actions did. The entire circum-Atlantic land experienced a period of extreme weather conditions characterized by colder temperatures and, often, prolonged and catastrophic drought. Mean temperatures were so clearly colder than in the period before or after that historical climatologists label this period the Little Ice Age. The evidence suggests that it began sometime in the fifteenth century, probably a few decades before Columbus's first voyage, and that it began to fade in the eighteenth century. Its cause is equally unclear, although one hypothesis is that the sun's output of energy decreased slightly; some say that the sun "blinked." Observers in the seventeenth century, especially those who had access to the newly developed telescope, noted a marked decline in sunspots, and modern scientists join their early modern counterparts in theorizing that sunspot diminution may have been a visible sign of the sun's declining activity. Others argue that the earth may wobble on its axis, somewhat like a spinning top. A slight change in the planet's tilt toward the sun might account for the Little Ice Age. Scientists also recognize short-term factors. Intensely cold runs of years resulted from the eruptions of volcanoes, such as Huanyaputina in southern Peru in 1600 and Mount Vesuvius in 1631. A large eruption throws massive amounts of sulfur dioxide into the upper atmosphere, which creates a mirror-like effect reflecting back the sun's light and heat.

In Europe, colder temperatures took marginal agricultural lands out of cultivation; the growing season had become too short to bring crops to fruition. Core samples taken from the bed of Lake Bosumtwi in Ghana demonstrate that West Africa suffered extreme drought conditions throughout the height of the Little Ice Age, 1450 to 1700. Central Africa also experienced long periods of devastating drought during this period, but eastern Africa was unusually wet. Pollen studies in archaeological sites show that the plant landscape changed across North America in this period; and evidence has emerged of periodic dry conditions throughout much of the sixteenth century. Drought plagued much of the western regions, resulting in abandonment of settlements and consolidation of peoples. Catastropic drought also affected wide swaths of land to the south.

Agriculture was always an uncertain and difficult pursuit in this period. Typically, farmers reserved a portion of the harvest as seed for next year's crop. If drought reduced the productivity of the land and its plants, it became harder and harder to reserve seed that people needed immediately for food. Gathering wild plants, also reduced in size and number, could help sustain communities over the first or second year of a drought, but prolonged drought depleted farmers' ability to recover. Thus, even after normal conditions resumed, recovery of normal yields might take years. Dispersal of population into smaller units spread over the countryside, where they could gather wild foods, was a natural response to drought all around the Atlantic.

In all cultures around the Atlantic, environmental distress caused more than physical disarray, as it led people to question their rapport with the deities they worshipped. Religious worship kept believers in the proper relationship to the divine, and the supernatural forces governing the universe responded by providing the cycle of rainfall and sunshine that allowed the crops to grow. If this cycle was disrupted, what did it mean about the people's links to the spirit world? Christians held days of prayer and fasting; congregations came together to try to examine their behavior and win God's approval. In Africa, worshippers performed rituals at sacred sites to propitiate powers who withheld needed rain.

In America, early European venturers sometimes reported that Indians came to them to see if the Christian God would give them rain when their own deities would not; the way they put it was that "their gods were angrie." Little Ice Age conditions affected all regions around the Atlantic, but in America the overwhelming sense that the people had been abandoned by their traditional spiritual forces was radically intensified as Old World diseases to which they had no acquired immunity mowed down Indian populations. Diseases endemic in the rest of the world were unknown on the American continents, and America's people thus had no immunity to pathogens ranging from those lethal in the Old World such as smallpox and typhus to the usually mild influenza and measles. Extreme environmental conditions affected everyone; all had to examine their own relationship to God in times of famine and hardship. But Indians who saw their communities struck down by epidemics had to come to terms with the fact that Europeans were not affected in the same way. It was hard not to draw the conclusion that the divine powers in the universe had somehow transferred their favor.

Diseases in a population with widespread acquired immunity tend to strike serially; as the first affected die or recover, others become sick, and in this way the disease moves through a community a few people at a time. Where there is no acquired immunity, the spread is very fast and victims all become sick at once. Thus there is no one to fetch firewood or water, and people may die of exposure and dehydration as much as of the disease itself. Traditional healing methods such as sweat baths may have accelerated debility. Observers described bones lying scattered on top of the earth where the living were too few or too weak to bury the dead. The sense of loss and abandonment, of living in a universe that had broken its agreement with humanity, must have been profound.

Everyone involved in new relationships and circumstances was forced to think about the meaning of what they had always taken for granted. Christopher Columbus resisted the idea that he had actually stumbled on continents of whose existence contemporary Europeans had previously been completely unaware; through his four transatlantic voyages he continued to insist that his landfalls had been on the coast of Asia. He had expected to find Asia at about the location of the Caribbean region where he landed because he based his calculations on the work of the ancient geographer Ptolemy, who had underestimated the circumference of the earth, and because reports of medieval travelers had exaggerated the extent of Asia so that maps showed it extending farther east than it actually does. Within his lifetime, however, voyages led by Amerigo Vespucci and John Cabot began the process of delineating the shape and extent of the eastern American coastlines, and Europeans quickly accepted the notion that an entirely new world had been found. Juan de la Cosa, who sailed with both Columbus and Vespucci, made the first world map with a sketchy representation of America on it in 1500, only seven years after Columbus returned from his first voyage with news of his discoveries. Two years later the Cantino Planisphere, a map acquired by Alberto Cantino, a diplomat from Ferrara, showed Portuguese discoveries including the outline of Brazil and a highly developed rendition of Africa's west coast. In 1507, Martin Waldseemüller created a map showing two continents on the ocean's western shores and wrote the name America on the southern one.

All of the lands surrounding the ocean were changed by the beginning of regular transatlantic contact. Continents whose great centers were inland became reoriented toward the coast, and previously marginal peoples and lands were now in the forefront of development. England, for example, went from being, as the poet John Donne wrote, "the suburbs of the Old World," to a position of leadership in the new commerce. On the African coast and in North America and Brazil on the western Atlantic, groups that had participated in trade and culture in very limited ways now became the brokers of the trades and amassed power as a result. The Sahara continued to function as a great inland

This world map, created by Martin Waldseemuller in 1507, was published just fourteen years after Columbus returned from his first voyage. It was the first map to apply the name America to the newly-revealed lands. Library of Congress, G3200 CT000725

sea and the trade caravans continued to travel across it, so the Atlantic trades were supplementary. These effects, the shift of power to formerly small groups on the Atlantic coast, were also felt less dramatically in the parts of America where the Spanish went because they entered through the Caribbean, America's counterpart to the Mediterranean, and thereby reached the great cosmopolitan centers within a few years. Whereas European outposts on the east coast of North America and in Brazil expanded slowly, the Spanish empire reached its full extent within the first few decades and kept these dimensions throughout the colonial period.

Although it would take generations for these effects to be fully assimilated, Americans very quickly became consumers of European and African products and culture. Time and again Europeans thought they were venturing into territory where no Old World people had ever been, only to find evidence that the Indians already knew about the people coming from across the sea. In 1501, eight years after Columbus returned from his first voyage, a Portuguese expedition led by Gaspar Corte Real, looking for the eastern end of the passage to the Pacific that all Europeans believed must exist, came onto the far northern American coast. They "forcibly kidnapped about fifty men and women of this country" and brought them back to Europe. Pietro Pasqualigo, the

Venetian ambassador in Lisbon wrote home the startling news that these Indians had items he recognized as coming from his own city: "these men have brought from there a piece of a broken gilt sword, which certainly seems to have been made in Italy. One of the boys was wearing in his ears two silver rings which without doubt seem to have been made in Venice." We do not know for certain the date at which large numbers of fishing ships began to converge on Newfoundland and Maine, but clearly the Indians of those parts knew much about Europeans at a very early date. We know about those forced migrants of 1501 because Italian diplomats were assiduous in finding out the news and sending it home. It was Alberto Cantino who wrote home to Ferrara the news that more than fifty Indians had been taken captive; the next year he would manage to acquire the map to which his name, rather than that of the maker, is forever attached.[8]

The search for the passage to Asia continued; it would not end until the expedition of Lewis and Clark in the early nineteenth century demonstrated that there is no system of waterways that allows navigation across the continent. A quarter of a century after Corte Real's voyage, a Portuguese navigator named Estevão Gomes, who sailed under a commission from Spain's Charles V, explored the coast of North America from New England northward looking for "a strait which may exist between Florida and the country called Baccalaos." According to Peter Martyr, who wrote his story, "rather than return with empty hands," he seized fifty-eight Indians, "all innocent and half naked." When he returned to Spain, rumors spread that he had brought "a ship-load of cloves and precious stones," because one man on the dock mistook the word *esclavos* (slaves) for *clavos* (cloves) and rushed to court with the news. Martyr derided "the partisans of Gomes" who, "without comprehending the stupidity of this man," celebrated his supposed cargo because finding cloves might have indicated that he had encountered people who had commerce with Asia. Martyr suggested that henceforth Spain should concentrate on the south: "It is towards the south, not towards the frozen north, that those who seek fortune should bend their way; for everything at the equator is rich."[9]

The north did have products very much desired in Europe, however. On many parts of the American coast the earliest relationships all required cooperation, or at least acquiescence, from the native people. In the north, hundreds of ships came every summer to take fish from the rich Newfoundland Banks back to a protein-starved Europe. Roman Catholics ate fish rather than meat on certain days every week as an act of piety, and the fish was largely supplied by America. The fur trade began as a spinoff from the fishing, and it was initiated and built by vast American networks. Indian hunters, often far in the Canadian interior, hunted the beaver and prepared the pelts. Because of these relationships, the coastal Indians, especially the Iroquoian-speaking Hurons, became very powerful, and Americans hundreds of miles from the European bases became owners of products they could not formerly have had. French venturers and entrepreneurs, who conducted the coastal portion of this trade, understood that it would be less viable if large numbers of Europeans came to settle. France, with its religious wars in the sixteenth century, did not see a need to export population. These two factors combined to make Canada more thinly settled by Europeans than other parts of the eastern Americas.

European commodities, especially metal tools and items such as beads, were central to the fur trade, but European involvement in this trade also facilitated widespread dissemination of native-produced goods. Wampum was one such commodity, and it was highly prized because it was spiritually charged. The best source of the quahog shells from which wampum was made is the shore of Long Island Sound, so the effects of the fur trade were felt profoundly there. Groups such as the Narragansetts and the Pequots, who lived along the Sound's northern shore, became very powerful as they took up the role of producing and controlling the flow of wampum. Steel drills from Europe made it possible for a single producer to make and pierce many beads in the time it formerly took to make only one and so these tribes became, as New England's William Wood wrote, the "mint-masters" of the northeast.[10]

The trajectory of Spain's early relationship with the Americas was different because entry through the Caribbean brought them close to the great population centers. In the first decades they had small agricultural settlements on the islands. Early experience led them to expect much richer commodities, because even the relatively poor groups they met on the islands had a bit of gold and they found that the streams had some gold dust that could be gained by panning. The hope of precious metals drove Spanish adventurers westward and within a few years they had encountered the fabulous wealth of the Aztecs and Incas. This discovery would spur on countless expeditions from many European nations hoping for similar finds, but failing. Jamestown's Captain John Smith tried to explain to a scornful English audience that it was not his or the settlers' fault that they had not found the prized metals and gems they had been instructed to look for, nor did Spanish success indicate any superiority on the Iberians' part: "It was the Spanyards good hap to happen in those parts where were infinite numbers of people, who had manured

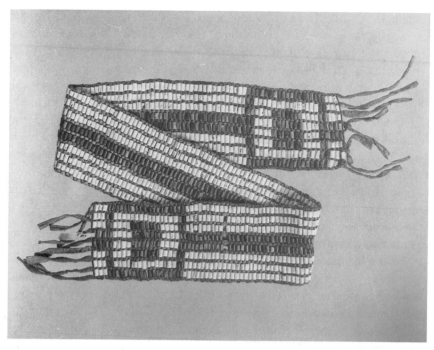

Wampum, made from quahog shells, had important spiritual and diplomatic functions. This Iroquois belt is an example of the kind of wampum belts that were exchanged to seal treaty negotiations. Courtesy of the Penn Museum, image NC35–12972

the ground with that providence, it affoorded victualls at all times. And time had brought them to that perfection, they had the use of gold and silver, and the most of such commodities as those Countries affoorded: so that, what the Spanyard got was chiefly the spoyle and pillage of those Countrey people, and not the labours of their owne hands."[11] Unlike the fur trade in the north, the extraction of gold and silver was not controlled by Americans and, foreshadowing developments throughout the Americas, it meant commandeering native labor and resources for the enrichment of the newcomers.

These early trades enhanced the lives of Europeans who had no other connection to America. Fish gave them essential protein, but many products allowed them to raise their standard of living and enjoy new luxuries. Literate Europeans began to avidly consume discoveries and overseas exploits. The printing press and movable type had spread across Europe in the decades before Columbus set sail. Increasingly, Latin, the international scholars' language, was being replaced in printed books by the vernacular, the language of ordinary people. Reformation leaders argued that all believers should be able to read the Bible for themselves; Luther translated the Bible into German, and translations into other vernaculars soon followed. Now reports of overseas voyages were printed and reprinted in editions that made them readily available. Their tales of dangers escaped and strange people with wondrous ways and possessions were the science fiction of their day for what one writer called the "mind-travelling Reader."[12] Ballads and engravings made new sensations available to the illiterate.

The humanist Gabriel Harvey, criticizing the old-fashioned literary efforts of his contemporaries, announced in 1593 that the "date of idle vanityes is expired . . . the winde is changed, & there is a busier pageant upon the stage." He advised his audience:

> But read the report of the worthy Westerne discoveries, by . . . Sir Humfrey Gilbert: the report of the brave West-Indian voyage by the conduction of Sir Fraunces Drake: the report of the horrible Septentrionall [northern] discoveryes by the travail of Sir Martin Forbisher: the report of the politique discovery of Virginia, by the Colony of Sir Walter Raleigh: the report of sundry other famous discoveryes, and adventures, published in one volume by M. Rychard Hakluit, a worke of importance.[13]

Every European group interested in American activities was constantly on the lookout for evidence of what others were doing and avidly read everything that was published. The Englishman John Florio translated the writings of Jacques Cartier, who explored the St. Lawrence River beginning in the mid-1530s, and in the book's dedication to "All Gentlemen, Merchants, and Pilots" he quoted Spanish analyst Francisco López de Gómara as saying that "The Spanyards never prospered or prevailed, but where they planted" and he argued that the same was true of the Portuguese.[14] Florio was working on an account originally written in French and translated into Italian, from which he rendered it in English. So, he was commenting on his own reading in Spanish sources while translating a French account from Italian for his countrymen and pointing out that England, which in 1580 had no plantations beyond those in Ireland, lagged behind.

One example of how information and images from across the Atlantic circulated in Europe can be seen in the literary career of the God Setebos. When Ferdinand Magellan's fleet set out on the expedition that circumnavigated the globe in 1519–22, Anthony Pigafetta signed on with the goal of making a record of the peoples, lands, and wonders to be seen on the voyage. Pigafetta was one of the fortunate survivors; he returned on the one ship of the original five that made it back to Spain. Magellan, like most of his sailors, had died along the way. Pigafetta's account was published in French in 1523, and in 1555 an English scholar and statesman, Richard Eden, published his own English translation. Pigafetta described how, in Patagonia, the expedition encountered people who worshipped a "greate devyll" whose name was "Setebos." This account, which also described St. Elmo's fire, the electrical effect that occurred around the masts in a "tempest," was reprinted many times in several languages. Francis Fletcher, who wrote an account of the second circumnavigation, that of Sir Francis Drake, said that the Indians they encountered along the South American coast worshipped "Settaboth" or "Settaboh."[15] Setebos figured in William Shakespeare's 1611 play *The Tempest* as the God worshipped by Sycorax, Caliban's mother. St. Elmo's fire, described by Pigafetta and others, appeared in the play as a manifestation of the spirit Ariel. Shakespeare's use of these images shows how widely reports from America circulated, but also how malleable they were. Sycorax is described in the play as coming from Algiers, not Patagonia, and the play is set in the Mediterranean.

Europeans consumed exotic cultures through people and artifacts that the early venturers brought back. The German artist Albrecht Dŭrer was entranced by an exhibition of Aztec gold figures he saw in Brussels in 1520; he wrote in his diary that

> I saw the things which have been brought to the king from the new land of gold (Mexico), a sun all of gold a whole fathom broad, and a moon all of silver of the same size, also two rooms full of the armour of the people there, and all manner of wondrous weapons of theirs, harness and darts, very strange clothing, beds, and all kinds of objects of human use, much better worth seeing than prodigies. These things were all so precious that they were valued at 100,000 florins. All the days of my life I have seen nothing that rejoiced my heart so much as these things, for I saw amongst them wonderful works of art, and I marvelled at the subtle Ingenia of men in foreign lands. Indeed I cannot express all that I thought there.[16]

Europeans also wondered at people brought from across the ocean. The French king Henri II was welcomed to the port of Rouen in 1550 by a mock battle of Brazilian Tupí warriors against Indian enemies. About fifty Tupís participated in this event; the other two hundred actors were French men who had been in Brazil dressed as Indians. This pageant supported a renewed French attempt to found a colony in Brazil in the middle of the sixteenth century; Jean de Léry went as part of this venture. Henri II also kept a zoo of African animals so he and his courtiers could experience the exotic in other ways. At the beginning of the next century, New England Indians demonstrated canoe handling on the Thames. And a German or Dutch visitor, Michael van Meer, invited a friend to paint a picture of Eiakintonomo, a Virginia Indian on display in St. James's Park, in his friendship album, a book that also included many pictures of English life and autographs of society's leaders, including the king and queen.

The great appetite for stories of "famous discoveryes, and adventures" combined with the relative ease of entering into print meant that ordinary people had the chance not only to undertake overseas exploits but also to star in their own stories. Bernal Díaz del Castillo, who participated with Hernan Cortés in the conquest of the Mexico, believed that Cortés had taken all the credit that belonged to him and others, so he wrote his own account. In it he compared himself to Julius Caesar, saying "I was present in many more battles and warlike encounters than those in which the writers say Julius Caesar was engaged, [that is] in fifty three battles, and to record his exploits he had consummate chroniclers, but he was not satisfied with what they wrote about him, so Julius Caesar himself with his own hand made a record in the Commentaries of all the wars he was personally engaged in." Captain John Smith, who also compared himself to Caesar, struck the same note when he concluded his books with the statement, "John Smith writ this with his owne hand." Eyewitness testimony trumped high status and scholarly credentials.[17]

Skill and daring counted for much in the early days of Atlantic relationships, and knowledge of languages was a central skill. In the trading centers on the African coast, many people knew a variety of languages as well as the trade pidgins, simplified composite languages, in which business was often conducted. These versatile actors were often African or of mixed African and European descent.

For those who ventured into the Atlantic, seamanship called forth new levels of expertise. Navigating out of sight of land using celestial navigation required some understanding of trigonometry. Sometimes such mathematical proficiency occurred in people who had little in the way of literacy, but everyone with any authority on the ship would have had some command of numbers. Speed and distance were measured by allowing a rope with knots at intervals to go over the side and counting the seconds between the knots' disappearance. Mariners and pilots also often had skills at drawing. They would make sketches of coastlines as the ships moved along them, with the depths they recorded. Raising the anchor required keeping time with chants and drums, so ships' companies included men with some musical training.

Privateering was an enterprise open to those willing to take great risks for the possibility of great rewards. Privateering was state-sanctioned piracy, and it was especially employed by countries that were too poor or backward to undertake colonization. European nations, such as England, that lagged far behind the Iberians in establishing formal relationships with America, still sought to divert some American profits to themselves. Technically, letters of marque that authorized privateering were supposed to be issued to shipowners who had suffered losses through depredations by ships from other nations. These licenses allowed them to attack ships from the nation that had violated their rights to recover the amount lost. Such patents were issued during times of war, such as between England and Spain in the last decades of the sixteenth century; it was a way of making war through private enterprise. Although it was limited and controlled in theory, in practice once a captain had authorization, he might commit attacks on ships of many nations.

English, Dutch, and French privateers centered their attention on the Caribbean, especially on the great fleets that carried all kinds of treasure, especially gold and silver, in convoy from Havana to Seville every summer. Although most privateers never made the big strike they hoped for, capturing one ship could set up a shipowner for life. Privateering also enriched the state; the English crown took one-fifth of the total value of any prize. The great Spanish Armada of 1588 that tried to take control of England was a direct response to the stepped-up level of privateering and the losses incurred. Because it was patriotic plundering and all the wealth, as the English saw it, had been extracted from innocent Indians by Spanish cruelty, even leaders such as Sir Walter Raleigh sent out privateering ventures, and the exploits of men such as Sir John Hawkins and Sir Francis Drake, who mixed privateering with their other goals, were celebrated. Dutch commander Piet Hein's capture of the Spanish treasure fleet in 1629 is still remembered in Netherlands popular culture today.

While some leaped at the chance to take advantage of the new possibilities that the ocean's rim offered, many continued to think of the sea as a barrier rather than a way of connecting. The dangers and discomforts of a transatlantic crossing were formidable; a familiar proverb held that those who ventured on the sea hung in a state between life and death. William Bradford described the Pilgrims' feelings on their arrival on the New England coast in 1620 after a voyage marked by fierce storms:

Being thus arrived in a good harbor, and brought safe to land, they fell upon their knees and blessed the God of Heaven who had brought them over the vast and furious ocean, and delivered them from all the perils and miseries thereof, again to set their feet on the firm and stable earth, their proper element. And no marvel if they were thus joyful, seeing wise Seneca was so affected with sailing a few miles on the coast of his own Italy, as he affirmed, that he had rather remain twenty years on his way by land than pass by sea to any place in a short time, so tedious and dreadful was the same unto him.

Bradford and his flock, fresh from the city of Amsterdam, saw nothing but thick woods before them, and they were always aware of the vast ocean at their back.[18]

CHAPTER 3

Atlantic People

Huge numbers of people migrated westward across the Atlantic in the centuries after 1492. Millions were enslaved and had no choice about either embarkation or destination. The others were free, but a very high proportion of the free migrants felt some compulsion in the choices they made. Many fled economic restrictions at home and signed up for a period of servitude to pay their way over. Others feared or experienced interference with their ability to practice their religion and chose emigration in hopes of being able to worship as they saw fit. The Americas offered opportunity to some, and the fortunate were able to make good on that promise.

The logic of colonization and plantation agriculture seemed to demand the forcible enlistment of unwilling labor. Sugar cultivation moved across the Atlantic with Portuguese venturers. Portuguese entrepreneurs created plantations in their Atlantic islands of São Tomé and Madeira, and exported their knowledge and their system of using enslaved labor when Portugal founded its American presence in Brazil in the very early sixteenth century. As Columbus was making his first voyage to America, São Tomé was populated by conscripts from Portugal most of whom were convicts. The population also included about 2,000 Jewish boys and girls under the age of nine who were taken from their parents and baptized before their embarkation, part of the campaign to rid Portugal of Muslim and Jewish presence. Enslaved Africans made up the rest of the labor force. The island was exporting sugar in large quantities by 1530.

Portugal's drive to colonize Brazil was hastened by the knowledge that French planters were trying to become established there. Once the Iberians transferred their production methods across the ocean, Brazil quickly became the world's largest sugar producer. Slaves—first Indians, and then, as the native population declined or moved into the interior, Africans—were the labor force on the plantations. Enslaved Africans had been coming into Europe along the trans-Sahara trade routes in small numbers. After Portugal established a formal relationship with Kongo, Portuguese ships began to carry enslaved war captives back to their home base. As their Brazilian sugar production grew with its escalating demand for labor, Portuguese entrepreneurs initiated the human trade between Africa and the Americas. Not only did the transatlantic trade in enslaved Africans begin earlier among the Portuguese than other European colonizers, but over the more than three centuries during which the trade persisted and grew, more Africans were imported into Brazil than into any other American region.

The settlement of Brazil was first undertaken with the creation of twelve hereditary captaincies, effectively lordships, to divide up land in the 1530s. As with feudal lordships in Europe, the king retained title to the land. Most captaincies did not develop thriving economies and were reclaimed by the royal government; Brazil became a royal colony in the mid-sixteenth century. Two of the captaincies, São Vicente and Pernambuco, formed alliances with local Indian leaders, and these became the most important sugar producers. Brazilian sugar output surpassed that from the Atlantic islands by the beginning of the seventeenth century. As Brazil took over sugar production, the islands became provisioning centers for ships crossing the ocean between Africa and Brazil; Portugal itself was not necessarily a port of call in this trade.

Brazil emulated the Portuguese Atlantic islands both in sugar production and in developing a mixed population. Although the migrant stream from Europe grew through the seventeenth century and especially in the early eighteenth, with whole families immigrating and towns growing up, people of European descent were always a minority in Brazil. Moreover, the settlements and plantations remained near the coast. The interior continued largely in the hands of native nations. French venturers again attempted to establish a presence in Brazil in the early seventeenth century, this time in the north, which provoked a Portuguese effort to build outposts there. These were mainly founded by Jesuits, who set up missions to convert the large native population; the Jesuits created their own large plantations to support the work. The discovery of gold and diamonds in the northeast at the turn of the seventeenth century occasioned a huge influx of Portuguese into the area.

The enslaved Indian population that worked on the plantations in the sixteenth century was replaced by Africans in the next. African cultural forms persisted in the Afro-Brazilian population. From the earliest days of sugar planting, enslaved Africans escaped from servitude and made their way into Brazil's interior, where they created or joined African-Indian communities. The federation of Palmares, which contained several communities, included Europeans as well as Indians and Africans; its population was reported at 20,000 people at its height. As happened throughout the Americas wherever enslaved Africans were present in large numbers, these settlements, whose populations became known as Maroons (from the Spanish word *Cimarrón*, or runaway), reproduced African forms of government and rituals of kingship. Religious rituals in Palmares, as in other Maroon communities, were apparently a mixture of Christian and African elements.

✤ Portugal's entrance into the transatlantic slave trade was possible because of the long Portuguese presence on the coast of West Africa, especially in the kingdom of Kongo. In the later sixteenth century, Portuguese representatives tried to take control of Angola; Portuguese

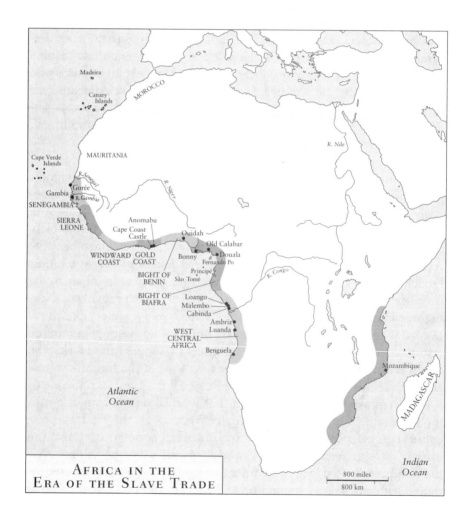

AFRICA IN THE
ERA OF THE SLAVE TRADE

800 miles

800 km

were present there into the eighteenth century, but Portugal never really controlled Angola. The Portuguese found a formidable adversary in Queen Njinga of Ndongo in Angola. She accepted baptism as a Roman Catholic and the Portuguese helped her to attain power, but she was never their pawn. Her first encounter with the Portuguese occurred when she was sent by her brother, who preceded her as ruler, as an envoy to the Portuguese court in Luanda. As she told the Capuchin missionary Giovanni Antonio Cavazzi da Montecuccolo many decades later, when she entered the room and saw that the Europeans were sitting on chairs but they had provided a cushion "on the ground according to the custom of black people" for her to sit upon, she called over one of her ladies in waiting and "sat on her as if she had been a chair," thus ritually occupying the same space as the European men.[1]

When she believed that the Portuguese were double-crossing her, Njinga renounced Roman Catholicism and placed herself at the head of a powerful army. In the 1640s her efforts were supported by Dutch venturers who were attempting to break into Portugal's West African relationships; Njinga was reported to have a Dutch woman among her ladies in waiting. The expansive Dutch had seized the province of Pernambuco in Brazil from the Portuguese in the early 1630s and would hold it until 1654. After the Dutch withdrew from Angola in 1656, Njinga returned to the Portuguese and their religion and accepted missionaries and Portuguese emissaries at her court, where European fashions reigned with her. Although Njinga fought against interference in West African affairs by meddling Europeans, the largest effect of the spreading war was to provide vast numbers of captives to the slave traders, both Portuguese and Dutch. The memory of Njinga and what she represented lived on in the traditions and ceremonies of Afro-Brazilians. Portuguese traders dominated the transatlantic trade in slaves from these early days until English merchants moved heavily into the trade in the middle of the seventeenth century.

The Portuguese presence in Brazil and on the west coast of Africa was marked by a willingness not to probe too deeply into people's culture and religion. In 1492, with the expulsion of Muslims and Sephardic Jews from Granada, the Sephardim moved to countries where they could pursue their professions. Portugal, right next door, was an attractive destination, especially as so many Sephardim already lived there. As many as 30,000 of those expelled from Spain found refuge there; others went to the Ottoman Empire and the Netherlands. Wherever they went, they were welcomed because of their knowledge of how the Atlantic mercantile system operated. As merchants from northern Europe attempted to find a foothold in the developing commerce, they had to try to break into Iberian trades, so Sephardic migrants and their knowledge of Spanish language and commercial practices were particularly useful.

Sephardim became a highly mobile group able to operate around the Atlantic and adapt to a wide variety of situations. They were a small minority wherever they were, and they knew that their situation was never secure, but their effectiveness was always recognized. Many Jews had converted to Christianity, and Portugal required that they be Christians. However, Portuguese authorities did not enquire too closely into their beliefs. New Christians, or conversos, had been suspect when they were in Spain, and many resumed practicing their Judaism openly once they were in Dutch or Turkish territory. The Sephardim worked through kin and religious ties; wherever they went in the Atlantic, they could always call on these networks for information, resources, and marketing. These Jews, who were always conscious that political change could threaten their bases, formed small communities where they could. Their establishment was marked by the arrival of Torahs from Amsterdam, and they centered their settlements around religious observance and the organization of their trade networks.

Spanish conquistadors moved quickly through the Caribbean and into Mexico and Peru within a few decades of Columbus's first voyage. Conquistadors established themselves on the land and received grants of *encomienda*, licenses that allowed them to tax and demand labor services from the native communities under their control. From the beginning, questions arose about the treatment of subject Indians. The Laws of Burgos in 1512 specified the rights of Indians under *encomienda* and laid down guidelines for their treatment. Not only were *encomenderos* supposed to protect the Indians within their grant but they were also required to give the Indians instruction in Christianity.

Major changes took place within the evolving Spanish system. New laws of 1542 stipulated that no Indians were to be enslaved. At the same time other challenges to the *encomienda* system arose. Newer colonists resented the *encomenderos'* immense privileges, which were obstacles to the newcomers' ambitions. With the opening of major silver mines in the 1540s, the demands on Indian labor began to change radically. Armies of bureaucrats were sent to administer the colonies and maintain them in the proper relationship to the crown, and to regulate the flow of goods to and from the Indies. The Council of the Indies and the Board of Trade in Spain oversaw the system of courts and administrators, and the networks of trade, in America. And they assiduously collected information about their rivals' activities.

This formal grant of encomienda included land and the right to command the labor of Indians on that land, in Argentina, 1594. The Schøyen Collection, Oslo and London, MS 2927/4

The early nineteenth century German traveler Alexander von Humboldt copied these images of Aztecs of various stations and roles from an early Mexican codex. The Indian artist who drew the originals was said to have lived in the time of Montezuma. HIP/Art Resource, NY, ART327665

New planters objected to the *encomienda* system because they saw it as unfairly privileging the earliest colonists. Religious leaders argued that the *encomenderos'* control over the Indians' spiritual lives was wrong; priests insisted that they alone should have the duty of religious instruction and conversion of the natives. Antonio de la Calancha, an Augustinian priest, argued that Jesus faced west as he died on the cross, thus foretelling the westward movement of Christianity. Priests started flooding into Brazil and the Spanish colonies in large numbers from the beginning, and in both empires there was a very close relationship between the religious orders and the crown. By the middle of the sixteenth century there were hundreds of priests and many religious establishments. Moreover, the priests were active on the fringes of settlement as well as in the centers, and they devoted all their efforts to converting the Indians who were in their charge.

A planter turned Dominican priest named Bartolomeo de las Casas had become convinced that Indians were treated inhumanely and that the duty to convert them was ignored. He pushed for changes in the laws, and the new laws of 1542 were passed in response to his urging. His continuing charges led to a full-scale investigation and debate in Spain about the best way to govern Indian communities and to incorporate them into Spanish colonial society. This debate produced a judgment that determined the legal status of Indians in the 1550s. The Indians of Spanish territories in America were formally declared to be capable of living as civilized Christians and were recognized as subjects of the king of Spain. Those who resisted, however, could still be dealt with harshly as long as they were in opposition to the Spanish, and the debate produced a set of criteria by which to judge whether Spanish actions against hostile Indians met the standards of Just War.

Not only did the priests position themselves as the Indians' protectors but many of them also devoted much of their energy to learning as much as they could about pre-Columbian Indian cultures and practices. They learned native languages so they could preach to Indians in their own terms, and sometimes they framed their lessons in ways that appealed to native practices. For example, Fray Bernardino de Sahagún depicted hell as populated by monsters from native lore, *tlatlatecolo* and *tzitzimime*, who have "metal bars for teeth, . . . they have tongues of flame, their eyes are big burning embers. They have faces on both sides. Their molars are sacrificial stones."[2] Sahagún preached in Nahuatl, the language of the people, and he wrote one of the most important books about native culture in Mexico. The preservation of many early manuscripts produced by American natives is due to the priests' efforts.

For their part, Indians within the areas claimed by Spain continued to live under their own government and customs. In Peru, colonial leaders adapted the *mita* system, a labor levy placed on subject populations by the Incas, to provide labor. We have many documents in which Indians delineated their own histories and expectations; these survived because Spanish authorities took them seriously and collected them. Magnificent maps such as the *Mapas de Cuauhtinchan*, created by American artists, recorded the people's sacred history, the story of their rulers, and their location in space. In creating these maps, the painters continued the pre-Columbian tradition of presenting history through art that could be read for the story it told. Sometimes storytelling maps were created as evidence in lawsuits or other court cases; they recorded landholdings that

This map of the Mexican territory of Tepetlaoztoc was created by native artists. It represents native landholding patterns from before the arrival of the Spanish and shows the persistence of indigenous conceptions alongside European landscape representations. ©The Trustees of the British Museum

dated from before the Spanish entrance. When Spanish authorities were instructed to prepare maps of their territories for transmission to Spain, they often turned to these Indian artists to make them. Natives also presented their claims to Spanish courts through written documents. These petitions told both of how the societies had been arranged and governed and of how the Spanish had encroached on those arrangements. All these sources attest to the continuing vitality of native communities even in the face of imported disease and Spanish invasion.[3]

The man who is known to history as El Inca Garcilaso de la Vega was the son of an Inca princess and a Spanish conquistador. At the end of the sixteenth century he wrote an extensive history of Peru before the arrival of the Spanish, describing both the behavior of leaders and the people's way of life, creating a crucial archive for the people and future historians. He compared the Incas to the ancient Roman empire and emphasized the benevolence of the rulers. He also wrote about the conquest of the last Inca emperor and of the struggles for dominance among the conquistadors. Although he was exiled from Peru at a young age and wrote in Spanish, he emphasized his dual heritage throughout.

As Indians were legally taken under the king's protection as subjects, colonists and promoters increasingly turned to enslaved Africans
to meet their labor needs. Potosí, the fabulous mountain of silver in
modern-day Bolivia, began to be developed as a mining operation in the
middle of the sixteenth century, and Africans were imported in large
numbers to work in the mines there and elsewhere. Revenues from mining
declined in the early seventeenth century, and plantation agriculture, a
similarly voracious consumer of labor, filled a larger and larger role in
the colonies' economic life.

Much of the movement of people westward across the Atlantic was
poorly recorded at the time, and not even all this documentation has
survived, so historians have pieced together estimates of numbers transported in various periods. All of these totals are approximations.
Although their figures may differ, historians do agree that Europeans
were vastly outnumbered by Africans before the early decades of the
nineteenth century. Many scholars suggest proportions of three or four
Africans for every European.[4]

The trade in Africans welded the western coast of Africa into the
Atlantic trades, and a huge infrastructure of intermediaries and other
workers kept the ports running, especially as African leaders firmly kept
European traders on the shore. These same leaders bolstered their
coffers by taxing the European bases.

During most of the eighteenth century, English ships dominated the
movement of people across the Atlantic, both Europeans and enslaved
Africans. Other European nations participated in the slave trade, and
Portuguese merchants, especially those based in Brazil, continued to play
an important part. Spanish ships occupied a relatively minor role in the
shipment of slaves. The latest estimates, based on ship and plantation
records and inferences from many other sources, posit that more than
eleven million Africans were forced onto ships from the beginning of
transatlantic voyages until the final days of the trade in the early nineteenth century. What is even more shocking is that the same collaborative
scholarly effort to comb all the relevant sources indicates that somewhere
around nine and half million arrived at American destinations. Thus in
the infamous Middle Passage, a million and half Africans were lost—some
to destinations outside the Americas, but most to death at embarkation or
on the voyage. Africans forced onto these ships did not take their situation
docilely; it is estimated that a shipboard rebellion occurred on at least one
in ten ships, and many of the deaths resulted from people choosing to end
their lives rather than spend them in slavery. Many, probably most, other
voyages were conducted in the face of fears of an uprising, and rumors

that a conspiracy was afoot were omnipresent. Death continued to stalk the enslaved after arrival. In the particularly brutal regimes of Caribbean sugar plantations, a high proportion of newly arrived Africans, one-fourth to one-third, died in the first few years after arrival, so the populations of the enslaved received constant replenishment from Africa.

African merchants and political leaders played key roles in the trade. Africans repelled efforts to establish plantations in Africa, so Europeans transferred African labor across the ocean for the burgeoning plantations there. European merchants established relationships with their African counterparts and would return again and again to the regions where their partners lived. European traders carried goods for the trade that were specially selected for those markets, and Africans and Europeans dealt with each other in the trade languages they all knew.

The majority of slaves for most of the period came from West Central Africa, the first region where the trade became established in the sixteenth century. The Bight of Benin, known to contemporaries as the Slave Coast, was the second largest source as the English islands in the Caribbean began to produce sugar in the middle of the seventeenth century. With the expansion of plantations, growing demand for labor led to the addition of regions farther north along the west coast of Africa—the Gold Coast (modern Ghana), Bight of Biafra (mostly modern Nigeria), and Upper Guinea, including modern Sierra Leone and Liberia as targets for slave-trading merchants. During the eighteenth century, at the height of English involvement in the trade, it is estimated that a large ship left England for the west coast of Africa every other day.

Until the later seventeenth century, merchants took on small numbers of captives at early ports of call as they moved down the African coast, and these men and women were placed as guardians, actually managers, of the main populations loaded onto the ships as they moved farther along the coast. This practice ensured that the guardians were from a different ethnic group than the bulk of the slaves. Disease in the crowded conditions of the slave ship was a threat that could be as terrifying as rebellion, and the guardians, who stayed among the enslaved cargo in the hold, were alert to signs of impending epidemics. These roles were extensions of the kinds of intermediary role played by Africans with linguistic and other skills in the trading ports initiated by the Portuguese. Once across the Atlantic, however, these guardians were probably sold into slavery in the same way as the cargoes they had guarded.

We have a window into the actual conduct of the trade on the coast of Africa through the experience of two young men: Little Ephraim Robin John and Ancona Robin Robin John from Old Calabar, a commercial hub on a network of waterways just inland from the Bight of Biafra. This region had been a trade center for a long time, mainly in food and other commodities with the African interior, but connections with the transatlantic slave trade began with the arrival of English ships in the later seventeenth century. Old Calabar quickly became a major center of the human trade, and rival groups of merchants vied for control of relationships with English merchants. Merchant clans created elaborate ceremonies by which to conduct the trade, and they traded only with Englishmen who observed those forms. Because outsiders were not allowed to live in the region, arriving ships came into the estuary only with permission and on payment of taxes. African merchants sent their children to England for education and they adopted European dress and manners when dealing with ship captains.

Ceremonies continued while they all waited for the arrival of enslaved Africans from the interior; these were not called for until after the merchants had concluded their bargain and the English had handed over goods to pay for the cargo they anticipated. In return, it was customary for the African merchants to send young men, often their own sons, to stay on the slave ships as pledges in the interim, which could be many weeks or even months. The Robin John brothers, along with many others, were invited onto an English ship in 1767, in a period when rivalries among African merchants had become extremely heated and English traders feared the conflict's effect on the trade. When fighting broke out on the ships, many Africans were killed and the Robin Johns were put in irons and enslaved. The entire system had thus broken down. The brothers were sold into slavery with a French doctor in the island of Dominica in the Caribbean. These men, who spoke English well and could read and write, had skills and knowledge of the system that allowed them to negotiate the experience of slavery in a way that most of the people from their country could not. But they were no longer in control of their own fate; their first two attempts at escape resulted in their being reenslaved. Both times they had put their trust in English ship captains who promised to help them. Perhaps in turning to these captains, they were attempting to employ the system they had known in Africa. But away from Old Calabar, different rules applied.

Most of the men and women who were enslaved were captives taken in wars farther inland. As time wore on, some warfare became slave-gathering operations, and children forced into the trade had often been kidnapped. Different regions also presented different gender and age mixes; women were a much higher proportion of the enslaved from the

Old Calabar was a major port in the slave trade. European traders were confined to the coast, and the organization of the trade was controlled by African merchants. Print and Picture Collection, Free Library of Philadelphia

Bight of Biafra than from other regions. The increase in the trade and changes in its locations reflected political change in the African regions involved as much as growth in transatlantic demand. One striking change concerned the age of the enslaved, as the proportion of children in the America-bound populations steadily increased over time.

By the beginning of the seventeenth century, Europeans began to emigrate to America in larger numbers and they came with the intention of living out their lives across the ocean. They came in great waves, these waves often reflecting difficult times at home. Periods of economic downturn or food shortages could strengthen people's resolve to emigrate. The 1690s, for example, were a decade of repeated crop failure and famine caused by the cold and drought of Little Ice Age conditions.

Mexico and Peru attracted settlers, but the Spanish crown regulated the flow of migrants and tried to make sure that only Roman Catholics went to their colonies. Castilian law required husbands who intended to remain in the colonies to send for their wives in Spain so they could reestablish their families in America. The presence of European women was always considered a marker of an empire's intention to create true societies abroad. In fact, Pedro de Zuñiga, the Spanish ambassador in London, sent a report saying the Spanish need not be too concerned about England's new settlement at Jamestown: "It appears clearly to me that is not their intention to plant colonies, but to send out pirates from thence, since they do not take women, but only men."[5]

Once populations became established and a semblance of familiar community was created, some chain migration began to occur. People in America sent back to their home areas to encourage friends, family, or co-religionists to come and join them. If they had done well in America, they sometimes offered to help pay the newcomers' passage over or to aid in setting up their households and workshops or farms. In this way, they recreated familiar relationships in a new setting and built communities that to some extent resembled those they had left behind. Chain migration was a phenomenon shared by all regions as they became established. The city of Puebla in Mexico drew a high proportion of its settlers from a single town in Spain—Brihuega in New Castile—initiating a process of people writing home to encourage their former neighbors to come; this was a system that the English settlers of New England also employed. Juan Fuero, who was living in Quito, wrote to his relative Juan Fernando Resto in Spain, urging him to emigrate with his family and offering to pay his passage in 1587:

> For the love of God, having seen this [letter] I hope you come at last with your wife and mother to where I am which is in Chimbo, where no more want shall come to pass, God willing. And to ensure your voyage, [I have entrusted] a merchant, Julio Ferrosin, with 700 ducats of eleven reales (less nine reales) which he carries in the form of one gold disk handed off to him by Pedro López de la Hera, as stated in the accompanying letter. Thus, when God is served to carry this money there, come straightaway, as it will bring you great contentment and fine old age. And I ask your Mercy [to use this money] to purchase a pair of black slaves, pretty, big girls to come and serve you, and bring all the white cloth you have in the house, because here it is highly esteemed, and the women go well-dressed in silk, because here it is quite expensive; and bring six pillows covered in velvet of various colors and a good rug, so that these 700 ducats will be well spent on necessary things, with just a little of the remainder for the trip to Nombre de Diós, since there I will have monies ready to pay your passage and also to get you here, where I am . . . [and] do me a favor and bring me a half-dozen good halberd and partisan blades and a saddle and a shield for yourself . . . and also bring a half-dozen lance heads—good ones.[6]

Fuero's letter allows us a glimpse of so many of the threads that made up the Atlantic, especially the role of trust. In the kind of transaction that was replicated thousands of times, he entrusted a merchant with gold to be given to his Spanish relatives, which they were to use in preparation for emigration. Any of these people could have defaulted on this trust and given a hundred reasons for being unable to fulfill it. Even in cases where all involved tried their best, illness or death often intervened to confound their plans. The letter also gives valuable information on

This image of the Spanish Caribbean port of Nombre de Dios in Panama dates from the 1580s. The harbor is full of vessels, showing how busy the port was. The Pierpont Morgan Library, New York, MA 3900

life in Quito at the end of the sixteenth century and the domestic arrangements in place then.

Women and men who migrated primarily for economic reasons tended to do so as individuals. Their passage over and the terms they accepted in order to pay for their passage were organized by merchants who made a business of signing up young people who were either desperate or hopeful enough to embark on a new transatlantic career. These migrants threw themselves into the unknown; they would have to work to pay off their passage, and unless they had very valuable skills, they had no control over where and for whom they would work. They cut themselves off from home, family, and friends, and they had no reasonable hope of ever returning.

In eastern North America, the great problem in populating American colonies with Europeans lay less in encouraging people to go than in organizing and financing such a large project as transporting thousands of people. Spain, with its newfound wealth, was able to control the whole process more than other nations that aspired to emulate that success. Populating French and English colonies in North America and the Caribbean required novel funding mechanisms, and the solution lay in sending young men and women, but mostly men, who agreed to serve terms of servitude as payment for their passage over. These indentured servants, or *engagés*, expected to get some help from former masters in setting up for themselves when their terms were up, but many became wage laborers after their servitude had ended.

Servitude was a normal phase of life in much of Europe. In England and France, people left home as teenagers and entered servitude, a condition in which they would remain until they were in their early twenties. This was the major form of education for most young men and women; apprenticeships had to be paid for and were out of reach for most families. In England, servants signed up for one year at a time and often moved to a new master or mistress every year. The turnover occurred at the annual autumn harvest fairs when all the servants and masters negotiated terms for the next year. This system gave servants a degree of leverage, as they exchanged gossip at the fair and avoided harsh or delinquent masters. The servants were supposed to have a marketable skill when their career of servitude was up, and they could avoid masters who had a bad reputation or who had defaulted on this promise for other servants.

In transatlantic indentured servitude, by contrast, the servant had much less leverage. Potential migrants were recruited by ship captains or merchants who then sold their time once they had landed in America. The very term "indentured" referred to the practice of laying the servant's copy of the contract on top of the merchant's copy and tearing a small indentation out of the two. The illiterate servant could then at least know that the contract to which he was subjected in America was the one to which he had put his X in England. The entirety of the servant's time, usually five to seven years, was already committed and would be sold to the highest bidder, so the newcomer had none of the flexibility of the system in England.

Servitude as a mode of populating the colonies also distorted the society's composition, as potential masters in the agricultural colonies generally wanted male servants to do the hard work of clearing land and farming staple crops. In New France, where the economy was based principally on the fur trade, there often were not enough positions for all the servants in the early years. Young women did go as servants, and colonial promoters always urged the colonies to make sending women a priority, but they faced life in largely male establishments with few of the protections they would have had at home. In the middle of the seventeenth century, the French government sent a large number of women under the age of twenty-five as potential wives for settlers. Each of these *filles du roi* (daughters of the king) received a dowry, and they were under the protection of nuns until they married. Except for one brief period in early Virginia when a similar drive was initiated, the servant trade to the English colonies in the Chesapeake and the Caribbean was conducted privately and responded to the market. By the later seventeenth century in both New France and the more southern English colonies, the possibility of a servant gaining land of his own at the end of his term had shrunk unless he was willing to move into newly opened areas.

Although most servants who went to America did live out their lives there, the firmness of their commitment was less sure. A late seventeenth-century letter from a father, Leger Adverty, to his son in New France offers a striking contrast to Juan Fuero's letter of the previous century:

> My dear son, I am most astonished to have met people from your country and not to have received a letter from you. It is true that I find it strange to have a son whom I have cherished more than my own self but who has no thought for me. I thought I would have the happiness of seeing him within four or five years of his departure. My dear son, I beg of you to try to find a way of coming back to France and of spending two to three months in your native town of La Flèche. I swear to you that you are your mother's heir and should you come to La Flèche you would have 800 livres. . . . I ask for nothing except that you show me the respect owed father and mother. Your father Leger

Adverty, not forgetting Marie Lemoine, your mother. Your uncle Lucas sends you his best, as do your aunt, his wife, and all your good friends in the good land of Anjou, where white wine costs a sol. My son, I do not yet take my leave. I still hope, God willing, to set my eyes on you in La Flèche before I die.[7]

Remigration was more common from New France than from other European colonies, but Maurice Adverty died in Canada, so his family's expectation that his residence there would be temporary was unfulfilled.

One compelling reason for emigration was religious persecution or the threat of persecution to come. The sixteenth, seventeenth, and eighteenth centuries saw the splintering of Protestant churches and the gathering of communities centered on shared beliefs and commitments. These communities placed their religious dedication before other loyalties and their members to some extent separated themselves from society at large. Puritans, Huguenots, and Baptists were among the earliest of the new sects, and like those that followed, their movement spread across national borders into an international brotherhood. Other Protestant groups such as Moravians and Labadists formed very large groups in central Europe, and Quakers were similarly numerous in Britain.

Puritan New England colonies that were settled at the same time as New France and the Chesapeake plantations differed in their pattern of migration. The migrants went as part of family groups, and the settlements more nearly reflected the communities from which they came in both gender and age profiles. About a third of the settlers were servants, but they often shared religious convictions and regions of origin with their employers. New England, like parts of Mexico, was populated by chain migration, as new migrants from the settlers' home areas joined the first settlers in a partial re-creation of the communities from which they came. New England was also unusual in that the bulk of the migration took place within a single decade, between 1630 and the outbreak of the English Civil War in 1642. With its relatively scattered agricultural population and cool climate, New England was one of the healthiest places on earth for Europeans, a place where endemic diseases largely died out. Puritans, like all early modern people, tended to have large families and the population very soon began to grow by natural increase.

Beginning in the later seventeenth century, European immigration to eastern North America increasingly came from new sources, especially Scots-Irish and mainland Protestants. The Scots-Irish, descendants of people who had previously migrated from Scotland to Ulster, the plantation in northern Ireland founded at about the same time as Jamestown in Virginia, settled in enclaves in the backcountry of the newly opening southern colonies. Colonial authorities saw them as useful people who could help to stabilize the frontier.

Protestants from all over Europe, especially those who belonged to the more radical sects, seized the opportunity to create superior versions of European communities in North America. Colonies ostensibly under British control welcomed Protestant incomers and gave them considerable latitude to govern themselves in their own plantations as long as they generally conformed to the basic outlines of colonial government. Many migrants from Germany and eastern Europe came as members of religious communities. Moravians were evangelical Protestants who lived in highly structured communities; Count Nikolaus Ludwig von Zinzendorf established the religion in Germany and he instituted a strict set of regulations by which Moravians lived. Like the Quakers who emigrated from England in the same period, the Moravians dressed in plain clothes and lived simple lives. When they moved to America, they replicated the community structure and voluntarily lived within its rules. Wealthy Moravians such as Zinzendorf acquired large estates to the west of settled areas in the Carolinas, Pennsylvania, and New York, so that Moravians could build their own lives undisturbed by intruding outsiders. English and other settlers who were attracted by the Moravians' beliefs and life were welcomed into the communities.

Emigration from central and eastern Europe steadily grew during the eighteenth century, as regular networks to attract and finance migrants emerged. As economies of countries bordering the Atlantic strengthened, Europe's interior continued to experience hard times that were intensified by religious strife left unresolved by the settlement of the Thirty Years' War in the middle of the seventeenth century. Most of the outmigration from Germany actually went east—to Russia and eastern Europe and even to the East Indies. The minority of Germans who went to America made their way to Rotterdam on the Rhine; they then were carried to an English port, where they received permission to travel to the port of Philadelphia. Whereas indentured servants in the seventeenth century were almost all young and single, Germans in the next century mostly traveled in family groups and included people with a degree of education and skills.

Gottlieb Mittelberger, a schoolmaster who traveled on one of these ships in 1750, wrote that the migrants were packed in "like herrings." He vividly described their suffering: "during the voyage there is on board these ships terrible misery, stench, fumes, horror, vomiting, many kinds of sea-sickness, fever, dysentery, headache, heat, constipation, boils, scurvy, cancer, mouth rot, and the like, all of which come from old and sharply salted food and meat, also from very bad and foul water, so that many die miserably." However poor their former circumstances had been, he wrote that those on the ships wished they could be home again; when land was finally sighted, they could only thank God for their deliverance.

Roughly half of the German migrants were able to pay their own way to America and were thus able to set up for themselves and their families on arrival. The others sailed on credit, and they needed to make a contract on arrival with the person who would "redeem" them by paying for their passage. The fortunate redemptioners had relatives already in America who would come to the port and satisfy their obligations; the rest entered servitude after making the best agreement they could. Those who had survived the journey in reasonable health, according to Mittelberger, made pretty good bargains, but the sick were deemed undesirable servants and had to sign on for long terms. Parents were forced to make bargains for their children, and families were often separated at the port not to be reunited for many years. Back in Germany in 1754, he wrote that many in America wished themselves back in their homeland.[8]

German redemptioner John Frederick Whitehead arrived in Philadelphia in 1773. He told of the arrival of two Quakers, Mordecai Lee and James Starr of Bucks County, seeking a servant for a relative.

> I happened to be under Deck when they arrived but by receiving Tidings that Masters were come I went up on Deck in order to look at them for little I expected, and they soon were inclosed by a ring of Men who offered their Service. [S]ome said they could plow and sow and others again could reap and mow, some could drive [a] Team and others were Tradesmen. I for my part thought it not worthwhile to enter the ring or to encroach upon them which made [me] keep off a small distance but it was my good fortune to be eyed by the said Mordecai Lee who beckoned to me to come near him, which I did joyfully. [H]e then, like the rest of Masters, first enquired after my Debt and having acquainted him with it, he replied it was very high and [asked] how long I purposed to serve for it, to which [I] replied I thought six Years were sufficient.

When asked about his skills, Whitehead replied that he had none but that he did have some education. Lee and Starr then discussed the situation, but as they spoke English he could not understand what they said. Finally, Lee told him that they would consider buying his contract if he added six months to the indenture, to which Whitehead replied,

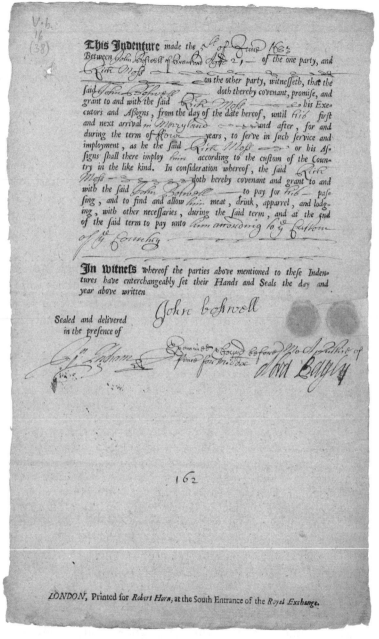

This Indenture made the ⁵ᵗʰ of *June* 1683
Between *John Boswell of Branford* *clerk* 2, — of the one party, and
Rich Moss — on the other party, witnesseth, that the
said *John Boswell* doth thereby covenant, promise, and
grant to and with the said *Rich Moss* — to his Exe-
cutors and *Assigns*, from the day of the date hereof, until *his* first
and next arrival *in Merryland* — and after, for and
during the term of *four* years, to serve in such service and
imployment, as he the said *Rich Moss* — or his Assigns shall there imploy *him* according to the custom of the Country in the like kind. In consideration whereof, the said *Rich*
Moss — doth hereby covenant and grant to and
with the said *John Boswell* to pay for *his* — passing, and to find and allow *him* meat, drink, apparel, and lodg-
ing, with other necessaries, during the said term, and at the end
of the said term to pay unto *him according to ye custom*
of ye Country —

In witness whereof the parties above mentioned to these Inden-
tures have enterchangeably set their Hands and Seals the day and
year above written

John Boswell

Sealed and delivered
in the presence of

Jn Indham

Examined & Signed before Mr Sandhis of
Peace for middx

Lord Bagley

162

LONDON, Printed for *Robert Horn*, at the South Entrance of the *Royal Exchange*.

Servants who agreed to go to America signed pre-printed indenture forms
such as this one from 1683. The phrase "custom of the country" meant
that the servant was engaged on the least favorable terms, and indicated
the low bargaining power of the prospective servant. By permission of
the Folger Shakespeare Library

"that it seemed a long Time to serve, especially if I should have the ill fortune to get an ill natured Master or Mistress, to which he said he could assure me if I was a good Boy I should have no reason to complain, but if I proved to the contrary I might also expect the same from my Master." Whitehead accepted their offer; he was reassured by the "sober yet chearful and familiar behavior" of the Quakers. After completion of his term Whitehead tried to enter several trades before settling down as a weaver; he supported a family on his income, but never owned his own home.[9]

Within these broad organized or semi-organized mechanisms for moving people across the ocean, some individuals found that the Atlantic setting offered them scope for taking uncharted paths. Personal identification was with the local community rather than the nation in this period all around the ocean, and those who recognized similarities in other communities found no difficulty in joining them. One early example attained mythic proportions in the many retellings of his story. Gonzalo Guerrero, as he came to be called, was a sailor shipwrecked in Yucatán in 1511. Another survivor of the same shipwreck, Jerónimo de Aguilar, was recaptured by Cortés after eight years with the Mayas and he and La Malinche or Doña Marina, a young native woman captured by Cortés, became the principal interpreters as the Spanish moved into Mexico. Reports of Guerrero said that he became a great fighter among the Mayas, which was how he got the name warrior, and that he had refused when Cortés offered to repatriate him. Bernal Díaz wrote that he did not want to rejoin the Spanish because his face was tattooed and his ears pierced. Also, he had become the father of a large family and that family became a crucial part of the way he was presented to European readers. Bernal Díaz wrote of his pride in his family: "And now you see these my children, how handsome they are. . . . Give me these green glass beads for them, and I will tell them that my brothers send them to me from my homeland."[10]

La Malinche's life demonstrates that mobility did not begin with Europeans' transatlantic adventures. She was an Aztec by birth but had been sent to live with Mayas when she was still a child. Thus, she had a range of linguistic skills and played a crucial role in interpreting native languages and cultures for the Spanish. She had a son with Cortés, who took the boy to live in Spain. In another example of the intersections of this newly interconnected world, Malinche's son Martín was said to have died fighting against the Moors.

In the Chesapeake, Pocahontas played a role somewhat like Malinche's. She was ten or eleven when Jamestown was founded, according to Captain

John Smith, and her father Powhatan, the paramount chief, placed her in the role of intermediary in the colony's early years. Powhatan, who had more than thirty tribes as clients in the region, decided to allow the English to plant on a peninsula in the James River apparently because he knew he could enhance his own power as he controlled the trade in European manufactured products to other Indian communities. Smith was captured early in the colony's life and experienced a ceremony in which he believed he was about to be killed until Pocahontas spontaneously intervened to save his life. Modern scholars believe he had actually gone through an adoption rite. After this episode, she became the principal emissary to Jamestown. Early reports told of her teaching the English boys to turn cartwheels, but also of her escorting shipments of food and other supplies to the needy colonists. Powhatan removed Pocahontas from contact with the colony as she matured, but an English expedition discovered her and brought her back to Jamestown as a captive. She became a Christian and married colonist John Rolfe; like Malinche, she had a son who was brought up in Europe.

In every chronicle, hints abound of people who chose to leave the groups with whom they traveled and who found new communities in which they felt comfortable. As Hernando de Soto led his meandering expedition through the North American southeast in the 1540s, at each stop they made, some people disappeared. These included Spanish Christians as well as Muslims from North Africa, and, if they survived, they would have lived out their lives in their new settings. That we never hear again of most of them is testimony to the possibilities of change and choice in this time and place. But sometimes people did turn up again. De Soto captured a Coosa woman, who was ultimately returned to her people near the Alabama-Georgia border by another expedition twenty years later; she had spent the intervening decades in Mexico. We can only imagine her feelings and those of her people; the sharing of information would have been invaluable for future dealings.

At about the same time that the unnamed Coosa woman came home, another expedition took a young Paspahegh man, Paquiquineo, on the Outer Banks of Carolina. He may have gone willingly as an emissary; the Spanish treated him as a prince. Paquiquineo lived with the Spanish for a decade; he was in Havana and Mexico City and even visited Spain. When he was baptized in Mexico City, the viceroy of New Spain acted as his sponsor and gave him his own name, so he appears in Spanish records as Don Luís de Velasco. He was brought back to his home in the Chesapeake by a party of Jesuits who wished to found a mission to the Indians there and expected Don Luís to be their entrée to his people. Instead, he was apparently deeply conflicted once he was back home—his people believed he had returned from the dead to help them in a time of deep distress—and he left the Jesuits to rejoin his own community. Ultimately, he led the party that wiped out the mission. His regret about the action he felt forced to take can be inferred from the careful Christian burial he arranged for the priests.

The Talon family offers a dramatic case of the utility of being able to reinvent yourself in new circumstances. The mother and father of this large family were French, but they married when both were in Quebec. They were back in France when René-Robert Cavaliere, Sieur de LaSalle, was planning an expedition to found a settlement that would secure the mouth of the Mississippi River in Louisiana in the 1680s. As experienced colonials, the Talons were members of the party, and LaSalle saw their children, who ranged in age from a few months to twelve, as important players. The explorer took ten-year-old Pierre with him when he went to the Hasinais (Caddos) with the intention of leaving Pierre with the Indians to learn the language. LaSalle's expedition disintegrated on this trek and he was killed by his own men. Pierre spent several years living with the Hasinais. Meanwhile, the rest of his family and the other colonists were attacked; four of his siblings were taken by Indians. Spanish expeditions into the region secured all the Talon children and took them to Mexico City. Robert, who was younger, went back to Spain with the returning viceroy. The three older boys, including Pierre, were sent to be soldiers in Veracruz; a year later their ship was captured by a French warship, so they were again returned to French custody. They demanded to be sent to Spain, but they were sent to France where Pierre and his brother Jean-Baptiste were again put into military service; their younger brother Lucien was made a servant.

French authorities, hoping to revive the project of a Louisiana settlement, interrogated the brothers intensively about native life along the Gulf Coast. The two soldier-brothers were persuaded to join the second expedition to this renewed colony, but they returned to Europe as soon as they could to seek their sister, Marie-Madeleine, who they learned had been taken to Spain from Mexico City. The quest for Marie-Madeleine was unsuccessful and the two young men were in a Portuguese prison two years later; the reasons they were in Portugal and why and for how long they were imprisoned are unknown. Some years later, Pierre and Robert were active along the Rio Grande. Jean-Baptiste and Robert ultimately settled down in Louisiana territory; Robert married and had children in Mobile. Marie-Madeleine is believed to have returned to Quebec, and Pierre died in France.[11] These were Atlantic lives indeed; the mobility and flexibility they exemplify, imposed or chosen, must stand in for the thousands of others who left no trace in the records.

Africans also entered into new relationships as their situations altered; like most of these actors, they could never be wholly secure. Samba Bambara was an interpreter working with French traders along the Senegal River in the early eighteenth century. Because the French authorities suspected him of plotting revolt, they decided to enslave him and send him to New Orleans in America, which already had a large Bambara population. Though he had been suspected of treachery, in Louisiana Samba was at first treated as a trusted person and placed as overseer of the Africans belonging to the *Compagnie des Indes* (Company of the Indies). He also continued to function as an interpreter. His treatment illuminates the way Atlantic arrangements were always perched precariously on makeshift foundations. Samba's skills made him too valuable to sideline until he was again accused of conspiracy. The small contingent of French colonists lived in terror of possible alliance between the transatlantic enslaved and the powerful Indian nations that surrounded them. Many of the Bambaras did leave the French settlements in the company of fellow slaves who were Indians and joined Indian communities away from the plantations. In this way, they emulated the Maroon communities in South America.

People caught up in Atlantic cultural cross-currents sometimes found avenues to new identities in ways of thinking previously unknown to them. Christianity in its various forms could be cultural aggression, but it also offered some converts empowerment and scope for new roles. Roman Catholics of African descent, like Europeans, formed religious brotherhoods known as *cofradías*. Black *cofradías* had existed in Iberia before the opening of the Atlantic, and in Latin America they were often organized along the lines of craft or profession. These brotherhoods offered members both support and a sense of corporate identity. They also allowed converts to make their religion their own.

The highly individualistic Christian communities that found refuge in America opened the door to a kind of independence of mind and spirit that affected enslaved Africans and American Indians as well as Europeans. Within Roman Catholicism, more mystical and charismatic strains emerged in this period, and some of those found expression across the ocean.

María de Jesús de Ágreda was a young Franciscan nun in Spain who, in the 1620s, began experiencing ecstatic visions in which her spirit left her body and was carried to America by angels to preach to the Indians who needed instruction to avoid damnation. What was astonishing was that a Franciscan friar in New Mexico, Fray Alonso de Benavides, believed he had encountered Indians who apparently had seen María. In fact, he first heard of this phenomenon when Jumano Indians traveled to his mission to request that he come to them; as he told it, they said they had been instructed to do so by a beautiful woman dressed in blue who talked to them in their own language and told them about Jesus. Soon other Indians came with their own stories of the lady's apparitions and her effect on them. Benavides made a trip to Spain to interview María about her experiences, and he became convinced that she was indeed the lady in blue his Indians had seen.

Marie de l'Incarnation was a nun who moved physically to America from her native France; she was inspired by a charismatic form of Christianity but found her ability to realize her dreams circumscribed at home. As a nun, she responded to calls issued by the Jesuit missionaries in New France for female religious leaders to come and help convert Indian women, and she emigrated at the age of forty, just a few years after Alonso de Benavides was seeking the truth about the lady in blue. She was able to make this move because she became associated with a wealthy young widow, Madeleine de la Peltrie, whose religious impulses mirrored those of Marie and who had vowed to create a convent among the Indians of New France. As Mother Superior, Marie ran her convent as a remarkably open place. She admired the spirituality of the Indian women she met and she was content to welcome them when they came to live with her and her nuns. She was also willing to allow them to leave periodically as they all did. Like María de Jésus de Ágreda, she believed that she had been given special abilities by divine intervention in order to bring the Gospel to those who had been denied it; in her case, she attained knowledge of Indian languages overnight by spiritual infusion.

Marie died in 1672. At about the same time, a group of religiously inspired native women living at Kahnawake near Montreal began a regime of extreme hardship in order to achieve spiritual transcendence. Kateri Tekakwitha, the leader of these women, defied her family and community to live as an unmarried virgin. Despite disabilities from a childhood bout of smallpox, she undertook the most extreme physical mortification, believing that her physical suffering brought her closer to God. So extreme were her practices that the Jesuits who had first brought her to Christianity tried to persuade her to lighten them. She died at the age of twenty-four and was immediately credited with miraculous cures; all who knew her were amazed at the joy and peace with which she faced her sufferings. In the late twentieth century, she was beatified by the Roman Catholic church and canonized in 2012.

Religion offered women avenues to independent action in this period. In 1710, in the midst of the War of the Spanish Succession, five Capuchin nuns set out from Spain to found a convent in Lima, Peru. They were captured by Dutch corsairs and taken to Portugal; after many adventures, they finally began their convent in Peru, on a foundation earlier created by an Indian man, Nicolás de Ayllón, and his wife María Jacinta, a mestiza, in 1713. On the eve of their convent's opening, "all the church bells were ringing and there were so many bonfires and luminarias that one could only praise God," the nuns reported.

> Actually it seemed as if God had come down from heaven to join in the celebrations that were taking place on earth, because from about four o'clock in the afternoon until eight o'clock in the evening there appeared a stunning palm tree in the sky. Its trunk sprouted out of a small cloud—the color of our habit—next to which was a cross made of stars. The Trinitarian nuns called us so that we could see it. Everyone was amazed, and they pointed out to us that there were five beautiful shoots coming out of the trunk and that their fronds were extended outward in a remarkable display of splendor and variety; everyone said that heaven had also set out luminarias.[12]

Protestant groups such as Quakers, Moravians, Baptists, and Labadists followed their doctrines to their logical conclusions as the constraints they had faced in Europe dropped away in America. One aspect of European practice that some transplants rejected was the construction of congregations along traditional lines of the social hierarchy. In America, many of these sects opened their doors to the excluded. Rebecca Protten was one such convert, an enslaved woman belonging to a Dutch planter in the Danish Caribbean island of St. Thomas who became a deaconess in the Moravian church and won her freedom. In her efforts to reach other enslaved women with her message of redemption, she faced a double barrier. Some plantation owners did not want their slaves converted, and representatives of the hierarchical Moravian system on the island were nervous about her attracting attention as a female preacher. Nonetheless, she converted hundreds of slaves and created a congregation of Africans. Protten was sent to Moravian communities in Germany along with her German husband, but finally achieved her goal and carried her mission to Africa. She had been born in Antigua, and died in Ghana.

Rebecca Protten's story is matched by that of the man who became known as Archibald Monteath. Aniaso, his original name, was born in West Africa, tricked into slavery at about the age of ten, and transported to Jamaica in the late eighteenth century. His talents were recognized, as he occupied the role of overseer as an adult. Archibald's case shows the complexity of American regions that attracted people of strong and independent religious opinions, as he was introduced to the Moravians by a pious plantation owner who was also a slaveholder. Archibald found a new set of roles among the Moravians, especially after he was able to purchase his freedom. They, in turn, thought his story was so inspiring that they published his autobiography.

Samson Occum was a Mohegan Indian who became a minister in the Congregational Church in eighteenth-century New England. He was considered the prime exhibit of Indian ability and was sent on a lecture tour in England by his mentor, Eleazor Wheelock. Audiences were astounded as he demonstrated his mastery of Greek and Latin as well as English. Occum was a missionary to Algonquian Indians in Long Island and in southern New England, but he, along with other Wheelock protegés, ultimately came to resent his position and believed that the money he had raised in England had been used for other purposes, not for helping and educating Indians as he had been led to expect. He believed that he had a better understanding of what it meant to be a Christian, and he and his congregation decided to move west away from the grasp of men like Wheelock. Occum and his followers moved first to Oneida country in northern New York and then, when they found European Americans encroaching on them again, to Wisconsin where their descendants live today.

For all these people, developing forms of Christianity offered unprecedented opportunities for defining and realizing their own dreams. Those who fashioned their own understanding of religion, even imported religion, made it their own even in defiance of those who had been their first instructors. New connections in the Atlantic made such innovations possible.

Commodities:
Foods, Drugs, and Dyes

Gold and silver were the American products that had the most stupendous effect in Europe, but the first great commodity brought from across the Atlantic into Europe and Africa was fish. Fishing was an extension of long-established Old World patterns. European fishermen began to move into the northern Atlantic in the late Middle Ages, and the Iceland fisheries were established by 1400. The fishing expanded to Greenland, and then to Newfoundland, where the steeply rising underwater land forms the Grand Banks. The underwater banks extend intermittently all along the coast as far south as New England. The deep sea currents hitting the banks cause nutrients to rise and with them rich stocks of fish, particularly cod, so this region is one of the prime fishing territories in the world. From the end of the fifteenth century, possibly even before Columbus's first voyage, hundreds of ships from all over western Europe began to converge on Newfoundland every spring. Basques and French predominated through most of the sixteenth century, but at the end of the century, English and Dutch fishermen began to participate in a major way. English and French fishermen also extended the enterprise southward to the New England coast.

From their bases on land, small boats went out daily; they caught fish with lines and hooks and returned when their boats were full. Preservation was the major concern, as fish spoil rapidly. Most fishermen used a combination of air-drying and light salting, although Basques tended to pack newly caught fish in the ship's hold in layers interspersed with lavish amounts of salt. How much salt was used depended on access to it but also on the tastes of consumers. During the seventeenth century, as many as 200,000 tons of cod were shipped eastward from America every year. Much of Europe depended on the Atlantic cod fisheries for protein; because codfish thrive at sea temperatures between 4°C and 7°C but cannot tolerate water below 2°C, reports of lean years in the cod fisheries can delineate colder times that occurred in the Little Ice Age.

American fish tied western Europe together, despite the animosity and even open warfare between the Protestant and Roman Catholic countries. Most fish, even that caught by English and Dutch fishermen, was sold to southern Europe; the rapidly growing populations of those Roman Catholic countries observed days every week when they ate no meat, only fish. In return, products of these warm countries, such as wine, raisins, and olive oil, were sold north. American fish allowed the northern countries to pay for the southern commodities they wanted.

Captain John Smith, pointing to the preeminence of the Dutch at sea, became an impassioned advocate of fishing as England's future in America. Gold and silver run out, and the markets for other products could become saturated. Unlike crops that required massive plantations, fishing would allow ordinary English people to support themselves and the nation and would spread the wealth. Smith concluded his argument with these words: "Therefore honourable and worthy Country men, let not the meannesse of the word fish distaste you, for it will afford as good gold as the Mines of Guiana or Potassie, with lesse hazard and charge, and more certainty and facility."[1] Not only was the sea off New England and the Newfoundland Banks teeming with fish, but this was, Smith argued, a fully renewable resource.

Fishing was conducted almost entirely with Old World labor. But the other major product from the north, furs, was controlled by American Indians. Native hunters and traders, forming vast networks that reached far into the Canadian interior, captured and processed the pelts, trading them for European goods and for native-produced wampum that was highly prized for its spiritual qualities. Only the final trade-off in the east involved Europeans. The earliest major fur trade, mostly in beaver skins, was conducted with the French along the St. Lawrence and with the Dutch at Fort Orange (Albany). Later, as beaver became extinct farther south, the trade centered on Hudson's Bay, and the British were the major European partners. As the trade moved north, the quality of the pelts improved, as the coldest regions produce the thickest fur. The fur trade, as with so many American products, afforded a new level of luxury to consumers in Europe where native species had been overhunted. The downy fur under the coarse guard hairs on the pelts was made into lustrous felt that was then turned into the beautiful large hats worn by fashionable, rich Europeans.

Spanish adventurers saw gold adorning high-ranking women and men in the Caribbean in their earliest years there; when they moved into

This proposed coat of arms for the Dutch settlement of New Amsterdam shows the huge importance of the trade in beaver pelts for the economic growth of the colony. Collection of the New-York Historical Society, Accession #1885.5

the mainland of Central America, they saw gold and other precious minerals that were beyond anything they had ever dreamed of. In the 1540s, Spaniards in Peru and in Mexico discovered the rich silver mines of Potosí and Zacatecas and began to organize the mining and processing of the ore. Silver became the principal export of Spain's colonies. In the first 150 years, as much as 181 tons of gold and 16,000 tons of silver went along official pathways into Europe; more probably came by informal avenues.[2] Moreover, precious metals went east as well as west; a substantial portion of the silver mined in Mexico and Peru went into the Pacific trades.

American silver dramatically changed the balance of power in Europe, with the emergence of Spain as a wealthy and powerful country. This treasure allowed Spain to undertake military campaigns against European countries that had rejected the authority of the Roman Catholic church, campaigns that culminated in the Thirty Years' War between 1618 and 1648. Silver's impact on Spain and the rest of Europe was ambiguous, however. It did not stay in Spain, as governments and merchants used it to buy needed commodities. So, despite bringing fabulous wealth that made it desired throughout Europe, silver did not encourage infrastructure development and new industries the way that far more humble commodities did. Precious metals flowing into Europe did lead to monetization of national economies. Gold and silver coins fostered standardization of values and enhanced trade. Creation of a system of standard coinage had begun with the gold coming into Europe from Africa, but American treasure greatly accelerated the process.

The most precious early commodity after silver is somewhat surprising: dyes. Pedro Álvares Cabral's India-bound fleet happened on the coast of Brazil in 1500, the beginning of Portugal's presence there. In the first decades of the relationship, the product brought home by the Portuguese and then by French interlopers was brazilwood, a wood from which dye was extracted. So important were new dyes from America that the land was named for the dyewood. Textile production was a growing industry in Europe, and producers avidly sought good dyes that would hold their color permanently. The Spanish soon procured dye-producing logwood from the Caribbean and the Yucatan. Both brazilwood and logwood produced a red dye, but they did not fulfill all the hopes placed in them because the red faded quickly to a muddy color.

Once they were in the Central American mainland, the Spanish found the true colorfast scarlet that Europeans had sought for so long: the rich red dye called cochineal. Cochineal comes from an insect that lives on the prickly pear cactus, the plant that served as the perch for the prophetic eagle whose appearance told the Mexica that they had arrived at their new home at Tenochtitlan. For centuries, Indians in Peru and Mexico had been growing the plants and their parasites and dyeing cloth with the red fluid that the insects emitted.

Spain's European rivals worked assiduously to find out where cochineal came from. Although knowledge of how to grow and process sugar and other crops spread throughout the plantations, cochineal was one product whose secret was kept for a long time. Spain sold cochineal to Italian dyers, and it spread throughout Europe in the sixteenth century, but most consumers who bought the expensive commodity yearned in vain for the secret of its origins. Spanish authorities zealously guarded the mystery and made revealing it a crime. Northern Europeans knew that cochineal was associated with a cactus, and they persistently believed that the dye was from the plant's seeds or berries. One reason why the secret could be kept was that although the prickly pear grows in a wide variety of environments, the cochineal insect survives only in a climate similar to Mexico's. Indians continued to be the principal cultivators of both the prickly pears and the cochineal insects as the amount of cochineal exported eastward across the Atlantic soared.

Fish, furs, cochineal, and precious metals extended and enlarged existing European patterns, but many American commodities led to the creation of new kinds of meeting places and new ways of consuming foods and drink. Their novelty is indicated by the names the Spanish gave them. Europeans' impulse was always to liken the new to something already known, but these foods were too strange and exotic to have familiar counterparts; their native names accompanied them across the ocean. Thus chocolatl became chocolate, tomatl became tomato, and mahiz became maize.

From the earliest contacts in Mexico, Spanish newcomers were introduced to chocolate. Although it was unlike any drink they had known before, they quickly realized that it played a very important role in social and religious life among the Aztecs. The Indians did not always sweeten their chocolate, but its bitterness was modified by the addition of vanilla or peppers; sometimes it was prepared with ground maize. As with other American crops, the growth, processing, and preparation of cacao as a food were highly technical and the Spanish had to be schooled in these procedures. Americans particularly valued the thick layer of foam that formed when especially skilled women prepared the chocolate drink. Spanish chroniclers also recognized that cacao beans were exchanged as a form of currency and that debts could be paid in cacao. Initially to gain access to the relationships in which cacao played such an important part, Spanish venturers took up drinking chocolate in American ceremonial ways, and chocolate-drinking expanded among Americans in response.

The English physician Thomas Trapham suggested that Jamaica's planters were unhealthy because they tried to continue to eat as if they were in England, with their diet centered on a large midday meal. Instead of perpetuating habits proper to the Old World, he said, they should learn "new Indian ones." He argued that chocolate should constitute half of their food intake. Breakfast should consist entirely of chocolate; then they should have a midday meal of fruit and meat in broth. At four in the afternoon, they should take more chocolate. After sundown they could have a plentiful meal. It was important to have a chocolate-centered diet because chocolate cooled the body and kept its functions lubricated. Moreover, it was a good indicator of one's state of health; if you could not digest chocolate, that was a sign that you needed to take a powerful purgative.[3]

Over the centuries, the entire Atlantic was tied together by the commodities that were exchanged along the coasts and across the ocean.

The principal export from Africa came to be people, the millions who were forced into slavery. In exchange, Africa imported textiles, iron, guns and other weapons, tobacco, and foods. The plantation colonies in America exported commodities that were deemed to make life better for those who consumed them all around the ocean: sugar, rum, tobacco, chocolate, and later cotton and coffee, which were introduced from Africa. Most of these actually created new tastes rather than replacing goods people already consumed, and, as prices fell with greater production, consumers down the income chain were able to join the wealthy in eating, drinking, and smoking the new luxury products. Demand grew alongside availability; these markets were not easily saturated. New and old products from the Americas poured value into the Old World. The fish from Newfoundland and New England and the tobacco from England and Spain's American colonies collectively generated far more revenue than the gold and silver from American mines.

Both coasts were joined by trades between south and north. Along the western Atlantic coast, England's mainland colonies were tied to the Caribbean. The northern colonies sold food—fish and farm produce— to plantation owners for their enslaved workforce. Sugar came back along the same routes and it was transformed into rum in the north. Manufactured goods from Europe went to all the other continents.

Plants and animals, some brought deliberately but many more unintentionally, dramatically changed life in lands bordering the ocean. European and African cuisines were transformed by previously unknown foods the explorers brought back from America. Not only did these foods provide new dimensions to the available fare, but they also made it possible for the poor to eat a more calorie-rich diet than ever before. Crops such as maize (which Americans call corn), potatoes, and cassava (also called manioc or tapioca) can produce crops in soil and climates in which other, more finicky, plants do poorly. Moreover, their yield per acre is tremendous compared to crops previously known on the eastern side of the Atlantic. Peppers, beans, and tomatoes added vitamins and variety, and it is hard to imagine many Old World cuisines today without these foods.

Fruits such as pineapples continued to be expensive rarities, but everyone who tasted them was entranced. Of pineapples that he encountered in Africa, the Dutch traveler Pieter de Marees wrote, "It has the best taste one can find among all fruits," and he insisted, "One cannot stop eating them." De Marees was aware that pineapples had come from America, and everywhere they were imported, the response was the same. One English source wrote that King James, when he tasted a pineapple, said that this must be the apple offered to Eve in the Garden of Eden, but de Marees insisted that the forbidden fruit was the "very delicious" banana.[4]

American crops were welcomed as miracle foods. Their productivity was truly astonishing. Thomas Harriot, sent to the early Roanoke colony by Sir Walter Raleigh to report on the American environment, excitedly compared corn yields to those typical of English agriculture. An acre would produce "at the least two hundred London bushelles" of corn and that was not all, because Indians grew beans and other plants among the corn stalks. At home, Harriot pointed out, "fourtie bushelles of our wheate yeelded out of such an acre is thought to be much."[5] What was not known at the time was that these crops were the results of painstaking hybridization by American farmers over many generations. Ancient forms of maize cobs were similar in size and shape to one grain of present-day corn, but by the time Europeans arrived Americans were growing maize that would be recognizable today. And maize had to be deliberately removed from its husk and sown by farmers; unlike other grains, it does not self-sow. Without human intervention there would have been no maize crop. So the beginnings of American agriculture thousands of years ago required people to make a commitment to try to grow food, whereas with other grains, potential farmers could notice that wheat or barley produced a new crop every year after the grain fell to the ground and adapt to that pattern. Maize is more a human invention than a simple fact of nature, and the word maize means that it is literally the substance that sustains life.

The name maize comes from a Taino word meaning "life-giver." Not only does it reach maturity much more quickly than other grains but it is also adaptable to a wide variety of environments. Unlike many New World crops that required relatively warm conditions, maize was grown throughout the Americas. This marvelous plant spread over Europe and Africa like wildfire, where it and other American imports quickly became mainstays of agriculture. In fact, Europeans often called maize "Turkey wheat," partly because it was growing around the Mediterranean so soon after regular transatlantic traffic began that many thought it had always been there. In France, according to the English philosopher John Locke, maize was called "Spanish wheat." Africans called it the grain from the sea or from across the sea, "overseas millet," or, sometimes, white man's corn, reflecting its initial appearance with European traders. Although Europeans called it Turkey wheat, in Turkey it was called "Egyptian grain," probably reflecting its route into the area.[6] Maize cobs began to appear in paintings and sculptures, and it figured in representations of Adam and Eve in the Garden of Eden.

Maize, a phenomenally productive crop, spread over the world very quickly after regular contact between Europeans and Americans began. One of the earliest images of maize was in an herbal book published by botanist Leonard Fuchs in 1542. The LuEsther T. Mertz Library of the New York Botanical Garden, Bronx, New York

TVRCICVM
FRVMENTVM.
Turcfifch forn.

Cassava was another American food that spread over the world. Gonzalo Fernández de Oviedo y Valdés, who grew up at the Spanish royal court and made twelve voyages to America, wrote a comprehensive history of the early years of the Spanish presence there and of the American natural world. Oviedo described how cassava was planted and rhapsodized on the beauty of the fields where it grew. Correct processing was crucial, as cassava contains deadly prussic acid. Oviedo observed native workers as they peeled the roots with clamshells and then grated them "on a few rough stones serving as graters for this purpose. The grated cassava is then carried to a very clean place in which they fill a *cibucán*, which is a round-shaped, loosely woven bag, ten or twelve spans in length, as wide as a human leg, approximately, made of soft tree bark, after the style of palm matting." Once the cassava was in the bag, it was pressed until all the liquid was drained away, carrying the poison with it. He described how they baked the dry cassava in round flat loaves; cassava bread, he wrote, "turns out to be a very good dish" and "quite nourishing." Moreover, it would keep indefinitely.

Oviedo also wrote that cassava served as a means of escape. Many Indians, he alleged, had committed suicide by consuming raw cassava in the early days of the Spanish presence to avoid the servitude imposed on them. He wrote of cases where as many as fifty Indians had "killed themselves together . . . by each taking a drink of this juice." Oviedo alleged that the devil whom they worshipped had told them to do this.[7]

American foods quickly became staple crops in West Africa. Cassava spread so widely that many Africans believed it was native to their lands. Pieter de Marees, who published his account of the "Gold Kingdom of Guinea" in 1602, wrote that maize grew everywhere. He described the bread that Africans made—some all maize, some mixed with millet—and compared it to "Leyden buns." He also wrote that the Africans made beer of maize, called "Poitouwe." Like Thomas Harriot, de Marees thought the yield of maize was miraculous and its variety of colors beautiful. He also pointed out that the entire plant was useful.[8]

West African farmers began to experiment with other starchy American foods, especially sweet potatoes and plantains. Sweet potatoes are rich in vitamins; they and plantains, although new to Africa, could be used in the same way as yams in familiar dishes and therefore found a welcome. American peanuts added protein, which cassava lacks, and chili peppers and tomatoes added vitamins and flavor. Africans forced into slavery in America found a familiar food environment as they had been growing, cooking, and eating New World foods at home.

The rapid influx of American foods may have made possible the huge population boom in Europe and Africa, and historians have argued that some powerful states emerged partly as a result of more abundant calories available to feed a burgeoning population. Maize, in particular, produces a crop much faster than the grains it replaced, and in parts of Africa two plantings can be harvested in a single season. Not only was it a calorie-rich source of carbohydrates for human beings, but its stalks were useful as winter animal fodder. But problems emerge when maize is too large a part of the diet, because niacin, an essential vitamin, is chemically bound in it and therefore unavailable to the human body. In Latin America, where women ground the corn with lime that liberated the niacin, this was not a problem. But the vitamin-deficiency disease pellagra could strike populations that imported the crop but not the preparation method.

Knowledge was essential to proper development, and in Spain's case, the focus on information-gathering emanated directly from the king. Spain's Philip II, whose reign spanned the second half of the sixteenth century, created a systematic effort to collect information on the resources of the West Indies, as all of America was called initially. He was obsessed with gathering data and personally read and annotated the reports that flowed across the Atlantic; he also directed the creation of archives to maintain all this information. As the courtier Don Juan de Silva remarked, somewhat sardonically, "His Majesty's brain . . . must be the largest in the world."[9]

The government sent out questionnaires to its representatives abroad to make sure that the right kind of information was gathered, a technique that was later emulated by others with American empires. Bureaucrats also directed officials in America to create maps of both Indian and Spanish holdings to complement the written record. Officials throughout the Spanish colonies were commissioned to find out as much as possible about local resources and report back to the colonial capitals, where all the reports were brought together and compiled. Much of the information contained in the replies came from interviews with Indians, and the accompanying maps were almost all drawn by native cartographers; the resulting collection is known as the *Relaciones geográficas*.

The monarch's charge particularly instructed officials to interview Indians in order to glean as much information as possible about the sources and uses of American products, and he singled out tobacco and chocolate for study. So seriously did Philip II take this endeavor that he sent his own physician, Francisco Hernández, to head up the project in the 1570s. Hernández's efforts identified and analyzed more than 3,000 new plants and incorporated centuries of experience with their properties. He drew on an illustrated herbal created by two American natives, Juan Badiano and Martín de la Cruz, who had learned Latin and European classical traditions from Spanish missionaries. None of the other European empires made such comprehensive attempts to acquire information about the American environment and its resources. Spanish missionaries' commitment to learning indigenous languages made it possible.

Across Europe, some wealthy people began collections of items from around the world and exhibited them in early museums known as cabinets of curiosities; people visited them to experience the awe that was inspired by seeing how other people lived. The Danish physician Ole Worm had a famous cabinet. Guidebooks increasingly indicated which were worth seeing so that travelers would not miss the most interesting ones.

Jean Moquet, who was the keeper of the French king's cabinet of curiosities, the royal collection of rarities, traveled extensively in the early years of the seventeenth century. He published his *Voyages en Afrique, Asie, Indes Orientales et Occidentales* in 1617. Similarly, John Tradescant, gardener to the king of England, voyaged in search of specimens for the royal gardens and for his own museum, which, evoking the biblical story of Noah collecting every known species for salvation, he named the Ark. His son, John Tradescant the younger, made several trips to America in search of rare specimens. The plant collected for the Tradescants in Virginia by another world traveler, George Sandys, is named *tradescantia* in their honor. The English merchant Peter Mundy wrote about his visit to the Ark, where he saw

> beasts, fowle, fishes, serpents, wormes (reall, although dead and dryed), pretious stones and other Armes, Coines, shells, fethers, etts. of sundrey Nations, Countries, forme, Coullours; also diverse Curiosities in Carvinge, paintinge, etts., as 80 faces carved on a Cherry stone, Pictures to bee seene by a Celinder which otherwise appeare like confused blotts, Medalls of Sondrey sorts, etts. Moreover, a little garden with divers outlandish herbes and flowers, whereof some that I had not seen elswhere but in India, being supplyed by Noblemen, Gentlemen, Sea Commaunders, etts.

Although Mundy himself traveled extensively in the Middle East and Asia, he wrote that one day spent in this museum would allow one to see "more Curiosities" than if "hee spent all his life in Travell."[10]

One result of the countless specimen-gathering expeditions as well as the more informal cases where colonists sent curiosities home to friends was unprecedented expansion of the number of plant species known to Europeans; whereas herbals had contained around 500 plants at the time of Columbus's first voyage, the plants cataloged by the end of the seventeenth century numbered more than 20,000. Prints of exotic plants decorated homes and offices. In Florence, Cosimo de Medici had fields of maize and gardens of tomato plants so that he could experience both the growth and taste of these plants firsthand. He also commissioned frescoes for the Palazzo Vecchio including garlands of fruits and vegetables such as maize and tomatoes.

From the earliest days of contact, medical specialists expected powerful new medicines to come from America, and these, having the same properties, could replace drugs from the East Indies. Many American crops were first greeted as potential medicines. The germ theory of disease did not yet exist, so all around the Atlantic sickness was treated as a disruption of the natural balance of the body. Europeans believed that good health was produced by the proper balance of the four humors—blood, phlegm, black bile or choler, and yellow bile or melancholy—that mirrored the four basic elements of nature—air, water, earth, and fire. Physicians treated the sick largely by trying to extract corrupted or excess humors through bloodletting and purging

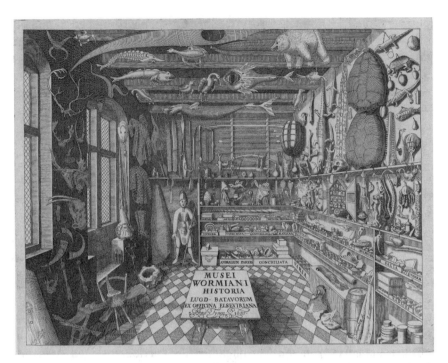

Ole Worm maintained a celebrated cabinet of curiosities in Copenhagen. His book about the collection showed the interior of his museum with its huge and varied collection of items from all over the world. Courtesy of the John Carter Brown Library at Brown University

using powerful laxatives or by making the patient vomit. Early reports of American medical practices spoke of practitioners blowing or sucking on the body; the assumption that American medicine was similar to European came naturally. Indians taught Europeans to use substances such as cocoa butter to heal cuts and sores, and the newcomers also learned about medicinal uses of tobacco. In American cultures, as in Europe and Africa, herbal medicines were the province of female practitioners, so newcomers attempting to gather information acknowledged the role of women in knowledge creation.

Along with medicines and treatments, an apparently new disease, syphilis, had appeared in Europe shortly after Columbus's return. It was particularly frightening because of its rapid spread and deadly effect. Girolamo Fracastoro, a humanist and member of the college of physicians in Verona, wrote an epic in the Virgilian mode on the devastating disease. He began to write his *Syphilis sive De morbo gallico* (*Syphilis, or the French Disease*) about 1510, and the book was published in 1530. Fracastoro introduced a shepherd named Syphilus, "the first man to display disfiguring sores over his body . . . and from this first victim the disease derived its name." As a physician, Fracastoro described the course of the disease, discussed theories about whether it was an American disease newly introduced into Europe, and described guiacum, the American wood that many doctors believed could provide a cure. He also associated the lore surrounding syphilis with the ancient story of the lost island of Atlantis, and presented Columbus as a new Aeneas.[11]

In 1539, the Portuguese physician Ruy Díaz de Isla published his theory that syphilis had been unknown in Europe before Columbus's men brought it back from the Caribbean. He wrote of treating men with the disease and called it *El Mal Serpentino*, because, like a snake, which is "hideous, dangerous, and terrible, this malady is hideous, dangerous, and terrible."[12]

Nicolas Monardes, a physician who lived in Seville, the port to which Spanish Atlantic crossings returned, created a garden in which he grew plants from around the world. Monardes, a university-trained physician, was also an active merchant in partnership with a Spanish businessman based in the Caribbean. They carried enslaved Africans westward and brought important New World products for sale in Spain. With his close connection to the docks and warehouses of Seville, Monardes was able to commission sailors to bring back plants and seeds for his experimental garden, which was a natural extension of his involvement in the Atlantic. Monardes celebrated the Indian origins of many cures and told of interviewing people returning from America to learn not only the properties of various substances but also how the migrants had learned about them from American teachers.

Monardes was particularly interested in syphilis, and like Fracastoro, he believed guiacum, "the wood of the Indies," was a cure. Monardes agreed with Ruy Díaz de Isla in thinking that syphilis had arrived in Europe in 1493 with Columbus's returning sailors. Physicians' advocacy of guiacum reflected the belief common among the learned that God had arranged the world so that the cure for any disease would be found in the same location where the disease originated. In the mid-sixteenth century, Monardes published his findings in a series of illustrated books so that doctors and patients all over Europe could benefit from his experiments. Whereas Ruy Díaz de Isla's book attracted little attention, Monardes's work was widely accepted, and was almost immediately translated into Latin, English, French, and Italian. Fernão Cardim, a Portuguese Jesuit in Brazil, referred to the recently published work of Monardes when he was describing the medicinal plants of Brazil.

Tobacco was a plant for which Europeans had high hopes. Early venturers to America from the far north to the south were fascinated by seeing Indians smoking, which they called drinking smoke. Jacques Cartier, who first traveled up the St. Lawrence River in Canada in the 1530s, wrote one of the earliest descriptions:

> They have a plant, of which a large supply is collected in summer for the winter's consumption. They hold it in high esteem, though the men alone make use of it in the following manner. After drying it in the sun, they carry it about their necks in a small skin pouch in lieu of a bag, together with a hollow bit of stone or wood. Then at frequent intervals they crumble this plant into a powder, which they place in one of the openings of the hollow instrument, and, laying a live coal of fire on top, suck at the other end to such an extent that they fill their bodies so full of smoke that it streams out of their mouths and nostrils as from a chimney. They say it keeps them warm and in good health, and never go about without these things. We made a trial of this smoke. When it is in one's mouth, one would think one had taken powdered pepper, it is so hot.[13]

Everywhere they went, Europeans learned to accept the greeting of a tobacco ceremony through which they were refreshed from their journey and welcomed into the ritual circle of the community. Only after proper relationships were established could discussions begin. Travelers reported that Indians could go for long periods without eating if they smoked, and they believed smoking tobacco induced heightened psychological states. Scientists believed that smoking might offer another mode of ridding the body of corrupt humors: the smoke would move through the body and open the pores, allowing poisons to escape. Monardes reported all manner of cures. For example he reported that a brew of the leaves, used as a salve, would cure many kinds of stubborn ulcers. Fernão Cardim described Indians in Brazil drinking smoke of "Petigma, by other name the holy herbe" much as Cartier saw it in Canada. He thought its effects were mixed. Some smokers became "dizzie and drunke," but "to others it doth much good, and maketh them voide a great deale of flegme at the mouth." Many of the Portuguese, he wrote, had taken up the habit.[14]

As Monardes was conducting his experiments and writing about them, Jean Nicot brought some tobacco plants back to France from a diplomatic mission to Portugal, where he had also conducted successful

André Thevet's book about his experiences in Brazil included this picture of Indians in their daily life. Thevet showed entire families, increasing his readers' sense that the Indians were not so very different from Europeans; the man in the center is smoking a roll of tobacco. This item is reproduced by permission of The Huntington Library, San Marino, California

trials of a salve made from tobacco leaves. When Carolus Linneas created the modern system of taxonomy in the eighteenth century, he preserved Nicot's association with the plant by naming its genus *nicotiana*. Linneas's genus *monarda*, which includes beebalm, honored Monardes.

Although European scientists were interested in tobacco, its importation into Europe was strangely delayed. It was not until the very end of the sixteenth century that Spanish ships began carrying it in large amounts eastward across the ocean. Much of this tobacco was grown in the Caribbean, and ships of many nations, especially Portuguese, sought entry into the tobacco-carrying trade.

Tobacco was an expensive product when it was first introduced into Europe; only the wealthy could have it. But in the early seventeenth century it very quickly went from being a luxury to becoming an item of mass consumption. Tobacco was the first consumer craze. This transition is exemplified in the genre paintings of the Dutch Golden Age, where scenes in taverns and other gathering places included people smoking tobacco in pipes.

Colonists in England's Jamestown colony in Virginia failed to find precious metals and met with no success in producing silk and other commodities in great demand in Europe. After about a decade, they turned to growing tobacco, having replaced the native *Nicotiana rusticum* with the variety colonists knew as Orinoco, *Nicotiana tabacum*. The sponsoring Virginia Company then moved to make land widely available to prospective planters. A boom in tobacco consumption ensued in England as the price plummeted; Chesapeake tobacco could be provided much more cheaply than that imported from the Spanish colonies, especially as economies of scale and efficiency were introduced over time. There was a series of crises of overproduction as tobacco plantations spread and the price course followed a roller-coaster pattern. English promoters did not like the prospect of building an empire on smoke rather than a commodity that could provide raw materials for substantial industries, but tobacco would dominate through the colonial period. Although tobacco grown in English colonies was supposed to be marketed only in the parent country, it is clear that many ships sailing eastward called in at other European ports first, and Chesapeake tobacco found its way throughout Europe.

Much as they admired the vibrant plant life they encountered in the Americas, Europeans always wanted to be able to replicate the basic elements of the cuisines they had known at home. Bread made from maize was crumbly and cassava dough was too stiff. They yearned for bread made from wheat, whose gluten created a dough that was supple and coherent. Those from warmer regions hoped to be able to resume eating rice.

More than just personal preference and a desire for comfort foods was at stake. When the Spanish first spread through the Caribbean and into Mexico, the priests were disturbed to find no grapes from which wine could be made. How were they to celebrate the mass without wine? What did the absence of grapes mean about God's intentions for these new lands? Was it possible that the wine referred to in the Bible was intended as a generic term and that substances used by the local people could be substituted for it? Oviedo claimed that Indians made good drinkable wine from cassava. Reports from all over the Americas said that Indians sacrificed tobacco in sacred ceremonies and consumed it in rituals. As with the wine and fasting associated with Christian worship, it produced an altered mental state. Venturers from Iberia were used to churches suffused with the smoke of burning incense, which had itself been incorporated into Christian worship from pagan practices in the Mediterranean region in late antiquity. In the frost-free parts of America where it could be cultivated, cacao was used in American Indian worship alongside tobacco; like the wine of the mass, it was associated with divine blood in religious uses, especially when it was brewed with the vegetable dye annotto, which gave it a deep red color.

None of these mood-altering substances was restricted to religious uses alone. As with wine in Europe, tobacco and cacao also had a role to play in creating social bonds and cementing relationships among Americans. Social rituals centered on tobacco and cacao did become fixtures for Europeans on both sides of the Atlantic, but Europeans never incorporated them into their own religious observances. As they moved farther into the South American mainland, the Spanish were relieved to find environments that supported grapevines. English colonists on North America's east coast were pleased to find abundant grapevines, but in the beginning they needed to import French vignerons to teach them the winemaking process.

Psychotropic substances played a large role in transatlantic trades, but not all of these products became popular. Kola nuts are native to West Africa; they contain caffeine and, like tobacco, were used as an appetite suppressor and mood lifter. They were important items of ceremonial exchange in Africa, and early European visitors certainly saw their use. Yet, until the emergence of cola drinks in the later nineteenth century, they were not consumed outside of Africa.

Coca, widely cultivated and used in Peru, was another potentially powerful commodity that did not enter the export trade. Spanish reporters sent descriptions of coca, which they found among Peru's Incas very early on. Pedro Cieza de Leon wrote in the 1530s that "Throughout Peru the Indians carry this Coca in their mouths; from morning until they lie down to sleep they never take it out. When I asked some of these Indians why they carried these leaves in their mouths, which they do not eat, but merely hold between their teeth, they replied that it prevents them from feeling hungry, and gives them great vigor and strength. I believe that it has some such effect, although perhaps it is a custom only suitable for people like these Indians." He noted that some Spaniards had become wealthy cultivating coca for sale to Indians, especially those working in the mines. A tax on coca, instituted by the bishop of Cuzco, sustained the church in Peru. The physician-merchant Nicolas Monardes grew and experimented with coca, and he wrote about his findings, but coca did not become a major trade item as tobacco did.[15]

Travelers continued to remark on how coca was used by the Indians they encountered in South America. At the beginning of the nineteenth century, Alexander von Humboldt tried chewing the leaves, and, like his sixteenth-century predecessors, commented on their mood-elevating and hunger-suppressing properties. The Italian neurologist Paolo Montegazza published a study of coca's effects, after experimenting on his own body: "I sneered at all the poor mortals condemned to live in the valley of tears while I, carried on the wings of two leaves of coca, went flying through the space of 77,438 worlds, each more splendid than the one before." The drug became a commercial success when Angelo Mariani, a chemist in France, infused it into Bordeaux wine and marketed it as a tonic. In the form of *vin mariani*, coca consumption became a consumer craze, as tobacco had done two centuries earlier, reaching to the top of the social order with praise from Buckingham Palace, the White House, and the Vatican. Nonalcoholic carbonated drinks that combined coca and kola to produce a tonic soon followed.[16]

Iroquois Indians used ginseng for a wide variety of medicinal purposes. Father François Lafitau, a Jesuit missionary in New France, had read widely on Chinese use of ginseng and searched for it as part of his mission in America. The burgeoning trade in ginseng was with China, not regions across the Atlantic. American ginseng is particularly strong, and tons of it dug on the New York-New France border and in Appalachia to the south made their way across the Pacific.

America had another psychedelic plant whose properties were recognized but which did not become a major trade item: jimsonweed. Jimson is a contraction of Jamestown, and the early settlers there had experience of its effects without recognizing their source. A group of soldiers from Jamestown in the early seventeenth century believed they had been bewitched in the night by the Indians who surrounded their camp. They heard strange chanting noises and actually attacked each other in their hallucinations.

Robert Beverly, writing at the beginning of the eighteenth century, described how soldiers in Bacon's Rebellion in 1676 were affected, and he identified the culprit as

> The James-Town Weed (which resembles the Thorny Apple of Peru, and I take to be the Plant so call'd) is supposed to be one of the greatest Coolers in the World. This being an early Plant, was gather'd very young for a boil'd Salad, by some of the Soldiers sent thither, to pacifie the Troubles of Bacon; and some of them eat plentifully of it, the Effect of which was a very pleasant Comedy; for they turn'd natural Fools upon it for several Days: One would blow up a Feather in the

Air; another wou'd dart Straws at it with much Fury; and another, stark naked was sitting up in a Corner, like a Monkey, grinning and making Mows at them; a Fourth would fondly kiss and paw his Companions, and snear in their Faces, with a Countenance more antic, than any in a Dutch Droll. In this frantic Condition they were confined, lest they should, in their Folly destroy themselves; though it was observed that all their Actions were full of Innocence and good Nature. Indeed they were not very cleanly; for they would have wallow'd in their own Excrements, if they had not been prevented. A Thousand such simple Tricks they play'd, and after Eleven Days, return'd to themselves again, not remembering any thing that had pass'd.[17]

However, jimsonweed, despite its spectacular properties, never became a transatlantic trade item.

As Cieza de Leon speculated that coca was only suitable for Indians, many people with roots on the eastern side of the Atlantic worried that their bodies would not be attuned to foods and medicines grown in the very different American environment. Following humoral theory holding that each environment produced its own balance, they assumed that moving from one environment to another placed a great burden on the body, and exotic foods might not be nourishing. Thomas Gage was an English Roman Catholic who joined the Dominican order in Spain and served as a missionary in Guatemala and Central America. He renounced his Catholicism after returning to England and wrote the first comprehensive book in English describing the Spanish colonies. He argued that the American environment was, ironically, too effective in growing plants; foods that grew too quickly did not accumulate the nutrients present in plants that came to maturity more slowly in less hospitable soil. Gage was puzzled by the fact that however splendid the food seemed, he was always hungry again two hours after a meal. A "Doctor of Physick" explained to him that the food he ate lacked "substance and nourishment." Gage's experience of seeing people around him with their stomachs "gaping and crying, Feed, feed" caused him to remember a story he had heard about Queen Elizabeth. When she was presented with fruits from America, she reportedly remarked that "surely where those fruits grew, the women were light, and all the people hollow and false hearted."[18]

Africans and Europeans in the Americas longed to have the food they were accustomed to at home. Every European transatlantic venture from the beginning brought seeds of familiar plants, from wheat and rye to peaches, and every early report glowed with the news that the seeds sprouted quickly and produced vigorous plants. As time went by, naive enthusiasm was tempered by experience. Most early venturers were not experienced farmers, and even later large migrations often brought more urban than rural people; the newcomers learned slowly and painfully that experience and experimentation were required to fit the crop to the environment. Rust or fungus attacked crops such as wheat, and colonists learned to think in terms of a double planting and harvest. They grew American crops alongside ones imported from Europe and Africa; if the imported crops failed, they could rely on what they called the Indian harvest.

Old World flora and fauna spread over the Americas far in advance of the people from across the ocean. Honeybees were one of the imports that became ubiquitous as they took up pollinating duties for plants both imported and native. Many incoming animals were useful to the Americans as well as the newcomers, and they adapted quickly to their new environments. Horses, escapees from Spanish forts and settlements, formed feral bands, and they were quickly incorporated into native life. Horses were native to the Americas but had died out in the Pleistocene era; they found the grasslands highly suited to their needs, and they enhanced the lives of the Indians by whom they were captured and trained. So central did they become that modern Americans' vision of Indianness centers on a mounted Indian man. Cows, similarly escaped from domestication, invaded meadows and plains.

Pigs were another import that thrived in the Americas without much human intervention. From the earliest days of contact, Spanish and Portuguese navigators developed the practice of dropping off a breeding pair on the islands where they touched in the hope that the pigs would provide a food supply for future fleets, an expectation that was often fulfilled. When the flagship of a Virginia-bound fleet was shipwrecked on Bermuda by a hurricane, they found the island overrun by pigs. Bermuda, which is extremely dangerous to approach because of the reefs that ring it, had been known as the "Isle of Devils," and the shipwreck victims were delighted to discover that the devils were actually a walking food supply.

All of these imported animals were mixed blessings, especially where their populations were unchecked by predators. Grazing animals in large numbers could turn lush meadows into deserts by their close cropping of new shoots. Pigs competed with Indians for gathered food—nuts and berries—and they invaded and often wrecked Indian agricultural fields and their stored produce. The net effect of Old World fauna in America may have been to reduce the complexity of the mix of plant life. Pigs may also have carried European diseases and spread them to

Indians who had not yet had dealings with the newcomers. Such "magical" appearances of epidemics fed the Americans' sense that their world was changing in ways they could not comprehend; they also contributed to Europeans' assumption that God somehow favored their enterprises.

Some animal imports were unintentional and devastating. Rats, which came off the ships as cargoes were unloaded, were a plague both to Indians and Europeans. They wormed their way into stored food supplies, sometimes even creating famines, and they preyed on growing crops. In Barbados, planters would sometimes burn an entire field of valuable sugar plants, setting the fires on all four sides to drive the rats to the field's center. They were willing to sacrifice the crop to kill the rats.

American crops spread over the world and fed the population boom that intensified in the seventeenth century. At the same time, plants imported into the Americas transformed life all around the Atlantic. Sugar made the greatest impact. Sugar production moved steadily westward from its ancient origins in the South Pacific. Sugarcane had appeared in India more than 2,000 years ago and was ultimately brought into Europe, as with so many other innovations, by North Africans.

Portuguese entrepreneurs cultivated it on the Atlantic islands and then in Brazil as more environments suited to its production were opened up. Brazilian sugar began an economic boom and a network of relationships that linked all of western Europe. The number of ships crossing the Atlantic grew exponentially, as they carried enslaved Africans and provisions to the plantations and sugar back to Europe. German, Dutch, and Italian merchants joined Portuguese and Sephardic entrepreneurs in financing the trades and providing ships. On the plantations, they processed the cane sufficiently to produce mostly brown sugar and molasses. These products were shipped to Portugal, and from there they were transported to countries in western Europe for further processing and distribution.

The Spanish followed Brazil in sugar production on their Caribbean islands. Columbus had brought sugar to the West Indies on his second transatlantic voyage in 1493, and Spanish colonists soon created plantations and processing works in the islands. By the seventeenth century, the Caribbean islands had become centers for growing and processing sugarcane, and the English plantations on Barbados and Jamaica moved into cane planting by mid-century.

From the beginnings of large-scale production of sugar, consumption has grown steadily, with no apparent limits to demand for it—although sugar made from cane has shared the stage in more recent times with beet sugar and corn syrup. Honey had been the principal sweetener in Europe before the advent of sugar there, and in its early days sugar was a luxury for the very rich. As it became more widely available and especially as its price fell, people further and further down the social and income scale were able to enjoy it, and cuisines were transformed in the process. During the eighteenth century, the amount of sugar each person in England consumed annually went up more than 400 percent.

The human cost of this new luxury for Europeans was the labor of countless enslaved Africans. Cultivation of sugarcane called forth new kinds of agriculture with huge plantations and economies of scale. Processing required hard-won technical knowledge, especially the ability to judge precisely when each stage of growth and treatment had been reached. Portuguese planters in Brazil perfected the modes of sugar cultivation for the Americas. Lengths of cane were laid in long trenches and new plants sprang from them. The mature cane was cut and then crushed in great rollers to squeeze out the sweet juice. Then the juice was heated to concentrate it and ultimately to produce crystals, the sugar that modern consumers use. In its early stages, the syrup is molasses and is quite dark in color. Crystalline brown sugar is a further stage, and white sugar is the final product. The great mills in the seventeenth-century Caribbean housed the most extensive and sophisticated industrial works anywhere in the world.

Sugar is both a sweetener, adding variety and intensity to the foods routinely consumed around the world, and a preservative. Previously, drying in the sun or in salt were the only modes for preserving food in most regions. Sugar allowed consumers to keep foods indefinitely, especially fruits and some meats, in ways that did not alter their texture and succulence.

Sugar was also greeted as a medicine. Honey had long been used to aid digestion, and sugar was pressed into service for that purpose. It also followed honey as a way to heal stubborn infected sores and wounds. Sugar draws out moisture and inhibits the growth of bacteria. In traditional medicine in Africa and Europe, sugar was put directly into intractable sores and the results were gratifying. In modern times, medical practitioners have rediscovered sugar's seemingly miraculous ability to heal.

Before antibiotics, inhaling the fumes in sugar refineries was a favored treatment for tuberculosis, and sugar's salutary effect on lung problems was noted even in the seventeenth century. Richard Ligon, who described the transition to large-scale sugar production on Barbados, wrote that as this plant has a faculty, to preserve all fruits, that grow in the world, from corruption and putrifaction; So it has a vertue, being rightly applyed, to preserve us men in our healths and fortunes too. Doctor Butler one of the most learned and famous Physitians that this Nation, or the world ever bred, was wont to say that,

If Sugar can preserve both Peares and Plumbs,
Why can it not preserve as well our Lungs?

And that it might work the same effect on himself, he always drank in his Claret wine, great store of the best refin'd Sugar, and also prescribed it several wayes to his Patients, for Colds, Coughs, and Catarrs; which are diseases, that reign much in cold Climates, especially in Ilands, where the Ayre is moyster then in Continents; and so much for our Health.[19]

Another very popular product emerged from the sugar plantations. In addition to crystal sugar and molasses, rum was distilled from sugar cane juice; after the middle of the seventeenth century, rum, with its far higher alcoholic content, took its place alongside wine, beer, and ale. "Strong waters," as distilled spirits were called, had been made in small quantities for centuries in Europe, but they were extremely expensive. Rum manufacture, as with all sugar products, introduced economies of scale that made the product widely and cheaply available.

Rum, called "Kill Devil," was distilled on the islands where the sugar was grown, but refining and distilling methods were also exported along with the raw materials. One center of sugar refining and its offshoot, rum distilling, was in northern Europe, particularly the Netherlands, Germany, and England. The mainland colonies of North America forged a relationship with the Caribbean that became even more important to developments on the western side of the Atlantic. The northern agricultural colonies provided food, animals, and timber to the islands; in return they received raw sugar, which was the foundation of a major rum industry. France closed its ports to rum in an effort to protect the wine and brandy industries, so French island colonies sold their raw sugar to the English colonies to the north.

Rum, increasingly inexpensive, was exported around the Atlantic. Much went to Africa, where it was exchanged by colonial merchants for enslaved Africans who were taken to the Caribbean. There, these same merchants loaded raw sugar, which would begin the cycle again when it was distilled in North America. Sailors in the British navy received a rum ration, which amounted to a full pint every day by the end of the eighteenth century.

These images show Africans being sold into slavery; at top, a prospective buyer examines a potential purchase. The lower picture shows newly purchased slaves being ferried to the ship that will carry them across the Atlantic while their friends and relatives mourn on the shore. Courtesy of the John Carter Brown Library at Brown University

Rice was another key crop that traveled westward across the Atlantic and enriched the plantations. Rice was apparently cultivated on the West African coast, in the wet low-lying areas, and many historians believe that the knowledge of enslaved Africans led to the design of the intricate water-management systems that allowed rice to become such a valuable crop in similar environments in America. Tools adapted to rice cultivation first developed in Africa and were taken for use in America, and African knowledge of the timing and preparation of the crop was essential.

Enslaved workers in the Caribbean were allowed to grow crops in small gardens, and in these, in addition to American foods such as maize and cassava, they grew vitamin-rich foods from Africa: yams and okra, traditionally cultivated by women, were particularly popular. Their garden-plot vegetables added variety and nutrition to the bland starchy diet they got from the planters.

All these newly available products had revolutionary effects. Crops from America radically changed consumer patterns in Europe. They also forced governments to think in new ways. Rulers needed to make money out of these new endeavors and the old procedures did not suffice. Previously monarchs had simply taken a cut of imports and exports, but now the trades were dispersed and had to be regulated in ways that would benefit the national economy and aid the royal treasury. Overseas exploits involved the nation in expensive wars and protections, so it was only right that merchants and planters should help to pay the bills. But too often the taxes seemed to fall on ordinary consumers in ways that actually retarded economic growth. In the absence of robust governmental bureaucracies, governments turned responsibility for some of their functions over to small groups of well-placed subjects through monopolies and other kinds of expediencies such as tax farming. Merchants bought the right to collect taxes. The benefit to the government was receiving the money up front, and the merchants found tax farming worthwhile because they were able to collect much more over the course of the year than they paid for the privilege of collecting the tax. In Spain and in England, the royal government enacted monopoly control over the import and sale of tobacco, a product that was not necessary for the people and that enriched importers. The hope was that substantial sums would flow into the national treasury from such controls.

National leaders thought about building European economies in other ways. One was to attempt to restrict trade with the colonies to ships going to and from the parent country. That would funnel all the new commodities into building that nation's economy, particularly when raw materials contributed to the creation of new or enhanced existing industries, like textile manufacturing in England. A product such as tobacco that vanished as it was consumed elicited hostility because it did not provoke infrastructure creation.

Dreams of a closed economic circle in which colonies fed raw materials into European industries were just that—dreams. There was at least as much informal commerce—smuggling—as that sanctioned by the law, and it is arguable that the colonies would have collapsed without the ships that brought supplies and carried their commodities to places where they could be sold to best advantage. Increasingly through the eighteenth century, tea, along with beef preserved in salt, was carried by smugglers to colonies all along the coast of America and in the islands. Ships carrying commodities from America back to Europe were required to make the home country their first port of call, but there is considerable evidence that many cargoes went to other countries where shipmasters could evade taxes and regulation. By sponsoring privateering at the inception of the Atlantic trades, nations had created a set of expectations and patterns of behavior that could not be fully controlled as the Atlantic economies developed.

CHAPTER 5

Eighteenth-Century Realities

At the opening of the sixteenth century, the Atlantic Ocean was transformed from a barrier that separated the American continents from Africa and Europe into a highway that united them through the myriad people and commodities that traveled on ships in both directions. By the middle of the eighteenth century, this highway was taken for granted; leaders on both of the ocean's sides believed they understood the relationship of the Old World and the new fairly well. Over the colonial period, European empires had moved periodically to change their relationship to their Atlantic holdings, and all tended to make similar moves at about the same time. All these initiatives were inspired by large-scale changes that affected conditions around the ocean, and all demonstrated the degree to which officials watched what was going on and responded to their understanding of everyone else's plans.

It is no accident that Spain, England, and France all built permanent colonies in previously neglected North America in the first decade of the seventeenth century: Jamestown in 1607; Quebec in 1608; and Santa Fe in 1608–10. All three empires were responding to changes in Europe as well as trying to preempt their rivals in America. Countries with American empires would again attempt to make changes more or less simultaneously in the later seventeenth century and, in a major way, after the middle of the eighteenth century. As the eighteenth century progressed, and often in response to these moves, officials were forced to recognize that their understanding was quite imperfect, and that society, culture, and economies all around the Atlantic had developed in ways they had not anticipated.

In the late seventeenth century, European leaders, especially in France and England, planned for a new relationship with America. They disliked the haphazard and varied ways their colonies had developed and now, feeling stronger and better organized, they hoped for what they saw as a more rational relationship across the ocean. As planners assimilated hard-won knowledge of realities on the ground, English and French empires moved in similar directions: they sought to tighten up administration of their colonies and they decided to emulate the Spanish example by sending over bureaucrats and using questionnaires to find out more about their American plantations.

Government attempts to gather information were accompanied by a new scientific interest in America, its plants, animals, and their uses. At the beginning of the seventeenth century, Federico Cesi organized the Academy of Linceans in Rome, its name referring to the lynx with its extremely precise eyesight, and they set out to catalog and portray all the world's species; Galileo was the best-known member of this scientific organization. Groups such as England's Royal Society, organized in 1660, and the French Academy of Sciences, founded in 1666, employed some of the same techniques as their governments, sending out questionnaires and collecting specimens gathered by agents around the world. These gentleman-scientists devoted much of their energies to analyzing and organizing data and creating systematic knowledge of the natural world. Spain sent out twenty-five scientific expeditions in the eighteenth century. The Spanish physician and botanist Casimiro Gómez Ortega argued that such enterprises were the best avenue to renewed power and influence for Spain: "twelve naturalists . . . spread over our possessions will produce as a result of their pilgrimages a profit incomparably greater than could an army of 100,000 strong fighting to add a few provinces to the Spanish empire."[1] Colonists were also active in these pursuits, and they organized comparable societies, such as the American Philosophical Society in Philadelphia and the Cercle des Philadelphes in St. Domingue.

Knowledge and power were very closely allied, and the gathering of information was meant to lead to more rationalized imperial control. The French Ministry of Marine assumed administrative control of New France in 1663 and Jean-Baptiste Colbert, the king's chief minister, hoped to make permanent settlement a priority. England also moved to investigate conditions in North America and to control the transatlantic trades and eliminate smuggling. Whereas the English colonies, most founded by corporations or proprietors, had grown up with a variety of governments and systems, the sprawling Spanish empire in America, divided into four viceroyalties and with an elaborate bureaucracy, was far more centralized. In the 1680s the English government began to implement a plan to get rid of the colonial charters, each of which outlined a slightly different system of government, and to consolidate all the mainland colonies in two great viceroyalties on the Spanish model. The plan was set in motion first in the north; all the colonial charters were recalled and the Dominion of New England stretching from New York to Maine was created. This bold plan was halted when Charles II's successor, James II, was ousted in the rebellion known as the Glorious Revolution. But the northern colonies, except for Connecticut, which had managed to avoid surrendering its charter, were given new charters that were far less favorable to their traditions of self-government. Government bureaucrats were sent over to see that regulations were enforced, and governors received questionnaires to fill out so that the Board of Trade could judge correctly what was going on in America.

English and French planners had focused their attention on the sugar islands of the Caribbean, the engines of so much wealth production, and on the trade in enslaved Africans across the Atlantic. Increasingly through the eighteenth century, however, the American landmasses, where people of European descent many generations removed from Europe had developed their own societies, drew leaders' interest.

North America was one such location. The colonies founded or acquired by England clung to the east coast, hemmed in by the Appalachian mountain range. New France to the north, with its thin sprinkling of Europeans in a sea of powerful native societies, looked to control the central artery, the Mississippi River, and the lands between it and the mountains to the east. As the population increased in the English colonies and their sense of security heightened, colonists wanted to cross the mountains and settle in the rich agricultural lands of the Ohio Valley. Many of the early charters had grandly granted lands between specified north and south latitudes "from Sea to Sea," so colonists, pointing to this language in their charters, argued that they had a perfect legal right to expand westward. As advance parties from the east began to survey and map the western lands, the French built a string of forts along the frontier to prevent settler movement into these territories.

The rich Ohio Country had drawn earlier migrants. Indians who had been pushed out of their lands to the east moved across the mountains to safety. Here powerful groupings emerged as remnants of eastern nations were absorbed into existing polities and a new phenomenon emerged: they began to think in pan-Indian terms and to see that they needed the strength that came of unity. Although they welcomed the many traders who operated in the interior because of the superior goods they brought, these Indians, like the French, wanted above all to block, or at least slow, the westward movement of settlers from the English colonies on the eastern seaboard. And the settlers who trickled westward were religious and economic refugees from Europe who had felt victimized in their homelands, had then found that there was no room for them in the settled parts of the colonies to which they had traveled, and now felt pushed out to be the buffer between increasingly hostile and powerful Indian groups angry over their displacement and eastern governments that seemed indifferent to their situation.

Reluctantly the European leaders began to take notice of what was happening in North America. Had they been more open in their perceptions, they would have begun to realize that societies on the western side of the ocean were developing in distinct ways and that they were no longer as responsive to interference from Europe as they had been. Creoles, people of European or African descent born in America, no longer shared formative experiences with those on the ocean's eastern side. Above all, American societies were not prepared to see their interests subordinated to those of the parent countries. France and Britain and their allies had been at war intermittently from the late seventeenth century. Ideally, these wars should have stayed in Europe, but increasingly they spilled over into the colonies, where unhappy settlers were forced to take roles in them. Europeans called these wars by names indicating their European causes, such as the War of the Spanish Succession or the War of the Austrian Succession, but Americans in the English colonies called them as they saw them: Queen Anne's War, King William's War, King George's War, and so on. Fighting wars in Europe was expensive, but abroad they were cripplingly so and the colonists did not like it when they were dragged into these conflicts. Indians also found the spillover of European wars into America and the influx of Europeans fleeing problems at home alarming. In 1752, Shawnee leaders told the governor of Pennsylvania that God had put the ocean between Europe and America to keep them separate and they should have been kept so.[2]

The Seven Years' War was the first of these inter-imperial conflicts that actually began in America and whose principal theater of action was not European; Britain's American colonists called it the French and Indian War and it became known as the Guerre de la Conquête (War of the Conquest) among French colonists in Canada. Everything changed because of the scale of this war. Previously, residents of the British colonies had fielded militias gotten up for specific campaigns. French soldiers, many with deep roots in Canada, had developed a set of military practices that recognized the key role of their Indian allies. As America became the center of the war, both France and Britain sent over large professional armies to fight it, with effects that no one foresaw. As Voltaire wrote,

France and England fought "over a few square acres of snow, somewhere in the vicinity of Canada." Even before the war was over, "they've already spent, on this lovely scuffle, far more than the whole of Canada is worth."[3] France lost the war in America and gave up all of Canada and its claims to the interior by the terms of the 1763 Peace of Paris. They could have kept Canada but chose instead to keep the sugar-producing island of Guadeloupe, while relinquishing Grenada, Dominica, and Tobago. France's colony of St. Domingue, on the island of Hispaniola, produced the most riches of all the islands. Spain, France's ally, also relinquished territory in North America.

The Seven Years' War was part of a massive shift in Atlantic relationships in the mid-eighteenth century that would ultimately lead to campaigns for independence throughout the Americas. The fielding of large professional armies brought ordinary people from both sides of the Atlantic face to face for the first time. French leaders were horrified by the style of warfare that had evolved in their colony, considering frontier fighting destructive of everything that French culture stood for. Similarly, the English thought American militias were sloppy and they detested the decentralization of decision making they insisted on. For their part, colonists saw the incoming Europeans as combining arrogance and ignorance, a deadly mixture in a setting where local knowledge mattered so much.

American Indians had the most to lose. Some, seeing the French as their only bulwark against the encroaching populations moving westward from Britain's colonies, had allied with French forces. All had become dependent to some degree on European trade goods, and many groups had split over how to conduct themselves in this conflict. At war's end, new settlers began to stream across the mountains, inundating the lands the Indians had carved out as their own, and a new militancy began to emerge among the American natives. This militancy had spiritual roots. In the 1750s, as tensions increased, a series of prophets had begun to emerge along the frontier; they all preached that the Indians must return to their old ways and reject European goods and, above all, alcohol. A Delaware man named Neolin had a powerful vision in which "the Master of Life" told him that if the Indians drove away the Europeans and prayed only to him, he would restore all the animals on whom they had relied and make their traditional life possible again. Most of the prophets had purely local audiences, but Neolin soon attracted a large following and helped to inspire the series of attacks on Britain's frontier posts in 1763 that became known as Pontiac's War.[4] Nothing could stem the flow of settlers westward, even though Britain issued the Proclamation of 1763 forbidding it. More people flowed into the British colonies in the years between the end of the Seven Years' War and the outbreak of the American Revolution than in the entire preceding century, and huge numbers of them went, or were sent, west.

In the middle of the eighteenth century, the Spanish crown, like the British, sought to tighten up administration of the empire and make it more rational from a European perspective. These Bourbon Reforms confronted a wide range of practices that had grown up over time and that looked chaotic from Spain's viewpoint. The Roman Catholic church had grown very powerful in Spanish America, and it was the reformers' first target. The Jesuit order was virtually autonomous and actually controlled large areas, including the colony of Paraguay. Their depth of commitment had made them dominant; the Jesuits ran 120 colleges in Spanish America and their missions ministered to many thousands of Indians. The Jesuits had already been expelled from Portugal and its possessions and from France when the Spanish monarchy ordered all the Jesuits to leave both Spain and Spanish territories in America in 1767. The reformers also focused on corralling the work of the brotherhoods known as *cofradías*. These were organized around a single racial or ethnic group and sometimes on professional lines, and were an important way to achieve a Christian life for Indians and Africans. They acted as advocates and as social welfare agencies for their members.

Spain's experience in the Seven Years' War revealed that the nation had lapsed into weakness, almost irrelevance, in international politics, and the reformers sought to reverse this slide. Official teams were sent to examine the colonies and their administrations, and offices that had been in the hands of American-born creoles were now filled by people directly from Spain. Old monopolies and restrictions on commerce were swept away and merchants were now free to conduct trade anywhere within the empire. Reformed administration was expensive and, as in other empires, new or increased taxes were imposed to pay for it. These strictures led to revolts around the colonies. A series of rebellions took place over decades in the Andean highlands, culminating in the Túpac Amaru revolt in 1780.

Its leader, Túpac Amaru, took the name of the last Inca emperor from whom he was descended. Like Neolin in North America, Túpac Amaru combined a message of spiritual renewal with resistance to the Spanish, but his appeal was to all who were born in the region regardless of their ancestry. Ultimately, however, the creoles of European extraction chose to side with the Spanish and the revolt was put down with deaths of over 100,000 Indians. At the same time, the Comunero revolt in the province of New Granada—modern-day Colombia and part of Venezuela—demanded an administration composed of the American-born and an end to investigatory intrusions from Spain. These rebels did not seek independence and they did succeed in stopping the trend toward greater centralization for their territories.

The Seven Years' War marked a turning point in Atlantic history because all the European imperial powers began to examine American arrangements with unprecedented intensity. The war's massive expense led all European powers to try to make their American colonies pay more for the cost of empire, and they sought to rationalize administration. France attempted to compensate for the loss of Canada and help provision its important colony of St. Domingue by fostering a huge initiative to build up the small colony in French Guiana on the northeast mainland of South America. Guiana had been the object of European aspirations since the beginning of contact; it was said to be the home of El Dorado, a ruler known as the gilded one, whose attendants blew gold dust over him.

Kourou, as the site was called, was a chance to start over, to create a more perfect colony, and many of the philosophes, French intellectuals associated with the Enlightenment, were interested in it. Unlike Canada, it would be in a location with a friendly climate, and the king decreed that it should be populated exclusively by Europeans. All colonists were to have land of their own, and freedom of conscience was guaranteed. Like the English colonies to the north, France looked to Germany and eastern Europe for colonists; they were promised free passage and food and clothing for two years. Concerned as they were to avoid the mistakes of earlier ventures, planners sent scientists, experienced farmers, and doctors to lead the colony, and they sent animals that they thought would thrive there.

The Kourou project drew prospective colonists in huge numbers that dwarfed even the multitudes going to North America at the same time. Thousands made their way to France, often traveling vast distances on foot, and 13,000 to 14,000 prospective planters actually shipped out for Guiana at the outset. The result was catastrophic. It is estimated that 9,000 people died in the first year, mostly in epidemics exacerbated by starvation. Yellow fever was probably the culprit; this disease, native to West Africa, thrived when huge numbers of previously unexposed people were brought together in the right climatic conditions. In the Caribbean, clearing the land for sugar plantations created ideal conditions for mosquito multiplication, partly by eliminating natural enemies. Heinrich von Uchteritz, who was in Barbados in the 1650s, described the effect of the denuded environment: "Although this island lies in a pleasant location, one hears no birds."[5] The mosquitos that carry yellow fever take blood from infected people and convey it to others; the cycle then continues with these new infections. Without a large and vulnerable population, the cycle will end. Large numbers of newly arrived Europeans living closely together in Kourou provided an ideal vector. About 3,000 debilitated migrants returned to France, and many of them died shortly after their return.

Kourou's experience encapsulates the intersection between the state of knowledge about American colonization after 250 years of experience and the logistics of transatlantic movement. Colonists embarked at the wrong time of year, so that they arrived in the rainy season; food shipments were not timed to be there when colonists needed them, so they either spoiled before they could be used or came too late. All colonization efforts were predicated on a best-case scenario, the assumption that everything would come together perfectly. In an age when transatlantic communication required months and shipping was subject to the vagaries of weather and commerce, such an assumption was risky at best.

While governments sought to tighten up administration and control, resistance to a closer relationship between Europeans and creole societies in America was felt on the eastern side of the Atlantic as it was on the west. Some political leaders in the Old World began to resist the growing influence of America on their own societies, and some intellectuals pointed to the ways in which American imports had distorted European experience. Voltaire's satirical novel *Candide, or Optimism*, published in 1759, was the greatest best seller of the eighteenth century, having been widely translated. Candide, a naive young man who had been taught that this world, as it had been created by God, was the best of all possible worlds, witnessed horror after horror as he moved around the Atlantic. He encountered his old teacher, Pangloss, who had been reduced to beggary and whose face was covered with "pus-filled sores" and his nose partially eaten away. Pangloss had syphilis, and he traced its transmission through a series of unfortunates, the first of whom "had gotten it in a straight line from one of Christopher Columbus's comrades."[6]

Leading Europeans grew uneasy about their implication in slavery through American colonies, especially as the volume of the trade in enslaved Africans continued to increase. Those in port cities were constantly reminded of the wealth accumulated by merchants involved in human trafficking, and their expanding influence. Voltaire's character Candide, in the Dutch colony of Surinam on the northeast coast of South America, saw a man of African descent lying by the side of the road. He was wearing blue canvas shorts and was missing his right hand and his left leg. Candide, horrified, asked if the man's master was responsible for his injuries. The man said yes and that such was the custom: "When we're working in the sugar mills and the grinding wheel catches a finger, they cut off a hand. When we try to escape, they cut off a leg." Through the voice of this man Voltaire vividly evoked the complicity of Europeans in the suffering of the enslaved: "This is what it costs, supplying you Europeans with sugar."[7]

Some residents in those same port cities disliked seeing people of African descent in their midst. In Iberia, with its long association with Africa, a cosmopolitan population was less remarkable, but in France and England the presence of Africans was startling. Encountering men and women who were completely deprived of rights, as in the writings of philosophes like Voltaire, forced Europeans to confront their own involvement in slavery across the ocean.

Some Europeans began to organize movements to abolish the slave trade; some hoped to abolish slavery itself. In France, the Societé des Amis des Noirs (Society of the Friends of the Blacks) and the English Society for the Abolition of the Slave Trade brought home the horrors of the traffic. Spanish law had always institutionalized pathways to freedom for the enslaved, and the Spanish colonies, unlike those of other European nations, contained many free people of color. Nonetheless, the numbers of enslaved Africans continued to grow.

Leading French intellectuals spoke out against French participation in the enslavement of Africans. The Abbé Raynal, a former Jesuit and leading philosophe, with the collaboration of such writers as Denis Diderot, wrote a history of European involvement in the Atlantic which contained a stunning denunciation of slavery: "Slavery is entirely repugnant to humanity, reason, and justice." These writers went on to declare: "He who supports the system of slavery is an enemy of the whole human race." In this book, published in Amsterdam in 1770, they warned of "the impending storm" and said "the negroes only want a chief, sufficiently courageous, to lead them to vengeance and slaughter." When this "great man" emerged, they predicted, the black code would be replaced with a white code carrying terrible consequences for the plantation owners.[8]

Little Ephraim Robin John and Ancona Robin Robin John, the young merchants from Old Calabar who had been illegally enslaved, benefited from growing abolitionist sentiment in England. The second time they were tricked and reenslaved, they were held on board ship at the English port of Bristol for several months, awaiting shipment. Now, in 1773, they were able to make use of their specialized knowledge as they wrote to influential Englishmen, including the slave trader Thomas Jones, whom they had known in Old Calabar, about their plight. Ultimately they wrote to the English chief justice, the earl of Mansfield, an act that demonstrates their intimate knowledge of English affairs. Mansfield had issued a ruling in the *Somerset v. Stewart* case in 1772. James Somerset was an enslaved man who had been brought to England from Jamaica by his master. After he escaped and was recaptured, his English godparents brought suit in his favor as he was held on board ship in a situation very similar to that experienced later by the Robin Johns. Mansfield ruled that Somerset, after having been free in England, could not be forcibly sent back to Jamaica.

Thomas Jones finally responded to the Robin Johns's pleas by obtaining a writ of habeus corpus that required their captor to put them on land, but when they were landed, they were put in jail. As Little Ephraim pointed out in his letter, they had been illegally enslaved in the beginning. Chief Justice Mansfield examined them in person. Ultimately they were freed through a process of arbitration rather than a formal court ruling. Once they were free, Jones, the slave trader, took them to his home and placed them in school in Bristol, where they were treated as the princes they were. They asked to meet the brothers Charles and John Wesley, the founders of Methodism, and asked for instruction in Christianity. The Wesleys framed the conversion experience of all who became Methodists as rescue from enslavement to sin. Finally, in 1774, seven years after they had been enslaved, they returned to Old Calabar, where Little Ephraim once again engaged in the trade in human beings.

The Robin Johns's experience was not typical. While native and creole societies in the Americas were moving toward control of their own course and Europeans began to question their implication in American commerce, the west coast of Africa continued to be drawn into the trade in slaves. The trade reached its height in the final years of the eighteenth century, with 80,000 people being sent across the Atlantic every year. Europeans were restricted to settlements on the coast as in earlier times, so the interior remained in African control. African and European merchants in the coastal trading centers maintained a cosmopolitan society. Muslim leaders in the interior resisted the intrusion of slave traders into their areas and in some cases took control of governments in coups designed to make sure that Muslims were not enslaved.

Muslim governments came to power in Guinea early in the eighteenth century, in Senegal in the 1770s, and in northern Nigeria, the Sokoto caliphate, in 1804.

Interest in collecting and classifying American products, and assimilating their meaning for European understanding of human history, intensified in the eighteenth century. The great French *Encyclopédie* project, led by Denis Diderot, sought to combat superstition by bringing together all knowledge in a single publication. American realities challenged inherited claims, and Diderot and his colleagues urged Europeans to look at the evidence with a clear-eyed gaze. The German scientist Alexander von Humboldt spent several years on his survey of South America at the end of the eighteenth and beginning of the nineteenth centuries and wrote extensively about his findings and theories.

The old idea that America was still in a primitive or earlier stage of development when Europeans first approached it appeared in the eighteenth century in the work of European intellectuals such as Cornelis de Pauw and Georges-Louis Leclerc, Comte de Buffon. Euro-Americans were more skeptical, especially as writers such as Buffon followed Bacon in arguing that nature in the Americas had been held back in its development by a catastrophic flood. Thomas Jefferson wrote his *Notes on the State of Virginia* to prove that the American environment was as developed as any other in the world and rejected the notion of a universal flood, using the best scientific reasoning of his time. He concluded: "Ignorance is preferable to error; and he is less remote from the truth who believes nothing, then he who believes what is wrong."[9]

Americans also questioned other theories. William Stith, who published *The History of the First Discovery and Settlement of Virginia* in 1747, scoffed at those who wanted to endow Europe's relationship to America with greater antiquity through "monstrous Legends" such as that of the Welsh bishop Madoc's legendary medieval voyages, and wrote, "Plato's Fable also of the Atlantick Islands has been applied to this Subject."[10] These writers and their contemporaries on the Atlantic's east side were establishing an independent history for America.

Many intellectuals wondered whether the path taken by the Americas through all those millenia of separation was different from that of Europe and Asia. Others hoped that study of America's people and their customs could lead to an understanding of the fundamental laws of human society, as Newton's three laws of motion had allowed scientists to understand the underlying physical laws on which the universe operated. Father François-Joseph Lafitau was a Jesuit missionary in New France in the early eighteenth century who wrote a major treatise on the customs of the Indians. His goal was to create a science of society, so he compared the Indians' customs to those of ancient cultures as a way of finding and isolating the most basic elements of human society. Lafitau's ultimate goal was to verify that all the world's peoples stemmed from the original creation in the Book of Genesis, a position he thought was best demonstrated by their shared cultural attributes. Everything he saw in America from snowshoes to scalping found analogues in his reading of ancient sources. He wrote that the Indians' pipe or "calumet of peace" was just like Mercury's staff, and he noted that dissemination occurred even in the ancient world: "Mercury was a foreign divinity for the Greeks who had taken him from the Egyptians and other barbarous peoples." In this discussion he also demonstrated his wide reading, as he referred readers to an engraving of a pipe adorned with feathers in Robert Beverley's *History and Present State of Virginia*, published in 1705.[11]

While eighteenth-century observers such as Lafitau continued the ethnographic practices of earlier centuries, their work found a mixed reception in Europe, partly because some thinkers now questioned the religious universalism it sought to establish. The great philosophe Voltaire ridiculed Lafitau's reasoning: "Lafitau has the Americans come from the ancient Greeks, and here are his reasons. The Greeks had fables, some Americans have them as well. The first Greeks went hunting, some Americans do so as well. The first Greeks had oracles, the Americans have sorcerers. The ancient Greeks danced at their festivals, the Americans dance, too."[12] Just as Voltaire questioned the wisdom of fighting wars for American land, he and those who thought like him questioned both the techniques and the motives of the writers who advocated involvement in American pursuits.

Despite the skepticism of the intellectuals, one result of Atlantic involvement for many was a greater sense of future possibilities for human beings. Many people, even among those who had been unwillingly thrust into unfamiliar pursuits, found new ways to exert a degree of control over their own lives. People who had migrated for religious reasons were a prime example of this newfound sense of empowerment. Others, who had fled economic distress, may have had limited control over their personal lives but still found that they could manipulate their circumstances to some extent. Even the total deprivation of rights for the enslaved, ironically, led to the notion that all those who were not enslaved owned a minimum standard of rights—or at least the men among them did. Another effect of population movements was the erosion of old notions of difference. As they shared experiences, people of American Indian, African, and European descent came to see that they had problems and interests in common. Old separations did not disappear, but the possibility of joint action seemed more realistic. This new sense of basic human rights and common heritage meant that people all around the Atlantic reacted in unexpected ways to government efforts to impose restrictions on them. The spread of coffee houses, where Atlantic-grown coffee was consumed along with news and rumors, created public spaces in cosmopolitan centers all around the ocean where new ideas and claims were discussed and disseminated.

Resistance took many forms in the Americas, only some of which involved formal revolution. From the beginning of slavery as an institution, individuals seized opportunities to take control of their own lives and escaped into inaccessible places, often the mountainous interior of islands or other equally difficult terrain, and formed communities. These self-liberated people were collectively called Maroons. As in other American situations, Maroon communities created a new sense of identity among people from many different sources in the Old World. They created their own economies but also lived by raiding the plantations. Those in authority periodically conducted campaigns against them but Maroon communities continued to exist and grow.

Britain, victorious in the Seven Years' War, decided to keep a huge standing army in North America, ostensibly to police the frontier and aid in the incorporation of the vast territories recently acquired from France. Authorities in Whitehall, the seat of government in London, also decided that the newly expensive empire must begin to pay its own way, and they dispatched officials to end the smuggling that had become a way of life and to oversee the collection of new and old taxes. The new British presence in their midst and the apparent assault on the traditions of self-government built over more than a century called forth resistance on the colonists' part. Their way of confronting the challenge, through agreements not to consume British goods, had an effect similar to the Indians' response to their prophets' calls to reject imported products: it built solidarity among populations that were so diverse in their origins and ways of life that leaders had despaired of ever achieving a sense of common cause.

The American War of Independence itself demonstrated what Europeans would learn over and over again when attempting to bring rebel populations under control: it is not enough to have a superior army and to hold the main population centers when all the people are potential combatants of one sort or another. Moreover, pacification campaigns, such as the one the British army conducted through the American South, are doomed to failure. The South contained many

Maroons were enslaved people who liberated themselves and built towns in inaccessible locations where fresh escapees were welcomed. Trelawney was one such community in Jamaica. General Research and Reference Division ID# 1228976, Schomburg Center for Research in Black Culture, The New York Public Library, Astor, Lenox and Tilden Foundations

loyalists, and British strategists hoped that they could be enlisted to extend control over pacified areas as the army moved on. But armies create enemies wherever they go and the supposedly pacified areas the British left behind quickly became more resistant than ever. Southerners were alarmed as news of revolutionary rhetoric spread among the enslaved, and they put their efforts into making sure that their workforce stayed under their control. When France entered the war on the American side in 1778 after it became apparent that Britain would not win the war easily, this conflict became, from the Atlantic perspective, just one more in the long series of wars between France and Britain and their allies. Ultimately, Britain did not so much lose the war as lose the will to continue a conflict that was draining the treasury and had no end in sight.

As the war was winding down in North America, a revolutionary movement whose call to arms was explicitly modeled on that of the United States was launched in the Netherlands, where opposition to the hereditary power of the House of Orange began to arise. The Patriots, as they styled themselves, called for the people to demand participation in government and presented this program as a return to the principles on which the Dutch Republic had been founded, the consent of the people. Emulating the Americans, the Patriots organized citizen militias to confront the forces of the stadholder, the head of government, and the movement spread over the whole country. Patriot writings were suffused with Enlightenment ideals, but, as a Dutch movement, it was also deeply imbued with the religious traditions of the republic.

Americans declared their independence claiming entitlement from "the laws of Nature and Nature's God" and said that human rights were "self-evident," not granted by government or any other human agency. As the American states inaugurated a constitutional government based on the consent of the people, France's government confronted the huge debt accumulated from the imperial wars of the eighteenth century, culminating in their part in the American Revolution. Louis XVI called an extraordinary meeting of the Estates General for May 1789. This national assembly had not met since the early seventeenth century. Louis expected the meeting to advise and assist him in paying the debt, but the process of selecting delegates and polling opinion throughout the country led to creation of thousands of formal lists of grievances. The lists were segregated by estate—the clergy, the nobility, and the commons—and so no general picture of what ailed the nation and especially of the cure for its ills emerged. The third estate, the commons, moved to create a national assembly in which the people as a whole would be represented.

The movement that culminated in revolution was widespread; all over the country groups of peasants attacked the estates of the nobility, and feudalism, which was defined as the privileges of the few over the great bulk of the people, came to be defined as the enemy. In August 1789, the National Assembly legislated the equality of all French and abolished inherited privilege. The Declaration of the Rights of Man, like the American Declaration of Independence, asserted that human beings are born with rights that pertain to all. Some members of the nobility, including the Marquis de Lafayette, who had participated in the French forces supporting the American Revolution, sympathized with the movement. Thomas Jefferson, author of the American declaration, was in Paris as ambassador at the time and Lafayette consulted him on the French declaration's wording. Whereas the American document had listed the rights of "men" as "life, liberty, and the pursuit of happiness," the French put them as "liberty, property, security, and resistance to oppression." Neither revolution in these statements meant to recognize full rights and membership in the political society for women or children; and slaves, as property, occupied an ambiguous role. Over succeeding months, the Roman Catholic church was disestablished in France and church properties were nationalized.

Popular movements—the Jacobins, who were named for the seized convent in which the original group met, and the *sans-culottes*, urban artisans who wore full-length trousers rather than the knee britches known as culottes worn by elite men—gained followings all over the country. Pressures from these groups led to the creation of a Convention to write a new constitution for the nation that would eliminate the monarchy. This same Convention, sitting as a court of law, decided that Louis XVI must die and he was publicly executed in 1793. Revolutionaries set out to create a new order based on reason rather than the accumulation of past decisions and compromises that had constituted the ancien régime.

The lesson Europeans drew from the French Revolution had more to do with the dangers of unlimited popular control than with the positive power of reason as France descended into the Terror, in which those who were considered insufficiently committed to the cause were hunted down. The revolution ended a decade after it began with the coup that brought Napoleon Bonaparte to power.

France claimed four sugar colonies in the Caribbean at the time of the revolution: Martinique, Guadeloupe, Cayenne, and Saint-Domingue, which occupied the western part of the island of Hispaniola; the Spanish colony of Santo Domingo on the other side of the central mountain range occupied the rest of the island. Although the French had been willing to trade all of Canada and the North American interior for Guadeloupe, the truly rich colony was Saint-Domingue, which produced half the coffee and almost half the sugar grown throughout the world. Planters in the colonies consumed products from home, including many luxury items. Saint-Domingue had a growing population of free people of African or mixed descent, which virtually equaled the population of Europeans. Both were dwarfed by the enormous number of enslaved Africans, the largest slave force in the Caribbean. After the Seven Years War, legislation attempting to create a rigid separation of people of color from Europeans and to limit free people of color's sphere of action created unrest. Like some Indians in North America, the excluded sometimes looked to the king for protection against local elites; independence and democracy were not necessarily guarantees of rights for all.

When the call went out in France for parishes to elect delegates to the meeting of the Estates General that began the revolution, planters in

Saint-Domingue held impromptu elections of their own and even sent delegates to be present at the meeting. Their charge was to argue that the colony was not a possession but had voluntarily put itself under the protection of France and that its survival required that it be allowed to trade freely with all comers. The first revolutionary impulse, as in North America, thus stemmed from the white planters' desire for greater autonomy.

Although planters thought they could insulate their islands from events in Europe and selectively introduce elements of the new regime, the massive population of enslaved workers quickly became aware that a new form of government based on universal human rights was emerging in France. They also knew that ending slavery was a subject of discussion for some influential leaders. Port cities throughout the Caribbean welcomed ships from all over the Atlantic, and the sailors brought news as well as commodities. A contingent of free colored soldiers from Cap Français (modern Cap Haitien) had been part of the aid France gave to the American revolutionaries, so the course of that revolution was well known in Saint-Domingue. Large Sunday gatherings of slaves disseminated their belief that the government had already taken steps to mitigate their plight but that the planters had illegally ignored those decrees. And the leaders that Raynal and Diderot had predicted emerged. Georges Biassou was born a slave on a sugar plantation near the cosmopolitan city of Cap Français on Saint-Domingue where he was exposed to news from all around the Atlantic. He began a movement with his friend Toussaint Louverture; Jean-François, a self-liberated slave, was also important in these events. Biassou held a leadership position on his plantation and therefore had greater freedom of movement than most of the enslaved workers; Toussaint, a skilled herbalist, had won his freedom twenty years earlier. In August 1791, slaves rose up all over Saint-Domingue and attacked and burned the plantations simultaneously, bringing production of coffee and sugar to a virtual halt.

The rebels acted on news from France, but they were also influenced by African inheritance. Many enslaved workers in Saint-Domingue at this time were African-born and they had brought their own traditional definitions of good government with them. A monarch who was in tune with the people's wishes was portrayed as descending from an original benevolent blacksmith; the blacksmith, as in the Ogun tradition, was a figure who brought people together. A monarch who kept the nation's resources for himself was seen as tainted by witchcraft.

Male African-born slaves in Saint-Domingue may have been soldiers in Africa; their engagement in warfare led to their enslavement in many cases. Civil war in Kongo between rival families with claims to

Cap-Français (now Cap-Haitien) was one of the centers of the Haitian Revolution. With the city in flames, people from a variety of origins flee the destruction, an image that is a vivid reminder of how revolution had changed everything. Manuscripts, Archives and Rare Books Division ID# 485443, Schomburg Center for Research in Black Culture, The New York Public Library, Astor, Lenox and Tilden Foundations

power and their followers had gone on intermittently from the mid-seventeenth century, like the conflict between England and France and their supporters in Europe. Fighting broke out with new intensity in the 1760s and continued until almost the end of the century. Many of the men sent into slavery, most under French auspices, had been participants in this war, and they were experienced soldiers whose weapons had been primarily French muskets. Wars in other African areas also supplied workers as the enslaved population of Saint-Domingue grew dramatically. When fighting broke out in Saint-Domingue, they brought their experience to the struggle. In the Saint-Domingue rebellion, companies of soldiers were organized along African lines of allegiance.

Commissioners sent from France tried to broker a settlement, but they only sowed confusion. Ultimately they were persuaded to issue a proclamation ending slavery, and the Convention in France ratified this for all French colonies in 1794. Meanwhile, Spanish armies composed mainly of people of color, both free and enslaved, moved into Saint-Domingue. British forces from Jamaica also intervened, as France had done when Britain's American colonies rebelled. The Spanish and the British, like the French commissioners, tried to lure the rebels to fight on their side by promises of freedom and status. Free people of color and the formerly enslaved had to decide whom to trust. Toussaint Louverture and Biassou agreed with those who thought the French commissioners could not be trusted; they had already shifted their positions too often as circumstances seemed to change. And the invading armies recognized the rights of people of color only as long as they were willing to take an active role in the fight on their side.

Initially the rebels joined the Spanish forces seeking to overturn French control, but ultimately the leaders split. Toussaint cast his lot with newly Republican France to defeat the Spanish invaders, and Biassou continued the alliance with the Spanish, who promised wide scope to the formerly enslaved. Spanish forces were defeated in 1795 and the British army also withdrew. Yellow fever had mowed down thousands of the vulnerable troops. People of African descent had a degree of immunity to yellow fever as they had to malaria, and the revolution's leaders realized their advantage; Toussaint had predicted that the invaders would be defeated by the rainy season. Many of the former slaves who had fought on the Spanish side left for Cuba; the Cuban governor was reluctant to admit them and they were dispersed to Trinidad and other islands. Georges Biassou and his family went to Spanish Florida.

Toussaint now embarked on a plan to recreate the plantation system without slavery. His invasion of the Spanish part of the island and unilateral promulgation of a constitution that guaranteed freedom and equality to all angered Napoleon; with the agreement of Britain and the United States, Napoleon sent a force to restore French control in 1802. The United States acquired the Louisiana Territory from France during these upheavals. Despite massive deaths among the men, the French army defeated the forces under Toussaint and the other generals, Henri Christophe and Jean-Jacques Dessalines; Toussaint and his family were sent to France, where he died in prison. As the French commander began to re-create the plantation system, complete with slavery, rebellions sprang up all over the island and were greeted with a systematic campaign to eliminate any people of color who were deemed to pose a threat. Devastated by the rebels and, as in previous campaigns, by yellow fever in epidemic proportions, the French army withdrew and Dessalines, restored to authority, proclaimed the republic of Haiti, named for what was believed to be the original Taino name for the island, at the beginning of 1804. As had happened in France, Haiti's government descended into dictatorship and further upheavals ensued, but Haiti continued as the first independent nation comprising and led by people of color that emerged from the early modern Atlantic system. Haiti was the first nation to abolish slavery; legally, all citizens of Haiti were

In acknowledgment of the nation's debt to Toussaint Louverture's "firmness, activity, and tireless zeal and rare virtues," St. Domingue's Constitution of 1801 named Louverture governor for life. General Research and Reference Division ID# 1228923, Schomburg Center for Research in Black Culture, The New York Public Library, Astor, Lenox and Tilden Foundations

designated as black; *blanc* (white) meant simply foreigner or outsider. Twelve years after Haiti was established, that country gave substantial aid to Simon Bolívar as he led the revolution that would end the Spanish empire in the Americas.

Back in Europe, although the French Revolution ended the monarchy, Napoleon continued its foreign policy trajectory with even greater vigor. Rather than just keeping Spain and Portugal as allies, he invaded them and put his own nominees on their thrones. The Portuguese crown and the country's elites moved the monarchy to Brazil in 1808 after Napoleon's invasion, the only time that an American colony became the principal site of a European empire's government. With the discovery of gold at the end of the seventeenth century, and diamonds a few decades later, Brazil had become ever more important in Portuguese thinking over the course of the eighteenth century. A series of rebellions in the later eighteenth century raised hopes and fears, as the interests of Indians, the enslaved, free people of color, and those of European descent seemed to be in conflict. Brazil had always had a thriving trade directly with Africa, and the number of Africans imported as slaves soared at the end of the eighteenth century; as Haiti's sugar and coffee production flagged, Brazil and other continental locations became important suppliers. English merchants formed relationships with Portuguese merchants in the Brazil trade, and the English government took an interest in fostering those relationships. But transfer of the court to Brazil meant less freedom and flexibility for American traders. The court returned to Portugal in 1821 and Brazil became an independent monarchy in 1822.

Authorities in Madrid continued to try to pursue the path of imperial reform and especially to tighten control of trade between the colonies and Spain. Successful rebellions, in which creoles saw their future in rejection of Spanish control, would not come for another two decades, and they, like the events following the Seven Years' War, involved the continuing spillover from the endless cycle of wars between Britain and France. With the king deposed by France, the bureaucratic system that had, at least in theory, directed the colonies' development became less powerful, and Spain's American colonies were now forced to begin charting their own course. Many were dismayed by the loss of the monarch as their reference point; others, distressed by the royal government's continuing campaign to put officials direct from Spain into offices that had traditionally been filled by creoles as part of the campaign to extract more revenue from the colonies, greeted this new situation as an opportunity and created self-governing councils throughout the provinces.

One issue for all rebelling American colonies was: Who were the people in whose name the revolutions were waged? The North American colonies all had traditions of self-government for male Europeans although the possibilities for participation for those below the social and economic elites varied. Deference, the accepted idea that society's glue was the universal acknowledgment that some men were natural leaders because of their place atop the community's pyramid, made the system work. People of African descent and American Indians were largely excluded from revolutionaries' definition of "We the People." In the Spanish colonies, definitions were much more complex. The Spanish empire had always had well-established legal avenues to emancipation for the enslaved and had recognized a range of categories of mixed descent.

In the changed situation in Spain's colonies, creoles of mostly European extraction initially called for creation of representative assemblies in the colonies after the king's removal; these calls assumed that the system of deference would continue to operate. These movements were quite localized and certainly were not yet cast in terms of creating independent nations. A few leaders, most notably Francisco de Miranda from Venezuela who had fought on the patriots' side in the American Revolution as a captain in the Spanish army, had looked forward to a similar movement among the Spanish colonies. But independence was still beyond the aspirations of most. The colonies' population was larger than that of Spain by this time and many of these organizers saw themselves as defending the empire against the depredations of the French.

The Spanish constitution, promulgated under French control in 1812, included a definition of Spaniard that encompassed people on both sides of the Atlantic including Indians and free people of mixed or African heritage. Within each colony, the Indian population and people of European and African descent were supposed to have been kept separate, although in practice such separation was rarely achieved, and much of the population was of mixed origin. Under the 1812 constitution, those who had some African mixture were offered a lower kind of citizenship. Slaves were completely excluded from Spanishness. The constitution declared that all the empire was a single administrative unit and would have ignored the different history and status of each of the American colonies. It also ended the special protected status of Indian polities, as they were folded into the general category of citizen. In practice, even if not in theory, Spanish Americans saw their interests as being neglected and curtailed by the new system. As revolutionary leaders increasingly used the language of slavery to describe Spanish control, the enslaved began to argue that their freedom must be on the agenda, especially as armies on both sides offered freedom to slaves who joined the armies. One Ecuadorian, Alejandro Campusano, testified that "the sweet voice of the patria came to my ears, and desiring to be one of its soldiers as much to shake off the yoke of general oppression as to free me from the slavery in which I found myself, I ran swiftly to present myself to the liberating troops of Quito."[13]

The implications all remained to be worked out when the Spanish monarchy was restored in 1814 after Napoleon's defeat at the Battle of Trafalgar and the subsequent pulling back of French forces from Spain. All those leaders who had seen themselves as defending the monarch in the face of French tyranny suddenly regarded Ferdinand VII in a wholly new light. The restored government rescinded all the acts of the previous regime, including the new constitution. Movements in Venezuela, New Granada, and Buenos Aires in Argentina began campaigns for independence, and Miranda's associate Simón Bolívar emerged as the leader in Venezuela by 1813. He was born in 1783, the year the American Revolution formally ended, into an elite Venezuelan creole family of European descent; Bolívars had been in America for almost two centuries. Bolívar completed his education at a military academy in Caracas and went to Europe at the age of fifteen, the first of several trips. He spent most of his time in Spain on his first trip, but lived in France and traveled in Italy,

Simón Bolívar argued that the colonies had been kept underdeveloped, their purpose being "to produce gold for the insatiable greed of Spain." Courtesy of the John Carter Brown Library at Brown University, Accession# 02–63

England, and Germany on his subsequent voyages and he avidly read the writings of the Enlightenment philosophers. While in England seeking support for Venezuela's cause, he met with the slave trade opponent William Wilberforce and other leaders. He also traveled through the United States. He formed the resolution to break "the chains with which Spanish power oppresses us" while standing with friends on Rome's Aventine Hill.[14] Bolívar also saw the logic of ending slavery: "It seems to me madness that a revolution for freedom expects to maintain slavery."[15]

King Ferdinand VII, on the advice of his ministers, decided that the American colonies had to be brought into line. In 1815 a large army arrived to restore the colonies to Spanish control. The fighting across the colonies went on for years and was extremely destructive. Mexico, Guatemala, and Peru had successful rebellions and Santo Domingo ultimately followed suit. Aspirations for a united states of the former Spanish colonies soon gave way before local loyalties in the huge and varied territories from which a variety of nations emerged at different times across the former empire.

Rebellion had not been the obvious choice for all subjects in every part of Spanish America; merchants and wealthy plantation owners did not necessarily see their future as brighter with independence, and some regions feared being subordinate to more powerful colonial centers. When members of the lower orders began to turn out in rallies in support of genuine independence, creoles sometimes had second thoughts about where their best interests lay. Indians, like those in the Ohio Country to the north, had to consider whether their concerns would be more respected by independent creole governments or by European authorities. The island colonies of Cuba and Puerto Rico did not rebel. The Spanish-born fled back to Spain as the rebellions achieved independence, just as many French and creole property owners had left Saint-Domingue for the United States after the Haitian Revolution. Loyalists in England's American colonies reversed the direction, as they streamed south into the Caribbean and north into Canada after the American Revolution.

Newly independent countries, emulating the French Revolution, proclaimed the equality of all free people, although, as in much of the United States, property qualifications regulated access to full participation. The abolition of slavery came in stages in the former Spanish colonies. In 1816, Bolívar promised freedom to all slaves who enlisted in his army. Several newly independent states took the first step by proclaiming that children born to enslaved mothers would be free; some stipulated that they would be free when they reached the age of majority. Slavery did not end in the United States until 1865. Many European nations and the United States formally ended the transatlantic slave trade in the first decades of the nineteenth century, but the illegal trade went on. The shift from legal to illegal trade meant that new locations on Africa's west coast became the principal sites of the trade; the old cosmopolitan centers went into decline. It also meant higher mortality rates on the transatlantic voyage, and a much higher proportion of children—more than 40 percent—in the human cargoes. Cuba and Brazil were the principal countries to which the enslaved were sold.

Modern nations were created around the Atlantic in these decades at the end of the eighteenth century and the beginning of the nineteenth. Definitions of citizenship remained murky in some cases, and the lines of inclusion and exclusion were still being defined, but previous ways that various classes of people had been delineated were eliminated or modified. Rights, a concept that had formerly inhered in specific groups defined by status, occupation, religion, or ethnicity, now increasingly came to be seen as pertaining to human beings in general. Free men had rights denied to women and the enslaved, and it would be a long time before all would be deemed to have the same status before the law. Modernity was in its infancy in this period, but the basis for modern systems had been laid.

The Atlantic

The early modern Atlantic was always a work in progress. How-ever much government planners, merchants, religious leaders, and ordinary migrants hoped for stability and permanence, all arrangements were subject to change. On the macro level, carefully bal-anced alliance systems crumbled when empires swapped territories. This happened on a large scale at the end of the Seven Years' War, the first time that European governments had focused their attention pri-marily on the Americas. When France decided to evacuate the mainland of North America, Indian nations that had built their strategy on bal-ancing between the French and the British suddenly confronted a situa-tion where they dealt with only one empire and their leverage was gone. French colonists found themselves now part of the British Empire and had to learn to live within it. Thousands of Acadians were expelled from the maritime provinces of Canada and forcibly moved south in a harrowing forced march; many ended up in Louisiana where they founded the Cajun culture. Throughout the Caribbean, also, people had to learn to cope with new systems and new leaders.

On the more personal level, people had always had to learn to improvise as their situation changed. A few stories have come down to us, but most of these people disappeared from the record. Presumably, the chameleons, those who were really successful at adapting to new cultures and circumstances, are the ones whose stories we do not know—they disappeared because they blended in so successfully. Those whose stories survive were either publicized as exemplary or they were caught repeatedly in the maelstrom of changes and competition so their names came up again and again.

Just as arrangements on the land were constantly in flux, how people conceptualized the ocean changed as well. From the time that the earliest maps of the lands bordering the ocean began to be drawn, some ob-servers pointed out that South America's east coast seemed to fit neatly into the coastline of West Africa. Abraham Ortelius, a sixteenth-century

Flemish geographer who created a world map and the first world atlas based on the new discoveries, was the first to make this connection in print. This perception provoked the idea that all the landmasses had originally been one and that some cataclysm in the distant past had split them apart. Thus the ocean, or at least the part that was usually labeled the Ethiopian Sea, had once not been there. Francis Bacon took up this idea, and Alexander von Humboldt added to the argument that the continents had not originally been separated by a vast body of water by pointing to the similarity of rocks and fossils on the corresponding shores.

Modern world maps have the Atlantic Ocean at their center, and this seems natural to us. But of course configuring our picture of the world as centered on this particular body of water is pure convention; it is no more right or natural than the medieval maps showing the known landmass surrounded by the world ocean. This convention implies that the initiatives and connections formed across this sea in the early modern period were, and are, the engine of growth and change in the world.

The Atlantic had never been a closed system. Even before commentators began to write of an Atlantic Ocean, goods and people had been connecting this ocean to the South Sea, as Europeans called the Pacific, the Indian Ocean, and the huge Arctic and Antarctic oceans. From early times the landmasses were as much barriers as opportunities, and venturers continued to look for even more waterways that would penetrate them. Following the waterways they found around continents, mariners inaugurated a global trade system in the sixteenth century and this system has grown and become ever more integrated ever since.

All these waters were variously conceptualized by participants, usually in ways that made them as favorable to new enterprises as possible. To speak of the Atlantic Ocean, as people came to do in the nineteenth century, was as much a matter of convention as to see several ocean bands between Africa and Europe and the Americas as earlier venturers had done, especially if the phrase Atlantic Ocean implies a bounded body of water. Modern oceanographers and climatologists suggest that Columbus's title, referring to the Ocean Sea, actually makes the most sense. We now understand that the world's oceans form a single unified system, so the medieval and Renaissance notion of a single World Ocean is not as far-fetched as previously thought. Clearly, developments in one body of water affect the entire system. Study of the phenomenon known as El Niño, in which warm water periodically appears on the surface off Peru's coast in the winter—the name El Niño refers to its coincidence with the celebration of the birthday of Jesus—has led climatologists to understand how interconnected the oceans are. El Niño interacts with changes in pressure across the Pacific Ocean, and the product of this interaction is widespread weather anomalies all around the world. The onset of the monsoon in South Asia is affected by El Niño, as is the timing of the appearance of cherry blossoms in Japan, and the height of the Nile River at flood. Atlantic droughts and storms can be traced to El Niño's effects. Because markers like the Nile flood stage and the onset of the monsoon have been recorded for centuries, historical climatologists have traced the incidence of El Niño back into the distant past. Thus the interconnected Atlantic Ocean becomes once again part of the Ocean Sea and connected to human activities and natural trends all over the world.

The interconnected ocean system was experienced especially by the Spanish in the early modern period. Some French and English in the north participated in the ginseng trade with Asia, but this was a limited enterprise. In Spanish America, where the colonies looked west as well as east, the Pacific and Atlantic oceans were indeed joined. From the middle of the sixteenth century, the Manila galleons brought spices, silk, porcelains, and other luxury goods in demand in Europe to the port of Acapulco and took silver back to Asia. Some of these Asian products stayed in the Americas and fueled trades; a delicate Wanli porcelain Chinese wine cup has been unearthed in the early fort at Jamestown in a context that shows it had arrived shortly after the colony had been founded in 1607 and just a few years after this porcelain technique had been perfected in China. Logs of these huge ships' voyages have proven useful in determining climatic conditions; the trips took much longer in the mid-seventeenth century than in periods before or after, indicating changes in the prevailing winds. Spain's presence on the Americas' western shore meant that it came closest to realizing the dream with which Columbus first set out: find a route to the rich Asian trades.

Chronology

360 BCE
Plato tells story of the lost continent of Atlantis

718
Muslims from North Africa conquer Spain; the province of Al-Andaluz is created

1000
Norse make settlements in Greenland, Newfoundland

1340s
Europeans encounter the Canary Islands

1352
Ibn Battuta crosses the Sahara to Mali

1400s
Europeans encounter Atlantic islands; Madeira, Azores, Cape Verdes; Songhay empire is established; Portuguese begin to trade with West African kingdoms; Mexica and Inca empires consolidate their power; Iroquois League, Hodeno-saunee, is formed; Europeans begin fishing in Iceland

1480s
Fishing expeditions from Europe to Newfound Banks begin

1492
Columbus crosses Atlantic; North Africans are expelled from Spain

1500
Juan de la Cosa creates the first map showing America; Portuguese land in Brazil

1512
Laws of Burgos are passed in Spain

1517
Martin Luther publishes his Ninety-Five Theses, arguing for the Bible as the sole source of authority in Christianity, and begins the Protestant Reformation

1521
Spanish conquer Tenochtitlan

1524
Verrazano sails along North American east coast

1530s
Brazil is divided into captaincies; Jacques Cartier explores St. Lawrence River

1535
Viceroyalty of New Spain is founded

1540s
Expeditions led by De Soto and Coronado cross the North American continent; silver mines are opened in Spanish America

1542
New Laws regulate treatment of Indians in Spanish colonies

1543
Viceroyalty of Peru is founded

MID-1500s
Mines are developed at Potosí

1550s
Status of Indians under Spanish law is established

1575
Portuguese build bases on Angolan coast

1591
Songhay empire is conquered by Morocco

c.1600
Brazilian sugar output surpasses that of Atlantic islands; Portuguese attempt to establish control in Angola; Lincean Academy is founded in Rome

1607
English settlement at Jamestown is founded; English create settlement in Ulster, Ireland

1608
French settlement at Quebec is founded

1610
Spanish settlement at Santa Fe is founded

1618–1648
Thirty Years' War in Europe between Protestant and Roman Catholic countries

1620s
Apparition of Lady in Blue appears in northern New Spain

1630s–1654
Dutch control Pernambuco

1641
Marie de l'Incarnation founds Ursuline convent in New France

1660
Royal Society is founded in England

1663
French Ministry of Marine takes control of New France

1666
French Academy of Sciences is founded

1680s
LaSalle leads expedition to discover mouth of Mississippi River; English government begins to implement plan to revoke charters of American colonies

1690s
Extreme Little Ice Age conditions are experienced

1710
Capuchin nuns travel to nunnery in Peru

1717
Viceroyalty of New Granada is founded

EARLY 1700s
Muslim government comes to power in Guinea

MID-1700s
Spanish empire institutes Bourbon reforms

1750s
Neolin experiences visions of Master of Life

1754–63
Seven Years' War (French and Indian War)

1759
Voltaire's *Candide* is published; Jesuits are expelled from Brazil

1767
Robin John brothers are captured on African coast; Jesuits are expelled from Spanish territories

1770
Muslim government comes to power in Senegal

1774
Robin John brothers are returned to Old Calabar

1776
Viceroyalty of Río de la Plata is founded

1776–1783
American Revolution

1780
Túpac Amaru revolt in Andean highlands; Comunero revolt in New Granada

1789
Outbreak of French Revolution

1791
Revolution in Saint-Domingue

1804
Sokoto caliphate is established in northern Nigeria; Republic of Haiti is proclaimed

1808
Portuguese court is moved to Brazil; revolutionary movement begins in Mexico (New Spain)

1811
Revolutionary movement begins in Venezuela

1814
Revolutionary movement begins in Peru

1821
Mexico becomes independent

1822
Brazil becomes independent

Notes

CHAPTER 1

1. On these points, see Martin W. Lewis, "Dividing the Ocean Sea," *Geographical Review* 89 (1999): 188–214.
2. "Eirik's Saga," in Magnus Magnusson and Hermann Pálsson, trans. and ed., *The Vinland Sagas: The Norse Discovery of America* (New York: Penguin, 1965), 98–100.
3. Richard Hakluyt, epistle dedicatory to Sir Robert Cecil, Vol. 3 of *The Principal Navigations, Voyages, Traffiques, and Discoveries of the English Nation* (London: Bishop, Newberie and Barker, 1600), sig. A3.
4. Michel de Montaigne, "Of Cannibals," *The Essayes or Morall, Politike and Millitarie Discourses*, trans. John Florio (London: Val. Sims, 1603), 100–101; Samuel Purchas, *Purchas His Pilgrimage*, 2nd ed. (London: Stansby, 1614), 719–26.
5. Luis Weckmann, *The Medieval Heritage of Mexico*, trans. Frances M. López-Morillas (New York: Fordham University Press, 1992), 19–20, 51. See also Howard Mancing, *The Cervantes Encyclopedia*, 2 vols. (Westport, CT: Greenwood, 2004).
6. Sir Walter Ralegh, *The Discoverie of the Large, Rich and Bewtiful Empyre of Guiana* (1596), ed. Neil L. Whitehead (Norman: University of Oklahoma Press, 1997), 145–46.
7. The accounts of Orellana and Acuña are in Clements R. Markham, ed. and trans., *Expeditions into the Valley of the Amazons, 1539, 1540, 1639* (London: Hakluyt Society, 1859), quotes 34, 122–23.
8. "The Written Record of the Voyage of 1524 of Giovanni da Verrazano as recorded in a letter to Francis I, King of France, July 8th, 1524," in Lawrence C. Wroth, ed., *The Voyages of Giovanni da Verrazzano, 1524–1528* (New Haven: Yale University Press, 1970), 137.
9. William Strachey, "A True Reportory of the Wreck and Redemption of Sir Thomas Gates, Knight," in Louis B. Wright, ed., *A Voyage to Virginia in 1609* (Charlottesville: University of Virginia Press, 1964), 78–79. See the *Aeneid*, Book I, lines 365–68.
10. Sir Francis Bacon, *New Atlantis, a work unfinished* (London: Thomas Newcomb, 1659), 12–14.
11. Jean de Léry, *History of a Voyage to the Land of Brazil, Otherwise Called America*, 2nd ed., 1580, trans. Janet Whatley (Berkeley: University of California Press, 1990), 144.
12. "A Treatise of Brasil, written by a Portugall who had long lived there," in Samuel Purchas, *Hakluytus Posthumus or Purchas His Pilgrimes*, 4 vols. (London: W. Stansby, 1625), IV:1289. C. R. Boxer identified the writer as Fernão Cardim.
13. G[eorge] S[andys], *Ovid's Metamorphoses Englished, Mythologiz'd, and Represented in Figures*, 2nd ed. enlarged (Oxford: John Lichfield, 1632), Book XV, 497.
14. Columbus to Ferdinand and Isabella, 1498, in J. M. Cohen, trans. and ed., *The Four Voyages of Christopher Columbus* (New York: Penguin, 1969), 220–26.
15. Menassah ben Israel, *Mikveh Israel. Esto es, Esperança de Israel* (Amsterdam: Semuel Ben Israel Soreiro, 5410 [1650]), translated as *The Hope of Israel* (London: R.I., 1650).
16. On these reports, see Matthew Restall, *Seven Myths of the Spanish Conquest* (New York: Oxford University Press, 2003), chap. 5.
17. Thomas Harriot, *A Briefe and True Report of the new found land of Virginia*, 1588, 1590 in David Beers Quinn, ed., *The Roanoke Voyages, 1584–1590*, 2 vols. (London: Hakluyt Society, 1955), I:379–81.

18. "A Treatise of Brasil" in Purchas, *Purchas His Pilgrimes*, IV:1305; Robert Harcourt, "A Relation of a Voyage to Guiana" in Purchas, *Pilgrimes*, IV: 1267.

19. Charles-Marie de la Condamine, *A Succinct Abridgment of a Voyage Made within the Inland Parts of South-America* (London: E. Withers, 1747), 51–55.

CHAPTER 2

1. Robert Dankoff, *An Ottoman Mentality: The World of Evliya Çelebi* (Leiden: Brill, 2004), 62–63. Columbus was originally from Genoa, and his name was Colombo. The Spanish version of Columbus's family name was Colón, which Çelebi rendered Kolon.

2. Francis Bacon, *Novum Organum* (London: Thomas Lee, 1676), 17. Bacon published the original in 1620 in Latin. This translation was in a collection headed by Bacon's *Sylva Sylvarum*.

3. *The Travels of Ibn Battuta, A. D. 1325–1354*, trans. H. A. R. Gibb and C. F. Beckingham, 4 vols. (Cambridge: Hakluyt Society, 1958–1994), IV: 946–78; Ross E. Dunn, *Adventures of Ibn Battuta: A Muslim Traveler of the Fourteenth Century*, rev. ed. (Berkeley: University of California Press, 2005), Introduction, chap. 13; a map of the Mali trip is on p. 277.

4. Kwasi Konadu, *The Akan Diaspora in the Americas* (New York: Oxford University Press, 2010), 58.

5. João de Barros, 1552, in Mary Louise Pratt, *Imperial Eyes: Travel Writing and Transculturation* (London: Routledge, 1992), 67.

6. Gaspar de Carvajal, "Discovery of the Orellana River," in José Toribia Medina, *The Discovery of the Amazon*, ed. H. C. Heaton, American Geographical Society Special Publication No. 17 (New York, 1934), 167–235, quote 218; material in brackets added by editor.

7. Paul LeJeune, "Relation of events in New France, 1640 and 1641," in Reuben Gold Thwaites, ed., *The Jesuit Relations and Allied Documents*, 73 vols. (Cleveland, OH: Burrows Brothers, 1896–1901), XXI:39.

8. The letters by Albert Cantino and Pietro Pasqualigo on Corte Real's return are printed in David B. Quinn et al., eds., *New American World: A Documentary History of North America to 1612*, 5 vols. (New York: Arno, 1979), I:148–51.

9. Peter Martyr, *De orbe novo decades* (1530), dec. VIII, trans. F. A. MacNutt, in Quinn et al., eds., *New American World*, I:274–75.

10. William Wood, *New Englands Prospect* (London: Tho. Cotes, 1634), 62.

11. John Smith, *The Generall Historie of Virginia, New-England and the Summer Isles*, 1624, in Philip L. Barbour, ed., *Complete Works of Captain John Smith*, 3 vols. (Chapel Hill: University of North Carolina Press, 1986), 2:206.

12. Wood, *New Englands Prospect*, title page.

13. Gabriel Harvey, *Pierces Supererogation* (London: John Wolfe, 1593), 48–49. Richard Hakluyt collected and printed accounts of voyages in editions that were extremely popular.

14. *A Shorte and briefe narration of the two Navigations and Discoveries to the Northweast partes called Newe Fraunce: First translated out of French into Italian, by that famous learned man Gio: Bapt: Ramutius and now turned into English by John Florio: Worthy the reading of all Venturers, Travellers, and Discoverers* (London: H. Bynneman, 1580), sig. B2.

15. Richard Eden, *The Decades of the newe world or west India* (London: William Powell, 1555), 220. Although Fletcher's account was not published until after Shakespeare's death, the manuscript apparently circulated widely. The manuscript can be compared with the printed version in Francis Fletcher, *The World Encompassed by Sir Francis Drake*, ed. W.S.W. Vaux (London: Hakluyt Society, 1854); mention of Settaboth is on p. 48.

16. *The Writings of Albrecht Dürer*, trans. William Martin Conway (New York: Philosophical Library, 1958), 101–2.

17. Bernal Díaz del Castillo, *The True History of the Conquest of New Spain*, trans. Alfred Percival Maudslay, 5 vols. (London: Hakluyt Society, 1908–1918), 5:290–91; Barbour, ed., *Complete Works of Captain John Smith* 2:41, 129, 437, 468; 3:29, 47, 302. Bernal Díaz's book was published a few decades after his death; Smith oversaw the publication of his own books.

18. William Bradford, *Of Plymouth Plantation, 1620–1647*, ed. Samuel Eliot Morison (New York: Knopf, 1952), 60–62.

CHAPTER 3

1. Giovanni Antonio Cavazzi da Montecuccolo, *"Missione evangelica al regno di Congo,"* MSS Araldi [Modena], vol. A, book 2, 24–25, quoted in Linda M. Heywood and John K. Thornton, *Central Africans, Atlantic Creoles, and the Foundation of the Americas, 1585–1660* (Cambridge, UK: Cambridge University Press, 2007), 124–25.

2. Sahagún's sermon is excerpted in Merry E. Wiesner-Hanks, ed., *Religious Transformations in the Early Modern World* (Boston: Bedford, 2009), 35.

3. For examples, see David Carrasco and Scott Sessions, eds., *Cave, City, and Eagle's Nest: An Interpretive Journey through the Mapa de Cuauhtinchan No. 2* (Albuquerque: University of New Mexico Press, 2007), and Barbara Mundy, *The Mapping of New Spain: Indigenous Cartography and the Maps of the Relaciones Geograficas* (Chicago: University of Chicago Press, 2000).

4. The W. E. B. Du Bois Institute of Harvard University has sponsored a large cooperative effort to produce a searchable database that aims to collect as many voyages as possible. It can be consulted at http://www.slavevoyages.org/tast/index.faces.

5. Pedro de Zuñiga to King Philip III, October 5, 1607, in Alexander Brown, ed., *The Genesis of the United States*, 2 vols. (1890, rpt. New York: Russell and Russell, 1964), I:118–19.

6. Juan Guero to Juan Fernández Resio, February 28, 1587, reproduced and translated in Kris Lane, *Quito 1599: City and Colony in Transition* (Albuquerque: University of New Mexico Press, 2002), 52. Nombre de Díos was the port in Panama where the ship from Spain landed.

7. Leger Adverty to the [Sieur] Maurice Adverty "resident in Canada," in Louise Dechêne, *Habitants and Merchants in Seventeenth-Century Montreal*, trans. Liana Vardi (Montreal: McGill-Queen's University Press, 1992), 25–26.

8. Gottlieb Mittelberger, *Journey to Pennsylvania in the Year 1750*, trans. Carl Theo Eben (Philadelphia: John Jos McVey, 1898), 25–31.

9. "The Life of John Frederick Whitehead Containing His Travels and Chief Adventers," in Susan E. Klepp, Farley Grubb, and Anne Pfaelzer de Ortiz, eds., *Souls for Sale: Two German Redemptioners Come to Revolutionary America* (University Park: Pennsylvania State University Press, 2006), 51–162, quote 138–39. On his life and career, see the introduction to his account, *Souls for Sale*, 27–49.

10. For Guerrero and Bernal Díaz's telling of his story, see Rolena Adorno, *The Polemics of Possession in Spanish American Narrative* (New Haven: Yale University Press, 2007), 229–40.

11. "The Talon Interrogations: Voyage to the Mississippi through the Gulf of Mexico," trans. Linda Ann Bell, in Robert S. Weddle, Mary Christine Morkovsky, and Patricia Galloway, eds., *La Salle, the Mississippi, and the Gulf: Three Primary Documents* (College Station: Texas A&M University Press, 1987), 209–58.

12. Sarah E. Owens, trans. and ed., *Journey of Five Capuchin Nuns* (Toronto: Iter, 2009), 187.

CHAPTER 4

1. John Smith, *The Generall Historie of Virginia, New-England and the Summer Isles*, 1624, in Philip L. Barbour, ed., *Complete Works of Captain John Smith*, 3 vols. (Chapel Hill: University of North Carolina Press, 1986), II: 474.

2. J. H. Elliott, *The Old World and the New, 1492–1650* (Cambridge: Cambridge University Press, 1970), 60.

3. Thomas Trapham, *A Discourse of the State of Health in the Island of Jamaica* (London: R. Boulter, 1679), 50–60, 67.

4. Pieter de Marees, *Description and Historical Account of the Gold Kingdom of Guinea, 1602,* trans. and ed. Albert van Dantzig and Adam Jones (Oxford: Oxford University Press for the British Academy, 1987), 161–63.

5. Thomas Harriot, *A Briefe and True Report of the new found land of Virginia* (London: R. Robinson, 1588), 13–15

6. Thomas D. Goodrich, *The Ottoman Turks and the New World: A Study of Tarih-i Hind-i Garbi and Sixteenth-Century Ottoman Americana* (Wiesbaden: Otto Harrassowitz, 1990), 67.

7. Gonzalo Fernández de Oviedo y Valdés, *Historia general y natural de las Indias,* 1535, in Jane Gregory Rubin and Ariana Donalds, eds., *Bread Made from Yuca* (New York: Interamericas, 2003), 24–29.

8. de Marees, *Description and Historical Account of the Gold Kingdom of Guinea,* 113–14.

9. Don Juan de Silva is quoted in Geoffrey Parker, *The Grand Strategy of Philip II* (New Haven: Yale University Press, 1998), 66–67.

10. Peter Mundy, *The Travels of Peter Mundy, in Europe and Asia, 1608–1667,* ed. R. C. Temple (London: Hakluyt Society, 1919), III, pt. 1:1–3.

11. Geoffrey Wheatough, trans. and ed., *Fracastoro's Syphilis* (Liverpool: Francis Cairns, 1984), 99–101, and passim. I thank Ralph Hexter for advice on this work.

12. Alfred W. Crosby, *The Columbian Exchange: The Biological and Cultural Consequences of 1492,* 30th anniversary ed. (Westport, CT: Praeger, 2003), 123, 139–40.

13. Jacques Cartier, "The Second Voyage," in Ramsay Cook, ed., *The Voyages of Jacques Cartier,* trans. H. P. Biggar (Toronto: University of Toronto Press, 1993), 69–70.

14. "A Treatise of Brasil, written by a Portugall who had long lived there," in Samuel Purchas, *Hakluytus Posthumus or Purchas His Pilgrimes,* 4 vols. (London: W. Stansby, 1625), IV:1292.

15. W. Golden Mortimer, *History of Coca: "The Divine Plant of the Incas,"* 1901 (rpt. San Francisco: Fitz Hugh Ludlow Memorial Library, 1974), 148–64.

16. Howard Markel, *The Anatomy of Addiction: Sigmund Freud, William Halsted, and the Miracle Drug Cocaine* (New York: Pantheon, 2011), quote 54.

17. Robert Beverly,*The History and Present State of Virginia* (1705), ed. Louis B. Wright (Charlottesville: University of Virginia Press, 1947), 139.

18. Thomas Gage, *The English-American, His Travail by Sea and Land* (London: R., 1648), 43, 200.

19. Richard Ligon, *A True and Exact History of the Island of Barbados* (London: Humphrey Moseley, 1657), 96.

CHAPTER 5

1. Casimiro Gómez Ortega to José de Gálvez, minister of the Indies, 1777, translated in Jorge Cañizares-Esguerra, "Iberian Colonial Science," *Isis,* 96 (2005), 69.

2. Donald H. Kent, ed., *Pennsylvania Treaties, 1737–1756,* vol. II of Alden T. Vaughan, gen. ed., *Early American Indian Documents: Treaties and Laws, 1607–1789* (Bethesda, MD: University Press of America, 1984), 262.

3. Voltaire, *Candide, or Optimism,* Burton Raffel trans. and ed. (New Haven: Yale University Press, 2005), 94.

4. Anon., *The Journal of Pontiac's Conspiracy,* 1763, in Milo Milton Quaife, ed., *The Siege of Detroit in 1763* (Chicago: Lakeside Press, 1958), 8–17.

5. Alexander Gunkel and Jerome S. Handlers, trans. and ed., "A German Indentured Servant in Barbados in 1652: The Account of Heinrich von Uchteritz," *Journal of the Barbados Museum and Historical Society,* 33 (1970), 91–100, quote 93.

6. Voltaire, *Candide*, trans. Raffel, 10–12. *Candide*'s circulation is described in the introduction to this volume by Johnson Kent Wright, p. xv.

7. Ibid., 68.

8. These quotations are taken from an English translation of the portion of Raynal's collaborative work that dealt with the slave trade published as the revolution was breaking out in Haiti; *Slave Trade. A Full Account of this Species of Commerce; With Arguments Against It, Spirited and Philosophical: by the Celebrated Philosopher and Historian, Abbé Raynal. Translated from the French* (London: T. Cox, 1792?), quotes 35, 37, 44. See also Hugh Thomas, *The Slave Trade: The Story of the Atlantic Slave Trade, 1440–1870* (New York: Simon and Schuster, 1997).

9. Thomas Jefferson, *Notes on the State of Virginia*, 1787, ed. Frank Shuffleton (New York: Penguin, 1999), 32–35.

10. William Stith, *History of the First Discovery and Settlement of Virginia* (Williamsburg: William Parks, 1747), 1–2.

11. Fr. Joseph François Lafitau, *Customs of the American Indians Compared with the Customs of Primitive Times*, 1724, ed. and trans. William N. Fenton and Elizabeth L. Moore, 2 vols. (Toronto: Champlain Society, 1977), II:128–29, 146–47, 180–81.

12. Voltaire, *Essai sur les moeurs et l'esprit des nations*, 1754 (rpt. Paris: Garnier Frères, 1963), I:30, translated in David Allen Harvey, "Living Antiquity: Lafitau's *Moeurs des sauvages amériquains* and the Religious Roots of the Enlightenment Science of Man," *Proceedings of the Western Society for French History*, 36 (2008), 75–92, quote 86.

13. Peter Blanchard, "The Language of Liberation: Slave Voices in the Wars of Independence," *Hispanic American Historical Review*, 82 (2002), 499–524, quote 518.

14. John Lynch, *Simón Bolívar, a Life* (New Haven: Yale University Press, 2006), 26.

15. Bolívar quoted in Blanchard, "The Language of Liberation," 514.

Further Reading

GENERAL WORKS

Abulafia, David. *The Discovery of Mankind: Atlantic Encounters in the Age of Columbus.* New Haven: Yale University Press, 2008.

Bailyn, Bernard. *Atlantic History: Concept and Contours.* Cambridge, MA: Harvard University Press, 2005.

Bailyn, Bernard, and Patricia Denault. *Soundings in Atlantic History: Latent Structures and Intellectual Currents, 1500–1830.* Cambridge, MA: Harvard University Press, 2009.

Benjamin, Thomas. *The Atlantic World: European, Africans, Indians and Their Shared History, 1400–1900.* New York: Cambridge University Press, 2009.

Canny, Nicholas, and Philip Morgan, eds. *The Oxford Handbook of the Atlantic World, 1450–1850.* New York: Oxford University Press, 2011.

Chávez, John R. *Beyond Nations: Evolving Homelands in the North Atlantic World, 1400–2000.* Cambridge: Cambridge University Press, 2009.

Elliott, J. H. *Empires of the Atlantic World: Britain and Spain in America, 1492–1830.* New Haven: Yale University Press, 2006.

Engerman, Stanley L., and Robert E. Gallman, eds. *The Cambridge Economic History of the United States*, Vol. I: *The Colonial Era.* Cambridge: Cambridge University Press, 1996.

Greene, Jack P., and Philip D. Morgan, eds. *Atlantic History: A Critical Appraisal.* New York: Oxford University Press, 2009.

Kupperman, Karen Ordahl, ed. *America in European Consciousness.* Chapel Hill: University of North Carolina Press, 1995.

McCusker, John J., and Kenneth Morgan, eds. *The Early Modern Atlantic Economy.* Cambridge: Cambridge University Press, 2000.

Pritchard, James. *In Search of Empire: The French in the Americas, 1670–1730.* Cambridge: Cambridge University Press, 2004.

CONTACT AND CONFLICT IN AMERICA

Barr, Juliana. *Peace Came in the Form of a Woman: Indians and Spaniards in the Texas Borderlands.* Chapel Hill: University of North Carolina Press, 2007.

Duval, Kathleen. *The Native Ground: Indians and Colonists in the Heart of the Continent.* Philadelphia: University of Pennsylvania Press, 2006.

Ethridge, Robbie. *From Chicaza to Chickasaw: The European Invasion and the Transformation of the Mississippian World, 1540–1715.* Chapel Hill: University of North Carolina Press, 2010.

Matthew, Laura, and Michel R, Oudijk, eds. *Indian Conquistadors: Indigenous Allies in the Conquest of Mesoamerica.* Norman: University of Oklahoma Press, 2007.

Restall, Matthew. *Seven Myths of the Spanish Conquest.* New York: Oxford University Press, 2003.

Van Zandt, Cynthia. *Brothers among Nations: The Pursuit of Intercultural Alliances in Early America, 1580–1660.* New York: Oxford University Press, 2008.

CROPS AND FOODS

Carney, Judith A. *Black Rice: The African Origins of Rice Cultivation in the Americas.* Cambridge, MA: Harvard University Press, 2001.

Carney, Judith A., and Richard Nicholas Rosomoff. *In the Shadow of Slavery: Africa's Botanical Legacy in the Atlantic World.* Berkeley: University of California Press, 2010.

Fields-Black, Edda. *Deep Roots: Rice Farmers in West Africa and the African Disapora.* Bloomington: Indiana University Press, 2008.

Gilman, Sander L., and Zhou Xun, eds. *Smoke: A Global History of Smoking.* London: Reaktion Books, 2004.

Markel, Howard. *An Anatomy of Addiction: Sigmund Freud, William Halsted, and the Miracle Drug Cocaine.* New York: Pantheon Books, 2011.

McCann, James. *Maize and Grace: Africa's Encounter with a New World Crop, 1500–2000.* Cambridge, MA: Harvard University Press, 2005.

Mintz, Sidney. *Sweetness and Power: The Place of Sugar in Modern History.* New York: Penguin Books, 1986.

Norton, Marcy. *Sacred Gifts, Profane Pleasures: A History of Tobacco and Chocolate in the Atlantic World.* Ithaca, NY: Cornell University Press, 2008.

Opie, Frederick Douglass. *Hog and Hominy: Soul Food from Africa to America.* New York: Columbia University Press, 2008.

Pope, Peter E. *Fish into Wine: The Newfoundland Plantation in the Seventeenth Century.* Chapel Hill: University of North Carolina Press, 2004.

Schwartz, Stuart B., ed. *Tropical Babylons: Sugar and the Making of the Atlantic World, 1450–1680.* Chapel Hill: University of North Carolina Press, 2004.

Spivey, Diane M. *Migration of African Cuisine.* Albany: State University of New York Press, 1999.

Warman, Arturo. *Corn and Capitalism: How a Botanical Bastard Grew to Global Dominance.* Translated by Nancy L. Westrate 1988, 1995; English ed. Chapel Hill: University of North Carolina Press, 2003.

THE EARLY ATLANTIC

Ben-Dor, Zvi. *The Ten Lost Tribes: A World History.* New York: Oxford University Press, 2009.

Ellis, Richard. *Imagining Atlantis.* New York: Knopf, 1998.

Fitzhugh, William W. *Vikings: The North Atlantic Saga.* Washington, DC: Smithsonian Institution Press in association with the National Museum of Natural History, 2000.

Levtzion, Nehemia, and Jay Spaulding, eds. *Medieval West Africa: Views from Arab Scholars and Merchants.* Princeton: Markus Wiener, 2003.

Lewis, Martin W. "Dividing the Ocean Sea." *Geographical Review* 89 (1999): 188–214.

More, Sir Thomas. *Utopia.* Edited by David Harris Sacks. Boston: Bedford Books, 1999.

Quinn, David Beers. *England and the Discovery of America, 1481–1620.* London: George Allen and Unwin, 1974.

Shaffer, Lynda. "Southernization." *Journal of World History* 5 (1994): 1–21.

Weckmann, Luis. *The Medieval Heritage of Mexico.* Translated by Frances M. López-Morillas. New York: Fordham University Press, 1992.

ENVIRONMENT AND INFORMATION-GATHERING

Anderson, Virginia DeJohn. *Creatures of Empire: How Domestic Animals Transformed Early America.* New York: Oxford University Press, 2004.

Barrera-Osorio, Antonio. *Experiencing Nature: The Spanish-American Empire and the Early Scientific Revolution*. Austin: University of Texas Press, 2006.

Cañizares-Esguerra, Jorge. *How to Write the History of the New World: Historiographies, Epistemologies, and Identities in the Eighteenth-Century Atlantic World*. Stanford: Stanford University Press, 2001.

Crosby, Alfred W. *The Columbian Exchange: The Biological and Cultural Consequences of 1492*. 30th anniversary ed. Westport, CT: Praeger, 2003.

Freedberg, David. *The Eye of the Lynx: Galileo, His Friends, and the Beginnings of Modern Natural History*. Chicago: University of Chicago Press, 2002.

Gill, Richardson. *The Great Maya Droughts: Water, Life, and Death*. Albuquerque: University of New Mexico Press, 2000.

Grove, Richard H. *Green Imperialism: Colonial Expansion, Tropical Island Edens and the Origins of Imperialism, 1600–1800*. Cambridge: Cambridge University Press, 1995.

McNeill, John. *Mosquito Empires: Ecology and War in the Greater Caribbean, 1640–1914*. New York: Cambridge University Press, 2010.

Richards, John R. *The Unending Frontier: An Environmental History of the Early Modern World*. Berkeley: University of California Press, 2003.

Schiebinger, Londa, Mark Harrison, Jorge Cañizares-Esguerra, Steven J. Harris, and Michael A. Osborne. "Forum, Colonial Science." *Isis* 96 (2005): 52–87.

Schiebinger, Londa, and Claudia Swan, eds. *Colonial Botany: Science, Commerce, and Politics in the Early Modern World*. Philadelphia: University of Pennsylvania Press, 2005.

REVOLUTIONS

Adelman, Jeremy. *Sovereignty and Revolution in the Iberian Atlantic*. Princeton: Princeton University Press, 2006.

Armitage, David. *The Declaration of Independence: A Global History*. Cambridge, MA: Harvard University Press, 2007.

Blackburn, Robin. "Haiti, Slavery, and the Age of the Democratic Revolution." *William and Mary Quarterly*, 3rd ser., 63 (2006): 643–74.

Dubois, Laurent. *A Colony of Citizens: Revolution and Emancipation in the French Caribbean, 1787–1804*. Chapel Hill: University of North Carolina Press, 2004.

———. *Avengers of the New World: The Story of the Haitian Revolution*. Cambridge MA: Harvard University Press, 2005.

Dubois, Laurent, and John D. Garrigus, eds. *Slave Revolution in the Caribbean, 1789–1804*. Boston: Bedford/St. Martin's, 2006.

Dubois, Laurent, and Julius Scott, eds. *Origins of the Black Atlantic: Rewriting Histories*. New York: Routledge, 2010.

Klooster, Wim. *Revolutions in the Atlantic World: A Comparative History*. New York: New York University Press, 2009.

Landers, Jane G. *Atlantic Creoles in the Age of Revolutions*. Cambridge, MA: Harvard University Press, 2010.

Lynch, John. *Simón Bolívar, a Life*. New Haven: Yale University Press, 2006.

Shy, John. *A People Numerous and Armed: Reflections on the Military Struggle for American Independence*. New York: Oxford University Press, 1976.

Thomson, Sinclair. *We Alone Will Rule: Native Andean Politics in the Age of Insurgency*. Madison: University of Wisconsin Press, 2002.

Thornton, John K. "'I Am the Subject of the King of Congo': African Political Ideology and the Haitian Revolution." *Journal of World History* 4 (1993): 181–214.

RELIGION

Davis, Natalie Zemon. *Women on the Margins: Three Seventeenth-Century Lives*. Cambridge, MA: Harvard University Press, 1995.

Greer, Allan. *Mohawk Saint: Catherine Tekakwitha and the Jesuits*. New York: Oxford University Press, 2004.

Lewis, Maureen Warner. *Archibald Monteath: Igbo, Jamaican, Moravian*. Kingston: University of the West Indies Press, 2007.

Owens, Sarah E., trans. and ed. *Journey of Five Capuchin Nuns*. Toronto: Iter, 2009.

Schwartz, Stuart. *All Can Be Saved: Religious Tolerance and Salvation in the Iberian Atlantic World*. New Haven: Yale University Press, 2008.

Seeman, Erik R. *The Huron-Wendat Feast of the Dead: Indian-European Encounters in Colonial North America*. Baltimore: Johns Hopkins University Press, 2011.

Sensbach, Jon F. *Rebecca's Revival: Creating Black Christianity in the Atlantic World*. Cambridge, MA: Harvard University Press, 2005.

Silverman, David J. *Red Brethren: The Brothertown and Stockbridge Indians and the Problem of Race in Early America*. Ithaca, NY: Cornell University Press, 2010.

Sweet, James H. *Domingos Álvares, African Healing, and the Intellectual History of the Atlantic World*. Chapel Hill: University of North Carolina Press, 2011.

SLAVERY AND THE SLAVE TRADE

Berlin, Ira. *Many Thousands Gone: The First Two Centuries of Slavery in North America*. Cambridge, MA: Harvard University Press, 1998.

Eltis, David, and David Richardson, eds. *Extending the Frontiers: Essays on the New Transatlantic Slave Trade Database*. New Haven: Yale University Press, 2008.

Gomez, Michael A., *Exchanging Our Country Marks: The Transformation of African Identities in the Colonial and Antebellum South*. Chapel Hill: University of North Carolina Press, 1998.

Heywood, Linda, and John Thornton. *Central Africans, Atlantic Creoles, and the Foundation of the Americas, 1585–1660*. Cambridge: Cambridge University Press, 2007.

Lovejoy, Paul E. *Ecology and Ethnography of Muslim Trade in West Africa*. Trenton, NJ: Africa World Press, 2005.

———. *Transformations in Africa: A History of Slavery in Africa*. 2nd ed. Cambridge: Cambridge University Press, 2000.

Morgan, Jennifer. *Laboring Women: Reproduction and Gender in New World Slavery*. Philadelphia: University of Pennsylvania Press, 2004.

Peabody, Sue. *"There Are No Slaves in France." The Political Culture of Race and Slavery in the Ancien Régime*. New York: Oxford University Press, 1996.

Price, Richard, ed. *Maroon Societies: Rebel Slave Communities in the Americas*. 3rd ed. Baltimore: Johns Hopkins University Press, 1996.

Schwartz, Stuart B. *Slaves, Peasants, and Rebels: Reconsidering Brazilian Slavery*. Urbana: University of Illinois Press, 1992.

Smallwood, Stephanie E. *Saltwater Slavery: A Middle Passage from Africa to American Diaspora*. Cambridge, MA: Harvard University Press, 2007.

Sparks, Randy J. *The Two Princes of Calabar: An Eighteenth-Century Atlantic Odyssey*. Cambridge, MA: Harvard University Press 2004.

Sweet, James H. *Recreating Africa: Culture, Kinship, and Religion in the African-Portuguese world, 1441–1770*. Chapel Hill: University of North Carolina Press, 2003.

Thomas, Hugh. *The Slave Trade: The Story of the Atlantic Slave Trade, 1440–1870.* New York: Simon and Schuster, 1997.

Thornton, John A. *Africa and Africans in the Making of the Atlantic World, 1400–1800.* 2nd ed. Cambridge: Cambridge University Press, 1998.

TRANSATLANTIC MIGRATION AND EUROPEAN SETTLEMENTS

Altman, Ida. *Transatlantic Ties in the Spanish Empire: Brihuega, Spain, and Puebla, Mexico, 1560–1620.* Palo Alto: Stanford University Press, 2000.

Altman, Ida, and James Horn, eds. *"To Make America": European Emigration in the Early Modern Period.* Berkeley: University of California Press, 1991.

Canny, Nicholas, ed. *Europeans on the Move: Studies on European Migration, 1500–1800.* Oxford: Oxford University Press, 1994.

Dechêne, Louise. *Habitants and Merchants in Seventeenth-Century Montreal.* Translated by Liana Vardi. Montreal: McGill-Queen's University Press, 1992.

Lane, Kris. *Quito 1599: City and Colony in Transition.* Albuquerque: University of New Mexico Press, 2002.

Rothschild, Emma. "A Horrible Tragedy in the French Atlantic." *Past and Present* 192 (2006): 67–108.

Wokeck, Marianne. *Trade in Strangers: The Beginnings of Mass Migration to North America.* University Park: Pennsylvania State University Press, 1999.

Websites

Afriterra
www.afriterra.org
   Digitized catalog of more than 2,000 maps of Africa dating from 1480 to 1900.

Common-Place
www.common-place.org
   Online only journal with a focus on early American history; sponsored by the American Antiquarian Society and the University of Oklahoma.

Early Americas Digital Archive
www.mith2.umd.edu/eada
   Full texts of printed works related to the Americas from 1492 to 1820.

Environmental History of Latin America
www.stanford.edu/group/LAEH/index.html
   Online bibliography of academic work on environmental history in Latin America. Includes links to related websites and videos.

The Early Modern World
www.fordham.edu/halsall/mod/modsbook03.asp
   A collection from Fordham University of primary documents and full texts related to the opening of the Atlantic world and beyond.

Harvard University Library Open Collections Program: Expeditions and Discoveries
http://ocp.hul.harvard.edu/expeditions
   Maps, photographs, letters, and other manuscripts related to expeditions undertaken between 1626 and 1953.

Huntington Digital Library
http://hdl.huntington.org/cdm
   A selection of manuscripts, maps, photographs, and digitized rare books related to British and American history from the eleventh century to today.

John Carter Brown Library
www.brown.edu/Facilities/John_Carter_Brown_Library
   Online exhibitions and digitized archival materials, maps, and images, drawing from the John Carter Brown Library's collection, which focuses on the history of the Americas from 1492 to 1825.

Latin American Travelogues
http://dl.lib.brown.edu/travelogues
   Collection of Latin American travel accounts between the sixteenth and nineteenth centuries.

Museum of Underwater Archaeology
www.uri.edu/mua
   Latest findings on archaeological and historical research in shipwrecks.

Time to Eat the Dogs
http://timetoeatthedogs.com
   Blog by historian Michael F. Robinson on topics in the history of science and exploration.

The Trans-Atlantic Slave Trade Database
www.slavevoyages.org/tast/index.faces
   Versatile search engine and research tool with information on nearly 35,000 slaving voyages from the sixteenth to the nineteenth centuries.

Yale Indian Papers Project
www.library.yale.edu/yipp
   With a focus on New England Indians, this online archive includes digitized original documents spanning 400 years, accompanied by scholarly commentary.

Acknowledgments

In preparing *The Atlantic in World History*, I have benefited from the advice and scholarship of many colleagues and students. Bonnie Smith has offered invaluable advice, as have Nancy Toff and Sonia Tycko of Oxford University Press. Colleagues and students in NYU's Atlantic History Workshop have contributed much to my understanding of the subject both through their own scholarship and their contributions to our ongoing discussion of the subject. Gabriel Rocha read the entire manuscript and offered valuable suggestions for change. He also helped with the compilation of the suggestions for further reading and the websites.

Chronological Volumes
The World from Beginnings to 4000 BCE
The World from 4000 to 1000 BCE
The World from 1000 BCE *to 500* CE
The World from 300 to 1000 CE
The World from 1000 to1500
The World from 1450 to1700
The World in the Eighteenth Century
The World in the Nineteenth Century
The World in the Twentieth Century

Thematic and Topical Volumes
The City: A World History
Democracy: A World History
Food: A World History
Empires: A World History
The Family: A World History
Genocide: A World History
Health and Medicine: A World History
Migration: A World History
Race: A World History
Technology: A World History

Geographical Volumes
The Atlantic in World History
Central Asia in World History
China in World History
Japan in World History
Mexico in World History
Russia in World History
The Silk Road in World History
South Africa in World History
South Asia in World History
Southeast Asia in World History
Trans-Saharan Africa in World History

Index

Aataentsic, 8
abolitionism, 105–6, 119, 121
Academy of Linceans, 99
Acadians, 122
Acosta, José de, 7
Acuña, Fray Cristobal de, 9, 19
Adverty, Leger and Maurice, 60–61
Africa. *See* North Africa; West Africa; and
   individual territories
Ágreda, María de Jesús de, 68–69
agriculture: crop transplantation and, 77–80,
   90–92, 96
   Little Ice Age and, 32–33, 56.
   See also individual crops
Aguilar, Jerónimo de, 65
Amadis of Gaule, 8
Amazon River, 3, 19, 30
Amazons, 8–9, 19
American Philosophical Society, 99
American War of Independence, 110–12
Angola, 26, 28, 46–47
animals, transplantation of, 41, 77, 91–92, 104.
   See also individual animals
Antilia, 9
Argentina, 119
Asia, western passage to, 20, 35–36
Atlantic Sea, 4
Atlantis, 6–8, 11, 13, 84. *See also* New Atlantis
Ayllón, María Jacinta de, 70
Ayllón, Nicolás de, 70
Azores, 5
Aztecs, 30, 37, 40, 50, 76

Bacon, Francis, 108, 123
   New Atlantis, 11–13, 23
Bacon's Rebellion, 89–90
Badiano, Juan, 81
Bambaras, 68
Baptists, 61, 70
Barbados, 92, 93, 94, 105
Barros, João de, 28–29
Basques, 72
Bayezid II (Ottoman Empire), 23
Benavides, Fray Alonso de, 69
Bermuda, 91

Beverly, Robert, 89–90
   History and Present State of Virginia, 109
Biassou, Georges, 114, 116
Bible, Book of Revelation, 15–16
Bight of Benin, 54
Bight of Biafra, 54–55, 56
Block Island, 10
Boccaccio, Giovanni, 4
Bolívar, Simon, 117, 119–21
Bonaparte, Napoleon, 113, 116–17, 119
Bourbon Reforms (Spain), 103
Bradford, William, 42–43
Brahe, Tycho, 16
Brazil: Africa and, 117
   Amazon basin and, 30–31
   diamonds in, 117
   early European accounts of, 13, 18, 30–31
   European migration to, 45
   France and, 40, 44–45, 75
   gold in, 45, 117
   Indians in, 13, 30–31, 40, 45, 86, 117
   Maroons in, 46
   missionary activity in, 45, 50
   Portugal and, 34, 44–45, 47, 75, 117–18
   slaves in, 44–45, 53, 117, 121
   Spain and, 30–31
   sugar and, 44–45, 92–93, 117–18
   tobacco and, 85–86
brazilwood, 75
Brihuega (Spain), 57
Buffon, Comte de (Georges-Louis Leclerc), 108

Cabot, John, 34
Cabral, Pedro Álvares, 75
cacao, 76, 88
Caesar, comparisons to, 41
Cahokia, 31
Calafía, 8
Calancha, Antonio de la, 50
California, 8
Calvert, George (Lord Baltimore), 22
Calvin, John, 21
Campusano, Alejandro, 119
Canada: Acadians and, 122
   French presence in, 37, 73

Canada (*continued*)
  fur trade and, 37, 73
  Loyalist settlement in, 121
  Quebec, 98
  Seven Years' War and, 101–2, 104
  tobacco and, 85. *See also* New France
Canary Islands, 4–5, 16
Cantino Planisphere, 34, 36
Cap Français (Cap-Haitien), 114–15
Cape Verde Islands, 5, 15
Cardim, Fernão, 13, 18, 84–85
Caribbean: Columbus' voyages and, 15, 17, 92
  England and, 54, 76–77, 92–93
  France and, 113
  gold and, 37–38, 73
  North American trade and, 94
  privateering and, 42
  rum and, 94
  slaves in, 54, 94–96, 113
  Spain and, 35, 37, 58, 73, 75, 84
  sugar and, 54, 92–93, 100, 102, 104–5,
    113–14
  tobacco in, 86
  African foods in, 96. *See also individual
    islands*
Carthaginians, 4
Cartier, Jacques, 39, 85
cassava, 77, 79–80, 87, 96
Castillo, Bernal Díaz del, 41
Cavazzi da Montecuccolo, Giovanni Antonio, 47
Cayenne, 113
Cayugas, 31
Çelebi, Evliya, 23
Cercle des Philadelphes, 99
Cesi, Federico, 99
Champlain, Samuel de, 18
Charles II (England), 100
Charles V (Spain), 21, 36
China, 89
chivalric romances, 8
chocolate, 76–77, 81
Christianity: belief in Revelation and, 15
  celestial signs and, 16
  Protestant Reformation and, 21–22. *See also
    missionary activities; and individual
    denominations*
Christophe, Henri, 116
Cíbola, 10
Cieza de Leon, Pedro, 88, 90
coca, 88–89
cochineal, 75–76
cod, 72–73
coffee, 77, 110, 113, 114, 117–18

cofradías, 68, 103
Colbert, Jean-Baptiste, 99
Columbus, Christopher: Asia and, 34, 124
  Atlantic navigation and, 3–4
  Canary Islands and, 5
  Caribbean and, 15, 17, 92
  funding for, 23
  Indians and, 17
  legends and, 8, 15, 17
  Ocean Sea and, 3, 123
  Orinoco River and, 15
  sugar and, 92
Comunero revolt, 104
Coñori, 9
Convention (France), 113, 115
conversos, 22, 48
Cooke, Francis, 13
corn. *See* maize
Corte Real, Gaspar, 35
Cortés, Hernan, 8, 41, 65
Cosa, Juan de la, 34
cotton, 77
cows, 91
creole communities, 101, 103, 105, 107,
  118–19, 121
creole languages, 28
Cruz, Martín de la, 81
Cuba, 116, 121
Cuzco, 30, 88

de Marees, Pieter, 77–78, 80
de Soto, Hernando, 31, 66
Declaration of Independence (American
  colonies), 112
Declaration of the Rights of Man (France), 112
Deganawidah, 31
Dessalines, Jean-Jacques, 116
Díaz de Isla, Ruy, 84
Diderot, Denis, 106, 108
disease: Indians and, 33–34, 52, 91–92
  interpretations of, 33, 92
  slaves and, 54
  syphilis and, 83–84, 105
  transatlantic travel and, 62–63
  yellow fever, 104–5, 116. *See also* medicine
Dom Garcia (Kongo), 27
Dominica, 102
Dominion of New England, 100
Drake, Frances, 39, 40, 42
Durán, Diego, 15–16
Dürer, Albrecht, 40
Dutch Republic and, 111–12
dyes, 75–76

Eden, Garden of, 15, 78
Eden, Richard, 40
Eiakintonomo, 41
El Inca Garcilaso de la Vega, 52
El Niño, 123–24
El-Ksar el-Kebir (Alcazarquivir), 28
Elizabeth I (England), 21–22, 90
encomienda system, 48–50
Encyclopédie project, 108
England: abolitionism in, 106–7
    Africans in, 106, 107
    American Revolution and, 110–11
    army, 101–2, 110
    Caribbean and, 54, 76–77, 92–93
    colonial bureaucracy, 96, 98–101, 110
    fishing and, 72–73
    fur trade and, 73
    Indians and, 17, 65–66, 101, 122
    mercantilism and, 96–97
    migration and, 56–57, 59–61
    privateering, 42
    religious conflict in, 21–22
    rum and, 94
    Saint-Domingue and, 115–16, 118
    Seven Years' War, 101–4, 110
    slave trade and, 53–55
    sugar and, 54, 77, 93, 100
    tobacco and, 87, 96
Erik the Red, 5
Erikson, Leif, 5
Estates General (France), 112, 113
Ethiopia, 10
Ethiopian Sea, 4, 10, 123
Europe. *See individual countries*

Ferdinand of Aragon, 20–21
Ferdinand VII (Spain), 119–20
fishing, 5–6, 36–38, 72–73, 77
Fletcher, Francis, 40
Florio, John, 39
Fort Orange (Albany, New York), 73
Fracastoro, Girolamo, *Syphilis sive De morbo gallico*, 83–84
France: abolitionism in, 106
    Africans in, 106
    American expeditions of, 19, 67
    American War of Independence and, 111
    army, 101–2
    Brazil and, 40, 44–45, 75
    Canada and, 37, 73, 98, 101–2, 104
    colonial bureaucracy and, 98–101, 104–5, 113–18
    fishing and, 72

fur trade and, 37, 73
Indians and, 67–68, 102, 122
migration and, 59–61, 67, 104–5
privateering and, 42
religious conflict in, 21–22
revolution in, 112–13, 117
Saint-Domingue and, 113–16
Seven Years' War and, 101–4, 110
Spain and, 117, 119
sugar and, 94, 100, 102, 113
tobacco and, 85–86
French Academy of Sciences, 99
French and Indian War. *See* Seven Years' War
French Guiana, 104. *See also* Kourou
French Revolution, 112–13, 117
Freydis, 6
fruits, 77–78, 90
Fuero, Juan, 57
fur trade, 36–37, 60, 73, 76

Gage, Thomas, 90
Galindo, Juan de Abreu de, 16
García, Gregorio, 7
Genesis, Book of, 13, 15, 16, 78, 82, 109
German migration, 62–63
ginseng, 89, 124
Gold Coast (Ghana), 28, 54
gold: Aztecs and, 40
    Brazil and, 45, 117
    Caribbean and, 37–38, 73
    coinage and, 75
    Portugal and, 45
    privateers and, 42
    rumors of, 8–10
    Spain and, 37–38, 73–74
    West Africa and, 3, 4, 20, 28
Gómara, Franciso López de, 39
Gomes, Estevão, 36
Gómez Ortega, Casimiro, 99
Gotland, 6
grapes, 87–88
Great Britain. *See* England
Greenland, 5, 72
Grenada, 102
Guadeloupe, 102, 113
Guatemala, 120
Guerrero, Gonzalo, 65
guiacum, 84
Guiana, 9, 18, 73, 104. *See also* French Guiana
Guinea, 80, 108

Haiti, 26, 116–17, 121. *See also* Saint-Domingue

Hakluyt, Richard, 7, 13, 39
Harcourt, Robert, 18–19
Harriot, Thomas, 17, 78, 80
Harvey, Gabriel, 39
Haudenosaunee (The Great League of Peace), 31–32
Hawkins, John, 42
Hein, Piet, 42
Henri II (France), 40–41
Henry the Navigator (Prince of Portugal), 5
Henry VIII (England), 11, 21
Hernández, Francisco, 81
Hiawatha, 31
honey, 93
horses, 28, 91
Hudson Bay, 73
Huguenots, 21, 61
human rights, 109–14, 121. *See also* abolitionism
Humboldt, Alexander von, 50, 89, 108, 123
humoral theory, 82–83, 85, 90
Hurons, 37
    creation story, 8
Hythloday, Raphael, 11

Ibn Battuta, 27–28
Iceland, 5, 72
Incarnation, Marie de l', 69
Incas, 30–31, 37, 51, 52, 88, 103
indentured servitude, 59–61, 62–65
Indians: Brazil and, 13, 19, 30–31, 40, 45, 86, 117
    coca and, 88–89
    conflicts with settlers and, 102
    disease and, 33–34, 52, 91–92
    dye trade and, 75–76
    England and, 17, 101, 122
    European experiences of, 36, 40–41, 71
    European theories about, 15–16, 108–9
    France and, 67–68, 102, 122
    fur trade and, 37, 73
    histories of, 52
    Jamestown and, 65–66
    medicine and, 34, 83, 89
    missionary activities among, 15, 30, 48, 51, 69–71, 103
    Newfoundland and, 5–6
    Ohio Valley and, 100–101
    Peru and, 51, 52
    Seven Years' War and, 101–4, 110
    Spain and, 17, 48, 50–53, 81, 119
    tobacco and, 85–87
    views of Europeans and, 17
    Vikings and, 5–6. *See also individual groups*

Iouskeha, 8
Iroquois, 31, 89
Isabella (Queen of Spain), 20
Islam: Africa and, 20, 23, 27–28, 107–8
    Iberian Peninsula and, 9, 20–22, 47
    Ottoman Empire and, 21
    slave trade and, 107–8
Israel, Ten Lost Tribes, 15–16

Jacobins, 113
Jamaica, 76, 92, 111
James I (England), 77–78
James II (England), 100
James River, 10, 66
Jamestown (Virginia), 10, 37, 56–57, 61–62, 65–66, 87, 89, 98, 124
Jean-François, 114
Jefferson, Thomas, 112
    Notes on the State of Virginia, 108
Jesuits, 45, 66–67, 69, 103
Jews: Netherlands and, 22, 47–48
    networks among, 47–48
    Ottoman Empire and, 22, 47–48
    Portugal and, 44, 47–48
    São Tomé and, 44
    Sephardim, 20, 22, 47–48, 92
    Spain and, 20, 22, 47–48
jimsonweed, 89–90
João I (Kongo), 26
Jones, Thomas, 107
Jumano Indians, 69

kola nuts, 88
Kongo, 26–27, 29, 45, 46, 114–15
Kourou, 104–5

La Condamine, Charles-Marie de, 19
La Flèche (France), 60–61
Labadists, 61, 70
Lafayette, Marquis de, 112
Lafitau, François, 89, 108–9
language acquisition, 41, 51, 69, 81
Las Casas, Bartolomeo de, 51
LaSalle, Sieur de (René-Robert Cavaliere), 67
Laws of Burgos, 48
Lee, Mordecai, 63, 65
Léry, Jean de, 13, 40–41
Levant, 3, 23
Ligon, Richard, 93, 94
Linneas, Carolus, 86
Little Ice Age, 6, 32–33, 56, 73
Loango, 26
logwood, 75

Louis XVI (France), 112–13
Louisiana Territory, 67–68, 116
Louverture, Toussaint, 114, 117
Luther, Martin, 21, 39

Madeira, 4–5, 16, 44
Madoc, 10, 108
Magellan, Ferdinand, 39–40
maize, 76–80, 82, 87, 96
Mali empire, 27–28
Malinche (Doña Marina), 65–66
Mansa Musa, 27
Mansfield, Earl of, 107
Mapas de Cuauhtinchan, 51
maps: presentations of history and, 51–52
    representations of Americas and, 34–35
    representations of the Atlantic and, 4, 10,
    122–23
Mar del Nort (Northern Sea), 4
Mariani, Angelo, 89
Mariners Mirrour (Wagenaer), 14
Maroon communities, 46, 110–11
Martinique, 113
Martyr, Peter, 36
Mary, Queen of Scots, 21–22
Maryland, 16, 22
Medici, Cosimo de, 82
medicine: ginseng and, 89
    humoral theory and, 82–83, 85, 90
    Indian practices of, 34, 83, 89
    sugar and, 93, 94
    tobacco and, 83, 85
    women and, 83. See also disease
Mediterranean region, 3–4, 10, 23, 26, 28, 40,
    78. See also North Africa
Meer, Michael van, 41
Manasseh ben Israel, Mikveh Israel
    (Hope of Israel), 16
mercantilism, 96–97
Mexica, 29–31, 75. See also Aztecs
Mexico: chocolate and, 76
    dyes and, 75–76
    migration to, 56, 57, 65
    missionary activities in, 51
    pre-Columbian empires in, 29–31, 75
    silver and, 74. See also Aztecs
Mexico, Valley of, 29
Middle Passage, 53–54
migration: chain migration, 57
    conditions of, 62–63
    economic reasons for, 44, 56, 59, 109
    England and, 56–57, 59–61
    France and, 59–61, 67, 104–5

Germans and, 62–63
    indentured servitude and, 59–61, 62–65
    laws governing, 56
    North America and, 56–57, 59–67, 102–3
    redemptioners, 63
    religious reasons for, 22, 44, 61–62, 70, 109
    scope of, 56
    Scotch-Irish and, 61–62
    South America and, 56–59, 104–5
    Spain and, 56, 57–59, 65
    women and, 59–60
    within the Americas, 65–67
mining, 53, 74
Ministry of Marine (France), 99
Miranda, Francisco de, 118–19
missionary activities: Africa and, 26–27, 47
    Brazil and, 45, 50
    cultural adaption and, 87–88
    Indians and, 15, 30, 48, 51, 68–69, 71, 81,
    103
    Mexico and, 51
    Peru and, 30
    reasons for, 15
    Spain and, 50–51, 81, 87–88, 103
    slaves and, 70
Mississippi River, 3, 31, 67, 100
mita system, 51
Mittelberger, Gottlieb, 62–63
Mohawks, 31
Monardes, Nicolás, 84–86, 88
Montaigne, Michel de, 7
Montalvo, Garci-Rodriguez de, Las Sergas del
    Muy Virtuoso Caballero Esplandián, 8
Monteath, Archibald (Aniaso), 70–71
Montegazza, Paolo, 89
Montezinos, Antonio de, 16
Moquet, Jean, 81
Moravians, 61–62, 70–71
More, Thomas, Utopia, 11–12
Morocco, 23, 26, 28
Mundy, Peter, 82

Natchez Indians, 31
National Assembly (France), 112
Native Americans. See Indians
navigational skills, 41–42
Ndongo, 26, 47
Neolin, 102
Netherlands: Atlantic trading network of, 2
    Azores and, 5
    Dutch Republic and, 111–12
    fishing and, 72–73
    fur trade and, 73–74

Netherlands (*continued*)
  Jews in 22, 47–48
  privateering and, 42
  Reformation in, 21–22
  sugar industry and, 92
  tobacco and, 86–87
  West Africa and, 47
New England: Dominion of, 100
  fishing and, 72–73, 77
  migration to, 22, 42–43, 61
New France (Canada), 60–61, 69, 99–100
New Granada, 104, 119
Newfoundland, 5, 6, 22, 36, 72, 73, 77
Nicot, Jean, 85–86
Njinga (Queen of Ndongo), 47
Noah's flood, 13, 16, 82
Nombre de Dios (Panama), 57–58
North Africa: ancient cultures in, 4
  Islamic populations in, 9, 20, 23
  trade and, 20, 23, 34–35, 92
  scholars from, 23, 26, 27
North America. *See individual territories*
Nzinga a Nkuwu. *See* João I

Occum, Samson, 71
Ocean Sea, 3–4, 15, 20, 123–24
Ogun, 26
Ohio Valley, 100
okra, 96
Old Calabar (Bight of Biafra), 54–56, 106–7
Oneidas, 31
Onondagas, 31
Orellana, Francisco de, 8–9, 19, 30–31
Orenoqueponi, 9
Orinoco River, 3, 15
Ortelius, Abraham, 122–23
Ottoman Empire: Byzantine Empire and, 21
  Jews in, 22, 47–48
  Atlantic World and, 23
Ovid, *Metamorphoses*, 13
Oviedo y Valdés, Gonzalo Fernández de, 7, 70, 79–80, 87

Pacific Ocean, 11, 35, 123–24
Palmares (Brazil), 45–46
Paquiquineo (Don Luís de Velasco), 66–67
Pasqualigo, Pietro, 35–36
Patriots (Netherlands), 111–12
Pauw, Cornelis de, 108
Peltrie, Madeleine de la, 69
Pernambuco (Brazil), 45
Peru: coca and, 88
  convent in, 70
  dyes and, 75
  historical account of, 52
  mita system and, 51
  rebellion in, 120
  silver and, 74
  Spain and, 48, 56. *See also* Incas
Petrarch, 4
Philip II (Spain), 28, 80–81
Phoenicians, 4
Pigafetta, Anthony, 39–40
pigs, 91–92
Pilgrims, 22, 42
pineapples, 77–78
piracy, 1, 2. *See also* privateering; smuggling
Plato, 7
Pocahontas, 65–66
Pontiac's War, 102
Pope Alexander VI, 15
Portugal: Azores and, 5
  Brazil and, 34, 44–45, 47, 75, 117–18
  Canary Islands and, 4
  Cape Verde Islands and, 5
  French Revolution and, 117
  gold and, 45
  independence of, 20
  Jews in, 44, 47–48
  Madeira and, 5, 16
  North Africa and, 26, 28
  São Tomé and, 5
  slave trade and, 44–47, 53
  sugar and, 5, 44–45, 92–93
  tobacco and, 86
  Treaty of Tordesillas and, 15
  West Africa and, 13, 15, 26, 28, 46–47, 54
Potosí silver mine, 53, 74
Powhatan, 66
Prester John, 10, 26
printing press and print culture, 38–39, 41
privateering, 42, 97
Protestant Reformation, 21–22
Protten, Rebecca, 70
Ptolemy, 34
Puebla (Mexico), 57
Puerto Rico, 121
Purchas, Samuel, 7–8, 13
Puritans, 22, 61
Purple Islands. *See* Madeira

quahog shells, 37–38
Quakers, 61, 62, 63, 65, 70
Quebec, 98
Quetzalcoatl, 17
Quito (Ecuador), 16, 57–59

Raleigh, Walter, 9, 42, 78
rats, 92
Raynal, Abbé, 106
redemptioners, 63–65
Relaciones geográficas, 81
revolutionary movements: English colonies and,
   110–11
  France and, 112–13, 117
  Netherlands, 111–12
  Saint-Domingue and, 113–17
  Spanish colonies and, 118–21
Rhode Island, 10
Rhodes, Isle of, 10
rice, 87, 96
Roanoke, 17, 78
Robin John brothers, 54–55, 106–7
Rolfe, John, 66
Roman Catholicism: Africa and, 47, 68
  charismatic movements in, 68–69
  French Revolution and, 113
  Maryland colony and, 16, 22
  nuns and, 68–70
  priests and, 45, 50–51, 66–67, 69, 103
  Protestant Reformation and, 21–22
  Spain and, 20, 56, 103
  Thirty Years' War and, 22, 62, 74. *See also*
   missionary activity
Royal Society (England), 99
rum, 77, 94

Sahagún, Fray Bernardino de, 51
Sahara Desert, 3, 20, 28, 34–35
Saint Elmo's fire, 40
Saint-Domingue: African influence in, 114–15
  England and, 115–16, 118
  free blacks in, 113–16
  French colonialism in, 102, 113–16
  planters in, 113–14
  revolution in, 114–17
  Seven Years' War and, 102, 113
  slaves in, 113–16
  Spain and, 115–16
  sugar and, 113–14, 117–18. *See also* Haiti
Sandys, George, 13, 82
sans-culottes, 113
Santa Fe, 98
Santo Domingo, 113, 120
São Tomé, 5, 44
São Vicente, 45
Scots-Irish, 61–62
Senecas, 31
Sephardic Jews, 20, 22, 47–48, 92
Setebos, 39–40

Seven Years' War, 101–4, 110
Shakespeare, William, *The Tempest*, 40
Silva, Don Juan de, 81
Silva, Feliciano de, *Lisuarte de Grecia y Perión
  de Gaula*, 8
silver: coinage and, 75
  European demand for, 72–75
  mining of, 53, 74
  Mexico and, 74
  Peru and, 74
  privateers and, 42
  Spain and, 38, 53, 74–75
Slave Coast, 54
slave trade: African wars and, 47, 54–55,
   114–15
  children in, 55–56
  commodity exchange and, 77, 94
  conditions of, 53–55
  England and, 53–55
  first-hand accounts of, 54–55, 106–7
  Muslim involvement in, 107–8
  Netherlands and, 47
  Portugal and, 44–47, 53
  scope of, 53, 107
  Spain and, 53
  West Africa and, 28, 53–55, 107
  women and, 55–56. *See also* abolitionism
slavery: Brazil and, 44–45, 53, 117, 121
  Caribbean and, 54, 94–96, 113
  disease and, 54
  missionary activities and, 70
  Saint-Domingue and, 113–16
  São Tomé and, 44
  sugar and, 44–45, 54, 93, 106
  women and, 55–56
Smith, John, 37, 41, 66, 73
smuggling, 97, 99, 110
Societé des Amis des Noirs (Society of the
  Friends of the Blacks), 106
Society for the Abolition of the Slave Trade, 106
Somerset v. Stewart, 107
Songhay empire, 27–28
South America. *See individual territories*
South Sea (Pacific Ocean), 11, 123
Spain: armada of, 42
  Brazil and, 30–31
  Canary Islands and, 4–5
  Caribbean and, 35, 37, 58, 73, 75, 84
  chivalric romances and, 8
  chocolate and, 76, 82
  citizenship and, 119
  colonial bureaucracy of, 48, 81, 96, 98–99,
   103–4, 118–119

Spain (*continued*)
  data gathering efforts of, 80–81
  dye trade and, 75
  emancipation and, 106
  encomienda system, 48–50
  French Revolution and, 117, 119
  gold and, 37–38, 73–74
  Indians and, 17, 48, 50–53, 81, 119
  Inquisition in, 22
  Jesuits and, 103
  Jews and, 20, 22, 47–48
  migration and, 56, 57–59, 65
  missionary activities and, 50, 81, 103
  Muslims and, 9, 20–23, 47
  North Africa and, 20, 28
  North American exploration and, 9–10, 31,
    36, 37
  Peru and, 48, 56
  privateering and, 42
  rebellions against, 103–4, 118–21
  Roman Catholicism and, 20, 56, 103
  Saint-Domingue and, 115–16
  silver and, 38, 53, 74–75
  slave trade and, 53
  slavery and, 119
  South American exploration and, 8–9, 30–31,
    40
  sugar and, 92
  tobacco and, 81, 86, 96
  Treaty of Tordesillas and, 15
specimen gathering and collections, 80–83, 84,
  99
Starr, James, 63, 65
Stith, William, *History of the First Discovery
  and Settlement of Virginia*, 108
Strachey, William, 10
sugar: Brazil and, 44–45, 92–93, 117–18
  Caribbean and, 54, 92–93, 100, 102, 104–5,
    113–14
  England and, 54, 77, 93, 100
  European demand for, 77, 92–93, 106
  France and, 94, 100, 102, 113
  Madeira and, 5, 44
  medical uses of, 93, 94
  plantation agriculture and, 44, 92–93
  Portugal and, 5, 44–45, 92–93
  preservative uses of, 93, 94
  São Tomé and, 44
  slaves and, 44–45, 54, 93, 106
  Saint-Domingue and, 113–14, 117–18
  Spain and, 92
Surinam, 106
syphilis, 83–84, 105

Talon family, 67
Tawiscaron, 8
taxation, 48, 53, 88, 96–97, 103,
  110
Tekakwitha, Kateri, 69
Tempest (Shakespeare), 40
Tenochtitlan, 30, 75
Tepetlaoztoc, 52
textiles, 28, 75, 77, 97
Thevet, André, 86
Thirty Years' War, 22, 62, 74
Thorfinn, Karlsefni, 5
tobacco: Brazil and, 85–86
  ceremonial use of, 85, 87
  early description of, 85
  England and, 87, 96
  European consumption of, 77, 86–89
  France and, 85–86
  Indian consumption of, 85–87
  medical theories about, 83, 85
  Portugal and, 86
  Spain and, 81, 86, 96
Tobago, 102
Toltec Empire, 29
Tradescant family, 81–82
Trafalgar, Battle of, 119
Treaty of Tordesillas, 15
Túpac Amaru, 103
Tupís, 40

Uchteritz, Heinrich von, 105
Upper Guinea, 54. *See also* Guinea

Venezuela, 118–20
Verrazano, Giovanni da, 10
Vespucci, Amerigo, 11, 34
Vikings, 5–6, 19
vin mariani, 89
Vinland, 5
Virginia, 10, 22, 60, 87, 108
Vodou, 26
Voltaire, 101–2, 109
  Candide, or Optimism, 105–6

Wagenaer, Lucas Jansson, *Mariners Mirrour*,
  14
Waldseemüller Map, 34–35
wampum, 37–38, 73
Wesley, Charles and John, 107
West Africa: American crops in, 80
  drought in, 32
  French presence in, 68
  gold and, 3, 4, 20, 28

iron and, 26, 29
Islam and, 23, 27–28, 107–8
Netherlands and, 47
Portugal and, 13, 15, 26, 28, 46–47, 54
rice and, 96
slave trade and, 28, 47, 53–55, 107
trade networks in, 27–28
trade with Europe and, 4, 28
wars in, 47, 54–55, 114–15
Wheelock, Eleazor, 71
Whitehead, John Frederick, 63, 65
Wilberforce, William, 120
wine, 87–88

women: as warriors, 8–9
medicine and, 83
migration and, 56–57, 59–60
religious convictions of, 68–70
slavery and, 55–56
Worm, Ole, 81, 83

yams, 80, 96
yellow fever, 104–5, 116

Zacatecas, 74
Zinzendorf, Nikolaus Ludwig von, 62
Zuñiga, Pedro de, 56–57